COMMERCIAL SPACE EXPLORATION

Emerging Technologies, Ethics and International Affairs

Series editors:

Jai C. Galliott, The University of New South Wales, Australia
Avery Plaw, University of Massachusetts, USA
Katina Michael, University of Wollongong, Australia

This series examines the crucial ethical, legal and public policy questions arising from or exacerbated by the design, development and eventual adoption of new technologies across all related fields, from education and engineering to medicine and military affairs.

The books revolve around two key themes:

- Moral issues in research, engineering and design.
- Ethical, legal and political/policy issues in the use and regulation of Technology.

This series encourages submission of cutting-edge research monographs and edited collections with a particular focus on forward-looking ideas concerning innovative or as yet undeveloped technologies. Whilst there is an expectation that authors will be well grounded in philosophy, law or political science, consideration will be given to future-orientated works that cross these disciplinary boundaries. The interdisciplinary nature of the series editorial team offers the best possible examination of works that address the 'ethical, legal and social' implications of emerging technologies.

Forthcoming titles:

Super Soldiers
The Ethical, Legal and Social Implications
Edited by Jai Galliott and Mianna Lotz

Legitimacy and Drones
Investigating the Legality, Morality and Efficacy of UCAVs
Edited by Steven J. Barela

Commercial Space Exploration

Edited by
JAI GALLIOTT
The University of New South Wales, Australia

ASHGATE

Published by
Ashgate Publishing Limited
Wey Court East
Union Road
Farnham
Surrey, GU9 7PT
England

Ashgate Publishing Company
110 Cherry Street
Suite 3-1
Burlington, VT 05401-3818
USA

www.ashgate.com

British Library Cataloguing in Publication Data
A catalogue record for this book is available from the British Library

The Library of Congress has cataloged the printed edition as follows:
Galliott, Jai.
  Commercial space exploration : ethics, policy and governance / by Jai Galliott.
     pages cm. -- (Emerging technologies, ethics and international affairs)
  Includes bibliographical references and index.
  ISBN 978-1-4724-3611-5 (hardback) – ISBN 978-1-4724-3612-2 (ebook) – ISBN 978-1-4724-3613-9 (epub) 1. Space tourism. 2. Space industrialization. 3. Outer space – Civilian use. I. Title.
  TL794.7.G35 2015
  338.4'79199--dc23

                                                                                        2015016911

ISBN 9781472436115 (hbk)
ISBN 9781472436122 (ebk – PDF)
ISBN 9781472436139 (ebk – ePUB)

Printed in the United Kingdom by Henry Ling Limited, at the Dorset Press, Dorchester, DT1 1HD

*This book is dedicated to all those men and women who contributed to
the government-led exploration of space*

Contents

Notes on Contributors

Keith Abney is Senior Lecturer in the Philosophy Department and a Fellow of the Ethics + Emerging Sciences Group at California Polytechnic State University, San Luis Obispo. Previously, he held academic appointments at Auburn University, Chesapeake Biological Laboratory and Calvin College. He is well published on the ethics of emerging technologies – including robotics, cybersecurity, AI, human enhancements, space exploration, bioethics and more – especially their national security implications. He has also participated in organisations such as the Consortium for Emerging Technologies, Military Operations and National Security (CETMONS) and hospital bioethics committees. He earned his BA in philosophy from Emory University, MA from Fuller Seminary and MA (ABD) from Notre Dame.

Jacques Arnould is Engineer in Agronomy and Forestry, has a PhD in History of Sciences and a PhD in Theology. He is taking an active interest in the interrelation between sciences, cultures and religions with a particular interest for two set of themes: the first related to the life sciences and evolution; the second related to space conquest. To the first he devoted several works and publications on the historical and theological aspect. To the second, he is the French Space Agency (CNES) ethics adviser, since 2001. He belongs to the International Academy of Astronautics, to the Académie d'Agriculture de France, to the Académie de Lorraine des Sciences and to the Académie Nationale de Metz. He received in 2004 the Labruyère Prize from the Académie Française and in 2011 the Audiffred Prize from the Académie des sciences morales et politiques.

Meera Baindur is Faculty at the Manipal Centre for Philosophy and Humanities, Manipal University. She has a doctoral degree from Manipal University in the interdisciplinary area of environmental philosophy which she completed through the National Institute of Advanced Studies, Bangalore. Her research interests include environmental philosophy and environmental humanities: conceptualisation of nature in Indian thought, ecological and environmental ethics. Her book on this area is forthcoming. Her recent work includes papers related to the idea of place and cultural geography, idea of place in digital games, sacred places and landscape conservation.

Matthew Beard graduated with a Bachelor of Philosophy (Honours) from the University of Notre Dame, Australia in 2010, having completed a thesis on the relationship of luck and happiness, entitled 'The Pursuit of Happiness: Fragility and Flourishing in New Natural Law'. He is currently Research Associate with the Centre for Faith, Ethics and Society at Notre Dame, as well as the Managing Editor for *Solidarity: The Journal for Catholic Social Thought and Secular Ethics*. Matt's expertise lies generally in the area of moral philosophy. Alongside several academic articles in international journals, he has published on *The Punch*, *The Conversation*, and has appeared on triple j's *Hack*. He is also the current holder of the Morris Research Scholarship at Notre Dame, where he is completing his PhD in the area of Just War Theory and Virtue Ethics, a subject on which he has spoken internationally.

Angie Bukley is Dean and Vice President for Academics and Research at the International Space University in Strasbourg, France. She has nearly 30 years of professional experience in defence and space systems and holds a PhD from the University of Alabama in Huntsville. Prior to joining ISU, Prof. Bukley served as Associate Vice President and Chief Administrator of the University of Tennessee Space Institute, USA. Before that she was the Associate Dean for Research & Graduate Studies in the Russ College of Engineering and Technology at Ohio University, USA. She spent five years with The Aerospace Corporation in Albuquerque, NM, USA. Prior to joining Aerospace, Professor Bukley worked with a number of defence contractors on a wide variety of programs. She also spent seven years at the NASA Marshall Space Flight Center in Huntsville, Alabama, where she directed the Large Space Structures Laboratory and worked on remote sensing applications. She is an alumna of SSP 1993 and ISU faculty member since 1998. Prof. Bukley has over 70 technical publications and has received over 20 awards for technical merit. She is active in the American Institute for Aeronautics and Astronautics (Associate Fellow), American Astronautical Society, International Federation for Automatic Control, National Space Society, American Society for Engineering Education and Women in Aerospace – Europe.

Nicholas Campion is Director of the Sophia Centre for the Study of Cosmology in Culture at the University of Wales Trinity Saint David. He read history at Queens' College, Cambridge, and gained an MA at the School of Oriental and African Studies, London, in Southeast Asian Studies, specialising in history, politics and international relations. His academic interests gradually moved to the history of esoteric, occult and magical ideas, especially astrology, and his PhD, awarded by University of the West of England in 2004, was a study of contemporary belief in astrology. Before joining Lampeter University in 2007, he was Senior Lecturer in History, and taught in the Study of Religions department, at Bath Spa University.

Brent Franklin is a Professor at Burlington Community College. He has an MA in Applied Ethics from Linköping University in Sweden and an MA in Philosophy from the Central European University in Hungary. His areas of specialisation include ethics, applied ethics and social/political philosophy. He is particularly interested in the ethical issues surrounding first contact with life beyond our planet.

Robert Frize is a Fellow of the Institute of Actuaries, a member of the American Institute of Aeronautics and Astronautics (AIAA), the Royal Aeronautical Society (RAeS) and the Society of Satellite Professionals International (SSPI). He also holds a Masters Degree from the International Space University (ISU), Strasbourg, where he specialised in the regulatory and personal insurance environment of the emerging Space Tourism industry.

Jai Galliott is a Research Fellow at the University of New South Wales in Sydney, Australia. His research interests revolve around emerging military technologies, including autonomous systems, soldier enhancements and cyber warfare. His secondary interests include military strategy and applied ethics. He holds a PhD in military ethics from Macquarie University and was formerly a Naval Officer in the Royal Australian Navy and now conducts contract research for the Department of Defence. His recent books include *Military Robots: Mapping the Moral Landscape* (Ashgate 2015) and *Ethics and the Future of Spying* (Routledge 2015).

Jane Johnson joined the Macquarie University Philosophy Department late in 2009 as a Postdoctoral Research Fellow in Clinical and Public Health Ethics working with Professor Wendy Rogers, and in 2012 she was awarded a three-year Macquarie University Research Fellowship. Her interests include animal ethics, surgical innovation and environmental ethics, among others.

Elizabeth Kanon is a Lecturer in Philosophy at Texas State University. She holds an MA from the University of Mississippi and a PhD from Florida State University. She teaches a wide variety of foundational philosophy courses and her research focuses on environmental ethics and its intersection with technology studies.

Christopher Ketcham is an expert in risk management and holds a PhD from the University of Texas at Austin. He writes on philosophy, educational theory and enterprise risk management. He formerly held senior professional appointments in the insurance industry, most recently Senior Director of Knowledge Resources at the Insurance Institute of America.

Armin Krishnan is currently an Assistant Professor for Security Studies at East Carolina University (USA) and has previously taught intelligence studies at the University of Texas at El Paso. He received his PhD in 2006 from the University of Salford, UK, and also holds a Masters Degree in Intelligence and National Security from the University of Salford (2004) and another Masters Degree in Political Science, Sociology and Philosophy from the University of Munich (LMU). He specialises in defence and intelligence and has published altogether three books on aspects of contemporary warfare. His most recent book was published in German language by Matthes & Seitz Berlin Publishing in 2012 and dealt with the topic of targeted killing as a tactic and strategy of war.

Sara Langston is a Lecturer at the University of Sydney in Australia. Her current research, books and publication projects cover space bioethics, space environmental ethics, medical risks for commercial spacefarers, legal implications and cultural implications of commercialising space and the comparative identity of an 'astronaut'.

Veronica La Regina holds a Masters Degree in Institutions and Space Policy (2009) at Italian Society for International Organizations (SIOI) in Rome, PhD Studies in Economic Sciences (2004) at the State University of Milan, Graduate Studies in Maths and Statistics (2001) at the University of Rome Sapienza and a Graduation in Law (1999) at LUISS G. Carli in Rome. She also attended several summer schools dealing with Law & Economics, Game Theory, Public Policies and technical courses for satellite applications. She is current space analyst at Italian Space Agency (ASI) at the National and International Relations Unit, where she is leading two main projects of international cooperation with Argentina and Japan under the coordination of Italian Ministry of Foreign Affairs. Formerly, she has been Visiting Research Professor at International Space University in Strasbourg, France, and Resident Fellow, seconded by the Italian Space Agency (ASI), at the European Space Policy Institute (ESPI) in 2010–11. Prior to joining ESPI, she was employed at Telespazio SpA, a satellite services provider, in Italy, where she worked in the department of business strategies and marketing since 2007. Previously, in her position as Experienced Research at Wave Energy Centre in Lisbon (Portugal), she took care of the public policy issues related with the development and deployment of wave energy in Europe. Prior to this, she was Economic Researcher at Osservatorio Filas, centre of socio-economic research for innovation of SMEs. She also has been invited to give lectures about energy economics and space issues. She is involved in the activities of the International Institute of Space Commerce (IISC) from The Isle of Man and research projects at the Italian Space Agency. Her research interests include SatCom Policy, Technology Transfer, International Relations and Business Development Strategies.

Patrick Lin is the Director of the Ethics + Emerging Sciences Group at California Polytechnic State University, San Luis Obispo, where he is an Associate Philosophy Professor. He is also affiliated with Stanford Law School (Center for Internet and Society), University of Notre Dame (Emerging Technologies of National Security and Intelligence) and Australia's Centre for Applied Philosophy and Public Ethics. Previously, he held academic appointments at Stanford's School of Engineering, US Naval Academy and Dartmouth College. Dr Lin is well published on the ethics of emerging technologies – including robotics, cybersecurity, AI, human enhancements, nanotechnology, space exploration and more – especially their national security implications. He has provided briefings and counsel to the US Dept of Defense, CIA, United Nations, International Committee of the Red Cross, National Research Council, Google and many other organisations. He earned his BA in philosophy from UC Berkeley and PhD from UC Santa Barbara.

Joel Marks is Professor Emeritus of Philosophy at the University of New Haven in West Haven, Connecticut. He has directed a symposium series at the University of New Haven on 'Ethics in the Workplace'; hosted the radio program, 'Student Scene', on WNHU, West Haven, and co-hosted 'The Professors' on WNHU and CTV; writes occasional columns on ethics, astronomy and other topics for the *New Haven Register*; and is a regular columnist for the magazine, *Philosophy NOW*.

Tony Milligan is a Lecturer in Philosophy at the University of Hertfordshire and specialises in normative and applied ethics with a particular emphasis upon the relation between the human and the non-human. In addition to various papers on space ethics, he is the author of *Nobody Owns the Moon: The Ethics of Space Exploitation* (2015), *Animal Ethics: The Basics* (2015), *Civil Disobedience: Protest, Justification and the Law* (2013), *Love* (2011), *Beyond Animal Rights* (2010) and the co-editor, with Christian Maurer and Kamila Pacovska, of *Love and its Objects* (2014).

Zeldine O'Brien is a Barrister at Law and Lecturer at the Institute of Public Administration, University College Dublin (UCD). Following an LL.B from Trinity College Dublin, she was conferred with a PhD also from Trinity in the field of space law under the supervision of the late Dr Gernot Biehler. During her years of doctoral research, she was a participant in the European Space Agency's student participation programme. She has lectured in space law and policy at the UCD School of Physics and guest lectured at the School of Engineering of the University of Glasgow. She has published widely in the field of space law in Ireland, the Netherlands and the US and has taught at Trinity's Law School. She has also taught in Kosovo with the Irish Rule of Law International's project there in coordination with the Kosovo Chamber of Advocates. In 2005, she won the Diederiks-Verschoor Award from the International Institute of Space Law of which she is a member. She is also a member of the Society of Legal Scholars. She was called to the Bar of Ireland in 2009 and has been in practice since. Her research interests include aviation law, space law and European and Irish space policy.

Chris Pak is a Researcher on the Leverhulme funded project, 'People, Products, Pests and Pets: The Discursive Representation of Animals', a corpus linguistics project involving the construction of a three million-word corpus of digitally stored texts about animals for analysis with specialist software. He is also drawn to the application of computer technologies to the humanities (digital humanities) more broadly conceived. He edits the *Science Fiction Research Association*'s *SFRA Review* and research science fiction literature, film and other media. He is especially interested in the ecological and environmental significance of stories of terraforming and pantropy. His scholarship focuses on terraforming and its link to climate change and geoengineering, global politics and the relationship between the sciences, philosophy and the arts. He recently expanded this research to consider in more depth the related issue of pantropy, technologies for shaping animal (including human) bodies. He maintains a broad interest in postmodern literature, American literature, fantasy, horror and noir.

Daniel Pilchman is a Visiting Assistant Professor at Chapman University, where he teaches Political and Legal Philosophy and Multicultural Ethics. He received his PhD in Philosophy of International Law at the University of California at Irvine in June 2014. His research focuses primarily on the intersection between moral philosophy and political science, but he also has significant interests in epistemology, social theory and philosophy of religion.

Robert Seddon is a Member of Durham University's Centre for the Ethics of Cultural Heritage and an Honorary Research Fellow of its Department of Philosophy, where he previously undertook doctoral research on moral obligations concerning cultural heritage.

Robert Sparrow is an Associate Professor in the Department of Philosophy at Monash University, Melbourne. At the highest level of description his research interests are political philosophy and applied ethics. He is interested in philosophical arguments with real-world implications. More specifically, he is working in or has worked in: political philosophy, bioethics, environmental ethics, media ethics; just war theory; and the ethics of science and technology.

Zümre Gizem Yılmaz is based in Ankara, Turkey, and works as a Research Assistant at Hacettepe University, where she is also a PhD student of British Literature. She obtained her Bachelor's degree in 2010, and her Masters Degree in 2012 at Hacettepe University, in the Department of English Language and Literature. Her Masters thesis, entitled 'The Illustration and Function of Epic Theatre Devices in Selected Plays by Caryl Churchill', was an analysis of nearly all of Churchill's plays, researched in terms of socialist feminism, gender studies, animal studies and Brechtian theatre. Her research interests include contemporary British literature, new materialisms, posthumanist studies, queer fiction, animal studies and gender studies.

Chapter 1

Introduction

Jai Galliott

As a fleet of private spacecraft prepare for routine operation, it is becoming ever clearer that the dawn of commercial space flight and exploration is just around the corner, if not already upon us. For the very first time since the beginning of the space age, space transportation and exploration is no longer a strictly government enterprise, nor is it limited to highly trained and well-disciplined military test pilots and rocket scientists. Largely gone are the days of astronauts such as Neil Armstrong, Buzz Aldrin and Yuri Gagarin. With the reinvigoration of the industry, we need to rethink the role of the National Aeronautics and Space Administration (NASA) and its overseas counterparts, such as the Russian Federal Space Agency and the European Space Agency. In fact, we need to rethink the entire Cold War-initiated space program as we have known it to date. We must understand that a new space enterprise is already on our horizon and accompanied by a multitude of moral concerns and challenges that warrant the attention of philosophers, policymakers, industry stakeholders and the general public.

As we have seen with our regular transportation and construction industries, competition and new markets reduce costs and encourage innovation. In much the same way, the commercial space industry seems bound to make it easier to get to space, conduct exploration missions and, potentially, live there. Unwilling to wait for government to lead the way, private enterprise has been quite aggressive in its efforts to introduce regular individuals to space tourism. In 1996, a wealthy entrepreneur offered a $10 million dollar bounty to the first privately financed team that could fly a passenger vehicle into space, fuelling unprecedented competition and investment (XPRIZE Foundation 2014). Sir Richard Branson's Virgin Galactic has garnered the most attention in the news media and 'twitterverse' for having already built and tested an orbital vehicle capable of lifting aspiring astronauts into near space, with several hundred people from around the globe now having paid a substantial deposit to secure their place in space, despite the company facing a serious safety probe having encountered a fatal accident (Gannon 2014). However, the commercial space industry extends well beyond space tourism. SpaceX, founded by billionaire Paypal and Tesla Motors co-founder Elon Musk, also made history in 2012 when it became the first private company to secure a contract from NASA and successfully send cargo to the International Space Station. A company by the name of Planetary Resources also has ambitious plans to mine asteroids for rare and valuable minerals that may prove useful in cutting edge medical and engineering applications.

There may also come a day when space exploration and colonisation becomes a necessity rather than a commercial choice. The meteor that struck Chelyabinsk, Russia, in February of 2013 served as an important wake-up call for many and highlighted that we live in a cosmic shooting gallery and are not immune to the damage of stray objects. Not only did a 100-foot wide chunk of the rock discovered only one year earlier pass by and miss us, but one small chunk – estimated to weigh several tonnes and be 50-foot wide – hit the atmosphere with the force of around 440 kilotonnes of TNT and broke up in spectacular fashion, blowing out windows as it broke the sound barrier and lit the sky like a nuclear explosion (NASA 2013). Later that evening, another asteroid was spotted over the San Francisco Bay Area, but caused no known damage. But while NASA detects, tracks and characterises asteroids and comets passing close to Earth using both ground and space-based telescopes, noting those that are dangerous to our planet, the fact is that we live in the midst of large falling rocks and rising seas and the next supposedly harmless falling object may be of cataclysmic size and effect. That is, there may come a day when we need to extend all aspects of living into space, meaning that we would need to work, study, have sex, fight, die, worship, raise children, age, pay taxes, vote and so on in space. Of course, the need to evacuate Earth may not eventuate in our lifetime, but the knowledge we gain from our investigations may assist future generations and also shed light on a range of other ethical challenges that we face here and now, whether they concern matters of property rights and economics or justice and government (Lin 2006).

Space has long been called the 'final frontier', but whatever the reasons for going there and whatever we do once we get there – whether it is tourism, mining meteorites or even forming colonies – we must once again take the time to think about our responsibilities as frontiersmen and space pioneers. Our level of scientific development and ability to influence international policy confers upon us an obligation to study the ethical and social considerations associated with next generation space exploration. When we compare space exploration to our conquering of other frontiers, we learn that understanding the potential consequences from the very beginning is critical. When Britain colonised the United States, Australia and its other former realms, it had no plan to deal with their indigenous populations, the introduction of disease or the management of resources. Likewise, when the United States began to embrace the Internet, there was no policy to deal with intellectual property, online sales taxes, cybercrime or domain naming (Lin 2006). In both cases, we are still recovering from the absence of a good plan, but we now have the benefit of hindsight and can begin to apply it in the case of space. The relevant enabling technologies are maturing rapidly and if we are to fulfil our obligations to present and future generations, we must begin to think more seriously about the issues associated with creating a private space industry and possibly sending people to live on far-away planets about which we know very little.

The existing literature on the emerging relationship between government, the aerospace industry and academia is most commonly found in the trade media and often accessed via social networking platforms by those who once dreamed of being an astronaut or are enamoured with the idea of leaving Earth and taking up residence in outer space. This is no bad thing, but more serious discussion is starting to take place, with stakeholder meetings and conferences taking place more frequently as we approach the more critical stages of mission planning and operations, but the proceedings are rarely disseminated to the wider public in a digestible but scholarly form. This presents a major problem for those who wish to question whether the assertions made about the effectiveness and efficiency of the novel relationship between government and private enterprise are supported by rigorous and sufficiently holistic analysis. The risk is that in attempting to meet tight deadlines and critical engineering milestones, philosophers and policy experts raising what might be considered to be 'abstract' matters may not always be given an appropriate place at the roundtable to discuss the important questions that face this burgeoning industry.

The aim of this collection is to provide the first comprehensive and unifying analysis of the moral and politico-social matters concerning twenty-first-century space exploration, with a view toward developing policy that may influence real-world decision-making. Upon close consideration, there is a plethora of old questions that need to be revisited and many new ones that demand urgent attention. This book addresses what are arguably the most important of them. The first section establishes some of the relevant terms and examines a number of justifications for and against space exploration and colonisation. More specifically, in Chapter 2, Nicholas Campion provides a thorough survey of the philosophical concept of space as it pertains to wisdom and morality in western debate and theories and practices from China, India, Africa and the Americas. In doing so, he provides a valuable historical background for current debates on ethics and space, most notably those found in this book. In Chapter 3, Brent Franklin takes a very unique approach in arguing for the moral permissibility of multi-million dollar efforts aimed at finding and establishing contact with intelligent extraterrestrial life on other planets, so long as proper restrictions and precautions are implemented to respect the culture and autonomy of others. In Chapter 4, Elizabeth Kanon provides a reasoned justification for diverting funds and resources to space travel through focusing on the inevitable importance of anthropocentrism, human aggression and manifest destiny. In applying these concepts to space travel, she demonstrates that all three are necessary for human sustainability and that space travel and exploration is paramount to our continued success as a species. In Chapter 5, Zümre Gizem Yılmaz argues that once humans overcome their fear of the 'unknown', destructive consequences will occur as a result of anthropocentric practices and ideologies of human chauvinism.

Part II explores the role of public and private enterprise in the new space age and considers what sort of alliance, if any, is optimal for society. In Chapter 6, Jacques Arnold argues that space cannot be claimed by the public or the private sector and that successful space exploration can only occur through a joint effort, even if history shows that one of these sectors has been the primary driver of innovation and change in the earlier episodes of the space age. The idea here is that while key developments in astronautics may be attributed to individual entrepreneurs and entrepreneurial groups, they were made possible and will continue to be made possible by the governments and political leaders who prepare the collectives that will ultimately bear the risk of space exploration endeavours. In Chapter 7, Joel Marks argues that in the domain of near-Earth object detection, projection and response, the burden rests squarely upon the shoulders of government and that the private sector must be applauded for taking charge of the detection of asteroids and the common defence of billions of people in the face of the governments' fallacious reasoning, namely concerning the statistical probability of the relevant dangers. Chapter 8 represents a slight shift in focus as we begin to look at the dangers associated with the exploitation of space by the private sector. In particular, Zeldine O'Brien looks at the desirability of space advertising and considers some of the regulatory challenges associated with this form of marketing. In Chapter 9, Angie Bukley, Robert Frize and Veronica La Regina provide an interesting and in-depth report from a workshop held by the International Institute of Space Commerce on the risks associated with space tourism. Panellists consisted of a broad range of stakeholder enterprises including space vehicle providers, ticket vendors, space tourists, insurance companies and brokers focused on risk management, all hoping to forge mitigation strategies and industry-wide policy.

Part III revolves around asteroid mining and environmental-esque concerns. It begins with Chapter 10 from Tony Milligan, who argues that while space tourism involves issues of risk, trust, luxury consumption, fuel-derived pollution and space debris, all of significant ethical concern, space mining is arguably more troubling in the sense that it introduces a threat which is continuous with that posed by terrestrial mining: a threat of destruction as the price of extraction. He goes on to argue that this may be problematic in the case of Mars or other planetary bodies, not only by virtue of the fact that they are culturally significant, but also because they hold what some have called 'integrity'. In Chapter 11, Daniel Pilchman continues to ask whether asteroid mining ought to be conducted through the examination of four arguments for a prohibition on asteroid mining, namely that the practice violates a rock's right to moral consideration, is incompatible with human flourishing, violates property acquisition rights and exacerbates economic inequality. Ultimately, through clear and concise consideration of these arguments, Pilchman arrives at the more moderate position that the practice is permissible if certain methodological questions about the form of mining can be appropriately answered. In Chapter 12, Robert Seddon considers in what ways, and to what extent, the roles which space has played within the cultures that have developed on Earth might place moral constraints upon private explorers of space. He argues that space qua heritage is best conceptualised as an intellectual resource and that ideas of stewardship, which have been influential in archaeological ethics, might put practical constraints upon the exploitation of planets as resources. In Chapter 13, Robert Sparrow applies virtue ethics to issues in environmental philosophy and argues that large-scale planetary engineering demonstrates at least two serious defects of moral character: an aesthetic insensitivity and the sin of hubris: in his view, trying to change entire planets to suit our ends amounts to vandalism.

Part IV contains chapters providing a critical look at the exploitation of space for military purposes. In Chapter 14, Armin Krishnan considers whether it is wise to subscribe to the rhetoric about seizing the high ground and calls into question the utility of space weapons. To his mind, the vulnerability and cost of space weapons, coupled with the environmental risks, means that time-proven terrestrial alternatives should be the preferred option upon which policy is based. Matthew Beard reaches a similar conclusion in Chapter 15, but via rather different means. He argues that weaponising space for the purposes of enhancing a particular nation's military force violates territorial and political sovereignty in the same way as would positioning military assets in offensive positions on the ground, potentially jeopardising the one opportunity that states have to join together and forge a truly collective response to the management and preservation of space. In Chapter 16, I outline how artificial intelligence is set to become more important to space robotics as we travel greater distances from Earth. Contrary to some theorists who suggest that strong artificial intelligence presents a dire threat to attempts to attribute responsibility, my purpose in this explorative paper is to demonstrate that whilst autonomous space-faring military technologies certainly exacerbate some traditional problems and cause us to rethink who we ought to hold responsible for military war crimes or other events occurring in space, our traditional notions of responsibility are capable of overcoming the supposed 'responsibility gap'.

Part V delves into the bioethical challenges that we face as we progress into the age of commercial spaceflight and even contemplate human voyages to Mars and beyond. In Chapter 17, Sara Langston poses a number of important questions: should physicians and medical facilities screening potential space flight participants be accredited or hold special aerospace medical knowledge and expertise? How do we define and regulate the relationship between corporate screening physicians and commercial space flight providers? What is the physician's duty to disclose potential health risks in order to allow for informed consent? How should physicians distinguish and balance health risks, caution and benefit in human spaceflight? How should health professionals reason when the associated health risk profiles are unknown or uncertain? In Chapter 18, Keith Abney and Patrick Lin take matters one technological step further and extend the human enhancement debate to the discussion of commercial spaceflight in considering the bioethics of enhancing humans specifically to meet the rigorous demands of space travel. They consider how we should account for the uncertainty inherent in enhancement practice, how we might determine the level of acceptable risk and who should be charged with making the relevant decisions. In Chapter 19, Jane Johnson turns to an old question with new relevance in thinking about the role of animal astronauts. She explains how these subjects of space research are inherently, situationally and pathogenically vulnerable. Existing mechanisms for addressing the vulnerability of animal astronauts are discussed and shown to be wanting since they generate further vulnerabilities that are ultimately overridden by a purported 'greater good' for humans, the plausibility of which slips away for those like Johnson, who find the justification for space research to be weak.

Finally, Part VI is broadly concerned with responsibility and governance. In Chapter 20, Chris Pak provides a unique look at space exploration through the lens of science fiction. Particular consideration is given to the portrayal of entrepreneurs who engage in space exploration, colonisation and the adaptation of planets for human settlement, with a view to exploring how these stories can aid real-world thinking about space policy. In Chapter 21, Meera Baindur seeks to philosophically understand the idea of place and territoriality in outer space. Unpacking the concept of place in such descriptions has implications, we are told, for both international policies on space exploration as well as the ethical issues around the equal sharing of outer space. In Chapter 22, Christopher Ketcham and I explore what India's foray into space means for economical space exploitation and how this complicates the duty of other countries to provide humanitarian aid. We also consider the requirement for laws and policies that encourage fair and open access to space resources and how the International Law of the Sea might provide a base upon which we can build a more modern space treaty. In Chapter 23, Christopher Ketcham goes on to provide a fictional narrative, detailing the wide variety of considerations that we must remain cognisant of in embracing international cooperation on space affairs and treaties.

References

Gannon, M. 2014, 'Is Private Spaceflight Safe? What Virgin Galactic's Fatal Crash Means', viewed 29 December 2014, http://www.space.com/27638-virgin-galactic-crash-private-spaceflight-safety.html.

Lin, P. 2006, 'Viewpoint: Look Before Taking Another Leap for Mankind – Ethical and Social Considerations in Rebuilding Society in Space', *Astropolitics*, 4(3): 281–94.

NASA 2013, 'Russia Meteor Not Linked to Asteroid Flyby', viewed 29 December 2014, http://www.nasa.gov/mission_pages/asteroids/news/asteroid20130215.html#.VKEQZKdlAQ.

XPRIZE Foundation 2014, Ansari XPRIZE Home Page, viewed 29 December 2014, http://ansari.xprize.org.

PART I
Space Exploration: Concepts and Justifications

Chapter 2

The Moral Philosophy of Space Travel: A Historical Review

Nicholas Campion

As human activity in the solar system intensifies, so the need for an ethical debate on its impact increases. But how should this be approached? In 2003 Mark Williamson published a paper in *Space Policy*, in which he argued (2003, p. 52) that, compared to other issues, 'space demands a somewhat different [ethical] philosophy, based on detailed knowledge of the space environment', and must progress from the 'philosophical and academic' and 'be targeted towards the design of an ethical code or policy' to be of any practical use. However, as Williamson also states, we have to consider 'who is asking [ethical] questions and who is answering them?' (2003, p. 49): no question is ever asked without a prior context or a set of assumptions about the way the world works. For current purposes I will adopt the same definition of ethics as Williamson (2003, p. 48) from the *Collins Concise English Dictionary* (1992, p. 439): 'the philosophical study of the moral value of human conduct, and of the rules or principles that ought to govern it', and 'a code of behaviour considered correct, especially that of a particular group, profession or individual'. Williamson had in mind a number of such groups and professions whose respective interests may be diametrically opposed: chiefly space scientists, on the one hand, and those who stand to exploit space commercially, on the other. In order to reconcile these competing positions it is necessary to formulate an ethical policy to which rival parties can agree. This is necessary if a legal framework for space protection is to be constructed (Williamson 2003, pp. 149–80). As Henry and Taylor (2009) demonstrate, the need to develop such a policy is of immediate concern. Such concerns include the threat of the militarisation of space (Arnopoulos 1998, pp. 189–212; Moltz 2014, pp. 121–45), as well as its 'commercialisation, privatization, and industrialisation', and terraforming (Arnopoulos 1998, p. 258; Hargrove 1986, pp. xii–xiii). And then, if ethics are designed to minimise the harm resulting from such activities, then what constitutes harm is not always clear (Moltz 2014, p. 192; Reiman 2010). If there is emphasis on sustainable development (Reiman 2010), then what constitutes sustainability?

In the popular view, space is often valueless, and described in language which suggests danger. Williamson (2003, pp. 47–8) summarised such views in which space is 'a limitless, alien void populated by huge and indestructible stars, a handful of barren planets and swarms of potentially dangerous comets'; according to this narrative, 'The space environment is hardly in need of protection'. Williamson added that, from the scientist's point of view, what needs preserving is the 'relative purity' of the space environment. The preservation of the space environment for its own sake is one priority. But to scientists the acquisition of scientific knowledge and a better understanding of what it is to be human are also important (Reiman 2010; Lupisella and Logsdon 1997, p. 8). In this sense outer space is a source potential of wisdom. Williamson highlighted the core problem of a successful space ethics policy: if success is defined by practical implementation, how is it possible to persuade people who see space as either empty or dangerous that it needs protecting? My suggestion is that notions of 'place' as special (Tilley 1994) and 'storied' (Lane 2001) can be brought to the debate. The problem parallels that faced by climate-change scientists in the USA, who find that their evidence is dismissed by emotional appeals to economic liberty as fundamental to American identity, and by opposition to exploitation of the environment as un-American (Lynas 2015). Scientists need a positive counter-narrative of their own. This is in contrast to the COMEST report (2000, p. 1), which explicitly ruled out emotional appeals, arguing that scientific evidence alone should be sufficient to formulate an ethical policy for outer space.

Dualism in Space

The question to consider is what value is put on 'outer space' – defined as the realm beyond the Earth's atmosphere – and what discussions are of value in the historical literature, particularly in the western tradition? Fundamental to such debates is the distinction between dualist models, which hold that the universe consists of two separate modes of existence (such as mind and matter, or Heaven and Earth) and monist ones, which hold that there are no clear boundaries between kinds of existence in different zones of space. The issue is complicated by a double meaning of the word 'space'. The first is specific: space as outer space. The other is general: space defined as the physical location that humans occupy, whether the immediate environment or the larger one. My use of each should be clear from the context, but I will use the term 'outer space' where necessary. We also need to understand the nature of 'place'. In one current usage 'space' in the general sense is valueless, meaningless, homogenous and has no boundaries, while 'place' is endowed with identity, quality, value, meaning and definition (Tilley 1994, p. 26). We need to consider how outer space was, and is, conceptualised and imagined as a 'place', in which case, by definition, it possesses value.

From an Earth-centred perspective, when we look up we see not outer space but sky. Even at night we may be looking at distant stars but we refer to the wonder of the night or starry sky, not to outer space. Little has been written about the relationship between 'sky' and 'place', but it can be useful to draw on the literature on landscapes. For example, Lane (2001, pp. 37 and 58) argued that 'The human spirit is inexorably drawn to the appeal of place, whether real or imaginary.

Landscape, after all, is a constructed reality – a form which is given to nature by a particular human perception'. As Lane points out, huge importance is devoted to the preservation of wilderness and the countryside in western countries; his point of reference is the landscape, but his ideas can be extended to the skyscape, defined as the ways in which we experience and conceptualise the sky (Silva 2015). To adapt Lane, 'Skyscape, after all, is a constructed reality – a form which is given to nature by a particular human perception'. Lane added: 'the poet also reminds us that sacred places are, first, of all, "storied" places – elaborately woven together on a cultural loom that joins every detail of the landscape within a given community of memory' (2001, p. 59). As I shall argue, outer space, then, is a 'storied' place. In particular, there is a persistent narrative in western culture, preserved in modern scientific discourse, which portrays outer space both as pristine and a source of wisdom; it is a valued place, rather than a valueless space.

Space is also sometimes divided between value-laden, meaningful 'sacred' space, on the one hand, and valueless, meaningless 'profane' space, on the other (Eliade 1959, p. 20). This rigid model has been critiqued by Tilley (1994) and Lane (2001), for whom it is no longer useful. Nevertheless, the sacred-profane dichotomy is such a central narrative in western philosophy that it cannot be ignored. It is rooted in classical cosmology, particularly in the Aristotelian (1921) conception of a fundamental break between the sublunar world (the space below the Moon, including the Earth) and the space beyond the Moon, up to the stars: for Aristotle, the sublunary world was inherently imperfect and subject to a perpetual cycle of growth and decay while, beyond the Moon, one entered a realm of increasing moral perfection, until one reached the stars. A parallel dualism occurs in the Abrahamic faiths in which a distinction is drawn between a perfect realm, 'Heaven', which is 'up there', and an imperfect world, the Earth, which is 'down here' (McDannell and Lang 1988).

The discussion of pure or pristine environments links the space debate to traditions of utopian thought (Levitas 1990, pp. 1–8). Utopias tend to exist in a place which is either far away in space, lost in the distant past or anticipated in the future. In the past many utopias occupied a physical location, even one which could no longer be entered, such as the Biblical Garden of Eden (Eco 2013). For many centuries, especially during the European voyages of discovery, Europeans searched for a new Eden, and sometimes thought they had found it, the apparent paradise of Tahiti being a prime example. Some have argued that such undiscovered physical utopias can no longer exist. Ben Macintyre expressed the view that 'Legendary lands are all but gone now. In the age of Google Earth and GPS, there is no terra incognita left' (Macintyre 2013, p. 11). Yet the astronomical discoveries of the last century have opened up areas of *terra incognita* – or, to coin a phrase, 'stellar incognita', which replicate the vast areas once defined by European conquerors as unknown and uninhabited. In so doing, certain ethical dilemmas which have arisen in recent times are replicated. For example, only recently has it been acknowledged that Australia, when the Europeans arrived, was neither empty nor unknown, but occupied and known. By the same token, to regard outer space as empty and unknown will always raise the risk of an ethical blunder. A utopia, though, is not just a place but a method, inspiring people to work for a better world. In this sense, an ethical approach to space becomes 'an ideal to be striven for rather than an answer to be filled in' (Arnopoulos 1998, p. 14). The belief in a better place encourages people to strive to create that place.

The Ascent to the Stars

While physical space travel is just over half a century old, the idea of a journey to other planets or stars is almost as old as recorded history. Such ideas were current in Old Kingdom Egypt, and were set out in the *Pyramid Texts*, probably beginning around 2400–2300 BCE (Smith 2009). Central to the texts was the Pharaoh's post-mortem ascent to heaven on the rays of the sun. For example, Pyramid Text Utterance 508 reads: 'I have trodden those thy rays as a ramp under my feet whereon I mount up to that my mother, the living Uraeus on the brow of Re' (Faulkner 1993, 606.1688–9). The celestial journey did not exist without morality, measured by the weighing of the soul after death (Stilwell 2005), and the success of the ascent to the stars was dependent on one's virtue, anticipating later Christian theories of celestial salvation.

The relationship between soul and stars finds its fullest expression in the fourth century BCE in Plato's psychological theory (his view on the nature and function of *psyche*, understood as soul, or consciousness). This, in turn, may be understood in terms of his theory of the soul's origin in the stars. Each soul, Plato wrote, has its own star (1931, 41E–42A). As he said, the 'soul … traverses the whole heaven' (Plato 1914, 246B–C). Consciousness, as *psyche*, therefore pervades the sky. Plato's theory was elaborated in the *Republic* (1937, X.614–621) in which the mechanics of the soul's incarnation into human form were set out: the soul originates in the sphere of the fixed stars, descending through the planetary spheres at birth, and then ascending at death. Again, morality is key to the success of the celestial journey: the virtuous go to heaven after death, 'raised up into a heavenly place by justice', while the others go to the 'places of correction under the Earth' (Plato 1914, 249A–B). Aristotelian ethical cosmology (Aristotle 2004) can also be located in debates concerning the soul's relationship with the cosmos (Aristotle 1986; Campion 2010). There may also be some correspondence with Indian beliefs about salvation in the sky. As the Vedas put it, 'the seers, thinking holy thoughts, mount him (Time)' (*Hymns of the Atharva-Veda* 2000, p. 224). 'That I do know of thee', the Atharva-Veda intones, 'O immortal, where thy march is upon the sky, where thy habitation is in the highest heaven' (*Hymns of the Atharva-Veda* 2000, p. 212).

There is no firm dividing line between the human and the divine in Platonic theory and, significantly for the understanding of Plato's astronomy, none between humanity and the stars: all are embedded in the world's soul, of which individual souls are, in turn, a part (1931, 41D–E). The Cosmos, for Plato, was a 'Living

Creature endowed with soul and reason owing to the Providence of God' (1931, 30B–C). The whole universe, being animated by soul, is alive. The distinction between organic and inorganic matter, let alone between different kinds of life, cease to be an issue because the entire universe is considered to be alive. The other consequence of the soul's connection with the stars, in addition to salvation, was wisdom. Plato described how the creator 'showed them [the souls] the nature of the Universe, and declared unto them the laws of destiny' (1931, 41E–42A). It follows, then, that the journey to the stars is a means of gaining both salvation and wisdom. Plato's ethical theory (Irwin 1995) is therefore an adjunct of the soul's journey to the stars as a quest for knowledge.

The soul's journey to the stars was theorised in the *Corpus Hermeticum* (*Hermetica* 1982), composed mainly in Hellenistic Egypt in the last two centuries BCE and ritualised in *The Roman World in the Mysteries of Mithras* (Beck 2006) and *Gnostic Christianity* (Jonas 1963). *Nousanodia*, defined by Idel (2005, p. 42) as 'the NeoAristotelian spiritualisation of the [soul's] ascent' was codified in Jewish practice between the third and eighth centuries CE, in *heikhalot* literature, so-called 'because it describes heavenly *hekhalot* (temples or palaces), in which the heavens as a whole constitute a single temple containing a varying number of shrines composed of 'firmaments, angels, chariots, legions, hosts, and other wondrous phenomena and beings' (Magness 2005, pp. 7–8). The individual adept attempted to travel to the seventh heaven (that of Saturn) in order to achieve a vision of God's glory, which itself lay beyond the eighth sphere, that of the fixed stars. In each case, Hermetic, Mithraic, Gnostic and Jewish, every stage of the ascent was equated with increasing degrees of moral perfection and purification. The ascent to the stars was psychic, but in a world in which the soul was a vital part of individual existence and identity, was no less real for that. Such ideas were carried into medieval and Renaissance Europe through Macrobius' fifth-century *Commentary on the Dream of Scipio* (1990), from which it was easy for Dante (c. 1265–1321) to dramatise the celestial journey in the *Paradiso* (1971). A separate route of transmission of the celestial journey trope from the classical world to Renaissance Europe was via Jewish Kabbalah (Unterman 2008), and the translation of the *Corpus Hermeticum* in the fifteenth century. A separate and more orthodox Christian form of celestial ascent drew on the biblical story of Jacob's Ladder (Genesis 28.10–19), which was used widely in Christian imagery: a notable example is found in the facade of Bath Abbey, in England.

The idea that the entire cosmos was alive and animated by soul, and that the individual soul might ascend to the stars was a commonplace in Renaissance Europe (Couliano 1991). It fell out of orthodox intellectual favour with the eighteenth-century European Enlightenment, but remained familiar to all students of the classics, which included all educated people until the late nineteenth century, and popular in mystic, esoteric and magical world views.

Concepts of Heaven

The Greek word *ourania* is usually translated either as 'sky' or 'heaven', words which have radically different meanings in English. 'Sky' is the space above us, normally regarded as neutral and valueless, whereas 'heaven' is a paradise; it is the realm of God in the Abrahamic faiths, the home of angels and saints and the destination of the virtuous. *Psalms* 19.1 clearly associates what would now be distinguished as 'space', 'stars' and 'heaven' as blended utopian concepts, located 'up there' in a zone which is effectively physically unreachable for human beings, but represents a source of power, wisdom or morality: 'The heavens are telling the glory of God, and the firmament proclaims his handiwork'. Outer space as Heaven is a storied place. The celestial bodies were placed in the sky to measure divine time and reveal God's wishes, as *Genesis* 1.14 made clear: 'And God said "Let there be lights in the firmament of the heavens to separate the day from the night; and let them be for signs and for seasons and for days and years"'. Such was the power of divine presence in the sky that both classical and scriptural cosmologies suggest that the stars are so special that even just to gaze upon them can make one a morally better person (Aurelius 1964, V.47, p. 112, IX.29, p. 144; Plato 1937, 516B; Campion 2011). To travel to it, then, was even more special.

The notion of a divinity set apart from, and above the world tends to reinforce the dualist elements of both Platonic and Aristotelian cosmologies, and is the basis of Eliade's sacred-profane dichotomy. In dualist conceptions of space, both morality and wisdom are, then, ultimately located in the 'up there', rather than in the 'down here'. The alternative tradition, though, finds divinity, and therefore morality and wisdom, more evenly distributed through the entire world. China occupied something of a middle position between the two options. The metaphysical structure of the Chinese cosmos was vertical, with Heaven above and Earth below, the two locked in a value-laden power relationship in which heaven is exalted, honoured and powerful, while Earth is lesser and lower. The way of Heaven (above) was round, the way of Earth (below) square, *chi* (energy) passed between them and the task of the ruler, living in the square, was to grasp the round – to understand heaven – in order to benefit the square (Lai 2008, p. 209): as the opening section of the *I Ching* puts it, 'Heaven is high, the Earth is low' (Wilhelm 1968, p, 280). Yet, the distinction between high Heaven and low Earth was moderated by the flow, as in classical Greek physics, of energy between them: thus 'macrocosm and microcosm became a single manifold' (Sivin 1995, p. 6). As Xiaochun Sun put it, in China, 'The universe was conceived not as an object independent of man, but as a counterpart of and mirror of human society' (2000, p. 425). An apparent Heaven-Earth dualism is therefore contained within a single, monist, cosmos. Similar ideas are found elsewhere, and Native North American cosmology, for example, has been described as a 'patterned mirroring' between sky and Earth (Griffin-Pierce 1995, p. 63). In many cultures the relationship between sky and Earth depends on intimate links between two different worlds. In sub-Saharan Africa there is no distinction between the world down here and the world up there any more than between the worlds of the living and the dead, or the worlds of visible beings and invisible beings (Zahan 1979). This is same as the animist, or pantheist, 'lifeworld', discussed by David Abram (2010), in which the entire world is one single organism. To complicate matters, Platonic cosmology (1931) can also be represented as monist, in view of the soul's permeation of the entire cosmos, providing an essential unity. Dualist and monist cosmologies tell different stories about place, but there is no clear boundary between them. They are not rigidly defined alternatives. They are reflected in ongoing debates about the universe (Cobb 1986, pp. 292–3) and it is necessary that they are acknowledged and understood.

The most persistent, overtly monist ethical-cosmological scheme in western thought is Stoicism, in which the purpose of life is to live in agreement with nature. Zeno of Citium's fourth century BCE work, *On the Nature of Man*, argued that human nature is identical with the nature of the universe, virtue is the goal to which nature guides us and a virtuous life is therefore a natural life and vice versa, and living in accord with nature means living in harmony with the entire universe (Laertius 1925, VII.88). In Stoicism, then, there is nothing but nature, and all parts of nature are potentially equally valuable. There is no Heaven which is more sacred than the Earth, and hence there is no excuse for the devaluing of the Earth through commercial exploitation, and neither is there any excuse for exploitation of other planets.

Modern theorists are tending to react against dualist models. Tilley, for example, in contrast to Eliade, has argued that there is no essential distinction between the polarities of sacred and profane, or heaven and Earth, upper and lower. But he parts company from some views of traditional animism and pantheism, by emphasising that space has no inherent value or context beyond the activities of the individuals within it. Tilley does not argue that space has no value. Instead, it has the value which human beings give it as a result of their conceptualisation of it, their engagement with it and their participation in it as actors in the wider environment (Tilley 1994, pp. 10–11). Space is relational in that everything exists in relation to everything else. Presumed values are derived from the relationships between the people and things which occupy it, not because of its inherent, or essential, quality. Place possesses no intrinsic value, but it has the value which we give it.

Ethics and Space

The relationship between space, morality and ethics can be traced back to the recorded origins of human speculation on the nature of the sky. However, whereas the two major strands of cosmology which I have discussed (the dualist and the monist) both see the sky as included in the ethical and moral order, modern environmental and ecological thought tends to focus on nature narrowly defined as existing on planet Earth, and ignore outer space (Weston 2009, pp. 109–30).

To that extent, environmental and ecological thought tends to replicate the dualist distinction between the 'up here' and the 'down here'. Planet Earth is seen as valuable and coincident with nature, while space, and the sky, are ignored. For example Dobson (2007) and Eckersley (1992) review environmental and ecological theories, from those which prioritise preservation and conservation to those which advocate radical solutions, from those which prioritise human welfare to those which subordinate humanity to nature as a whole and from those which reject capitalism to those which accept it. None have anything to say about outer space, confining their theories to the terrestrial environment. They are still in thrall to an eighteenth-century rejection of any connection between Earth and sky (Westrum 1978, pp. 462–3).Yet, there is no boundary which separates the terrestrial environment from the celestial, or life on Earth from life in outer space (Lee 1994, p. 93). We therefore need to consider how environmental thought can expand to include outer space (Reiman 2010). A knowledge of ancient and classical theories of the value of outer space in western thought can assist this process.

Current Green ethical thought distinguishes two fundamental approaches. One fault line is between those who prioritise human interests, often short-term ones, and those who identify the wider environment as the central focus (Reiman 2010). First, environmentalism depends on a pragmatic, utilitarian, managerial approach to environmental problems which is designed to save the planet for humanity (Curry 2011, p. 45). As applied to space, it aims minimise the harm from industrial exploitation (Briggs 1986). As Article 1 of the 1979 Moon treaty stated, space 'is the province of all mankind' (UNOOSA 1979; Moltz 2014, p. 49). Environmentalism generally assumes a clear boundary between the living, biotic, environment, on the one hand, and the abiotic environment of dead, that is, non-replicating, matter, on the other (Lee 1994). Boundaries, though, are everywhere difficult to define and the distinction between matter which is alive and that which is not can also be arbitrary (Callicott, 2013, p. 309; Lupisella and Logsdon 1997). Second, ecologism (Curry 2011, p. 45) argues for 'radical changes in our relationship with the non-human natural world, and in our mode of social and political life' (Dobson 2007, pp. 2–3). At the radical extreme, ecocentrism subsumes humanity entirely within the ecological system (Rowe 1994, pp. 106–7), much as did Stoicism. The extremes of environmentalism and ecologism/econcentrism are related to the distinction between that version of Christian comsology which places humanity at the heart of the universe (Callicott 1986, p. 233; Cobb 1986, p. 297), as opposed to those classical cosmologies in which the cosmos is central, and humanities' welfare is dependent on its relationship with the wider cosmos. Ecologists and eco-centrics tend to 'de-anthropocentrize the world' (Weston 2009, pp. 109–30; Midgley 1994), recognising that human interests should not be central. To extend ecocentrism, an ethic which de-prioritises human interests could be known as 'cosmocentric' (Lupisella and Logsdon 1997).

Curry (2011, p. 45), identified three major ethical schools of Green thought; two are modern, one, 'deontology', concerns duty and a second, 'consequentialism', is related to utilitarian, managerial, environmentalism. He explicitly located the third, 'virtue ethics', in classical philosophy. Classical ethics – by which I mean Platonic, Aristotelian and Stoic – has a number of characteristics. First, it is teleological, assuming a goal which already has a kind of existence in the future and which lends existence in the present a purpose. It also, significantly for the traditions of thought which I have summarised, equates ethics with wisdom. As Francesco Varela (1992, pp. 3 and 4) wrote, ethics 'is closer to wisdom than to reason, closer to understanding what is good than to correctly adjudicating particular situations ... [A] wise (or virtuous) person is one who knows what is good and spontaneously does it'. This would have made perfect sense to Aristotle (Urmson 1988, p. 11), as well as to the Stoics, but begs the question of who is to judge what is right if there is no common source of revealed wisdom. Platonic cosmology can also be represented in terms of Green politics, as either anthropocentric and environmentalist, in that the welfare of the human soul is seen as either transcendental and independent of nature, or ecological and eco-centric, in that it is entirely embedded in nature, that is, the cosmos.

Extending classical 'virtue ethics', Curry proposes a Green Virtue Ethics (GVE) – which escapes the anthropocentrism which prioritises human interests alone, and, instead, sees humanity as embedded in nature ('nature takes its proper place at the heart of all things, not merely an add-on extra to make us better humans') and which must therefore include nonhumans (Curry 2011, pp. 51 and 55). Curry's inspiration is drawn partly from those traditional cosmologies which locate all nature as valuable, as well as from those elements of classical philosophy which embed humanity in nature, and by Abram (2010). Curry, who is no fonder of excusive ecocentrism than he is of anthropocentric environmentalism concludes that 'we are beings not only on, but of the Earth' (2011, p. 51). As Rowe (2006, p. 21) said, 'We are Earthlings first, humans second'. To embed human interests in nature, as well as the wide cosmos, does not mean devaluing it, but instead binds human welfare to the health of the wider environment.

To adapt Curry and Rowe, I propose that 'we are creatures not only in, but of space' (and of outer space), and 'we are Spacelings first, humans second'. In a recent influential discussion of sacred space, Thorley and Gunn (2007) rely heavily on the testimony of indigenous people. To extend their approach and taking the Earth as whole, situated in outer space, the entire human population is indigenous. Whether Earthlings or Spacelings, humanity exists on this tiny planet and its interests as a whole depend on the welfare of both Earth and space. My point here is that, to follow Tilley's argument that valueless space becomes valued place by virtue of its relationality, the Earth does not exist in isolation, but in terms of its relationships with other celestial bodies. It is actually in outer space, surrounded by it, part of it. In that sense, the boundary between space on Earth and the 'outer space' beyond the Earth's atmosphere disappears. Organic life is only sustained on the Earth by its relationship with the Sun and Moon and, in turn, our solar system only exists in relation to the Milky Way, our galaxy, and our galaxy is part of a greater structure which underpins our entire universe.

The Overview Effect: An Ethical Impulse

Williamson (2003) and Reiman (2010) identified the key task of a space-ethics policy as reconciling the competition between capitalist, commercial and industrial interests on the one hand, and scientists on the other. However, these arguments have no emotional component, only an appeal to all to respect science. However, emotional support for space ethics comes from the Overview Effect, the experiences reported by some astronauts when seeing Earth from space (White 1987). The cultural impact of the first photographs of a spherical Earth taken by Apollo astronauts and their impact in galvanising the political push for environmentally sustainable economics has been well documented (Brand 1977; Cosgrove 2001; Briggs, 1986, p. 114).

Interviewed on BBC Radio 4's *IPM* programme on 25 May 2013, the astronaut Geoff Hoffman spoke about the Overview Effect and was happy to describe the condition that he experienced on his mission as being a 'state of grace', words which he said had been suggested to him by a Jesuit priest. The 'Overview Effect' has been institutionalised in the 'Overview Institute' (Planetary Collective 2013; OI 2012a). The Institute's environmental agenda is clearly spelled out on its website (OI 2012b): identifying an unparalleled crisis in the history of the Earth, it argues 'for a global vision of planetary unity and purpose for humanity as a whole'. Such views are closer to ecologism than they are to environmentalism, with their implicit plea for a radical revision of humanity's relationship with the entire planet. For some astronomers, experiences such as Hoffman's provide a radical step into a 'new' politics. As formalised by the Overview Institute and placed into a historical context, they are reminiscent of utopian dreams of new worlds and journeys into space that have characterised western thought since the ancient world. In particular, the Overview Institute sees the Overview Effect as a source of wisdom and a possible path to salvation for an Earth under threat, narratives which are recognisable from classical sources. In the Overview Institute's philosophy, caring about the Earth is derived from an emotional experience. As Held (2006, p. 10) argued, 'the ethics of care values emotion'.

Conclusion

Williamson's solution to the ethical problem was to adopt environmental managerialism, or consequentialism, seeking pragmatic solutions. He correctly argued that 'philosophical and academic' discussions alone are inadequate to the task of developing a space ethics policy, when faced with immediate practical problems. Yet a successful ethical policy can only be enforced if its supporters have an emotional commitment to it. To this end we can deploy a number of narratives which are deeply embedded in western thought. In particular, we can conscript the long tradition in which outer space – the realm of the stars – is seen as special. We can replace the story of space as empty, dangerous and dead, with one in which it is teeming with life and enormous potential for enhancing science and knowledge. We can adapt dualist cosmologies, in which the realm of the stars is a source of wisdom and salvation, and monist cosmologies, in which humanity is seen as embedded in nature, humanity's welfare therefore being dependent on nature's. To extend this principle, humanity's welfare is dependent on the welfare of space – and outer space. Both monist and dualist cosmologies have something to bring to the debate and are evident in modern 'Green' philosophy. Of particular use is Curry's Green Virtue Ethics which, in turn, refers explicitly back to classical and other traditional cosmologies, especially emphasising humanity's integration in nature, with its consequences for morality, wisdom and salvation, and with space. In this sense, the universe, as Lane reports is 'storied', and the moral value we place on it is inseparable from the stories we tell about it. A practical space ethics policy is necessary, but it cannot leave philosophy behind. Instead it must make full use of philosophical and academic input.

References

Abram, D. 2010, *Becoming Animal: An Earthly Cosmology*. New York: Pantheon Books.

Aristotle, 1921, *On the Heavens*, translated by W.K.C. Guthrie. Cambridge, MA: Harvard University Press.

Aristotle, 1986, *De Anima*, translated by Hugh Lawson-Tancred. London: Penguin.

Aristotle, 2004, *The Nicomachean Ethics*, translated by J.A.K. Thomson, revised by Hugh Tredennick. London: Penguin.

Arnopoulos, P. 1998, *Cosmopolitics: Public Policy of Outer Space*. Toronto: Guernica.

Aurelius, M. 1964, *Meditations*, translated by M Staniforth. Harmondsworth: Penguin.

Beck, R. 2006, *The Religion of the Mithras Cult in the Roman Empire: Mysteries of the Unconquered Sun*. Oxford: Oxford University Press.

Brand, S. 1977, 'Why Haven't We Seen the Whole Earth?', in L.R. Rost (ed.), *The Sixties: The Decade Remembered Now, By the People Who Lived It Then*. New York: Random House/Rolling Stone, pp. 168–70.

Callicott, J.B. 2013, *Thinking Like a Planet: The Land Ethic and the Earth Ethic*. Oxford: Oxford University Press.

Campion, N. 2011, 'Enchantment and the Awe of the Heavens', in E Corsini (ed.), *Proceedings of the Sixth Conference on the Inspiration of Astronomical Phenomena*. Utah: Astronomical Society of the Pacific, **Prvo**, pp. 415–22.

Campion, N. 2010, 'Astronomy and Psyche in the Classical World: Plato, Aristotle, Zeno, Ptolemy', *Journal of Cosmology*, 9: 2179–86.

Collins Concise English Dictionary, 1992. London: Collins.

COMEST (World Commission on the Ethics of Scientific Knowledge and Technology), 2000, Sub-Commission Report on 'The Ethics of Outer

Space', UNESCO Headquarters, New York, http://unesdoc.unesco.org/images/0012/001220/122048E.pdf.

Cosgrove, D. 2001, *Apollo's Eye: A Cartographic Genealogy of the Earth in the Western Imagination*. Baltimore, MD: Johns Hopkins University Press.

Couliano, I.P. 1991, *Out of this World: Otherworldy Journeys from Gilgamesh to Albert Einstein*. Boston, MA: Shambhala.

Curry, P. 2011, *Ecological Ethics: An Introduction*, rev. edn. Cambridge: Polity Press.

Dante, A. 1971, *The Divine Comedy*, 3 vols, translated by Mark Musa, Harmondsworth: Penguin.

Dobson, A. 2007, *Green Political Thought*, 4th edn. London: Routledge.

Eckersley, R. 1992, *Environmentalism and Political Theory*. London: UCL Press.

Eco, U. 2013, *The Book of Legendary Lands*. London: Thames & Hudson.

Eliade, M. 1959, *The Sacred and the Profane; the Nature of Religion*. New York: Harcourt, Brace & World.

Faulkner, O.R. 1993 [1969], *The Ancient Egyptian Pyramid Texts*, 2 vols. Oxford: Oxford University Press, 2nd edn, Warminster: Aris and Phillips.

Griffin-Pierce, T. 1995, *Earth is My Mother, Sky is My Father: Space, Time and Astronomy in Navajo Sandpainting*. Albuquerque, NM: University of New Mexico Press.

Hargrove, E.C. 1986, *Beyond Spaceship Eerth: Environmental Ethics and the Solar System*. San Francisco, CA: Sierra Club Books.

Held, V. 2006, *The Ethics of Care: Personal, Political, Global*. Oxford: Oxford University Press.

Henry, H. and Taylor, A. 2009, 'Re-thinking Apollo: Envisioning environmentalism in space', in D. Bell and M. Parker (eds), *Space Travel and Culture: From Apollo to Space Tourism*. Oxford: Blackwell, pp. 191–203.

Hermetica: the Ancient Greek and Latin Writings which contain Religious or Philosophic Teachings ascribed to Hermes Trismegistus 1982, translated by W. Scott. 4 vols. Boulder, CO: Shambala.

Idel, M. 2005, *Ascension on High in Jewish Mysticism: Pillars, Lines, Ladders*. Budapest: Central Europe University Press.

iPM 2013, audio podcast, BBC Radio 4, London, 25 May. Interview with the astronaut Geoff Hoffman, viewed 5 July 2014, http://www.bbc.co.uk/programmes/b01sjn9l.

Hymns of the Atharva-Veda 2000 [1897], translated by M. Bloomberg. Delhi: Motilal Banarsidass.

Irwin, T. 1995, *Plato's Ethics*. Oxford: Oxford University Press.

Jameson, F. 2010, 'Utopia as Method, or the Uses of the Future', in M. Gordin, H. Tilley and G. Prakash (eds), *Utopia/Dystopia: Conditions of Historical Possibility*. Princeton, NJ: Princeton University Press, pp. 21–44.

Jonas, H. 1963, *The Gnostic Religion: The Message of the Alien God and the Beginnings of Christianity*, 2nd edn. Boston, MA: Beacon Press.

Laertius, D. 1925, 'Zeno', in *Lives of Eminent Philosophers*, translated by R.D. Hicks. London: William Heinemann, pp. 110–263.

Lai, K.L. 2008, *An Introduction to Chinese Philosophy*. Cambridge: Cambridge University Press.

Lane, B. 2001, *Landscapes of the Sacred: Geography and Narrative in American Spirituality*, expanded edn. Baltimore, MD: Johns Hopkins University Press.

Lee, K. 1994, 'Awe and Humility: Intrinsic Value in Nature. Beyond and Earthbound Environmental Ethics', in R. Attfield and A. Belsey (eds), *Philosophy and the Natural Environment*. Cambridge: Cambridge University Press, pp. 89–101.

Levitas, R. 1990, *The Concept of Utopia*. Hemel Hempstead: Allen Lane.

Lupisella, M. and Logsdon, J. 1997, 'Do we need a Cosmocentric Ethic?', International Astronautical Congress (Turin, Italy), IAA-97-IAA.9.2.09, International Astronautical Federation, 3–5 Rue Mario-Nikis, 75015 Paris, France.

Lynas, M. 2015, 'We must reclaim the climate change debate from the political extremes', *The Guardian*, 12 March. http://www.theguardian.com/commentisfree/2015/mar/12/climate-change-reclaim-debate-political-extremes.

McDannell, D. and Lang, B. 1988, *Heaven: A History*. New Haven, CT: Yale University Press.

Macintyre, B. 2013, 'A guided tour from Avalon to Eden', review of Umberto Eco, *The Book of Legendary Lands*, Thames and Hudson, *The Times*, Saturday Review, 9 November 2013, p. 11.

Macrobius, 1990, *Commentary on the Dream of Scipio*, translated by W.H. Stahl. New York: Columbia University Press.

Magness, J. 2005, 'Heaven on Earth and the Zodiac Cycle in Ancient Palestinian Synagogues', *Dumbarton Oaks Papers*, 59: 1–52.

Midgley, M. 1994, 'The End of Anthropocentrism', in R. Attfield and A. Belsey (eds), *Philosophy and the Natural Environment*. Cambridge: Cambridge University Press, pp. 103–12.

Moltz, J.C. 2014, *Crowded Orbits: Conflict and Cooperation in Space*. New York: Columbia University Press.

Morenz, S. 1992, *Egyptian Religion*. Ithaca, NY: Cornell University Press.

UNOOSA (United Nations Office for Outer Space Affairs) 'Agreement Governing the Activities of States on the Moon and Other Celestial Bodies', 1979, http://www.unoosa.org/pdf/publications/ST_SPACE_061Rev01E.pdf.

Planetary Collective 2013, *Overview*, online video, n.d., viewed 5 July 2014, http://vimeo.com/55073825.

Plato 1914, *Phaedrus*, translated by H.N. Fowler. Cambridge, MA: Harvard University Press.

Plato 1931, *Timaeus*, translated by R.G. Bury. Cambridge, MA: Harvard University Press .

Plato 1937, *Republic*, 2 vols, translated by P. Shorey. Cambridge, MA: Harvard University Press.

Reiman, S. 2010, 'On Sustainable Exploration of Space and Extraterrestrial Life', *Journal of Cosmology*, 12: 3894–903.

Rowe, S. 1994, 'Ecocentrism: The Chord that Harmonizes Humans and the Earth', *The Trumpeter*, 11(2): 106–7, viewed 19 May 2014, http://www.ecospherics.net/pages/RoweEcocentrism.html.

Rowe, S. 2006, *Earth Alive: Essays on Ecology*. Edmonton: NeWest Press.

Silva, F. 2015, 'The Role and Importance of the Sky in Archaeology: An introduction', in N. Campion and F. Silva (eds), *Skyscapes*. Oxford: Oxbow, pp. 1–7.

Sivin, N. 1995, 'State, Cosmos, and Body in the Last Three Centuries B.C.', *Harvard Journal of Asiatic Studies*, 55(1): 5–37.

Smith, M. 2009, 'Democratization of the Afterlife', in J. Dieleman and W. Wendrich (eds), *UCLA Encyclopedia of Egyptology*, **Los Angeles**, pp. 1–16, viewed 3 July 2014, http://repositories.cdlib.org/nelc/uee/1147.

Stilwell, G.A. 2005, *Afterlife: Post-Mortem Judgments in Ancient Egypt and Ancient Greece*. New York: iUniverse Inc.

The Overview Institute 2012a, OI, viewed 5 July 2014, http://www.overviewinstitute.org.

The Overview Institute 2012b, *Declaration of Vision and Principles*, viewed 25 May 2013, http://www.overviewinstitute.org/index.php/about-us/declaration-of-vision-and-principles.

Thorley, A. and Gunn, C. 2007, *Sacred Sites: An Overview*, Gaia Foundation, n.p., viewed 7 July 2014, http://www.earthskywalk.com/SacredSiteReport.pdf.

Tilley, C. 1994, *A Phenomenology of Landscape*. Oxford: Berg.

Unterman, A. (ed.) 2008, *The Kabbalistic Tradition*. London: Penguin.

Urmson, J.O. 1988, *Aristotle's Ethics*. Oxford: Blackwell.

Varela, F. 1992, *Ethical Know-How*. Stanford, CA: Stanford University Press.

Weston, A. 2009, *The Incompleat Eco-Philosopher: Essays from the Edges of Environmental Ethics*. Albany, NY: State University of New York Press.

Westrum, R. 1978, 'Science and Social Intelligence about Anomalies: The Case of Meteorites', *Social Studies of Science*, 8(4): 461–83.

White, F. 1987, *The Overview Effect – Space Exploration and Human Evolution*. Boston, MA: Houghton-Mifflin.

Wilhelm, R. 1968 [1951], *The I Ching or Book of Changes*, 3rd edn. London: Routledge and Kegan Paul.

Williamson, M. 2003, 'Space ethics and protection of the space environment', *Space Policy*, 19: 47–52.

Xiaochun, S. 2000, 'Crossing the Boundaries between Heaven and Man: Astronomy in Ancient China', in H. Selin (ed.), *Astronomy Across Cultures: The History of Non-Western Astronomy*. Dordrecht: Kluwer Academic Publishers, pp. 423–54.

Zahan, D. 1979, *The Religion, Spirituality and Thought of Traditional Africa*. Chicago, IL: University of Chicago Press.

Chapter 3
The Permissibility of First Contact

Brent Franklin

If intelligent alien life is discovered, should we make contact? For decades now, scientists have been actively involved in efforts to locate intelligent life elsewhere in our galaxy. Their efforts are collectively known as the Search for Extraterrestrial Intelligence (SETI). SETI has been almost entirely privately funded since the United States government stopped its funding of these activities in 1993 (Shuch 2011, pp. 6–7). The recent expansion of private sector involvement in human space endeavours is likely to benefit SETI, directly in the form of funding and indirectly with the increased human presence in space. As such, it is an appropriate time to begin grappling with some of the moral issues inherent in first contact between alien civilisations.

Most doubts about pursuing contact have centred on concerns about the consequences this would have for humans. The potential for hostile encounters with a more advanced civilisation has been one major concern. Many have also questioned how well human societies would be able to handle the news that we are not alone in the universe, though opinions differ on whether there would be widespread social upheaval or if people would mostly take it in their stride (Harrison 2011). To help quantify the potential impact of discovering an alien signal, SETI researchers have developed a metric called the Rio Scale (Almár and Shuch 2007, p. 58). Subsequently, the San Marino Scale was developed to measure the risk of messages we actively broadcast into space (Almár and Shuch 2007, p. 57). Both scales are, naturally enough, concerned exclusively with the impact on *us*. While the interests of humanity are certainly of moral relevance when considering whether we want to pursue contact, it is important to expand the scope of discussion to involve the impact of contact on *others* as well. For this reason, I will be considering the ethics of first contact in terms of the interests of the party being contacted and whether it is permissible from the standpoint of the party initiating contact.

Of particular concern in a first contact scenario are the cultural consequences, which will be my focus here. The introduction of new ideas, technologies and other cultural products can have extensive, transformative repercussions on the world view and practices of a society. This may be seen as what makes first contact between two previously isolated civilisations a unique moral problem. There are of course other important moral considerations, as the many instances of violence and subjugation throughout the history of first contact between human cultures should remind us. But it is rather straightforwardly the case that we should aim for peaceful, equitable relations in this regard. The question of how to respect cultural interests is less transparent.

This chapter begins by discussing reasons for opposition to contact that arise out of respect for cultural interests. Following that, I examine the concept of cultural survival and the extent to which this requires that a culture be protected from change. I argue that the self-determined process by which a culture controls its own development should be protected, but that there is no particular cultural state of affairs that must be protected. Just what should count as interference in this process is then discussed. Finally, I briefly argue against the proposition that contact should specifically be avoided with cultures that are perceived as less advanced. The conclusion is that the obligation to protect cultural interests by exercising caution and sensitivity does not require a general prohibition on contact.

Opposition to First Contact

To understand why first contact might be seen as morally unacceptable, this section looks at three examples of policies that oppose initiating first contact. The first example is the policy of Brazil regarding first contact with uncontacted indigenous tribes. As the country with the most uncontacted tribes within its borders (Survival International n.d., para. 1), Brazil's Indian protection agency, Fundação Nacional do Índio (FUNAI), operates a special department tasked with protecting these tribes (Terborgh 2012, para. 10). FUNAI's policy is to prevent contact and preserve the isolated status of these tribes. In the words of Sydney Possuelo, the creator of this policy and a famous veteran of FUNAI, 'We should avoid contact by all means, protect their environment, demarcate their lands and let them live their traditional lives' (Angelo 2007b).

The second example is the Prime Directive policy from the *Star Trek* science fiction franchise. The universe of *Star Trek* is populated by many alien species and issues surrounding first contact are the centrepiece of many episodes. The Prime Directive, which is the 'highest law' and guiding moral principle of the show's protagonists, prohibits contact with civilisations that have not yet developed the technology of interstellar spaceflight ('Who watches the watchers' 1989).

The third example comes from a hypothetical policy that some SETI researchers believe can explain why, despite their calculations that extraterrestrial intelligence should be commonplace, we have not been contacted by any (a puzzle known as the Fermi Paradox). The so-called Zoo Hypothesis holds that alien civilisations exist but are deliberately avoiding contact with us because they recognise some value in leaving us alone. A wide range of reasons for such a quarantine have been proposed, but the general theme is that the Earth is being isolated as a kind of biological or cultural preserve that would be spoiled by exposure to the wider galactic community (Webb 2002, pp. 46–51). The Zoo Hypothesis is named after a paper by John Ball (1973), but a similar idea was also developed earlier in the work of Russian astronautics theorist Konstantin Tsiolkovksy (Lytkin, Finney and Alepko 1995). Since the Fermi Paradox is based on the supposition that intelligent life is abundant, the Zoo Hypothesis implies that many civilisations have converged upon the same decision to avoid contact with us. This suggests there is a good reason for avoiding contact that we would also want to respect in our dealings with any alien civilisations we eventually discover.

These policies do not represent fully articulated moral arguments, but they are useful for identifying the type of thinking that grounds moral opposition to first contact. To begin with, there is clearly concern over the well-being of the people to be contacted. One of the many reasons given in defence of the Prime Directive in *Star Trek* is that 'history has proven again and again that whenever mankind interferes with a less developed civilisation, no matter how well-intentioned that interference may be, the results are invariably disastrous' ('Symbiosis' 1988). Indeed, the main motivation behind Brazil's policy is to avoid the disastrous consequences that have been so common in the past. Exposure to new diseases often decimates the population of newly contacted tribes. Violent confrontations and exploitation occur not only at the time of contact, but throughout attempts at integration (Terborgh 2012; Angelo 2007a).

The potential for harm, however, is not limited to violence, exploitation and disease. It is the potential for *cultural* harm which is at issue in this chapter. Even Brazil's earlier, well-intentioned policies of integration proved destructive: 'even peaceful contact with such groups often destroyed their native culture and self-sufficiency' (Angelo 2007a, para. 7). As it pertains to cultural harm, the driving idea behind these policies seems to be that contact would introduce an unacceptable influence over the development of the culture. This concern over exogenous influence can be broken down further into two issues: it might be considered objectionable because of the resulting changes to the culture or because it interferes with cultural self-determination.

The first concern is that a unique culture may lose its distinctive character. In *Star Trek*, the Prime Directive is supposed to prevent 'cultural contamination' so that a society can 'progress in [its] own way' ('Who watches the watchers' 1989). Tsiolkovsky's version of the Zoo Hypothesis shares this thinking. He believed extraterrestrials had avoided contact with Earth so as not to 'extinguish the unique evolutionary streams' of our planet. By leaving us alone they could instead 'allow our species to evolve to perfection and thereby bring something unique to the cosmic community' (Lytkin, Finney and Alepko 1995, pp. 374–5).

The second concern is that a culture may no longer be responsible for its own cultural development. The idea that a culture must be allowed to develop in its 'own way' could be interpreted as a matter of self-determination rather than a matter of protecting some unique cultural outcome. The Prime Directive's constraints on first contact are in fact part of a more general policy of non-interference in the internal affairs of other cultures. Supporters of FUNAI's policy express this concern as well. Possuelo and Survival International believe the decision to establish contact should belong to the tribes, not outsiders (Terborgh 2012, para. 21; Survival International n.d., para. 27).

Lastly, another theme found in these policies is the notion that not all cultures are *ready* for contact and so contact is only appropriate after a given threshold point is reached. The Prime Directive, for example, only forbids contact until a society has achieved a certain level of technology. Likewise, Tsiolkovsky's version of the Zoo Hypothesis is orientated towards eventual contact, after a species has reached maturity.

Cultural Survival

Establishing contact with a new culture certainly introduces a risk for the survival of that culture. Throughout human history, cultures have met their demise at the hands of others through acts of oppression and even genocide – intentionally malicious acts of the sort not being discussed in this chapter. However, cultures are also lost through peaceful cultural intercourse, as traditional practices and values are abandoned and new ones are adopted from other cultures. The focus of this section on cultural survival is therefore the possibility that a people may suffer the loss of their culture through exposure to and interaction with foreign cultures.

Put in those terms, it may sound like this would only be of concern to people who fear 'that intermingling with a different culture will inevitably weaken and ruin their own', to borrow a phrase from Salman Rushdie (as cited in Waldron 1992, p. 751). But it is possible to think that cultures deserve to be sheltered from change to *some* extent or in *some* circumstances without necessarily believing cultural interaction itself is a bad thing. First contact may be one such exceptional case, where the very survival of the culture or its distinctive character could require isolation.

The Value of Cultural Survival

A related issue that has been discussed extensively by philosophers is whether minority cultures should be given special rights and accommodations to protect the survival of their cultural traditions. The case in favour of cultural survival starts off by asserting the value of culture. Culture is said to play a crucial role as the framework through which an individual can relate to the world, relate to others and form his or her identity. Charles Taylor puts it like this: '[a] crucial feature of human life is its fundamentally dialogical character. We become full human agents, capable of understanding ourselves, and hence of defining our identity, through our acquisition of rich human languages of expression' (Taylor 1994, p. 32). Will Kymlicka draws a stronger connection between culture and individual interests: 'freedom involves making choices amongst various options, and … culture not only provides these options, but also makes them meaningful to us' (Kymlicka 1995, p. 83).

Simply recognising the importance of culture in itself would not imply that any special value should be attached to a particular culture. For this reason, Jeremy

Waldron argues that an individual's cultural needs can be satisfied by access to *any* 'cultural materials' (1992, p. 784). However, this neglects the fact that these needs are not satisfied if individuals are unable to understand or relate to the cultural setting around them. In addition, Kymlicka has pointed out that it can be a difficult and costly process to move between cultures. The attachment that people have to their own culture is therefore a strong reason to support their efforts to maintain that particular culture (Kymlicka 1995, pp. 85–6). Since cultures serve a valuable function and are not easily replaced, every culture has special value to its members. This makes the survival of a living culture an important moral concern.

Two Conceptions of Cultural Survival

But what is meant by cultural survival? I think it is helpful to differentiate between a substantive conception of cultural survival and a procedural conception. On a substantive conception of cultural survival, it is the *content* of the culture which matters, by which I mean its practices, institutions, systems of belief, technologies and other products. Taylor's views are an example of this. He believes cultural groups ought to be allowed to take measures which will ensure the continued use of their language as well as ensure the community will continue to have members (1994, pp. 52–3, 58–9). In other words, cultural survival is accomplished only if there continues to be a community that shares the content of its forebears. A similar view of culture has been observed in American courts. When minority cultures have asked for certain accommodations in order to maintain their way of life, they are usually not seen as having a valid claim if the culture has already changed a good deal over time, implying that cultural survival has already failed (Deveney 1992, p. 869).

In contrast, a procedural conception of cultural survival would aim to protect the integrity of the process by which a culture perpetuates itself over time. Cultures survive by changing and adapting over time. According to Jürgen Habermas, for example, what needs to be protected is the ability for individuals to carry on their cultural practices if they so choose – but not a guarantee that certain practices be continued indefinitely (1994, p. 130). When following this model, 'the only traditions and forms of life that can sustain themselves are those that bind their members while at the same time subjecting themselves to critical examination and leaving later generations the option of learning from other traditions or converting and setting out for other shores' (Habermas 1994, pp. 130–31). In other words, cultural content must earn the allegiance of its members. Kymlicka also believes that it is not the particular content of the culture that deserves protection and that the point of protective cultural rights is to enable members to manage the development of their culture themselves: 'It is right and proper that the character of a culture change as a result of the choices of its members' (1995, p. 104).

The substantive view of cultural survival fails to capture the dynamic nature of cultural phenomena. The process by which cultures adapt to circumstances and produce their valued content would have to be frozen. Survival in the substantive sense is perhaps better described as preservation. In Waldron's words, 'To *preserve* a culture is often to take a favoured "snapshot" of it, and insist that this version must persist at all costs' (1994, p. 788). Furthermore, this attempt to preserve particular content conflicts with the function of culture. Waldron points out that a culture cannot plausibly be seen as facilitating autonomy unless individuals are free to evaluate and reconsider the content of their culture (1994, pp. 786–7). Under the substantive conception of cultural survival, the content of a culture would have to be given priority over the role it plays to its members.

In the context of avoiding first contact, the goal may not be to preserve a particular past but rather to ensure a particular future untouched by outside influence. Nonetheless, this falls under the substantive conception of cultural survival, by setting the content or character of the culture as the goal of protection. The problem is the same in that a particular cultural outcome is being protected regardless of whether the members of that culture want it and regardless of whether they benefit. Protecting this content thus cannot be seen as serving the cultural interests of those people. The procedural view in contrast holds that the content of a culture should be preserved according to whether the members of that culture actually continue to value and identify with it (Deveney 1992, p. 874; Habermas 1994, pp. 130–32). Procedural survival therefore fits better with our reasons for protecting cultural survival as well as the nature of culture as a changing entity.

Cultural Autonomy

I have argued against pursuing the goal of cultural survival if that goal is interpreted as preserving the particular content of that culture. Rather, it is survival through unimpeded 'cultural reproduction', to use Habermas's phrase, that deserves protection (1994, p. 130). This does not mean that cultural interests have been respected regardless of what happens to that culture. For a culture to survive in the procedural sense still requires that its members not be deprived of control over its development. I will refer to this basic condition of procedural cultural survival as *cultural autonomy*. Roughly, cultural autonomy can be thought of as self-determination in cultural matters. Legal scholar Joakim Parker has defined cultural autonomy as 'the present ability to control activities relating to culture, and the power to guide the future development of a culture' (1993, p. 220).

Who is in Control?

The most obvious way in which cultural autonomy can be lost is when some outside party assumes authority over cultural affairs. The deliberate obstruction of self-determination (in cultural matters or otherwise) is typically unjustifiable. But even assuming well-intentioned first contact, there may be other ways in which first contact would violate autonomy by assuming too much control over events.

A first concern of this type is that any outside influence with extensive repercussions for that culture would be a violation of cultural autonomy. To respond to this, it is important to distinguish cultural autonomy from other perceived merits of isolation. David Brin, for example, has expressed the opinion that it would be regrettable if extraterrestrials contacted Earth any time soon, because he would like to see humanity continue along the path of progress it has been making *on its own*. He is concerned in particular that we would not be responsible for any of the social and scientific advances that would arise from interventions by a more advanced civilisation – advances we might otherwise have achieved ourselves (Fudge 2010, para. 12). We might be tempted to associate cultural autonomy with this ideal of self-sufficient, entirely independent progress. However, cultural autonomy as defined above and as a means to ensuring procedural cultural survival only requires that a culture retains effective control over its own development. In this example, autonomy is only jeopardised if humans are not free to turn down alien assistance.

Indeed, the freedom to choose a cultural path would still allow for the sort of independent progress preferred by Brin. A newly contacted society that retained effective control over its own development could carefully resist dramatic changes to their culture or could request that the outsiders leave. The point of cultural autonomy is that any cultural outcome should be conditional on the choices actively made by its members. Interaction with an alien civilisation may unavoidably alter the path of a culture, but it does not in itself change who is in control of directing that path.

Losing Control

Cultural autonomy is compromised when there is a loss of control over cultural development. But this does not necessarily have to take the form of outsiders assuming control. The following account of how first contact affected some Amazonian tribes illustrates that it is possible for people to lose the ability to steer their own cultural development, even when there is not another party that has *taken* control:

> The lure of 'things' (including alcohol) was irresistible and led to dependencies. …
> With the convenience of matches, one quickly loses the knack for starting a fire.
> Shotguns decisively outperform bows and arrows, but cartridges must be bought
> at a good price. Such newly acquired dependencies fundamentally altered the life
> of the Indians, who were compelled to work for wages instead of spending their
> days hunting, fishing, and tending their gardens. (Terborgh 2012, paras 24–5)

> Pacification was accomplished through the proffering of Western goods,
> including machetes, axes, metal pots, fishhooks, matches, mosquito netting, and
> clothing. The seductive appeal of such things was nearly irresistible, for each of
> these items can make a quantum improvement in a sylvan lifestyle. Acquisition
> of several or all of these goods is a transformative experience that makes contact
> essentially irreversible. Once a person knows such things exist, then that person

> and his entire community are irrevocably changed. Missionaries trying to make contact to save souls know this and exploit it to lure people into a trap of dependency. Dependency instantly demotes proud, confident, and independent people to a mendicant status that is pitiable to behold. (Terborgh 2012, para. 28)

Situations like this can be seen as compromising cultural autonomy by depriving people of the ability to return to the way of life they prefer and locking them into a cultural path they consider objectionable. Although the example involves some deliberate acts of exploitation, the 'trap of dependency' or other destabilising effects could occur unintentionally as well. Being simultaneously introduced to alcohol, new tools and modern economies, it would have been difficult for the indigenous people to understand the path represented by the pursuit of these things.

To some extent this mirrors the situation faced by any society when a new practice or technology emerges. The long-range consequences of any innovation can be difficult to predict and the short-range benefits attractive enough that unintended consequences arise only after it is too late to avert them. It would be a significant overreaction to say that we should resist change to the extent that such risks are never taken. Is it any different when introducing change to another culture? If they freely choose to adopt our cultural products, are we responsible for the results?

Precautions for Respecting Cultural Autonomy

If we are concerned about the effects of our actions when making first contact, it is not enough to deal peacefully and equitably. We must also be careful not to cause any unintentional harm. Having identified loss of cultural autonomy as a potential harm, we would be responsible for taking measures to prevent it. However, this does not imply we should refrain from ever establishing contact with another society; it seems far more reasonable to avoid contact only in cases where the risk is unacceptably high. Nonetheless, certain precautions can and should be taken to prevent the unintentional introduction of cultural content that could destabilise a culture.

There is an important difference between changes that emerge within a culture and those that are introduced from outside. In the latter case, whether we are talking about a technology, institution or belief system, the culture where it comes from will have a greater supply of experience and information that is useful in determining whether the other culture wants to adopt that cultural product. It may be an unavoidable risk that when a practice or product emerges for the first time, there will be unforeseen costs. But once those costs are better understood, others do not have to be left in the dark when the practice or product is introduced to them.

Therefore, once the transfer of culture begins, care should be taken to make sure that the relevant knowledge about cultural consequences also be transferred. For example it is more or less obvious that if blueprints for a technology like nuclear power plants were being transferred, then some information about the safety and environmental hazards should be attached. What I am proposing is that a broader range of supplemental information would be appropriate, such as our observations about the economic and social impact it has had in human societies. More importantly, this sort of information should be attached to a broader range of cultural products, since it can be difficult to predict which ones may turn into a 'trap' for an alien society.

Thresholds

One final consideration that appeared to motivate opposition to first contact was that some cultural groups – namely, those that are 'less advanced' – would not be 'ready' for contact. There is something very plausible about this claim, but in this section I will briefly argue that there is far less reason to support it than we might initially think. As such, I believe we do not need to apply a different approach to contact with less developed societies.

To be clear, I do not doubt that a society with more powerful technology, more effective organisation and similar strengths could exploit those advantages to the detriment of societies that lack those things. What I question is whether these disparities also translate to an increased risk of *cultural* harm when we are assuming a peaceful, cautious approach to contact.

The preceding discussion of cultural survival and cultural autonomy removes some of the motivation for treating less advanced civilisations any differently. If what I have argued so far is correct, then there is no special destiny or historical path that a culture is entitled to. Nor does respect for cultural autonomy require that a culture be left alone to develop entirely independently, unless of course that is their informed (post-contact) decision. Instead, if some cultures require special treatment due to their level of development, the concern must be that they are more vulnerable or at greater risk from first contact.

There is a very plausible line of thinking that appears to support the idea that there would be a threshold of readiness for contact. Experience with a given practice or technology enables people to manage it better. Since practices and technologies tend to emerge out of earlier ones that are related to them, those earlier developments should make people better prepared for the later ones. Thus, we can imagine there are certain developmental prerequisites for safely handling the introduction of new cultural practices and products. According to this way of thinking, until a given society has reached a certain point, it will be ill-equipped for dealings with a more advanced society. Although plausible, there are grounds to doubt this reasoning.

The main issue with this argument is that it relies on the widely discredited theory of unilineal cultural evolution, the idea that societies progress through a uniform sequence of developmental stages. On the contrary, cultures should not be expected to follow any one pattern of development. Although it may be possible to compare two cultures in terms of something like a technological index, this does not imply unilineal evolution. Two cultures could have reached the same level by different developmental paths that have little else in common. More importantly, this technological progress may not have any definite implications for the state of other aspects of culture like belief systems and social practices. It is reasonable to suppose that a culture could be more or less vulnerable to the potential impact of first contact regardless of its level of technology. Without the assumption of unilineal evolution, there is much less reason to suppose that reaching a proposed threshold point would make any difference in a culture's ability to handle the introduction of content from an entirely different culture.

Conclusion

In conclusion, the cultural consequences of first contact should be taken seriously, but cultural interests can be respected without having to avoid contact entirely. The strongest reason to prohibit first contact would be if contact in and of itself threatened an important cultural interest. This might have been the case if cultures needed to be sheltered from change in order to preserve an authentic character or achieve a particular cultural outcome. However, I have argued that such goals misplace the value of culture in its content rather than the value it has to its members. Respect for cultural interests is better served by protecting cultural autonomy, so that people may develop their culture however they choose, including the preservation of content they still value.

At a minimum, respect for cultural autonomy would mean not taking any actions intended to prevent the other society from directing their own cultural development. Yet it is also possible that the introduction of cultural content from another world may unintentionally weaken or destabilise autonomy. Therefore, caution should be exercised to prevent this. Predicting which cultural content will pose a threat to another culture may be difficult. I have also argued that we should not expect there to be a linear scale of cultural development to which this vulnerability can be neatly mapped. I have sketched some suggested precautions, but more work would need to be done in this area. Finally, it should be remembered that cultural issues do not exhaust the moral concerns involved in first contact. A comprehensive first contact policy would integrate other concerns, including the aim of peaceful and equitable relations, and address the relationship between these various considerations.

References

Almár, I. and Shuch, H.P. 2007, 'The San Marino Scale: A new analytical tool for assessing transmission risk', *Acta Astronautica*, 60: 57–9.
Angelo, C. 2007a, 'Prime directive for the last Americans', *Scientific American*, 14 April, viewed 1 July 2014, http://www.scientificamerican.com/article/prime-directive-for-the-1.

Angelo, C. 2007b, 'Q&A with iconoclast who makes first contact with amazonian tribes', *Scientific American*, 18 April, viewed 1 July 2014, http://www.scientificamerican.com/article/sydney-possuelo-sertanista/ Interview with Sydney Possuelo.

Ball, J.A. 1973, 'The zoo hypothesis', *Icarus*, 19: 347–9.

Deveney, M.R. 1992, 'Courts and cultural distinctiveness', *University of Michigan Journal of Law Reform*, 25: 867–77.

Fudge, T. 2010, 'Be careful what you say to space aliens', *KBPS*, 21 October, viewed 1 July 2014, http://www.kpbs.org/news/2010/oct/21/david-brin-wants-us-keep-low-galactic-profile. Interview with David Brin.

Habermas, J. 1994, 'Struggles for recognition in the democratic state', in A. Gutmann (ed.), *Multiculturalism: Examining the Politics of Recognition*, Princeton, NJ: Princeton University Press.

Harrison, A. 2011, 'After contact, then what?', in H.P. Shuch (ed.), *Searching for Extraterrestrial Intelligence: SETI Past, Present, and Future*. New York: Springer.

Kymlicka, W. 1995, *Multicultural Citizenship: A Liberal Theory of Minority Rights*. Oxford: Oxford University Press.

Lytkin, V., Finney, B. and Alepko, L. 1995, 'Tsiolkovsky, Russian cosmism and extraterrestrial intelligence', *Quarterly Journal of the Royal Astronomical Society*, 36: 369–76.

Parker, J.E. 1993, 'Cultural autonomy: A Prime Directive for the blue helmets', *University of Pittsburgh Law Review*, 55: 207–37.

Shuch, H.P. 2011, 'A half-century of SETI science', in H.P. Shuch (ed.), *Searching for Extraterrestrial Intelligence: SETI Past, Present, and Future*. New York: Springer.

Survival International n.d., 'The uncontacted Indians of Brazil', viewed 1 July 2014, http://www.survivalinternational.org/tribes/uncontacted-brazil.

'Symbiosis' 1988, *Star Trek: The Next Generation*, television broadcast, 18 April.

Taylor, C. 1994, 'The politics of recognition', in A. Gutmann (ed.), *Multiculturalism: Examining the Politics of Recognition*, Princeton, NJ: Princeton University Press.

Terborgh, J. 2012, 'Out of contact', review of *The Unconquered: In Search of the Amazon's Last Uncontacted Tribes*, by S. Wallace, *The New York Review of Books*, 5 April 2012 issue, viewed 1 July 2014, http://www.nybooks.com/articles/archives/2012/apr/05/out-contact-amazon-tribes/?pagination=false.

Waldron, J. 1992, 'Minority cultures and the cosmopolitan alternative', *University of Michigan Journal of Law Reform*, 25: 751–93.

Webb, S. 2002, *If the Universe is Teeming with Aliens ... Where is Everybody?: Fifty Solutions to the Fermi Paradox and the Problem of Extraterrestrial Life*. New York: Copernicus Books.

'Who watches the watchers' 1989, *Star Trek: The Next Generation*, television broadcast, 16 October.

Chapter 4

How Space Travel Will Save the World:
An Anthropocentric View of Sustainability

Elizabeth Kanon

Given the resources needed to obtain the ability to travel safely through space, a reasoned justification for doing so is needed. This argument consists of three pivotal foci – anthropocentrism, aggression and manifest destiny – demonstrating space travel is a necessary endeavour for human sustainability. Human sustainability is challenged by large population sizes, areas of the planet which are uninhabitable and human practices that pollute the air, land and water. The first premise argues anthropocentrism is the only world view upon which to ground the importance of sustaining the human species through space travel. The second establishes aggression as a natural drive with positive effects, which, if redirected, outweigh the negative. Finally, the third premise seeks to re-establish enthusiasm for exploration through the use of 'manifest destiny'. Each premise is sufficient to support the desirability of developing space-faring technology; together these three premises make the conclusion that human sustainability and space travel are paramount to our success as a species a truism.

Anthropocentrism

When discussing sustainability the underlying question is, 'what should be sustained?' For many, human beings is the obvious answer. The question becomes, 'should only humans be sustained'? The question is too simplistic, as humans are dependent upon resources found upon planet Earth. Oxygen, water, food and shelter are provided by interdependent ecosystems. So it necessarily follows that in order to sustain humans, the resources humans need to survive must also be sustained. Weak anthropocentrism is a world view that values humans and their needs but not to the exclusion of ecosystems. A competing world view, biocentrism, holds that value inheres only in ecosystems and human beings may be excluded if need be. The implication of biocentrism is that humans need not necessarily be sustained. Space travel is viewed as intrinsically human, thus many biocentrists deride the need to pursue such an endeavour. Hence, in order to procure policy and resources towards space travel, an anthropocentric world view is necessary.

Weak anthropocentrism is the belief that humans 'be valued more highly than other things in nature – by humans' (Murdy 2004, p. 281). This suggests that the individual doing the valuing is justified in valuing himself and others similar to him. Hence the reason for placing the highest value upon humans is simply the ability of humans to value. Critics of this world view charge 'speciesism'. Similar to racism and sexism, speciesism is a type of bigotry to be avoided. Anthropocentric views are deemed bigoted because such views place human beings above other species without providing good reasons for doing so. Paul Taylor questions anthropocentrism's dogmatism. 'In what sense are humans alleged to be superior to other animals? We are different from them in having certain capacities that they lack. But why should these capacities be a mark of superiority? From what point of view are they to be judged to be signs of superiority and what sort of superiority is meant?' (Taylor 2008, p. 148). He claims that humans cannot justify valuing humans more than other species since we are bound by our own species ability to view and value the world. He argues that we must revise our valuing system to incorporate a recognition that other species have values. Anthropocentrism is compatible with such a recognition; one can agree with Taylor and still reject biocentrism.

The biocentric assumption that humans are acting unnaturally when placed beyond, or above, all other species by anthropocentrism is false. In fact, valuing one's own species is quite natural: '[b]y the same logic, spiders are to be valued more highly than other things in nature – by spiders. It is proper for men to be anthropocentric and for spiders to be arachnocentric. This goes for all other living species' (Murdy 2004, p. 281). The charge of unnaturalism is turned upon the biocentrists in that they require humans to deny the natural instinct to preserve one's species. Richard Watson argues that '[h]uman ways – human culture – and human actions are as natural as are the ways in which any other species of animals behaves. But if we view the state of nature or Nature as being natural, undisturbed and unperturbed only when human beings are not present, or only when human beings are curbing their natural behaviour, then we are assuming that human beings are apart from, separate from, different from, removed from or above nature' (Watson 2008, p. 238). It becomes apparent that it is natural to insure the sustained continuance of one's own species.

Claiming that it is natural for humans to adopt a hierarchy of values, placing human interests over nonhuman interests, is guilty of the 'is/ought fallacy' and has a *prima facie* persuasiveness. It seems to suggest that because it is an instinctive behaviour to ensure the survival of one's species, it follows that we ought to do so. A closer look at the limits of moral behaviour show the weakness of this charge. Morality is strictly speaking a human construct. Only human beings can be injured in a moral sense; from this it follows that only humans can be restricted by moral prescriptions. If the basis of morality is to ensure social cohesion and thereby human species survival, then the charge of committing the naturalistic fallacy is a first order problem. In other words it is suggesting that morality ought to be based upon something other than survival of the human species. What would such a grounding look like? Human survival is the basis of moral culture so the 'is/ought fallacy' is misapplied since it only resonates at a second order level of moral consideration.

It is also apparent that humans have made ecological mistakes counterproductive to our sustainability. Weak anthropocentrism can support correcting our use of natural resources and implementing conservation policies. Further, space travel can aid in developing new technologies that will aid in such endeavours. Recognising that it is natural to want to preserve humanity is the first step towards accepting weak anthropocentrism's ability to justify expenditures towards such an end. Once we acknowledge we are natural beings with natural inclinations, we can begin to understand the natural drives which motivate us.

Aggression

It is important to understand the true nature of aggression; is it a biological drive or a response to environmental stimuli? Humans must base our control or utilisation of aggression upon how we understand the phenomenon. Therefore the first step would be to establish the true nature of aggression. Once the concept is understood, how we respond to this phenomenon is the next step. If it is shown that aggression is a natural biological drive, then a process must be found to bring out the positive implications of this drive and defuse the negative ones. If aggression is a learned behaviour, the need to relearn different behaviours in order to accomplish the same positive outcomes becomes apparent. This section will attempt an understanding of the nature and implications of aggression.

Obviously from our lexical conception of 'aggression', this concept has a negative connotation. In Webster's *New Universal Unabridged Dictionary*, the following represents the ordinary understanding of the term. Aggression is 'the action of a state in violating by force the rights of another state, particularly its territorial rights; an unprovoked offensive, attack, invasion or the like. 2. Any offensive action or procedure' (Webster 1989, p. 28).

In the first definition, we see aggression reserved for reference to governments or societies. In the second, the scope is enlarged to encompass any activity that exhibits 'offensiveness'. Ultimately the ordinary understanding of the concept implies that it is a behaviour that ought to be curtailed, if not expunged. Yet, aggression also has a positive understanding. If one were to look at 'aggressive' in a thesaurus, words like 'energetic, forceful, vigorous, competitive, ambitious ...' are attributed as synonyms (Landau and Bogus 1977, p. 16).

How are we to understand this seemingly contradictory concept? Perhaps an investigation into the various theories of its nature might clarify whether aggressive behaviour should be eliminated or encouraged. There are opposing views regarding the nature of aggression. One theory holds that it is an instinctual behaviour or drive while the other maintains it is strictly a learned behaviour. Each explanation suggests that aggressive behaviour can, and ought to be, controlled. This is the only point upon which these competing views agree.

Ethnologist Konrad Lorenz suggests that aggression is a biological drive or instinct which results in establishment of social bonds and, ultimately, survival.

In his book, *On Aggression*, Lorenz argues that humans, as animals, share many of the biological drives found in other animals. Lorenz defines aggression as 'the fighting instinct in beast and man which is directed against members of the same species' (Lorenz 1966, p. ix). He notes this instinct can be detrimental in that 'what directly threatens the existence of an animal species is never the 'eating enemy' but the competitor' (Lorenz 1966, p. 25). Yet he maintains that aggression has an 'indispensable' motivation in species survival regarding territorial distribution and establishment of intimate bonds (Lorenz 1966, p. 43). Drives could be understood as instinctual triggers for behaviour. Hence the uses of 'drive' and 'instinct' are often interchangeable within Lorenz's work. According to Lorenz, drives are important towards an animal's survival, without such drives the success of the individual and its species is at risk. Lorenz theorises from the fact that human physiology is a direct result of evolving from the same beginnings as animals – such that there is no significant difference between human and animal physiology – it follows that human psychology also has no significant difference. Thus, if animals have instincts, humans have the same instincts. He bolsters his claims by noting that Darwin's theory of evolution supports his own argument regarding intra-species aggression in that the 'struggle for existence' is a 'competition between near relations' with natural selection determining the winner (Lorenz 1966, pp. 23–4).

Lorenz has many critics of his characterisation of the nature of aggression. The opposing view on the nature of aggression claims that it is a learned behaviour thus rejecting the notion of drives or instincts in favour of rational choice. This 'nurture' view thus has no need to establish a positive function for aggression and can instead advocate the eradication of aggressive behaviour through socialisation and indoctrination. Rejecting the role of 'drives' is imperative as drives are beyond rational control. All behaviour must be grounded in a desire/belief condition. Drives do not conform to such a view, they are neither desires nor beliefs. One specific criticism of Lorenz's claims that aggression is a drive is based upon what is deemed an unsupported leap from commonality in that one area supports commonality in another. Ashley Montagu claims Lorenz's argument is flawed: '[t]here is, in fact not the slightest evidence or ground for assuming that the alleged "phylogenetically adapted instinctive" behaviour of other animals is in any way relevant to the discussion of the motive-forces of human behaviour. The fact is, that with the exception of the instinctoid reactions in infants to sudden withdrawals of support and to sudden loud noises, the human being is entirely instinctless' (Montagu 1973, p. 10). Unfortunately, Montagu never offers proof of this claim, instead the reader must infer Montagu's commitment to the belief that human behaviour is exclusively rational. Throughout his essay, 'The New Litany of "Innate Depravity"', he merely states that Lorenz is 'unacquainted with the facts' and lacks an 'understanding of the uniqueness of man's evolutionary history' (Montagu 1973, p. 11). Without offering the alternative facts and implications from these facts, Montagu remains vague and unpersuasive. Morton Hunt fares a little better with his denial of aggression as instinctual. He notes that within the community of ethnologists, agreement is not assured.

Many zoologists, biochemist and animal psychologists reject the theory that most behaviour is preprogrammed and stored in the genes. They agree that, for biochemical reasons, animals have built-in 'tendencies' to behave in certain ways but that these are specific and automatic only in lower animals; the higher the animal on the evolutionary scale, the more its tendencies are shaped, developed and organised into behaviour by its interactions with its environment (Hunt 1973, p. 21).

While Hunt does not produce the facts and theories of Lorenz's contemporaries, he does provide reasonable doubt on the strength of Lorenz's claims. An example provided by Hunt to support this claim notes that crickets chirp given the proper stimulus without having learned this ability, but that since humans must learn their language it is a sign that human speech is not instinctual (Hunt 1973, p. 21). But might the desire or drive to 'speak' be the same in both cricket and human? Can we truly ignore the fact that 'speaking' is a response to stimulus? Thus, while the manner in articulation may be learned in humans, the drive to articulate is similar to lower animals. Montagu himself notes that young humans articulate in response to the stimulus of hunger or withdrawal of support. The fact that we later learn a more complicated method to articulate does not imply that the 'drive to articulate' is dissimilar from lower animals.

Another rejection of Lorenz's use of analogy between animal and human behaviour is presented by Asad Shahzad. Shahzad states: '[t]he method of analogy, on many occasions cannot be applied even from man to man, let alone from animal to man. For example, if a blue-eyed man kills a person who has slapped him it cannot be concluded that all blue-eyed men are very likely to kill anyone who slaps them' (Shahzad 2010, p. 762). The problem with this counter-example is that the target property – killing – is not relevant to the primary property of having blue eyes; whereas, Lorenz's target property of aggression is relevant to the primary property of being a member of the animal kingdom.

The disagreement that aggression in humans is a natural drive rather than a learned behaviour centres on the ability to derive analogous behaviour between nonhuman animals and human animals. Either position requires commitment to a presupposition that cannot be irrefutably proven. If you agree with Lorenz, you accept that humans are similar enough to animals in possessing instincts. If you oppose Lorenz, you accept that humans are distinct from the other members of the animal kingdom in that humans do not have instincts. The rejection of Lorenz's use of analogues lies simply in a difference in accepting as fact an incompatible presupposition. A complication for Lorenz's opponents is the recognition of the human fight or flight response, which is often perceived as instinctual. If humans have one instinctual behaviour, it seems highly probable humans have others. It could be argued that the real difference in presuppositions is not about the presence of instincts but rather the ability of humans to not be ruled by instincts. Thus, the argument is humans can learn to not react to instinctual drives, whereas animals cannot. This suggests that humans can be taught to behave non-aggressively, despite an aggression instinct. Thus when Lorenz notes animal aggression results in fighting behaviour, it does not follow that human aggression must result in fighting behaviour. Instead, human reason can mediate a different behaviour. Regardless, aggression, mediated by reason or not, influences human behaviour.

Perhaps a good reason for accepting Lorenz's concept of aggression is the positive implications of aggression as a survival instinct. He argues that aggression aids in population dispersal within a territory and in establishment of close social bonds (Lorenz 1966, p. 43). Lorenz suggests that aggression contributes largely to both these positive factors. Without population dispersal, '[t]he danger of too dense a population of an animal species settling in one part of the available biotope and exhausting all its sources of nutrition … can be obviated … effecting their regular spacing out … [t]his in plain terms, is the most important survival value of intra-specific aggression' (Lorenz 1966, p. 31). However, Lorenz qualifies this claim by noting that 'unless the special interests of a social organisation demand close aggregation of its members …' (Lorenz 1966, pp. 30–31). Critics of his view could point out that humans fall under his qualification, since throughout history humans tended to congregate in large numbers. A further complication for Lorenz lies in the fact that currently there are no new territories available for humans 'spacing out', thus aggression undermines survival.

Lorenz's other positive factor for aggression might provide an answer to the previously mentioned criticisms of survival requiring population dispersal. He claims that close social bonds can only be established within species possessing a strong aggressive instinct. He notes types of social organisation formed through the degree of intra-specific aggression. Two will be discussed here for the purpose of showing the importance of aggression in forming 'love' bonds. The first type of social organisation – anonymous crowds – are formed by species lacking intra-specific aggression. Examples of anonymous crowds or 'herds' include some fish, birds and even mammals adopting this form of organisation, 'determined by the fact that individuals of a species react to each other by attraction and are held together by behaviour patterns which one or more individuals elicit in the others' (Lorenz 1966, p. 139). He notes that 'herd' organisation can aid in an individual's survival from predation by being one of many despite the difficulty for the herd to hide from predators. The herding instinct aids survival of the species in that a predator cannot catch every member and often fails to get even one due to the difficulty in concentrating upon one individual amid a swarming group (Lorenz 1966, p. 142). This form of social organisation is often found in species that cover vast areas, thus no close bonds are established amongst its members or with a certain biotope. Lorenz notes that humans may 'regress' into such a form of social organisation but only if 'certain horrible conditions' exist (Lorenz 1966, p. 139).

The social organisation most often associated with humans is referred to by Lorenz as 'the bond'. Whereas the previous social organisation permitted the impersonal exchange of one individual for another, 'the bond' exhibits personal ties formed through mutual attraction (Lorenz 1966, p. 165). Lorenz contends that central to forming 'the bond', 'individual animals should be capable of reacting selectively to the individuality of every other member' (Lorenz 1966, p. 166). Thus, an ability to distinguish one from another is paramount to forming such personal ties. The ability to develop special inhibiting mechanisms which redirect intra-specific aggression is also essential to forming 'the bond'. Thus, personal ties require aggression and the ability to redirect it (Lorenz 1966, p. 215). Lorenz notes that some non-aggressive species form life-long flocks, but these are always devoid of permanent friendships or brotherly love. Such long-term formations amongst species with low degrees of intra-specific aggression are 'always entirely anonymous' associations (Lorenz 1966, p. 216). So Lorenz argues that '[a] personal bond, an individual friendship, is found only in animals with highly developed intra-specific aggression; in fact, this bond is the firmer, the more aggressive the particular animal and species is' (Lorenz 1966, p. 216). Humans do form personal bonds and individual friendships. Thus, if Lorenz is correct, human social organisation is due to our strong intra-specific aggression as well as our ability to redirect our aggression.

Shahzad argues that Lorenz has the priority wrong when he claims love forms from aggression. Instead, Shahzad argues that love is the basis of aggression. Imam Ghazali (as cited by Shahzad 2010, p. 758) categorises aggression upon objects of love. The first is material, love of necessities or basic social goods. Benign aggression is considered by Ghazali is acceptable and justifiable. The second type of aggression for Ghazali is formed upon love of nonessentials like social status and affluence or over-consumption. This malignant aggression ought to be controlled (Shahzad 2010, p. 758). However, Shahzad seems to equivocate upon the 'object' of love. Lorenz is referring to other members of one's species and Shahzad is referring to things. One might note that in Maslow's hierarchy of needs, that is, list of basic necessities, he lists interpersonal relationships. Hence, Shahzad could claim that love of one's personal relationships could result in benign aggression. Shahzad or Ghazali need some kind of explanation of 'love' to make their argument stronger. Such an explanation is not given, leaving the reader to infer that love is either instinctual or a feeling. Lorenz's explanation is more complete in that it provides an explanation involving the instinctual basis for the feeling of love.

Sublimation of Aggression

Most humans would like to believe that our social organisation is based upon 'love and friendship' rather than anonymous 'herding'. Thus it seems reasonable to encourage the ability to feel love. If Lorenz is correct, the aggressive drive is central to such an ability. However it is not sufficient to ensure the development of 'the bond'. The second condition for 'the bond' is the notion of redirecting aggression in order to inhibit aggression's self-defeating outcome of total annihilation of both aggressors.

Lorenz claims that:

> the inestimably important fact that by the process of phylogenetic ritualisation a new and completely autonomous instinct may evolve which is, in principle, just as independent as any of the so-called 'great' drives, such as hunger, sex, fear or aggression and which – like these – has its seat in the great parliament of instincts. This again is important for our theme, because it is particularly, the drives that have arisen by ritualisation which are so often called upon, in this parliament, to oppose aggression, to conditions that are injurious to the survival of the species. (Lorenz 1966, p. 67)

This ritualised redirecting is the second condition Lorenz submits for forming 'the bond' and he notes further that the ritualisation itself becomes a drive that is beneficial to species survival. In the last chapter of *On Aggression*, Lorenz suggests that sports provide the much needed ritualised behaviour that serves such a purpose.

Once again Shahzad disagrees with Lorenz's claims. As an objection, he reminds us that Hindus and Muslims have been fighting for centuries. Thus he concludes that 'love does not seem to be the creation of aggression … rather aggression seems to be the tool of love' (Shahzad 2010, p. 757). This is in keeping with his position that love of things produces aggression on both a beneficial and malignant scale. However, Lorenz addresses this very concern. He notes that 'militant enthusiasm is a specialised form of community aggression … it has its own appetitive behaviour, its own releasing mechanisms. [and] can be elicited with the predictability of a reflex …' (Lorenz 1966, pp. 268–72). Lorenz identifies the initial stimuli for militant enthusiasm as being when the individual determines an outside threat to his social group by a traditionally hated enemy. Combined with a charismatic leader and a conglomeration of like-minded individuals, hostile behaviour results in war (Lorenz 1966, p. 272); this would explain Shahzad's example, as it is well known that a traditional hatred exists between the Hindus and Muslims of India. However, war is the very behaviour both Lorenz and Shahzad are determined to redirect. Shahzad suggests that war is a result of malignant aggression, based upon love of non-material things; whereas Lorenz claims it is the conditioned response to specific stimuli. What is interesting is that both authors have a commonality in the solution: for Shahzad and Lorenz, indoctrination has a role in changing this behaviour. Shahzad claims we can educate ourselves to not love the non-material and thus will not aggress in order to attain it. Lorenz suggests that humans are capable of adapting their values: '[d]uring and shortly after puberty human beings have an indubitable tendency to loosen their allegiance to all traditional rites and social norms of their culture, allowing conceptual thought to cast doubt on their value and to look around for new and perhaps more worthy ideals' (Lorenz 1966, p. 267). This is, according to Lorenz, the time to create to new 'object fixation'. Both authors are committed to the idea that humans can redirect their values into more positive behaviours. Perhaps space travel can become humans' new 'object fixation'? The next section considers the ability of space exploration providing 'more worthy ideals'.

Manifest Destiny

National Aeronautics and Space Administration (NASA) has used manifest destiny as an appeal to justify governmental expenditures. Steven Dick, a chief historian for NASA, reports that '[e]xploration is certainly part of the American character and Federally funded exploration has been a significant part of American history – from land exploration beginning with Lewis and Clark, to the U.S. Exploring Expedition headed by Charles Wilkes from 1838–1842' (Dick 2014). Hence, space is the next logical step in fulfilment of our character and history. Critics are concerned with the implication of imperialism inherent in manifest destiny and thus see the final frontier as another opportunity to exploit and assimilate other cultures. The positive features attributed to manifest destiny are acquisition of territory and innovative new technologies. Some question if these goals will be met and at what cost?

The term 'manifest destiny' originated as a slogan promoting United States' expansion into the western territories in the middle of the nineteenth century. Manifest destiny, at that time, conveyed the belief that through 'divine right' Occidental culture is destined to inhabit the whole continent of Northern America. This idea aided in establishing policy and concentrating resources towards conquering the lands west of the Mississippi River. Neo-manifest destiny slogans are utilised today to promote the expansion of human life into space. The traditional rejection of the reasonableness of manifest destiny is based upon the symbiotic inclusion of imperialism that occurs when one culture replaces another. Imperialism combined with religious zealotry have permeated the connotation of manifest destiny. A study conducted by MIT students in *Tomorrow's Frontier* exemplifies the disdain for use of terms like 'manifest destiny' – they state: '[m]uch of the language that appears in justifications for ambitious exploration missions exhibits a simple-mindedness rooted in an unchallenged desire to expand the "frontier"' (MIT 2007).

It is the frontier mentality, as described by Pete Gunter and Max Oelschlaeger in their book *Texas Land Ethics*, which offers a failed world view as 'the notion that nature's bounty is unlimited, virtually free for the taking ... [a] myth configures itself in many ways, such as in the belief that new resources will always be found to meet the expanding demands of a physically growing, materialistic society' (Gunter and Oelschlaeger 1997, p. ix). These authors advocate replacing the economic world view of frontier mentality since there is no frontier remaining. Yet as long as a frontier exists, this economic approach has demonstrated some success in human sustainability. Thus, declaring space a new frontier might allow continued success of such an economic world view.

Imperialism, or at least cultural assimilation, is a rational concern and yet how can human expansion into space risk such behaviour? Setting aside the question of extraterrestrial life, there are no cultures to be exploited or assimilated, all known 'territories' are uninhibited. In fact, these territories do not seem to offer any known resources that can sustain life. Thus, there is a significant difference between the old and new frontier – space. Some proponents of neo-manifest destiny in space exploration claim that space can offer minerals that could be utilised by humans on Earth. However, such a small gain does not provide the impetus that originally spurred the ordinary individual's drive to participate in conquering the old frontier. The only tangible benefit discerned in conquering the new frontier is the technological gains which might eventually trickle into common consumerism. In 'Top 10 NASA Inventions' Patrick Kiger and Marianne English list several technologies that were invented to solve NASA problems that have since been implemented into technologies for common, terrestrial uses. Their list includes memory foam, anti-corrosion coating, ArterioVision, scratch-resistant eyeglass lenses, remulsified zero-valent iron, insulin pump, lifeshears, charge-coupled devices and water filters (Kiger and English 2011). Past experience does support some technological gains have resulted from our space programme. Yet, some opponents claim such technologies do not justify the expenditure. David Bell and. Martin Parker, in their introduction to *Space Travel and Culture*, observe this objection '… the trump card – that all that money could have spent on eradicating poverty, building schools and keeping taxes down …' (Bell and Parker 2009, p. 2). It is widely claimed that the money spent by governments and private enterprise would be better spent on solving terrestrial problems; however, some critics take it a step further and claim that third world countries will be harmed due to being left out of the process. This is the viewed as a new type of imperialism where the cultures of non-industrialised nations will be undermined or impoverished from their inability to participate in the gains from the new frontier. Alan Marshall observes that claims of benefits from extraterrestrial expansion merely reflect an imperialistic search for resource surplus only benefitting the political and military programs of the nation seeking such a surplus (Marshall 1995, p. 43). Thus, poorer nations and peoples will only be harmed by space expanision due to first world countries controlling both the terrestrial and extraterrestrial resources.

Because one can infer that space exploration reflects imperialistic dominance, it need not be the case. Neo-manifest destiny proponents claim that technologies developed for space travel will have a global, beneficial effect since these will eventually be available to non-participating cultures despite their non-contribution towards the development of such technologies. The process would be similar to communication technologies that are now available and being utilised by individuals in poorer countries. Similarly, as this technology has improved quality of life in these impoverished nations, so too will the anticipated 'new' technologies. Some possible technologies that may emerge are water recovery and oxygen generation as well as agricultural advances. These technologies have an obvious application in areas of the world that currently suffer from poverty due to a lack of clean drinking water and arid growing conditions. Many believe that the ability to correct environmental damages due to industrial wastes will also emerge from the need to develop life-sustaining habitats in space. They claim that third world countries will reap benefits from industrial nations' efforts to colonise close astral bodies such as the Moon and Mars.

Conclusion

Given the postmodern perspective, how can concepts of anthropocentrism, aggression and 'manifest destiny' be used as persuasive tools? Space travel is exclusively human and thus requires a commitment to sustain human life. Aggression as an instinct can undermine our ability to sustain our species but can also provide a strong bond between nations if it is redirected towards a shared endeavour. Neo-manifest destiny must distance itself from the manifest destiny of the past. It must be emphasised that we mean to sublimate our natural aggressive drive towards a positive outcome. The basic resources for survival of our species here on planet Earth can be revitalised by the technologies and methods implemented in space travel. We seek to manifest humans in space in order to provide more territory for the expansion of our populations and to foster a common struggle which can only be achieved through cooperative efforts of all nations. Policy and practices need to be developed that reflect neo-manifest destiny ideals and reject past imperialistic tendencies. Technologies derived from sustaining life in space must have terrestrial applications that will benefit those of us who choose to remain behind. If we proceed with checks and balances upon our natural tendency to seek advantage over others, then a global effort will succeed in conquering the difficulty of living in extraterrestrial environs and space travel will save the world.

References

Bell, David and Martin Parker (eds), 2009, *Space Travel and Culture: From Apollo To Space Tourism*. Malden: Blackwell Publishing.

Dick, Steven J., 2007, 'The Importance of Exploration Part 2', *Why We Explore*, NASA History Program Office, viewed 3 June 2014, http://history.nasa.gov/Why_We_/Why_We_01pt1.html.

Gunter, Pete A.Y. and Max Oelschlaeger, 1997, *Texas Land Ethics*. Austin, TX: University of Texas Press.

Hunt, Morton, 1973, 'Man and Beast', in Ashley Montagu (ed.), *Man and Aggression*, 2nd edn. New York: Oxford University Press.

Kiger, Patrick J. and Marianne English, 2011, 'Top 10 NASA Inventions', HowStuffWorks, viewed 28 May 2014, http://science.howstuffworks.com/innovation/inventions/top-5-nasa-inventions.htm.

Landau, Sidney I. and Ronald J. Bogus (eds), 1977, *The Doubleday Roget's Thesaurus in Dictionary Form*. Garden City, NY: Doubleday & Company, Inc.

Lorenz, Konrad, 1966, *On Agression*. New York: Harcourt, Brace & World, Inc.

'Language of the Frontier and Manifest Destiny', *Tomorrow's Frontier: A Study of Possibilities for Future Space Exploration and Their Supporters* 2007, Massachusetts Institute of Technology, viewed 25 May 2014, http://web.mit.edu/demoscience/TomorrowsFrontier/Language1.html.

Marshall, Alan, 1995, 'Development and imperialism in space', *Space Policy 1995,* 11(1): 41–52.

Montagu, Ashley (ed.), 1973, *Man and Aggression*, 2nd edn. New York: Oxford University Press.

Murdy, William H., 2004, 'Anthropocentrism: A Modern Version', Susan J. Armstrong and Richard C. Botzler (eds), *Environmental Ethics: Divergence and Convergence*, 3rd edn. New York: McGraw-Hill.

Shahzad, Asad, 2010, 'Incoherences in Konrad Lorenz's Concept of Aggression', *Pakistan Business Review*, January, pp. 753–81.

Taylor, Paul, 2008, 'Biocentric Egalitarianism', Louis P. Pojman and Paul Pojman (eds), *Environmental Ethics: Readings in Theory and Application*, 5th edn., Belmont, CA: Wadsworth.

Watson, Richard, 2008, 'A Critique of Anti-Anthropocentric Ethics', Louis P. Pojman and Paul Pojman (eds), *Environmental Ethics: Readings in Theory and Application*, 5th edn. Belmont, CA: Wadsworth.

Webster's New Universal Unabridged Dictionary 1992. Avenel: Barnes & Noble Book.

Chapter 5

Who is Afraid of 'The Dark'? Familiarising the Unknown

Zümre Gizem Yılmaz

Beginning with the Enlightenment period and Cartesian dualism, ontology and epistemology have been separated, which has resulted in the separation of mind and body. Hence, humans have granted themselves privilege, claiming that they are the only beings that have an intellectual capacity, which has subsequently become the basic discourse used to justify the exploitation of racial and sexual minorities, of nonhuman animals, of the physical environment and lastly of outer space. As a combination of both mind and body, humans have entitled themselves to the right to colonise the other bodies that supposedly lack in mind according to the anthropocentric point of view. Therefore, on the Earth, and now in space, the human kingdom has been established out of human chauvinism. At the heart of this discursive formation lies the idea of untouched and pure humans that are thought to be exempt from the material formations in the universe, which puts emphasis on the position of humans as separate observers. However, the notion of untouched human beings has long been eroded through the posthumanist point of view, since posthuman studies clearly break 'the outline of human and consider the forces, substances, agencies, and lively beings that populate the world' (Alaimo 2011, p. 282) together, and tries to demonstrate that, as Karen Barad contends, humans' 'practices are not the only practices that come to matter' (2007, p. 206). Hence, eliminating the role of human beings as the only actors in the world, posthumanism and new materialisms draw attention to intra-action, which is interaction stressed both between and within all the beings inhabiting the universe. Drawing upon the entanglement of the observer and the observed in quantum physics, posthumanism illustrates that human beings do not observe the world separately, and their bodies are in a constant relationship with the other bodies. The aim of this chapter is, thus, to point out one perspective of the exploitation discourse, which is the discrimination of the unknown, and to illustrate space colonialisation as a consequence of an anthropocentric viewpoint.

A Space Phobia

Most of the phobias arise out of a sense of unknown, which generally makes humans link evil with the unknown. For instance, homophobia is a reaction of heterosexual humans who associate homosexuality with dark and devil simply because it is unknown to them. Similarly, ecophobia, coined by Simon Estok, also hints at the fear of the unknown 'as an irrational and groundless fear or hatred of the natural world' (Estok 2011, p. 4). In order to cope with the unknown, humans either try to assimilate it through the long-established discourses or familiarise that unknown into the dominant ideology. For example, while homosexuality was reacted against, treated as a disease and forbidden in the past, it has gradually started to be accepted politically and socially since the rights of homosexual couples have been acknowledged by a number of countries and states, just because homosexual discourse has merged with the dominant ideology through the familiarisation process, and it has found a place for itself to survive in a hetero-patriarchal society. While homophobia and ecophobia are one perspective of the reaction against the unknown, humans generally get afraid of the unknown, the unseen and the incomprehensible by connecting it with threatening demonised shapes.

The Scottish writer Ali Smith, in *The Accidental* (2005), portrays a family threatened by an unknown visitor, whereby she points to the psychological breakdown coming with the unknown. Although the family gets used to the unknown at first, and familiarise the visitor as a part of the family, it is later revealed that the visitor is there just for financial gain. Apart from this thematisation of the unknown throughout the novel, Smith (2005, pp. 14–15) also points to the psychological perception of the dark by humans:

> A man is standing there. He has no face. He has no nose, no eyes, nothing, just black skin. Astrid is terrified. Her mother will be furious with her. It is her fault he is here. You can't come in, she tries to tell him, but she has no breath. We're not here, she breathes. We're on holiday. Go away. She tries to shut the door. A mouth appears in the skin and a great noise roars out of it like she is standing too close to an aeroplane. It forces the door back. She opens her eyes, rolls straight off the bed on to her feet.

It already appears in human psyche that the incomprehensible, the unseen and the unperceived in human terms is accepted to have evil intentions and is associated with dark as it is unknown to humans. Since humans have limited sight to perceive and know the dark as it is, they psychologically suppose that the dark includes some evil spirits trying to conquer humanity in the world. Likewise, as humans cannot comprehend outer space in its full form, and as they cannot colonise and exploit all of it, they develop a kind of spacephobia, which is 'fear of outer space' (Doctor and Kahn 2008, p. 456). Spacephobia is automatically correlated to the fear of the unknown since, despite a number of explorations of space nearby the orbit, outer space yet remains 'dark, still, and mysterious' (Doctor and Kahn 2008, p. 457). Hence, as a result of anthropocentric binary oppositions, they first use nonhuman animals in explorations of the unknown and dangerous, that is, space, as they are believed to have lesser value in the hierarchy of beings, on top of which humans reside.

Hierarchy and Nonhuman Animals

Throughout centuries there have been many blurrings in the borders of the hierarchy, especially with the feminist and postcolonial discourses, and animal rights rising. Yet, still, the hierarchy of beings can roughly be accepted as starting with humans at the top with a racial and sexual discrimination; nonhuman animals in the second place with a differentiation between tamed (including pets) and wild animals, as well as mammals and the other kinds; plants; and lastly the other beings and matter in the world. Humans have been inclined to include the ones resembling human forms most to the higher status in the hierarchy as they tend to think in a human-centred perspective. First of all, the discrimination between humans against homosexuals and black people is a result of hetero-patriarchal hegemony, which has started to loosen these days. On the other hand, the differentiation of nonhuman animals as pets and wild ones brings about the idea that humans give more value to the ones that are closer to them. In other words, pets are like friends of humans and fill the emotional gaps in their lives. So it can be stated that while wild animals do not mean much in the personal lives of humans, pets become substitutes for family and friends; thus, they deserve more value. Moreover, the separation of mammals and the other kinds of animals such as reptiles is also a direct result of anthropocentrism because the former resemble humans more in terms of bodily functions such as reproduction. So, it is accepted to be their rights to have a more valuable status in the hierarchy. Similarly, plants and the other beings in the world are excluded from the higher places since they are really different from humans in terms of their shapes or functions.

Hence, as a result of these binary oppositions resulting from the anthropocentric discourse, in the first space explorations through the heart of the unknown, the lives of the nonhuman animals were risked rather than those of human beings. Animals have always taken the place of humans in these dangerous space adventures: recall that 'the dog Laika went before the Russian Yuri Gagarin and the chimpanzees Ham and Enos went before the American Alan Shepard' (Arnould 2011, p. 144). Therefore, space research and exploration centres of each superpower have become 'institutions of species imprisonment, enslavement, and slaughter' (Gaard 2012, p. 19). Consequently, the intrinsic value of nonhuman animals sent to space was denied and only their instrumental value for humans has been acknowledged. The English writer Lavinia Greenlaw, especially in her poem entitled 'For the First Dog in Space', underlines that it was accepted by the Russian scientists that Laika would be incapable of thinking as well as feeling any emotions simply because of her species. Throughout that particular poem, Greenlaw contends that, for the scientists, Laika is just another 'Russian mongrel bitch' (1993, p. 52) that can be easily sent to absolute death in Sputnik 2 without any regrets. Furthermore,

Greenlaw also criticises anthropocentric arrogance by means of the portrayal of the Russian scientists as at ease feeling secured and presupposing that an instrumentally valuable being will grant them enough knowledge about space, which will eventually lead them to the discovery of safer space. So, nonhuman animals have been seen as a substitute for humans especially in space exploration as they have been sacrificed to obtain knowledge about the safety of the point in space where the scientists want to reach. In addition to the criticism of the human-centred perspective, Greenlaw (p. 52) ruptures anthropocentrism by giving voice to Laika's feelings and her process of thinking:

> You will have no companion,
> no buttons to press, just six days' air.
> Laika, do not let yourself be fooled
> by the absolute stillness
> that comes only with not knowing
> how fast you are going.

She ends her poem advising Laika not to forget her language and to trust her fear on the edge of death. These recommendations determine Greenlaw's stance against speciesism conducted during the first space exploration age. By claiming that Laika is also able to feel fear and pain just like human beings, the figure of a senseless and mindless nonhuman animal, promoted by the scientists in that age to justify their use, has been eradicated. Furthermore, the stress upon Laika's use of her own language is also of significance in terms of recent biosemiotic evidences. One dimension of the exploitation of nonhuman animals was based on the claim that their lack of ability to communicate with humans in human language is the biological indicator that they do not have any intellectual development; hence, they can be treated just the same way as any object. Because humans have reduced 'the use of language to the status of sole certain indicator of the presence of rationality' (Cavaleri 2001, p. 44), they have attributed the status of object to those who do not speak human language. But, they totally forget about a fundamental scientific finding, which is each being, including humans and nonhumans, have his/her/its own way of communication. Hence, to claim that human language is the only way of communication, therefore, the only way to find the traces of an intellectual capacity in a being would be wrong.

So, there are two basic approaches towards the unknown as understood from the use of nonhuman animals in space discoveries and the denial of presence based on the use of human language; in the first case, although space remains unknown to humans, nonhuman animals are sent to the unknown sacrifice zones just because space provides another place for humans to exploit and make profit; in the second case, the unknown in the animal world, in terms of human limitations to understand the biosemiotics, is not discovered and even denied since to acknowledge their rational communication process would give birth to the need for a new ethical formation in the above-mentioned hierarchy of beings.

Entanglement and Doom

The perception of the unknown as a threat to humankind is a direct result of anthropocentrism because, by laying stress on merely discursive formations as the products of the distinctive mind and intellect of humans, anthropocentrism denies the fact that human beings exchange meanings with other bodies, which, in return, provides the simultaneous change of the discursive and material conditions: 'A piece of glass from the Empire State. You are what you breathe' (Winterson 1997, p. 211), or what you eat and drink, because in that process one shares the molecules and atomic particles between bodies. Posthumanist and new materialist studies 'see the "dance" of matters and meanings in the entire worldly reality: in the behaviour of subatomic particles, in the co-evolutionary dynamics that characterize the paths of life on Earth' (Oppermann and Iovino 2012, p. 450). Thus, it can be stated that we, as humans along with nonhumans, 'are and we are not our bodies' (Winterson 1997, p. 162), because our bodies are not fixed entities close to the outer factors of material formations. We are our bodies, but that body is co-shaped with other bodies, as well. Therefore, we are not fixed, pure, untouched beings; rather, we are constantly becoming.

With the new material turn in the literary and ethical arena, whereas the past epoch reinforced the superiority and uniqueness of human beings, contemporary ideas and theories accept the inevitable connection and intra-action between and within all the beings. 'Everything that is, is alive. Life did not come into this world. The life forms of the Earth are a natural product of the Earth, as the living planet is a natural product of the living universe' (Llywelyn 1993, p. 281). Hence, humans are not before or after the material formations of the universe; on the contrary, they are, just like the other beings, a product of simultaneous intra-action of bodies. Moreover, attributing existence only to human beings and reducing the status of nonhuman animals to the instrumental means of humans is criticised since the existence and liveliness of other beings and bodies have gradually been accepted especially with posthuman studies. Hence, a new argument about life and the limits of liveliness has been brought forward. Previously attributed to only human beings who believed themselves to be the sole intelligent ones, the definition of liveliness has been extended and nonhuman beings, and even matter, have also been included. Being alive was described within agency, which is the capacity to be acted upon and act upon something. In this context, dichotomies of Cartesian dualism based on mind and body separation have been shattered. Moreover, the limits of natural and pure human have been challenged, as well. With the acknowledgement of the presence of many other beings and bodies inside the supposedly 'untouched' and 'pristine' human body as a result of intra-action, there has become 'a reconsideration and re-acknowledgement of the material properties of human co-existence with the human and nonhuman' (Johns-Putra 2013, p. 126). To achieve thinking through both material and discursive formations at the same time, agency and the agential capacity of each being and matter should be recognised.

There are a number of stories about the gloomy and apocalyptic future of humans as, on the condition that human beings insist on not accepting the entanglement of all the beings in the world, an ecological catastrophe will await them in the future. Knowing how much they have already harmed nature, human beings continue their arrogant practices by exploiting nature as if any environmental degradation and material collapse will not have an influence on human societies. Yet, humans, who believe themselves to be separate observers in front of the material formations of the world, are not exempt from the degradation of nature because, along with the natural and ecological crisis, all the social and discursive institutions also collapse. This ideology brought about a number of dystopic and apocalyptic scenarios where all kinds of social institutions have disappeared, human beings have turned out to be barbaric monsters eating whatever they find (even each other) in this gloomy atmosphere and nature has come to a point where the damages humans have made cannot be reversed. Most of people agree on the fact that we are already in an irrevocable position in terms of environmental degradation, and that there are already a lot of signs of a dying environment and decaying human institutions around us. Greenlaw, in one of her poems, 'The Recital of Lost Cities' (1993, p. 15), summarises the beginning of an apocalyptic end:

It started with the polar ice caps,
A slight increase in temperature and the quiet
was shattered. The Australian Antarctic
wandered all over the Norwegian Dependency
as mountainous fragments lurched free
with a groan like ship's mahogany.

So as to prevent the foreseen negative future, anthropocentric rule should be abandoned and a new perspective about humans and other bodies should be gained through the posthumanist theories. It should be emphasised that the distinctive place of humans in the hierarchy has already been ruptured through the scientific findings on the material formations of the human body. Nevertheless, whereas 'science and technology are preoccupied with answering the question of our origins – whether it be through theories of the Earth's formation such as the Big Bang, or the mapping of the human genome' (Toffoletti 2007, p. 134), it has also eradicated what is human in its original form, as well. However, this representation of a new type of human, changing and evolving through the tools s/ he has made, has created techno-apocalyptic scenarios, and film and book themes about technophobia and virtual identities have been demanding subjects. Humans felt threatened in confrontation with 'a modern science whose pragmatic successes were threatening to confirm the picture of the universe as a godless machine' (Bennett 2010, p. 64). However, this phobia against the unknown and unpredicted consequences of the technological and scientific developments again arises out of anthropocentrism since it breaks human culture from the material formations in the world. Meanwhile, although all the examples are from the human world, it should also be recognised that the other bodies have their own co-evolution regardless of human intervention.

In relation to the concept of technological breakdown cast upon future human generations, Katherine Hayles (2006, p. 164) states: 'What we make and what (we think) we are co-evolve together' as the change of human biology is an ongoing process influenced by the tools or machines human beings have produced. Both human and nonhuman biology change under different circumstances. As an example, Hayles (2006, p. 164) states that 'tool use and bipedalism co-evolved together. Bipedalism facilitated the use and especially the transport of tools; tool use in turn bestowed such decisive fitness advantage that it had the effect of accelerating bipedalism'. As a result of this co-evolution, both cultural and biological changes took place. Hence, it is apparent that cultural and social practices are part of this co-evolution because what tools are made and how they are used are determined according to the cultural practices. Likewise, the tools produced out of the cultural and social needs have biological consequences on human bodies, as well as the bodies surrounding them in the physical environment. So, matter and discourse, material and discursive formations, co-evolve and co-constitute together. This evolutionary process can best be understood from the example of DNA, which 'transmits more than genetic information or life codes. It is more than an evolutionary record of the development of life on Earth. In the twenty-first century it has become the symbolic repository of epistemological, ideological, and conceptual change' (Roof 2007, p. 2). Hence, the acknowledgement co-constitution of matter and knowledge, just like in the embodiment of DNA, is essential in making full sense of the world in which we live together with the other beings.

Now in today's world humans have co-evolution with intelligent machines together with other living organisms and material forms, and through the acknowledgement of this co-evolution, it can be appreciated that 'recent developments in techno-science have unsettled many of the assumptions of humanist discourse' (Badmington 2004, p. 87). On the other hand, technology also influenced the adaptation process of human bodies to their environment, which is also stated by Jonathan Pritchard: 'For a number of the challenges currently facing our species – global climate change and many infectious diseases, for example – natural selection probably occurs too slowly to help us much. Instead we are going to have to rely on culture and technology' (2013, p. 100). Therefore, the nostalgic sense of human has been lost in the face of new developments, just as the nostalgic sense of human had been lost in the face of new developments 150 years ago. The unknown of the past has become the reality of today's world.

It is concluded from all the explanations that throughout ages human beings first reacted against, feared and hated the unknown, but later familiarised by accepting it to their discursive formations. However, nowadays this familiarising process towards the physical environment has proved to have fatal consequences for all the beings including humans. Demonised places that were once feared, hated and blamed for being the reasons for social collapse, in other words, shown as scapegoats (Estok 2011, p. 78), have become today's barren lands that have been exploited as a result of capitalist initiatives. This supposedly human enthronement over nature has apparently resulted in recent climate change about which 'science is split on what to do' (Hulme 2013, p. 85): should technology be made use of recovering the Earth? Or should technology be abandoned to give time to the Earth for it to turn back to its past sustainable form? Nonetheless, within all these discussions, human factor in the climate change is ignored and it 'is framed as a scientific or environmental phenomenon, to be explained in science-driven terms rather than as a result of social or political choices and with no reference to human interaction' (Howard-Williams 2009, p. 30). Denying the role of humans in recent ecological breakdown is an indicator of the fact that humans still continue to think in anthropocentric points of view. Just like Icarus who 'grew drunk with the joy of his flight and soon forgot his father's words' (Zoja 1995, p. 110), humans forgot about the possible disasters as a result of their unlimited exploitation of the physical environment. Yet still, with the awareness of to what extent humans have made the world unlivable, technological solutions are being searched, which brings up the idea that new life forms and new planets on which humans can survive can be found in outer space, where the exploitation and colonialisation of space starts.

Today, a number of science fiction scenarios about settling down on a new planet are at issue. The survival instinct in humans will play an important role when things come to a point in which we can no longer survive on this planet. However, this is not only an ecological question as there are many ethical, political and social problems alongside. First of all, when it is determined that new life conditions for humans will be established on another planet similar to ours in terms of survival requirements, the countries that hold political and capitalist power in their hands will provide opportunities in exchange for money, whereby the poor will be discriminated one more, and left to die in a dying and toxic world. Apart from this, humans will probably go through the same processes on the other planet as well, simply because they will not give up thinking in accordance with anthropocentrism. The British writer Jeanette Winterson illustrates a story of re-establishment of humans on a new planet with the hopes of not falling into the same faults in *The Stone Gods* (2007). In the novel, Winterson tells the story of extraterrestrial migration from Orbus to the Planet Blue (2007, p. 8):

> Orbus is not dying. Orbus is evolving in a way that is hostile to human life.
>
> OK, so it's the planet's fault. We didn't do anything, did we? Just fucked it to death and kicked it when it wouldn't get up.

Underlying the reasons of migration is human arrogance since humans are selfishly seeking a new home without care for the other bodies and beings on Orbus. Furthermore, Winterson also allows for the doubts of the characters about leaving this world for another one (2007, pp. 105–6):

What if this new world isn't new at all but a memory of a new world?

What if we really do keep making the same mistakes again and again, never remembering the lessons to learn but never forgetting either that it had been different, that there was a pristine place?

Perhaps the universe is a memory of our mistakes.

As a matter of fact, their doubts came true and the new planet they chose as their home returned into a toxic place hit by the ideological and discursive wars. Moreover, it can be seen in the novel that before leaving the toxic planet in which humans cannot walk without wearing a pollution filter, humans still think about making money out of decay and annihilation. They make a TV programme to get ratings about settling down on a new planet, and the key question is: 'If you were in charge of Planet Blue, what would you do first? Tell us and Win!' (p. 40). Hence, traces of the same mentality that caused the disastrous fall of humans on their original planet can still be found. So, it can be claimed that although humans have a chance to start over in a clean and untouched (by humans) planet, the consequences will be the same as long as they do not abandon the joys of flying, just like Icarus, coming with the discourses of the anthropocentric view, which centralises humans as the ruling beings.

Underneath the anthropocentric arrogance, ecophobia also lies: 'Nature's unpredictable – that is why we had to tame her. Maybe we went too far, but in principle we made the right decision. I want to be able to go out for a drink without getting hassled by some gawp-eyed museum-quality cod' (Winterson 2007, p. 88). As nature has remained unknown in its wild spots, humans have felt the urge to tame and bring civilisation to it through intervention. However, ironically enough, 'the more control we seem to have over the natural environment, the less we actually have' (Estok 2011, p. 6) as we can never predict what the consequences will be like as a result of our intervention. In Winterson's scenario of *The Stone Gods*, humans have to leave their own planet which has been destructed through anthropocentric practices, and find a new home in the 'unknown wilderness' of outer space.

Conclusion

Although the unknown is an essential factor of phobias, once humans have familiarised it, destructive consequences happen as a result of anthropocentric practices and ideologies of human chauvinism. Similar to ecophobia and homophobia, spacephobia also hints at the unknown dark beyond the perceptions of humans. However, contemporary literature draws attention to the colonialisation process of outer space as a result of familiarising the unknown. Yet, in order to prevent the destruction and annihilation of the human life forms on Earth, human intervention into the ecological system that is sustainable by itself should be stopped. Furthermore, if humans continue their civilised mission to tame outer space through the high technologies human discourses have created, they may cause an extraterrestrial catastrophe.

References

Alaimo, S. 2011, 'New Materialisms, Old Humanisms, or, Following the Submersible', *Nora: Nordic Journal of Feminist and Gender Research*, 19(4): 280–84.

Arnould, J. 2011, *Icarus' Second Chance: The Basis and Perspectives of Space Ethics*. Vienna: Springer-Verlag.

Badmington, N. 2004, *Alien Chic: Posthumanism and the Other Within*. New York: Routledge.

Barad, K. 2007, *Meeting the Universe Halfway: Quantum Physics and the Entanglement of Matter and Meaning*. London: Duke University Press.

Bennett, J. 2010, *Vibrant Matter: A Political Ecology of Things*. London: Duke University Press.

Cavaleri, P. 2001, *The Animal Question: Why Nonhuman Animals Deserve Human Rights*. Oxford: Oxford University Press.

Doctor, M.R. and Kahn A.P. 2008, *The Encyclopedia of Phobias, Fears, and Anxieties, Third Edition*. New York: Infobase Publishing.

Estok, S.C. 2011, *Ecocriticism and Shakespeare: Reading Ecophobia*. New York: Palgrave MacMillan.

Gaard, G. 2012, 'Feminist Animal Studies in the U.S.: Bodies Matter', *DEP Deportate, esuli, profugbe*, 20: 14–21.

Greenlaw, L. 1993, *Night Photograph*. London: Faber and Faber.

Hayles, K.N. 2006, 'Unfinished Work: From Cyborg to Cognisphere', *Theory, Culture and Society*, 23: 159–66.

Howard-Williams, R. 2009, 'Ideological Construction of Climate Change in Australian and New Zealand Newspapers', in T. Boyce and J. Lewis (eds), *Climate Change and the Media*. New York: Peter Lang.

Hulme, M. 2013, *Exploring Climate Change in Science and Society: An Anthology of Mike Hulme's Essays, Interviews and Speeches*. New York: Routledge.

Iovino, S. and Oppermann, S. 2012, 'Theorizing Material Ecocriticism: A Diptych', *Interdisciplinary Studies in Literature and Environment*, 19(3): 448–75.

Johns-Putra, A. 2013, 'Environmental Care Ethics: Notes Toward a New Materialist Critique', *Symploke*, 21(1–2): 125–35.

Llywelyn, M. 1993, *The Elementals*. New York: Tom Doherty.

Pritchard, J.K. 2013, 'How We Are Evolving', *Scientific American*, 22(1): 99–105.

Roof, J. 2007, *The Poetics of DNA*. Minneapolis, MN: University of Minnesota Press.

Smith, A. 2005, *The Accidental*. London: Penguin Books.

Toffoletti, K. 2007, *Cyborgs and Barbie Dolls: Feminism, Popular Culture and the Posthuman Body*. London: I.B. Tauris.

Winterson, J. 1997, *Gut Symmetries*. London: Granta.

Winterson, J. 2007, *The Stone Gods*. London: Penguin Books.

Zoja, L. 1995, *Growth and Guilt: Psychology and the Limits of Development*. London: Routledge.

PART II
Public Meets Private: An Emerging Space Enterprise

Chapter 6

Space Exploration: An Alliance
Between Public and Private

Jacques Arnould

Humanity has never done more to create and fulfil its destiny than by stepping outside the bounds of its houses, fields and countries, by venturing into the unknown. There have been many *terrae incognitae*, unknown lands which are the cradles of an ever-evolving humanity: the continents of Africa, Europe, Asia and then America, settled by our long-strided ancestors, boundless territories roamed and created by the cultural imagination and the spiritual quest, large and small infinities gradually discovered and described by the modern sciences. Today, as science fiction novels and space law teach, exploring space is a province of all mankind and celestial bodies a common heritage which remains partly unknown. To fulfil its exploration and exploitation, alliance between public and private sectors is required, as so many examples of macro-engineering projects from the past. If we cannot ignore the destiny of the Earth, we have to admit that exploration belongs to our human condition.

Exploring Space, a Province of All Mankind

Earth, August 2019. The Arecibo radio telescope picks up a musical signal of unknown origin. It appears to be coming from the Alpha Centauri star system, more than four light-years from our planet. Under the leadership of one of their members, a brilliant Puerto Rican linguist, the Jesuits decide to finance a space exploration mission to explore and study the mysterious 'Singers' ahead of any other international initiative ... The indisputable success of *The Sparrow* by Mary Doria Russell, published in 1996, surely owes to the fact that, more than a work of science fiction, it is a philosophical tale of good and evil, as humans experience these opposing forces in the most ordinary of situations (love, power, death) and in encounters with other forms of life and intelligence, other cultures and other civilisations. Russell reminds us that, for humans, exploration in any form is an experience as exhilarating as it is dangerous.

Exploration is unique to humans. While the human species shares a sense of curiosity with many living creatures, it alone has the ability to imagine – to project oneself beyond the immediate boundaries of space and time. Thus, the notion could be suggested that humans have never set out to explore worlds that they have not first imagined or seen in their dreams. And thus, through exploration, humans have never stopped examining their identity, their origins and their destiny. There are different types of answers to these ancestral questions: those which are the focus of the sciences – whether cosmology, particle physics, biology, anthropology or psychology – and those that belong to our own individual philosophical and spiritual quests. In *The Sparrow*, Russell shows how these different spheres – public and private, scientific and philosophical, secular and religious – continually influence each other in a constant process of joining together or, on the contrary, opposing each other.

Those who worked on establishing a legal framework for space in the 1960s seized on this unique aspect of exploration. The first Article of the Outer Space Treaty, drawn up in 1967, states: 'Article I: § 1. The exploration and use of outer space, including the Moon and other celestial bodies, shall be carried out for the benefit and in the interests of all countries, irrespective of their degree of economic or scientific development, and shall be the province of all mankind'. Thus, before giving space a status of its own (this status will be discussed below), the treaty first focused on the status of the human activities. What does 'province' mean? During the era of royalty in France, the term province (in French, *apanage*) referred to the share of the royal kingdom granted to the younger sons of the royal family in compensation for their exclusion from the throne. Since then, the term has become more generalised, meaning property, inheritance; it retains a notion of elitism. The use of the notion of province, to refer to space, is interesting. On the one hand, it offers mankind a rightful position: not that of domination (mankind does not rule the universe), or that of submission (no less deserving of its share), but more that of an heir benefitting from the work, power and potential troubles of its predecessors, who would like to be able to provide its descendants with the same possibility. On the other hand, still referring to space law, what mankind claims as its inheritance is not actually a territory, but a mission: that of exploring, exploiting and using a portion of the universe, for its own interests and that of future generations.

It is undeniable that space tools, starting with those most useful to us, are becoming ordinary to us. Inhabitants of Earth so quickly got used to being flown over by communication, observation and positioning satellites that they forgot about them, surprised that they are still being designed and constructed, launched into orbit and maintained, to provide the multiple remote services these same people rely on in their everyday lives – from weather forecasts and navigational tools to communication networks, observation and surveillance. They may be discrete and invisible to the naked eye, but these satellite systems have a price, comparable to that of equivalent services on Earth when these exist. They have a price, but are not cost-prohibitive; they have a price that needs to be, or should be, compared and evaluated in terms of achieving a mission, reaching a goal. So it is not surprising that some of these satellite systems are now not only operated, but also financed and set up by private operators who, according to the aforesaid, take advantage of previous public funding.

However, there is also another occupation in space, which will be our focus here: space exploration, which involves space telescopes, planetary probes and manned flights. Whether the price tag of these missions is relatively low – France's Corot telescope, which recently completed its mission to detect extrasolar planets, cost €170 million – or higher – an automatic Mars mission today costs several billion dollars – or exorbitant – whether for an Apollo programme or a manned mission to Mars – that these space exploration activities have no equivalent means that they have to be evaluated in other terms than price. To increase human knowledge of the universe, about life and its origins, to face worlds of which we were previously unaware, to risk challenging ideas, theories and certainties: what would have become of our species if, since its birth, it had not stayed true to its natural curiosity and penchant for exploration? Space exploration *is* a noble activity, a province of all mankind which, even more than major financial investments, has cost sweat, tears and sometimes even human lives. But is this not a way of acknowledging its worth beyond its financial cost, I mean: its dignity?

An Unknown Heritage

For a long time, what we now call space was completely inaccessible and off-limits to humans. Not because it was at a height which, without the least astronautical technology or principles, was unattainable, but because, in the West in any case, of the reigning cosmic and dualistic representation of reality: the world was divided into two parts – the sublunar and the supralunar. Humans, who belonged to the former, did not have access to the latter – at least not physically. At the start of the seventeenth century, the work of Galileo and his colleagues made this cosmology obsolete, and as early as 1610, Johannes Kepler wrote in his *Conversation with the Starry Messenger:* 'There will certainly be no lack of human pioneers when we have mastered the art of flight. Who would have guessed that navigation across the vast ocean is less dangerous and quieter than in the narrow, threatening gulfs of the Adriatic, or the Baltic, or the British straits? Let us create vessels and sails appropriate for the heavenly ether, and there will be plenty of people unafraid of the empty wastes. In the meantime, we shall prepare, for the brave sky-travellers, maps of the celestial bodies – I shall do it for the Moon and you, Galileo, for Jupiter' (Koestler 1968, p. 378). The explicit parallel drawn between the sea and space is not anecdotic, and cannot be reduced to the simple observation that we do indeed use the same terms for marine navigation as for air and space navigation. Kepler believes that the sky represents to the people of the West a new world. A new world that is just as compelling as the lands 'discovered' by Christopher Columbus were and still are. A new world that will soon attract not only explorers and scholars, but merchants and soldiers as well! But this parallel also points to a key difference between space and the sea, that is, their legal status.

While the similarities and parallels between maritime, air and space law are undeniable, it must not be forgotten that their chronologies are quite different.

When the Maltese ambassador Arvid Pardo presented the notion of 'common heritage of mankind' to the United Nations General Assembly on 1 November 1967, he suggested also applying it to the seabed and ocean subsoil. We are gaining knowledge of these vast territories of our planet, particularly deposits of polymetallic nodules: declared a common heritage of mankind, they legally belong to everyone and may not be privately exploited. When surface waters, otherwise known as the high sea, are found in international zones, they are treated as common property (*res communis humanitatis*) shared by all of mankind. This means no state can claim any form of sovereignty and no national law applies; they are accessible to all, to be utilised and exploited by all, within certain potential limits or a regulatory framework, subject to application of international agreements stipulating the national intervention systems and fishing quotas. Based on these principles, the international Montego Bay Convention on maritime law was signed in December 1982; the same principles were used to define space law.

The fact is that, though we do not even know its bounds and have only explored a minute part of it with our men and machines, space is not a 'no man's land' that could be occupied and exploited by the first to arrive, or by any subsequent parties. Law defines space as having an international character and cannot be claimed or appropriated by any State. It must be considered as a public domain where everyone must ensure order, peace and equality between States. To have established this, even as the two largest world powers, the US and the Soviet Union, were going head to head in a race to the Moon, and against the backdrop of the Cold War, was a major feat. Despite this context, the first space lawyers and the politicians who listened to their proposals boldly proposed to protect space from any national claim and any military hankering, offering it equally to all mankind. This assertion was generous, prophetic and even utopian, and met with mixed reactions. The Outer Space Treaty, which concluded on 27 January, was ratified by 97 States and signed by 27 others. The Moon Agreement was only ratified by 12 States and signed by four others.

This treaty and this agreement have divided space activities into two frameworks. Earth's orbits are exploited according to the status of *res communis*: satellites are placed in these orbits, in positions managed by the International Telecommunications Union (ITU), and public and private companies make profits on them. No one really wants to point out that occupying an orbital position is in fact a form of temporary appropriation of space – or not so temporary, as the case may be, since these satellites may remain in space in the form and with the status of debris even after they are no longer in operation.

The 'rest' of space, particularly the celestial bodies, was implicitly declared the common heritage of mankind. This concept was part of a wider political context: the decolonisation and bipolarisation of international relations and the emergence of a new North-South perspective. It was tied to the notion of a 'new international economic order', founded on equity, interdependence, sovereign equality and cooperation between States, which the newly decolonised States were calling for at the time. The western countries, the US in particular, readily agreed, but the Soviets claimed that this notion could not exist in societies based on Marxist ideology ... In any case, space law considers *terrae incognitae*, territories in space that are yet unknown, as a heritage, and thus sets out precisely the conditions under which projects aimed at exploring them must be conducted: non-militarisation, non-appropriation and consideration for future generations.

Another key legal notion of space law, and which is particularly relevant to the relationship between the public and private sectors, is that of the launching State. The term 'launching State' refers to a State which launches or procures the launching of a space object, as well as a State from whose territory or facility a space object is launched. Ultimately, this notion pertains to the question of liability: the launching State shall be absolutely liable to pay compensation for damage caused by 'its' space object on the surface of the Earth or to aircraft in flight. There is no statute of limitations on this liability, which creates a new legal problem in and of itself, because objects launched into orbit can remain there for centuries; only a public structure would be capable of ensuring liability on this type of time scale.

The Public and Private Sectors: An Alliance as an Old Entrepreneurship

As it were, Kepler's intuition proved accurate: almost four centuries after the astronomy revolution of the seventeenth century, there are many similarities between space and sea exploration and exploitation. Of course, he could not have imagined that there would also be parallels with a third domain, air.

On 15 May 1918, even before the Armistice had been signed, ending World War I, a young manufacturer from the region around Toulouse presented his project to open a Toulouse-Dakar air service line to an Italian pilot officer, Beppo de Massimi. Pierre-Georges Latécoère concluded his presentation with the following words: 'I've recalculated everything, and come to the same conclusion as the specialists: it cannot be done. So there is only one thing left for us to do, and that is to do it' (Chadeau 1990, p. 99). As soon as the war was over, Latécoère embarked on this adventure and created the mythic 'La Ligne', which would one day become the aviation company L'Aéropostale. This was a true MEP, Macro-Engineering Project, to borrow the term introduced by Eugene S. Ferguson (1978, pp. 6–18). MEPs, explains Ferguson, are on the cutting edge of the knowledge and resources of their time: they are complex, long and costly to carry out. They often come about thanks to visionaries and enthusiasts, rather than those concerned with the immediate needs of a society or the effects they will have on this society! Yet, they cannot ignore the socio-political conditions of their time.

La Ligne was truly an MEP and an exploratory endeavour, even if it was also commercial in aim: Latécoère's planes were flying through uncharted skies and often over virgin territories. Yet, though inspired by one man's genius, driven by his enthusiasm and financed with his own resources, this was not only a private undertaking. Like extra-atmospheric space today, air space too was subject to conventions and regulations as from the 1920s, if only in France and Spain, and even though air law was still very rudimentary. Landing, taking off, transiting; carrying mail and passengers, crossing borders; using foreign military fields; competing with national postal services: the least innovation, or simply the operations required to set up La Ligne, involved 1) queries for a body of law that was still in its infancy and 2) working with the public sector. Latécoère presented his project to the French government and created a structure that he hoped would be recognised by the State and receive government funding. Finally, on 25 December 1918, two months after the Armistice, the first Toulouse-Barcelona air connection was realised. Latécoère was the only passenger on board. La Ligne's subsequent growth and development into L'Aéropostale could never have happened without the aid of the French government – aid which was legal, political and financial. This example sheds an interesting light on the question of the privatisation of space and when it is appropriate to use this term.

When a Dragon capsule launched by a Falcon rocket docked at the International Space Station (ISS) on 22 May 2012, the operation was announced as a turning point in the history of space activities and the first foray into privatisation. But as aptly noted by Eric Dautriat, 'Privatisation, yes – but of what?' (2013, p. 99). NASA had undoubtedly relinquished the role of contracting authority for the launcher and the capsule, acting instead as the customer of SpaceX. NASA has already been the customer of another company, Orbital Science, for the past 20 years – for development of the airborne Pegasus launcher, which is, granted, a smaller-scale project. And, after the Challenger accident in 1986, NASA had already entrusted operational management of its space shuttles to the private sector.

Moreover, 90 per cent of the development costs for the launcher and capsule built by SpaceX were paid with public funding. This situation is reminiscent of another involving a different private company, Arianespace, with which SpaceX will be competing for the launching of commercial satellites – although unlike SpaceX, which was founded by a multi-billionaire CEO who, in addition to investing profits from PayPal (the online payment system), also sought to implement modern industrial management methods, Arianespace was born of an EU policy initiative. However, Elon Musk's endeavour has very little in common with the battle between Apple and IBM in the 1980s: even if SpaceX thumbs its nose at the famous model of the American military-industrial compound, such as Boeing and Lockheed-Martin, it is the focus of a great deal of attention and concern from the public, civil and military agencies. In short, this situation shows a new form of partnership between the public and private sectors, allowing the benefits of competition to work to everyone's advantage, rather than implementing complete privatisation.

Now, to return to Latécoère and La Ligne: are Musk and SpaceX space-era heirs of this legendary company? They surely have continued in the same tradition by adopting an innovative managerial and industrial approach, and especially by closely interweaving public and private powers and interests. Another similarity lies in their limited reliance on technical innovation: at least when La Ligne was being opened and before the creation of L'Aéropostale and the trans-Atlantic lines, Latécoère used proven aircraft, such as the Bréguet XIV which was built during World War I; Musk also made conservative and simple technical choices. Where the parallel is lost, however, is when it comes to actual exploration and facing the unknown: the pilots of La Ligne created airways and flew where few had flown before, over territories that were still considered virgin, whereas SpaceX launchers and capsules today, and perhaps its teams of astronauts in the future, travel along well-established courses, known for more than half a century. And space tourism, which is still marginal in more ways than one, will likely not change much about this. According to some, space tourism will soon be to space exploration (that is, the 'stuff of heroes') what visiting a botanical garden is to Charles Darwin's round-the-world-trip aboard the Beagle in the mid-nineteenth century. Only now can we fully appreciate the impact of this exploratory journey on our understanding of life, its history and humanity's place in it.

Restructuring Space Exploration

Investigatory and commission reports, following an accident or when drafting a new policy, are customary in the field of space. But the report published in 2009 by the commission headed by Norman Augustine contains a paragraph that is unusual for this type of literature:

> We explore to reach goals, not destinations. It is in the definition of our goals that decision-making for human spaceflight should begin. With goals established, questions about destinations, exploration strategies and transportation architectures can follow in a logical order. While there are certainly some aspects of the transportation system that are common to all exploration missions (e.g. crew access and heavy lift to low-Earth orbit), there is a danger of choosing destinations and architectures first. This runs the risk of getting stuck at a destination without a clear understanding of why it was chosen, which in turn can lead to uncertainty about when it is time to move on. (US Human Spaceflight Plans Committee, 2009).

Expressed here, for the first time in such official and clear terms, is the bidding to specify the ethical, or even philosophical, foundations of space exploration, and to indicate goals as well as destinations. For the Augustine commission, what this meant in particular was to determine whether the objective of going back to the Moon was actually a goal or merely a destination.

At a time when the earliest rockets were still not even reaching the limits of the atmosphere, one of the fathers of modern astronautics, Konstantin Tsiolkovsky, avoided any confusion of goal and destination. On 23 July 1935, in the Soviet newspaper *Komsomolskaïa Pravda*, he wrote:

Is there anything nobler than becoming master of all the Sun's energy, two
billion times greater than the energy that reaches the Earth?! Is there anything
more beautiful than escaping our humble planet, to enter the greater cosmos and
to offer mankind the opportunity to move beyond the tight constraints of life on
Earth and to break free from the chains of gravity?!

Tsiolkovsky was not concerned with a destination, but with a true goal. And in
fact, escape – somehow breaking free from Earth – is indeed one of the oldest
and most powerful motivations behind space travel, and surely remains so to this
day, even if dreams of one day reaching and colonising other celestial bodies have
been largely undone by actual astronomical knowledge, revealing space to be
apparently hostile to life and human survival.

But in any case, forms of escape necessarily raise serious ethical questions,
particularly with regard to fairness and justice: who benefits from the means
implemented to break free from our terrestrial prison, to send teams of astronauts
and especially satellites and probes outside its bounds? Issues such as the use of
space-based communication technologies and the destination of Earth observation
data are already, today, key aspects of the interesting debates on the meaning
of common heritage and common assets of mankind (Arnould 2010). Charters
already exist, or will be created, to give stricken populations access to the means
and data provided by space technologies. However, undeniably, these questions
are now also the subject of bitter battles between competing interests – pitting
nations against each other in some cases, and (more or less private) companies
in others. Space is no longer a territory for exploration, but the subject of power
struggles and battles over profits – a different response to the ethical question of
the ultimate purpose of space.

What would happen if living conditions on our planet were one day drastically
degraded, while at the same time high-performance spacecraft had been developed –
making it both necessary and possible to move part of the human population into
space? Who would be chosen? What system of justice would ensure fairness?
Many questions come to mind, but answers to these questions are virtually non-
existent; all that we know is that these answers would need to strike a delicate
balance between knowledge and power.

Conclusion

Oh! This vessel built of numbers and dreams
Would dazzle Shakespeare and delight Euler.

These verses by Victor Hugo, published in *La Légende des siècles* (Legends of
the Ages), were the inspiration for the title of Jacques Blamont's *Le Chiffre et le
Songe*, a 'political history of discovery'. What he proposes and argues in this book,

which, as he explains, he could also have called *The Dialectics of Knowledge and Power*, is as follows:

> Even if a few rare minds have had a monopoly on new concepts and creative initiatives, their work was not born in solitude, but within or at the edge of an Institution, which imposed an intellectual and social framework, defining the problems to be addressed and pointing the way to the solutions. The Institutions would have obtained nothing without the genius of a few great men; these great men would have produced nothing without the Institutions. Both sides would have remained sterile without the prince. Scientific advances, meaning the invention of both phenomena and the concepts used to handle them, is a political process. (1993, p. 8)

Blamont is right to point out the intrinsic and dialectic union between knowledge and power. And he is right to recall, at the end of his essay, the tragic story of the prisoners at the Dora camp who were forced, at risk of death, to build German V-2 missiles. The darker side of the space adventure cannot, and should not, be denied; on the contrary, it needs to be remembered so there is greater vigilance – to never let it surge up and overpower the lighter side. On one level, allying the public and private sectors, bringing them together to work on a common goal, such as exploring space, perhaps provides some protection against tragic outcomes.

As I have written, exploration is not optional for our species. Exploring is part of our condition: it feeds our curiosity, nourishes our imagination and is even necessary to our survival by providing other resources for our needs, other horizons for our creativity, other fields for us to study and other possibilities for the existence of others. Exploring is one of the roots and foundations of our possible future. Yet, exploring is not an imposed obligation, an inevitable fate or a predestined certainty: as a human being, one is free to say no to one's desires, impulses and passions for exploration, free to weigh the pros and cons, to set a time limit for oneself and to revise one's goals. Moreover, as Jean-Jacques Salomon explains: 'Despite advances in science and technology, our human horizon has not yet broken free from the bounds of Earth' (Arnould 2001, p. 216). Both the wording and the comment strike me as relevant: human exploration has not yet 'broken free' of Earth's horizon. However, with humans continuing to face these two infinities, the silence of which filled Blaise Pascal with dread, a breakthrough or 'breaking free' could finally end up happening – triggered by advances in astronautics or human genetics. Is humanity prepared to go the distance? Does it really want this? Is the constant thirst for new discoveries, sensational experiences and emotional thrills that drive some of its members enough to push humanity towards an adventure such as this? Is the motivation high enough to accept the dangers? Taking this step would require no less than for all forms of enthusiasm and all minds, all knowledge and all technologies, all means and all purposes – some of which we have discussed herein – to come together and be combined: Tsiolkovsky, Goddard, Esnault-Pelterie and all scientists and engineers, Latécoère, Musk and all bold entrepreneurs, Wright, Lindbergh, Mermoz, Armstrong and all human explorers, Cyrano de Bergerac, Verne, Clark and all masters of the imaginary. If we are to take humanity's exploratory tradition to this new level, moving far beyond the confines of African lands, as in times past, and truly breaking free of Earth's horizon ... if we are to make this happen, we clearly need to forget and eliminate any distinction between public and private that would be a handicap or obstacle rather than an additional asset. On the contrary, we need to align and ally the individual and collective efforts which, since the dawn of humanity, have allowed humans to explore or realise the unknown lands they have imagined.

References

Arnould, J. 2001, *La seconde chance d'Icare. Pour une éthique de l'Espace*. Paris: Editions du Cerf.

Arnould, J. 2010, *La Terre d'un clic*. Paris: Editions Odile Jacob.

Blamont, J. 1993, *Le Chiffre et le Songe*. Paris: Editions Odile Jacob.

Chadeau, E. 1990, *Latécoère*. Paris: Editions Olivier Orban.

Dautriat, E. 2013, *L'Espace en quelques mots*. Paris: Le Cherche-Midi.

Ferguson, E.S. 1978, 'Historical Perspectives on Macro-Engineering Projects' in F.P. Davidson and R. Salked (eds), *Macro-Engineering and the Infrastructure of Tomorrow*. Boulder, CO: Westview Press.

Kant, I. 1785, *Fundamental Principles of the Metaphysic of Morals*, viewed 23 November 2013, http://www.gutenberg.org/cache/epub/5682/pg5682.html.

Koestler, A. 1968, *The Sleepwalkers: A History of Man's Changing Vision of the Universe*. London: Pelican.

Outer Space Treaty or Treaty on Principles Governing the Activities of States in the Exploration and Use of Outer Space, including the Moon and Other Celestial Bodies 1967, viewed 23 November 2013, http://www.oosa.unvienna.org/pdf/publications/st_space_61E.pdf.

US Human Spaceflight Plans Committee 2009, *Seeking a Human Spaceflight Program worthy of a Great Nation*, viewed 23 November 2013, http://www.nasa.gov/pdf/396093main_HSF_Cmte_FinalReport.pdf.

Chapter 7

Heaven Can't Wait: A Critique of Current Planetary Defence Policy

Joel Marks

It is now generally recognised that Earth is at risk of a collision with an asteroid or a comet that could be devastating to human civilisation. Impressive strides in our understanding of this threat have been made in recent decades, and various efforts to deal with it have been undertaken. Intuitively the problem seems suited for governmental direction because of both the magnitude of the risk and the magnitude of the required response to that risk. However, the pace of government action hasn't kept up with the advance of our knowledge. This is certainly not an unusual situation, given the indirect connection between real hazards to the populace and the way governments function. A gap has therefore opened up for a nongovernmental initiative. Despite the daunting dimensions of planetary defence, one intrepid NGO in particular has stepped up to the plate: the B612 Foundation has embarked on a half-billion-dollar project, called Sentinel, to map the estimated one million near-Earth objects (NEOs) that could wipe out a city or worse (B612 Foundation [B612] n.d.a).[1] This chapter will offer an explanation of how we have arrived at this curious state of affairs, where private citizens have assumed what is arguably government's primary mandate to 'provide for the common defence' (quoting the preamble to the US Constitution), and examine some of the practical – or, if you will, ethical – risks that may be attendant on such a shift of responsibility. Finally, a new policy emphasis will be proposed.

Humanity's interaction with space rocks has a long history and no doubt prehistory, but the last half-century has been especially noteworthy. The period is aptly bookended by the 1963 publication of planetary geologist Eugene Shoemaker's paper proving the meteoritic origin of Barringer Crater in Arizona (Shoemaker 1963), and the explosion of a meteor over Chelyabinsk, Russia, in 2013, which indirectly injured 1,000 people and narrowly missed killing a million (Durda 2013). In between we have seen – to give just a partial list of highlights – the discovery of a likely meteoritic (that is, asteroidal or cometary) cause of the

---

1   The technical, and confusing, definition of 'near-Earth object' encompasses even objects that may now be vastly distant from Earth, so long as at perihelion they would be closer than 1.3 AU to the Sun (where 1 AU is the mean distance of Earth from the Sun). In this chapter I will be using the term more intuitively, as others have done, to refer to objects whose orbits are within the inner solar system. Cf. also B612 Foundation n.d.b.

extinction of the dinosaurs (Alvarez et al. 1980; Schulte 2010); the collision of a comet with the planet Jupiter (Jet Propulsion Laboratory [JPL] 2000) – perhaps the most titanic event ever witnessed in the solar system by human eyes, including my eyes (Marks 1994); the initiation of a dedicated survey of near-Earth objects that could threaten humanity (Morrison 1992); and the realisation that our planet is immersed in a sea of such objects (Morrison 2005).

Yet these have been both the best of times and the worst of times for planetary defence. For hand in hand with these impressive revelations and undertakings has been an odd complacency. To slightly mix metaphors: despite any number of wake-up calls, humanity keeps hitting the snooze button. Why is this? No doubt the answer is complex, with economic, political and other contingent factors in play; but as a philosopher with an interest in this issue, I have been particularly attuned to the role of various fallacies of reasoning in bringing us to this pass.

The logical crux of the matter is the nature of risk. The standard formula for assessing risk is to multiply the (negative) value of a prospect by the probability of its occurring. Thus, suppose you were on your way to an important meeting and came to a fork in the road. You had been intending to take the left branch, but now a sign warns you of possible flooding after the last few days of heavy rainfall. The right branch also leads to your destination, but, although high and dry, is a longer route. Your choice is therefore whether to take a small chance of missing the meeting entirely or almost certainly to arrive late. Given the importance of your presence at the meeting, you take the route on the right. To have ignored either of the two sorts of consideration – the relative costs of your missing all or part of the meeting and the respective likelihoods thereof – would have led to an unsound decision.

The risk of impact by space rock presents a similar crisis. On the one hand we will want to consider the severity of the feared outcome: the destruction of a city, the disruption of a region, the wrecking of human civilisation, even the extinction of our species. On the other hand we will want to consider the probability of these eventualities.[2] My diagnosis of the current state of affairs is that the relative lack of urgency in humanity's response to this threat has in large part been due to the failure to carry out this analysis properly.

How could this be? Are not the components of the formula straightforward? What is peculiar about the case, however, is twofold: the value of the outcome seems virtually infinite, while its probability seems virtually infinitesimal. The former is so because the end of humanity would be the ultimate catastrophe (for humanity), not only killing billions of human beings but also aborting all future human beings and in the process stripping the lives of those who had lived of a great deal of their meaning (in progeny, reputation and survival of projects and institutions to which people had contributed, or for which they had sacrificed, or

---

2   Strictly speaking, one's deliberations would not be complete until one had also tallied up for comparison the likely net costs, including opportunity costs, of *attempting to avoid* the various possible outcomes.

with which they had identified or about which they simply cared). But the latter is so because such events take place in geologic time and not in the short span of a human generation or even a culture.

So what do you get when you multiply infinity times infinitesimal? The answer is not really mathematical since both of these quantities are only virtual or suggestive. The actual numbers to be assigned are very large or small but not genuinely infinite. But who is to say what those precise numbers are?[3] The best we can do is compare relative magnitudes in an intuitive way; but this could be enough for practical purposes. Thus for example: a tiny chance of annihilation by space rock could be compared to the near-certainty of global disruption from climate change, leading to the conclusion that the latter be given priority.

But in reaching such a conclusion, fallacious reasoning has already been employed, I submit. I see the chief mistake in the way probability has been utilised. This is a deep problem, not just an error of calculation. It turns out that there are many ways to misunderstand the implications of minuscule probabilities when taking decisions based on them, and, indeed, in the process sometimes to misunderstand the nature of probability itself.

The relevant fact about asteroids and comets is that the larger they are, the fewer of them there are. This is known as a power law, and it has been empirically arrived at through extrapolation from observations. Furthermore, it is obvious that the smaller objects are less dangerous; the vast majority of them burn up in the atmosphere before they can cause any damage at Earth's surface. In addition, even larger objects that can penetrate the atmosphere, or descend far enough to cause surface damage if they exploded, can be mostly discounted because most of Earth's surface is uninhabited – in particular the oceans that cover 71 per cent of the globe.

A critical point is reached only when a space rock is a kilometre or more in diameter, at which point the consequence of colliding with it would be regional or global no matter where it hit; for example, even plummeting into an ocean could result in a tsunami that devastated an entire coastline. And a true extinction event would require an object 10 times that size. Now it is true that the Spaceguard survey mandated by Congress has already shown that there are roughly 1,000 kilometre-plus objects in Earth's immediate neighbourhood (JPL 2013b). However, every one that has been tracked shows no risk of impact on Earth for at least the next century; and this only confirms the independent geologic evidence that mass extinctions on Earth have been exceedingly rare, regardless of extraterrestrial cause.

Is all of this cause for reassurance? *NASA* Administrator Charles Bolden seems to think so, for he recently testified, 'This is not an issue that we should worry

---

3   Goodin (1995, chapter 17) deals with the same sort of problem in a discussion of nuclear disarmament, where he proposes a 'shift from probabilistic to possibilistic reasoning' to resolve it. I cannot help but wonder if Goodin's defence of disarmament would have withstood factoring in the impact threat. See also my discussion of anti-nuclear resistance in the sequel.

about in the near term' (House Science Committee 2013, minute 104:50). Others have gone so far as to deem planetary defence entirely unnecessary. I shall argue, to the contrary, that the only way to arrive at the conclusion that anything less than a sense of urgency on this matter is appropriate is to commit one or another of the following fallacies.

The Fallacies

Argument from Ignorance

While it is true that no object yet discovered poses an imminent risk to humanity, and also true that most (over 90 per cent) of the extinction-size objects that are estimated to exist in Earth's vicinity have already been discovered, it does not follow that there is no such object. Yet we have this remark from Phil Plait (2012), a popular expert on astronomy:

> We know there are no rocks that big [that is, extinction-size] headed our way anytime soon, at least not for centuries.

It is even scarier when the Near-Earth Object Program Executive at NASA says the same thing:

> We know everything out there that is that big, and there is just nothing right now that's in an orbit that's any threat toward the Earth (Lindley Johnson as quoted by Wall 2012a).

These statements are simply false; we *know* no such thing. Not knowing that there are any is not the same as knowing that there aren't any. To think otherwise is to commit the fallacy of arguing from ignorance. Indeed, Phil Plait (2013) was obliged to chew (if not eat) his words a year later when he reported:

> Three new near-Earth asteroids[4] have been discovered, one of which can actually get pretty close to Earth, close enough to categorize it as 'potentially hazardous'. Now, don't flip out about that. ... this new one ... only gets to about 5.5 million kilometers (3.4 million miles) form [sic] Earth. ... so in real-world terms, this rock isn't too big a worry. Which is nice, because it's about two kilometers across, so we really don't want it hitting us! ... The other two asteroids never get near the Earth, which really is good news, since they're both roughly 20 km (12 miles) across! ... So really, none of these three new asteroids is a threat.

---

4   Plait updated this to report that one of these asteroids has been reclassified as a comet, which could help to explain why it had never been observed before. But this is small consolation, as I explain in the sequel.

However they underscore the need for more survey observatories to go sniffing around the sky. I don't like that objects that big can still hide from us.

Fallacy of Composition

But let us suppose that we do have or will shortly have a comprehensive inventory of the objects near Earth that would wreak havoc were we to collide, and sufficient prognostication to assure us that we won't any time soon. It still would not follow that we are not at risk of a catastrophic collision in the near future. Why not? Because such objects, which are predominantly asteroids, do not constitute the only relevant category. Our planet is also vulnerable to collision with comets, and, in particular, long-period comets (Chapman, Durda and Gold 2001). What is distinctive about the latter is that they are approaching from such a great distance that their speed would be tremendous by the time they reached the inner solar system. The result is that, at the point that a long-period comet targeting Earth were actually near Earth, it would almost certainly be too late for humanity to launch an effective defence against it. According to planetary scientist Donald Yeomans (2013, p. 120), the time-to-Earth-impact after detection of a long-period comet at the distance of Jupiter – typical for this kind of apparition – could be as short as nine months. Meanwhile, in his testimony before the House Science Committee on 10 April 2013 (at minute 68:00), astronomer and NASA principal investigator Michael A'Hearn explained that, under present circumstances, two to four years would be needed to launch a payload to deflect such an object. And A'Hearn's comment pertains only to time-to-launch and perhaps time-to-intercept; the actual *deflection* of an *extinction-size* object with present technology could take from decades to a century.[5]

Yet the term 'asteroid' dominates the present discussion of the space-rock threat, carrying with it the unspoken implication that comets are safely ignored. Thus, the name of recent Congressional hearings on planetary defence was 'Threats from Space: A Review of Efforts to Track and Mitigate Asteroids and Meteors'; the name of a new United Nations plan for planetary defence is the 'International Asteroid Warning Network', and of the press conference announcing it, 'Defending Earth from Asteroids'; the name of a recent White House/ NASA Grand Challenge on planetary defence was the 'Asteroid Initiative'; the slogan accompanying the logo of B612, the premier NGO on planetary defence, is 'Defending Earth Against Asteroids';[6] and, taking their cue from the experts, just about any news report on planetary defence you are likely to come across will highlight asteroids usually to

---

5   Cf. this typical statement regarding even the smaller asteroids: 'The B612 Foundation Sentinel Space Telescope … will give humanity *the decades of warning needed* to prevent asteroid impacts with existing technology' (Lu 2013; my emphasis).

6   The B612 Foundation's website does, however, discuss the cometary threat (B612 n.d.b).

the total exclusion of comets, for example Moscowitz 2013, in which 'asteroid' appears 16 times and 'comet' not once, being utterly typical in this regard.[7]

That this is not just a matter of nomenclature is borne out by the plans currently under way to implement planetary defence. The most notable of these is B612's Sentinel telescope: as their website explains, 'Our mission is concerned with objects that are orbiting within the inner solar system' (B612 n.d.b). Dealing with the threat of long-period comets is explicitly ruled out. As Ed Lu, physicist, former astronaut and current B612 CEO, put it to me in a recent conference call (9 August 2013): 'we would have to come up with something fundamentally different' to meet it. To my knowledge, there are no plans by B612 or anyone else to do that. My point now is that the incentive to mount such an effort is being systematically dismantled by the drumbeat of fallacious asteroid/space-rock equations in the public discussion of the overall threat, and perhaps even in the minds of some of the experts. This is an example of the Fallacy of Composition, by which a feature of a part, in this case the manageability of asteroids, is attributed to the whole, in this case, the population of potential impactors.

What is particularly amazing and dismaying to me is that, with all the recent talk of the Chelyabinsk meteor explosion (plus the near-simultaneous buzzing of Earth by the even larger object DA14) being a wake-up call to the threat of impact by an asteroid, the far more ominous discovery of Comet Siding Spring the previous month elicited only exclamations of joy at the potential spectacle (Beatty 2013). At that time, *C/2013 A1 (the comet's technical name)* was estimated to be of dinosaur-killer size or larger, and predicted possibly to collide with Mars in October of 2014 (a mere 20 months after discovery). It turned out to be smaller and a near-miss. But had such a comet as originally characterised been headed towards us instead, we would be toast.

The Clockwork Fallacy

Another fallacy in the thinking about and public discussion of the impact threat has been spawned, apparently, by a locution, namely, 'once per', or 'once in' or 'once every' (or just 'every'). Consider the following wholly representative instances of its use:

> ... the frequency of NEO collisions where kinetic impact cannot accomplish deflection is low: approximately *once every* 100,000 years. (Schweickart et al. 2008; my emphasis)

---

7   This particular article is noteworthy for its neglect since two of the speakers at the press conference it was covering (American Museum of Natural History 2013) actually did mention, indeed highlighted, the comet threat (and in a way that could be interpreted as critical of their colleagues): astrophysicist Neil DeGrasse Tyson (at minute 42:53) and former astronaut Thomas Jones (at minute 57:08).

The first thing to appreciate is that although Earth has been and will get clobbered, it doesn't happen very often. Impacts from objects 10 km across, energetic enough to sterilize Earth, or nearly so, are *once-per*-100-million-year events – a good thing! (Beatty 2011; my emphasis)

Fortunately, the risk of The Really Big One – 10 kilometers (6 miles) across or bigger – is rare. Near Earth Objects (NEOs) that hit the Earth and do what the one 65 million years ago did to the dinosaurs and most other life on the surface – wiped them out – occur on the order of *once every* hundred million years or so. (Ropeik 2011; my emphasis)

The phrase is commonly used to express statistical facts, as in, 'You can expect a three to come up once every six throws of the die'. This is not meant literally, of course, since there could well be seven or 30 or even, I suppose, 100 throws of a fair die before a three came up again. And even more to the point of planetary defence, you could get two in a row. As Arizona Congressman David Schweikert put it at a hearing on planetary defence: 'It's a 500-year flood except we had three of them in the last ten years' (House Science Committee 2013, minute 79:14). The point is that 'once every' is a manner of speaking and should not be taken to imply regular periodicity.

Yet such mental slippage is a definite possibility, and can have very real-world consequences. This could not be more perfectly illustrated than by the following remark by Russian Emergency Minister Vladimir Puchkov regarding the lack of preparedness for what took place in Chelyabinsk:

We thought that humanity would not have to face such an attack for another couple of thousand years, but the opposite happened and Russia was hit with a large-scale natural emergency. (RT News 2013)

In addition to the basic fallacy, I would point out two concomitant temptations. First is that the specific numbers given appear to be made out of whole cloth. Obviously they are all rounded, and each must be based on something arbitrary or assumed. My strong suspicion is that the 100-million-year figure in particular is an extrapolation from a single event, namely, the Chicxulub impact at the Cretaceous–Paleogene *boundary. Second,* even taking the numerical assertions at face value, they are typically employed in an absurd manner; it is as if there were a resetting of the cosmic clock every time one of these timespans is cited. Thus, when I hear someone say that a catastrophic impact occurs 'once every' umpteen million years, and reflect that it has been umpteen million years since the last one, I think, 'Then perhaps we are due for another!' But the clear intent of the speaker is, 'Therefore it will be umpteen million years before there is another'. Here is a possible example:

> It turns out that [a large] asteroid ... only comes along every 10 million years or so, but there are plenty of lesser asteroids that could make life unpleasant for you or someone you know *much sooner*. (Huebert 2006; my emphasis)

The essential fallacy remains that a regularity is sometimes presumed where only randomness reigns. The next Big One could come in a 100 million years or next year. We simply have no idea.

The Actuarial Fallacy

A close cousin to the 'once every' fallacy is the actuarial fallacy. As that 'bad' astronomer (his nickname) Phil Plait put it:

> Allowing for the number of Earth-crossing asteroids – the kind that can hit us because their orbits around the Sun intersect ours – as well as how much damage they can do (which depends on their size), [astronomer Alan Harris] calculated that any person's lifetime odds of being killed by an asteroid impact are about 1 in 700,000. ... As a comparison, you're more likely to die in a fireworks accident. (Plait 2008)

This may be true, but what follows? Although Plait is definitely a supporter of redoubled efforts on behalf of planetary defence, he nonetheless echoes Bolden by inferring that:

> One out of seven hundred thousand! That's still pretty low ... and certainly not enough to lie awake at night worrying about it. (ibid.)

Ditto[8] for Yeomans:

> No one should be losing sleep over this issue ... . We've got much bigger problems, such as global warming or firearm safety. (quoted by Boyle 2013)

The fallacy, indeed absurdity, of this inference is that it ignores the unique significance of an extinction event. An actuarial calculation makes sense for an insurance policy, where premiums and compensations for loss need to be mutually

---

8   I find it ironic that both Yeomans' statement and this more specific claim by a reporter writing about the actuarial aspect of asteroid impacts – 'With another asteroid scare coming up later this month (spoiler alert: we won't die), it's time to put the danger of "impact events" – when comets and asteroids crash into Earth – in perspective' (Nerney 2013) – came just weeks before the meteor explosion over Chelyabinsk, which narrowly missed killing one million people. Director of the White House Office of Science and Technology Policy, John Holdren, skewered the actuarial fallacy in his Congressional testimony after Chelyabinsk (House Science Committee 2013, minute 105:30).

adjusted, and for other kinds of cost/benefit situations. But there can be no compensation for the loss of our entire species. One does not want an insurance policy to cover such a loss; one wants only to prevent it.

False Analogy

A similar criticism applies to yet another variation on the same theme, this time by analogy to a lottery (and also being killed by a terrorist). In the same column quoted above, Plait notes that:

> Despite propaganda to the contrary, the odds of any given person being killed
> by a terrorist attack are incredibly low. While terrorist attacks in the long run are
> a near certainty, the odds of *you* getting killed are very low. It's like the lottery:
> someone wins every time (eventually), but chances are it won't be you.

Ergo: it's stupid to play the lottery. Just so, there will be annihilation by space rock, but the chance of your being a victim is minuscule. But what does this show? *Don't worry – be happy?* I don't think so! To conclude thus is fallacious, and in more than one way. For one thing, it is a kind of *ignoratio elenchi*, which is to say, beside the point. For the dreaded outcome is not necessarily one's own death but rather the end of human civilisation. The second problem is that it leads to an irrational policy recommendation. This can be demonstrated by means of a *reductio ad absurdum*, as follows:

> Suppose it were true that the vanishingly small probability of annihilation
> by space rock in the near future made it irrational to strive to make adequate
> preparations to prevent it (since there will always be more pressing priorities).

> Then there would never be a good reason to make adequate preparations to
> prevent annihilation by space rock.

> But there is certainly a good reason to make adequate preparations to prevent
> annihilation by space rock (since it will occur someday unless we prevent it).

> Ergo: It is not true that the vanishingly small probability of annihilation by space
> rock in the near future makes it irrational to strive to make adequate preparations
> to prevent it.

Fallacy of Division

Another way to diagnose the above mistake in reasoning is as an instance of the Fallacy of Division, by which a feature of a type is attributed to each instance of the type. Consider that somewhere out there is an asteroid or a comet that will be the next large object to hit Earth unless we stop it. In particular there is an object of diameter 10 or more kilometres (> 6 miles), which is large enough to wipe us out. Call this object NEPI, for Next Extinction-size Potential Impactor. What we want to know, therefore, is when NEPI will be at our doorstep, which is to say, close enough to be of real concern and yet far enough away to allow us enough time to prepare an effective defence against it.

Since NEPI has not yet been identified, we have minimal information to go by in answering our question. Currently all estimates are made on the basis of the relative frequency of extraterrestrial objects of various sizes. The fallacy is to suppose that the latter knowledge gives us knowledge about NEPI, or about NeLO – the Next Large Object – to be discovered. This manifests a confusion about the nature of probability. It often seems to be treated as if it were an objective quality of an object or an event. Thus, when we ponder the likelihood that NeLO will be none other than NEPI, we seem to be attributing a particular probability to that hypothetical object.

Suppose, for example, that the Minor Planet Center in Cambridge, Massachusetts, announced that a new object had been discovered. Based on the orbital and other characteristics known or estimated to that date, the Center might also specify a probability that the object would hit Earth. However, as the object's properties became better known, that probability could be considerably downgraded. This is in fact what happened after the asteroid Apophis was discovered in 2004 (JPL 2013a). It was at first given a small but real chance of impacting Earth in 2029; but over time that likelihood was reduced to negligibility. So, did Apophis's physical properties change in the interim? Not at all. Therefore its probability of impacting us is not one of its properties. Rather, probability is a function of our knowledge of something, not a property of the thing itself.

That is, with two exceptions. For in reality – whether we know it or not – Apophis has either a zero or a 100 per cent probability of hitting us (unless we destroy or divert it). In other words, by the deterministic laws of the universe, a given object either will or will not hit Earth (unless we stop it). We now believe Apophis won't. Meanwhile, *ex hypothesi*, NEPI has a probability of hitting us of 100 per cent (unless we stop it). The problem is: we don't know when this will happen (or, more to the point of our real concern, when this would happen if we didn't prevent it).

But there is a much more immediate problem. The confusion about probability makes it seem as if we *do* know when this *won't* happen, namely, in the near future. For by interpreting the probability that NeLO will be NEPI as a quality of NeLO itself, we lull ourselves into a dangerous complacency about the prospect of extinction. We are lulled because the probability in question is exceedingly small, given the size class to which NEPI belongs. So why is the resultant complacency dangerous? Because the next large object to come down the cosmic turnpike does not itself have an exceedingly small probability of wiping us out. It has either a 0 per cent or a 100 per cent probability of wiping us out, and we don't know which.

The classic case of the Fallacy of Division is that the average American family has 2.6 children. Does this tell us that the next American family we encounter will have 2.6 children? Of course not. Indeed, no American family has 2.6 children, even though the 'average one' does. Just so, there is not a single asteroid or comet in the solar system that has a .000001 probability of being NEPI. There is only NEPI and then there are all the others that are not NEPI. And no statistical or frequency probability will tell us if the next large object to show up at our doorstep will be it. In fact, if NEPI were to surprise us and then wipe us out because we had been insufficiently prepared, the statistical probability of such an event would *still* be vanishingly small – 'once per' umpteen million years. But it would be little consolation when the doomsday rock is bearing down upon us to be able to exclaim, 'This is highly unlikely!'

Begging the Question

Yet another way to conceive the same error of reasoning is as an instance of question begging. For when the inference is made from a frequency probability ('once every hundred million years') to an assessment of risk ('exceedingly low probability'), it is really only a change of language that is taking place, rather than a production of knowledge. The 'conclusion' is just a redescription of the premise (which has itself been misleadingly described), but appears to be telling us something new. We seem to know something about the next object to be discovered, but in fact all we know is the relative frequency in a population of objects of a certain size. Yet on this basis we go on to make predictions and decisions of great moment.

Improper Transposition

A distinct error of reasoning that bears on the impact threat is the formal fallacy of improper transposition. A pessimist might cite a famous assertion by Socrates as an example. For when the snub-nosed sage proclaimed that the unexamined life is not worth living, it is commonly assumed that he meant to be making the much stronger claim that the *examined* life *is* worth living. This, however, would not follow. The mistake is to take a necessary condition (for life to be worthwhile, it must involve critical reflection) as a sufficient condition (habitually engaging in critical reflection will make life worthwhile). But, even granting the truth of the premise (that reflection is needed for the good life), additional conditions may need to be met before a life could be deemed a good one, for example that you have friends.

This fallacy is hovering in the vicinity whenever someone says, 'You can't stop a rock you haven't found'. This has become a mantra of the planetary defence movement; for example, it is the cornerstone of B612's Sentinel mission:

> We have the technology to deflect asteroids, but we cannot do anything about the
> objects we don't know exist. To date, less than 1% of asteroids larger than the
> one that leveled Tunguska in 1908 have been tracked. (Lu 2013)

The problem is to rely on detection as *sufficient* for planetary defence. Yet this
is the natural, albeit fallacious, inference to draw. Our human tendency to do so
is exploited, for example, in promotions of lotteries, as in the slogan, 'You can't
win if you don't play'. But of course, if you *do* play the lottery, this surely does
not mean that you *will* win the jackpot. Just so, we could have a highly developed
monitoring capacity for space rocks, and, yet, it would do us little good if, as noted
earlier, what we discovered were a 10-kilometre comet speeding right toward us
from the vicinity of Jupiter.

Contradiction

Finally there is outright contradiction or inconsistency with respect to another
mantra of the movement:

> Although the annual probability of the Earth being struck by a large asteroid
> or comet is extremely small, the consequences of such a collision are so
> catastrophic that it is prudent to assess the nature of the threat and to prepare to
> deal with it. (Morrison 1992)

This is of course an application of the standard formula for risk, which considers
not only probability but also the value of the outcome. However, in the current
climate, it tends to be invoked to spur action to ward off rogue asteroids but not
long-period comets, and, even so, the city-busters rather than the dinosaur-killers.
The reason given? In direct contradiction to the mantra: because the latter are so
unlikely! *But they are also more calamitous!*[9]

Policy Errors

My concern, then, is not to be a logical nit-picker, but to show the dire practical
consequences of widespread illogical thinking about the impact threat. For it is
clear to me that policy issues about the danger of extinction by space rock are

---

9   I will admit that there may be a reasonable limit of concern in terms of what is
technologically feasible. Consider for example the recent surmise that there are billions
of planets in our galaxy not orbiting any star (Wall 2012b). This would then suggest the
possibility of a *When Worlds Collide* scenario, against which we would, presumably, be
truly helpless. Yet I note with mixed feelings the White House's tongue-in-cheek dismissal
of a recent popular petition to build a Death Star (https://petitions.whitehouse.gov/petition/
secure-resources-and-funding-and-begin-construction-death-star-2016/wlfKzFkN).

being decided in part on the basis of logical miscues, and that, as a result, despite impressive achievements to define and meet the threat, humanity is leaving itself unnecessarily vulnerable. The specific policy mistakes I see are these:

- To focus on smaller rocks to the almost complete neglect of extinction-size ones.
- To focus on asteroids to the almost complete neglect of comets, and, in particular, long-period comets.
- To focus on detection to the relative neglect of deflection.
- To focus on deflection of small objects with long advance-warning times to the almost complete neglect of deflection of extinction-size objects with short advance-warning times.

Other Factors

There are certainly other factors supporting these policies besides fallacious reasoning. This is obvious because, as I have already indicated, the planetary defence community *has* shown an awareness of at least some of these logical pitfalls, and, more generally, the problematic nature of our epistemic situation.[10] But that awareness has apparently been blunted by considerations such as the following.

Cognitive Bias

There is a cottage industry of social scientists who have isolated various irrational biases that are inherent in human psycho-logic. The most obvious one relevant to the present question is the human tendency to exaggerate the risk of certain types of outcomes, despite their low or relatively low probability. This is why human beings are much more prone to dread flying than driving, even though the former is far safer. So it is commonplace to come upon items such as a column by science writer Jeff Wise in *Time* magazine, which places 'Asteroids' in the What We Fear [but is] Not Dangerous quadrant because 'Astronomers already have a track on everything big enough to destroy civilisation' (Wise 2012). Besides the outright falsity and illogic of this premise – the main theme of my chapter – I would also argue that the implied analysis is flawed. For the flying/driving example takes the relevant outcome to be death as such, in which case driving is surely more risky than flying. But would it not be more apt to conceive the outcomes as contrasting, say, instantaneous death from crashing through a windshield, on the one hand, and, on the other, minutes-seeming-like-an-eternity of terror in a plummeting

---

10   For example: 'It is this juxtaposition of the small probability of occurrence balanced against the enormous consequences if it does happen that makes the impact hazard such a difficult and controversial topic' (NASA 1998).

aeroplane and then death? If so, then the higher risk attributed to the less likely event might be quite legitimately based on a much more dreaded outcome. And, of course, what could be more dreadful than the end of our entire species?[11]

Anti-nuclear Resistance

There is also a popular movement to eliminate nuclear weapons, and to keep them out of outer space in particular. Consider this statement from a report co-signed by former US Senator Chuck Hagel just before he became Secretary of Defence:

> No sensible argument has been put forward for using nuclear weapons to solve any of the major 21st century problems we face … . (Global Zero 2012, p. 2).

But this flatly contradicts the finding of the most comprehensive and authoritative report on the impact threat to date:

> Unless a large flotilla (100 or more) of massive spacecraft was sent as impactors, nuclear explosions are the only current, practical means for changing the orbit of large NEOs (diameters greater than about 1 km). They also remain as a backup strategy for somewhat smaller objects if other methods have failed. They may be the only method for dealing with smaller objects when warning time is short … . (National Research Council 2010, p. 84)

The current state of this controversy is admirably reported by Birch (2013).

Budgetary Resistance

There is also abroad in the land (of the US in particular) a very budgetary-minded antipathy to creating new government programs. The satirical newspaper *The Onion* captured the sentiment perfectly in an article titled:

> Republicans Vote to Repeal Obama-Backed Bill that Would Destroy Asteroid Headed for Earth (http://www.theonion.com/articles/republicans-vote-to-repeal-obamabacked-bill-that-w,19025/)

Nor is this mere satire; the situation characterised in the following quotation from 2007 remains unchanged today:

> NASA officials say the space agency is capable of finding nearly all the asteroids that might pose a devastating hit to Earth, but there isn't enough money to pay for the task so it won't get done. (Borenstein 2007)

---

11   That is, dreadful to us; for certain other species might send up a cheer at the prospect of our, albeit not their demise.

And during the government shutdown in October 2013, NASA, the agency that is *de facto* in charge of American planetary defence efforts, turned out to have the largest percentage of 'nonessential' employees of any large government agency who were sent home – 97 per cent (Borenstein 2013)!

Yet the simple fact is that the tremendous progress made to date has been done on the cheap – mere millions, not billions of dollars of federal moneys. And even if the cost of a comprehensive planetary defence were significantly higher, it might still be comparable to portions of the budget that we take for granted, such as national defence and health care. Consider how much the money spent on the Iraq War could have furthered the protection of our species! The issue, therefore, I would maintain, is not one of affordability but of priorities.[12]

Furthermore, it is not really an either/or proposition for a wealthy nation – for example defending against terrorists or defending against space rocks, or defending against city-busters or defending against dinosaur-killers – no more than is providing *both* food and shelter for an average American family. The cost argument could therefore be considered another fallacy of reasoning: *false dichotomy*. For example:

> ... most people continue to drive their automobiles regardless [of there being '31 million accidents ... per year, at an annual cost of almost $100 billion']. For the same reason, that we can't live our lives paralyzed by the fear that something bad may happen, we shouldn't let the remote possibility of being struck by a meteor or asteroid rule our lives. (NASA 1998)

This makes it sound like the situation is that either we go crazy with worry and go broke funding feverish efforts to avert a very unlikely catastrophe, or else we live a sane existence with no sense of urgency whatever. But of course there is plenty of room between these extremes for a rational but still urgent effort to address the possibility of a catastrophic impact.

The Private Sector Response

All of these factors[13] have come together to inspire the B612 Foundation's initiative to build and launch its own space telescope (B612 Foundation [B612] n.d.a). The aptly named Sentinel will be placed in a Venus-like orbit, which will allow for continuous scanning of the near-Earth vicinity while looking away from the Sun. In addition, the outer-space vantage will avoid the water vapour in Earth's atmosphere, which impedes the infrared radiation that emanates from charcoal-

---

12   See Gerrard (2000) for an exploration of how such priorities are set.

13   Easterbrook (2008) offers yet another hypothesis: NASA's institutional instinct is not to ask, 'What can we do in space that makes sense?' Rather, it is to ask, 'What can we do in space that requires lots of astronauts?'

black asteroids. Sentinel's sole purpose is to fill the existing gaps in our knowledge of which objects orbiting near Earth pose a potential impact threat. It is expected to complete the inventory of the estimated one million such objects that would be large enough to destroy a city (or worse).

I personally am astounded that a nongovernmental organisation has the wherewithal – or at least the chutzpah – to take this near-definitive step to save the world. There is no question in my mind that people like Rusty Schweickart and Ed Lu are heroes of the highest order for seeing what needed to be done, and could be done and then doing it. (Full disclosure: I am a proud contributor to their organisation.)

But I am equally astounded that humanity has come to this pass, that an NGO wholly dependent on donations from private citizens needs to take such an initiative; for it represents a colossal failure of government to carry out one of its fundamental charges. In addition, I am dismayed by the further hardening of policy positions that I have characterised as irrational, which seems to be an inevitable result of the privatisation of this governmental function. For consider that B612, which must quite properly focus on a project that is doable by private means, may consequently be obliged to withdraw from, if not outright discourage, public discussion of the broader conception of planetary defence, lest that divert interest and funds away from its own herculean enterprise. This leaves it to outliers like myself[14] to perform this educative and political function – to play Chicken Little (or Don Quixote?) to an unknowing and sceptical world, and to a government that would be only too happy to discount the larger threat so as to focus on more local and electable concerns. The problem with relying on the private sector to conduct planetary defence, therefore, is that the fallacies I have highlighted in this chapter become not so much mistakes of reasoning as business and practical imperatives.[15]

Conclusion

I therefore propose as a principle of planetary defence that we act on the assumption that the next extinction-size object targeting Earth will be discovered the day after we have prepared an adequate defence against it were we to begin to prepare with all deliberate speed today. This further implies, I submit, that we cannot wait until we detect a specific threat to prepare to deflect it, but must have a deflection

---

14   And www.gaiashield.com.

15   But perhaps the same could be said as well about government, *mutatis mutandis*. Hence the perennial need for the role I have assumed in writing this chapter – the philosopher as gadfly. It does not take a rocket scientist to observe that it is better to be safe than sorry or that, while hoping for the best, it is wise to prepare for the worst.

infrastructure in place prior to detection.[16] Further, the scope of detection efforts must also be increased, specifically beyond the orbit of Jupiter and outside the ecliptic plane, in order to provide the advance warning we would need to deflect a long-period comet with our name on it. Any less robust planetary defence policy strikes me as irrational and potentially fatal to the human race.

References

Alvarez, L.W., Alvarez, W., Asaro, F. and Michel, H.V. 1980, 'Extraterrestrial cause for the Cretaceous-Tertiary extinction', *Science*, 208: 1095–108.

American Museum of Natural History 2013, 'Defending Earth from asteroids', press conference video, 25 October, viewed 3 March 2015, http://www.youtube.com/watch?v=Hi54HYX9pWc.

B612 Foundation n.d.a, 'Sentinel mission', viewed 3 March 2015, https://b612foundation.org/sentinel-mission.

B612 Foundation n.d.b, 'NEAs, NEOs and comets', viewed 3 March 2015, https://b612foundation.org/asteroids-101.

Beatty, K. 2011, 'If an impact looms, then what?' *Sky and Telescope blog*, web log post, 18 November, viewed 3 March 2015, http://www.skyandtelescope.com/community/skyblog/newsblog/If-An-Impact-Looms-Then-What-134136683.html.

Beatty, K 2013, 'Mars has front-row seat for 2014 comet', *Sky and Telescope blog*, web log post, 1 March, viewed 3 March 2015, http://www.skyandtelescope.com/community/skyblog/newsblog/Mars-has-Front-Row-Seat-for-2014-Comet-194306441.html.

Birch, D. 2013, 'Hunting rogue asteroids could be a new use for nuclear weapons', *Huffington Post*, 16 October, viewed 3 March 2015, http://www.huffingtonpost.com/2013/10/16/nuclear-weapons-asteroids_n_4107236.html.

Borenstein, S. 2007, 'NASA can't pay for killer asteroid hunt', Associated Press, 5 March, viewed 3 March 2015, http://www.nbcnews.com/id/17473059/#.USQdd6VvNtA.

Borenstein, S. 2013, 'The numbers that show how essential an agency is', Associated Press, 2 October, viewed 3 March 2015, http://bigstory.ap.org/article/numbers-show-how-essential-agency.

Boyle, A. 2013, 'Asteroids vs. comets: NASA expert assesses the cosmic threats to Earth', *NBC News Science blog*, web log post, 25 January, viewed 3 March 2015, http://cosmiclog.nbcnews.com/_news/2013/01/25/16702712-asteroids-vs-comets-nasa-expert-assesses-the-cosmic-threats-to-earth?lite.

---

16 Compare Chapman, Durda and Gold (2001, p. 13): 'Instead of waiting to characterize threatening objects only after they are discovered, consideration should be given to the advantages to building a capability in advance'.

Chapman C.R., Durda, D.D. and Gold, R.E. 2001. 'The Comet/Asteroid Impact Hazard: A Systems Approach', white paper, 24 February, viewed 3 March 2015, http://www.internationalspace.com/pdf/NEOwp_Chapman-Durda-Gold.pdf.

Durda, D.D. 2013, 'The Chelyabinsk super-meteor', *Sky and Telescope*, 125(6): 24–31.

Easterbrook, G. 2008, 'The sky is falling', *The Atlantic*, 1 June, viewed 3 March 2015, http://www.theatlantic.com/magazine/archive/2008/06/the-sky-isfalling/306807.

Gerrard, M.B. 2000. 'Risks of hazardous waste sites versus asteroid and comet impacts: Accounting for the discrepancies in U.S. resource allocation', *Risk Analysis*, 20(6): 895–904.

Global Zero Commission 2012, *Modernizing U.S. Nuclear Strategy, Force Structure and Posture*, viewed 3 March 2015, http://dl.dropbox.com/u/6395109/GZ%20US%20Nuclear%20Policy%20Commission%20Report.pdf.

Goodin, R.E. 1995. *Utilitarianism as a Public Philosophy*. Cambridge: Cambridge University Press.

House Science Committee 2013, 'Threats from space: A review of U.S. government efforts to track and mitigate asteroids and meteors', hearing video, 19 March, viewed 3 March 2015, http://science.house.gov/hearing/full-committee-hearing-threats-space-meteors-and-comets-part-1.

Huebert, J.H. 2006. Review of *Catastrophe: Risk and Response*, by Richard A. Posner. *Journal of Libertarian Studies*, 20(4): 71–7.

Jet Propulsion Laboratory 2000, 'Comet Shoemaker-Levy collision with Jupiter', California Institute of Technology and NASA, viewed 3 March 2015, http://www2.jpl.nasa.gov/sl9.

Jet Propulsion Laboratory 2013a, 'Predicting Apophis' Earth encounters in 2029 and 2036', California Institute of Technology and NASA, 16 April, viewed 3 March 2015, http://neo.jpl.nasa.gov/apophis.

Jet Propulsion Laboratory 2013b, 'Ten thousandth near-Earth object unearthed in space', California Institute of Technology and NASA, 24 June, viewed 3 March 2015, http://www.jpl.nasa.gov/news/news.php?release=2013-207.

Lu, E. 2013, 'Our cosmic challenge', B612 Foundation, web log post, 15 February, viewed 3 March 2015, https://b612foundation.org/news/ed-lus-message-our-cosmic-challenge.

Marks, J. 1994, 'Despite relative safety of Earth, Jupiter makes you stop and think', *New Haven Register*, 29 July, p. A9.

Morrison, D. (ed.) 1992, *The Spaceguard Survey: Report of the NASA International Near-Earth-Object Detection Workshop*, NASA/Jet Propulsion Laboratory/California Institute of Technology.

Morrison, D. 2005, 'Defending the Earth against asteroids: The case for a global response', *Science and Global Security*, 13: 87–103.

Moscowitz, C. 2013, 'United Nations to adopt asteroid defense plan', *Scientific American blog*, web log post, 28 October, viewed 3 March 2015, http://www. scientificamerican.com/article.cfm?id=un-asteroid-defense-plan.

National Aeronautics and Space Administration 1998, 'Is Earth in danger of being hit by an asteroid?' *Ask an Astrophysicist blog*, web log post, viewed 3 March 2015, http://teacherlink.ed.usu.edu/tlnasa/reference/imaginedvd/files/imagine/ docs/ask_astro/answers/danger.html.

National Research Council 2010, *Defending Planet Earth: Near-Earth Object Surveys and Hazard Mitigation Strategies*, National Academies Press, Washington, D.C., viewed 3 March 2015, http://www.nap.edu/catalog/12842. html.

Nerney, C. 2013, 'Good news! The odds are slim that you'll be killed by an asteroid or comet', *From the Lab blog*, web log post, 1 February, viewed 3 March 2015, http://www.itworld.com/software/339884/good-news-odds-are-great-you-wont-be-killed-asteroid-or-comet.

Plait, P. 2008, 'Death by meteorite', *Bad Astronomy blog*, web log post, 13 October, viewed 3 March 2015, http://blogs.discovermagazine.com/ badastronomy/2008/10/13/death-by-meteorite/#.Usq6_PRDts1.

Plait, P. 2012, 'How to defend Earth from asteroids', *Huffington Post*, 21 December, viewed 3 March 2015, http://www.huffingtonpost.com/phil-plait/defending-earth-from-asteroids_b_2341804.html?utm_hp_ref=science&ir=Science.

Plait, P. 2013, 'Good news, everyone: Asteroid 2013 TV135 no longer a threat', *Bad Astronomy blog*, web log post, 7 November, viewed 3 March 2015, http:// www.slate.com/blogs/bad_astronomy/2013/11/07/good_asteroid_news_ tv135_no_longer_a_threat.html.

Ropeik, D. 2011, 'The sky IS falling. Should we worry?' *Big Think blog*, web log post, 17 November, viewed 3 March 2015, http://bigthink.com/ ideas/41151?page=all.

RT News 2013, '"Meteor threat wasn't expected for another 2,000 years" – Russian emergency minister', *RT News blog*, 22 February, viewed 3 March 2015, http://rt.com/news/meteor-attack-not-expected-284.

Schulte, P. et al. 2010, 'The Chicxulub asteroid impact and mass extinction at the Cretaceous-Paleogene boundary', *Science*, 327: 1214–81.

Schweickart, R. et al. 2008, 'Asteroid threats: A call for global response', Association of Space Explorers, 25 September, viewed 3 March 2015, http:// www.space-explorers.org/ATACGR.pdf.

Shoemaker, E.M. 1963, 'Impact mechanics at Meteor Crater, Arizona', in BM Middlehurst and GP Kuiper (eds), *The Moon, Meteorites, and Comets*, 4, *The Solar System*. Chicago, IL: University of Chicago Press.

Wall, M. 2012a, 'End may be nigh for asteroid disaster movies', *Space.com*, 21 June, viewed 3 March 2015, http://www.space.com/16251-asteroid-impact-disaster-movie-facts.html.

Wall, M. 2012b, '"Orphan" alien planet found nearby without parent star', *Space.com*, 14 November, viewed 3 March 2015, http://www.space.com/18461-rogue-alien-planet-discovery.html.

Wise, J. 2012, 'Fearing well', *Time*, 9 January, p. 36.

Yeomans, D.K. 2013, *Near-Earth Objects: Finding Them Before They Find Us*. Princeton, NJ: Princeton University Press.

Chapter 8

Advertising in Space: Sales at the Outer Limits

Zeldine O'Brien

There have been a wide number of projects embracing many different aspects of space advertising over the years – some only proposed and others brought to fruition. In April 1993, an American corporate entity, Space Marketing Concepts Inc., proposed the use of a 'Space Billboard' – a mylar sheet to be launched into space of approximately 1 km² – to convey a commercial communication as well as carry scientific instruments (IAU 2001, p. 4; Balsamello 2009–10, p. 1791; Tomlinson and Wiley 1995, p. 539). It would have rivalled the full Moon in size and brightness, 'obliterated most astronomical observations' and was 'estimated to receive some 10,000 impacts of space debris per day with associated debris proliferation' (IAU 2001, p. 4). The project did not get off the ground figuratively or literally. This was not the first project with a space advertising aspect. In 1989, it had been proposed to celebrate the bicentennial of the French Revolution and the centennial of the Eiffel Tower by the launch of a ring of bright satellites to be known as 'The Ring of Light' (IAU 2001, p. 4). The project did not proceed following international opposition. A proposal that the Olympic Games in Atlanta be advertised by a reflector of 1,000 m x 400 m in space was put forward in 1996 (Huebert and Block 2006, p. 1; Balsamello 2009–10, p 1792) but failed to attract funding (IAU 2001, p. 4). In 2000, Pizza Hut paid to place a 30-foot logo on the external housing of a Proton rocket (Harwood 2000). Similarly, Columbia Pictures advertised the movie *The Last Action Hero* on the side of a rocket (Tomlinson and Wiley 1995, p. 541). An advertisement for Japanese noodles has been shot on the International Space Station (Balsamello 2009–10, p. 1772) and in 2009, the Moon Publicity Corporation proposed the use of shadow shaping technology on the Moon for advertising purposes (Moon Publicity Corp. 2009).

This chapter will consider advertising in space, including the definition of advertising, the international law relevant to this activity, relevant national laws and a brief discussion of the interests at stake, including identification of some of the challenges in regulation at national level.

Defining 'Space Advertising'

Advertising

There is no definition of 'space advertising' in general international space law. Advertising has been defined as 'any form of marketing communications carried by the media, usually in return for payment or other valuable consideration' (ICC 2011, p. 4). In EC law, it is defined as 'the making of a representation in any form in connection with a trade business, craft or profession in order to promote the supply of goods or services including immovable property, rights and obligations' (Directive 2006/114/EC, Art. 2(a)). Its purpose is both to *inform* consumers, existing or potential, of new or existing products/services in the market or the identities of sellers/suppliers ('informative advertising' (Lambin 1976, p. 3)) and *persuade* them to purchase or avail of it or continue to purchase or avail of it (Lambin 1976, p. 7). The definition in EC law offers much to recommend it as it is not mired in problems of multi-functionality nor following flows of revenue (cf. IAU 2001, p. 4). In requiring a representation and a promotional element, it does not become unduly focused on the nature of the promotion, that is, whether it is informative or persuasive or both. It also offers tangible proof that it is possible to define advertising in a manner acceptable to both common law and codal systems at a supranational level.

Space

In terms of defining 'space advertising', this chapter considers space advertising in relation to the locus of its occurrence rather than by topical relationship between the representation and space activities. What is outer space is a question that has been considered in depth in a great number of works, such as Cheng (1983), Diederiks-Verschoor (2008, pp. 15–20), Goedhart (1996) and Lyall and Larson (2009, pp. 153–74). Accursius of Bologna's oft-quoted proposition of '*cuius est solum eius est ab inferos usque ad coelom*' provides little assistance. There is no definition of 'airspace' in international air law or 'outer space' in international space law. While there is consensus that terrestrial airspace is synonymous with the Earth's atmosphere, its upper limit remains in doubt. Some assistance may be found in national law. Under the US National Aeronautics and Space Act 1958, as amended, 'aeronautical and space activities' is referable to 'research into, and the solution of, problems of flight within and outside the Earth's atmosphere' (s.20103(1)). Section 1(xv) of the South African Space Affairs Act 1993 defines 'space' as 'the space above the surface of the Earth from a height at which it is in practice possible to operate an object in orbit around the Earth'. The definitional reluctance is easily explained. While outer space is not subject to any claim of appropriation by any state (The Outer Space Treaty 1967, Art. II), airspace is subject to territorial claims (Paris Convention 1919, Art. 1; Chicago Convention 1944, Art. 1). To draw the line between the two is to state the limit of a state's sovereign territory – a singularly unattractive political proposition for many states, save for Australia. Applying this spatialist approach, advertising constitutes *space* advertising where it occurs or is intended to occur beyond a legally cognisable boundary between air and outer space. In Australia, this is in effect 100 km above sea level (s. 8 of the Space Activities Act 1998, as amended). The alternative to spatialism is functionalism. Functionalism draws its distinction on the basis of the function of the object. Thus any object launched or attempted to be launched in order to travel into, to or through outer space and/or to the Moon or other celestial bodies and its component parts, including its launch vehicle (Liability Convention 1972, Art. I(d); Registration Convention 1975, Art. I(b)), may be properly considered a space object and the subject of international space law. This approach avoids the need to delineate a clear boundary between air and space and thus the need to state any limitation on states' territorial sovereignty in air space but may be challenged by hybridised technology (see Christol 1992). Applying a functionalist approach, whether advertising is *space* advertising is answered by regard to the intended function of the object on or in which the advertisement is placed. The use of the term 'space object' reflects the usage of same in the *corpus iuris spatialis*. Advertising as an activity occurring in outer space on the Moon or other celestial bodies, as opposed to in, on, constituting or otherwise connected to a space object, will also be subject to state supervision by way of applicable national space laws.

To this definition of 'space advertising', a distinction has emerged between 'obtrusive space advertising' and 'non-obtrusive space advertising'. This distinction is reflected at international levels and in US space law.

Obtrusive and Nondestructive Space Advertising

The UN Committee on the Peaceful Uses of Outer Space (UNCOPUOS) recommended that its Scientific and Technical Subcommittee consider the issue of limiting *obtrusive* space advertising, a recommendation endorsed by the UN General Assembly in 2001 (UNGA Resolution A/RES/56/61 2001, s.15(c)(ii)). The distinction was recognised in US law and by the IAU where it quoted the definition of obtrusive space advertising as set out in the United States Code (2001, p. 3) as follows:

> advertising in outer space that is capable of being recognised by a human being on the surface of the Earth without the aid of telescope or other technological device. (49 USC §70102(9) *cf.* H.R. 2599, §2(c)(2))

'Non-obtrusive' is not defined although it is exempt from this definition (49 USC §70109(c)). It may be defined negatively (that is as advertising which is not 'obtrusive advertising'). Non-obtrusive space advertising would include product placement used in broadcasts from space objects, logos on uniforms of persons in space and logos on space objects themselves (Lyall and Larson 2009, pp. 298–9; IAU 2001, p. 3). In terms of practice, the logo of the European Space Agency is protected under Art. 6 of the Convention for the Protection of Industrial Property (ESA) and appears on, *inter alia*, the Ariane launch vehicle, space suits of ISS personnel and other goods and products. This practice has not raised any complaint. Indeed, the identification of space objects requires the presence of some identifying marks, although these do not have to be on exposed elements. The IAU set out three basic characteristics for assessing obtrusiveness:

a. Brightness as seen from the surface of the Earth;
b. Time of visibility from a given observing point on Earth;
c. Extent and positional control of the illuminated area on Earth (IAU 2001, p. 4).

Definitions of 'obtrusive space advertising' and 'non-obtrusive space advertising' still fundamentally require a promotional representation *and* presence in outer space. Classification of a marketing communication as either obtrusive or non-obtrusive space advertising is significant as the balance of interests to be struck varies with that classification.

The relevant provisions of international space law and some national space law as they bear on space advertising, both obtrusive and non-obtrusive will be considered.

Space Advertising and International Space Law

The launch of Sputnik 1 provided great impetus for the development of space law. Outer space 'was a new field and there were no vested interests to prevent the international community from embarking on a regime of co-operation rather than of conflict' (Rao K, quoted by COPUOS Legal Sub-Committee 1964, p. 78). It was in this context that UNCOPUOS developed five multilateral instruments concerning outer space at the heart of the *corpus iuris spatialis* (Outer Space Treaty 1967; Rescue Agreement 1968; Registration Convention 1975; Liability Convention 1972 and the Moon Agreement 1979).

The first of these instruments, the Outer Space Treaty ('OST'), recognises 'the common interest of all mankind in the progress of the ... use of outer space for peaceful purposes' (preambulatory cl.2). It establishes the free use of outer space, the Moon and other celestial bodies by all states and provides that activities in space 'shall be carried out for the benefit and interest of all countries' (OST, Art. I). This requirement for activities to be carried out for the 'interests of all countries' has not precluded commercial activities. State practice evidences a general acceptance of such activities. The ISS has been used on a commercial basis (see generally Von der Dunk and Brus 2006). However, the limits of this acceptance remain to be tested. If revenue from space advertising is used to fund expanding access to and exploration of space, Balsamello suggests the activity could be considered as being in the common interest of all mankind (2009–10, p. 1784 cf. IAU 2001, p. 3).

All activities must be carried out by state parties 'in accordance with international law' (OST, Art. III). States bear international responsibility for national activities in outer space, including the Moon and other celestial bodies, whether they are carried on by governmental agencies or by nongovernmental entities (OST, Art. VI). They also have international responsibility for assuring that national activities are carried out in conformity with the provisions of the OST (Art. VI) and, therefore, in accordance with international law. The activities of nongovernmental entities in outer space require authorisation and continuing supervision by states (OST, Art. VI).

Liability for launching of space objects will fall on launching states under both Art. VII of the OST and Art. II of the 1972 Liability Convention. Launching states include states which launch or procure the launch of a space object and states from whose territory or facility a space object is launched (Liability Convention 1972, Art I(c)). Due regard in licensing national activities must be had under international law to the 'corresponding interests of other states' (OST, Art. IX). These interests include the freedoms of other states to use and access space which includes the making of astronomical observations. Further, activities which may give rise to 'potentially harmful interference' to the interests of other states will trigger the need for consultation with other states (OST, Art. IX). This is significant as proposed space advertisements may pose a risk arising from an unacceptable contribution to the proliferation of space debris. In addition to this, other environmental concerns relating to aesthetics have also been noted by the IAU (2001, p. 3). Ownership remains unaffected by presence in outer space (OST, Art. VIII). Jurisdiction over the space object is determined by the state of registry, that is, the state upon whose national registry the space object is registered (OST, Art. VIII).

The import of these provisions is that there is no outright ban on *all* space advertising either expressly or impliedly part of the *corpus iuris spatialis*. State practice shows an acceptance of some space advertising. Advertising on the ISS is permitted where it is subject to guidelines regulating commercial activity (Belingheri 2006, p. 38). Space advertising as an activity falls clearly within the scope of activities that are under the supervision and the responsibility of states, whether it occurs in outer space, on the Moon or on other celestial bodies. As such, states have a clear duty to ensure that such advertising activities of their nationals are conducted with due regard to the rights of other states, the duties under the OST and in accordance with general international law. It is by national laws licensing space activities that state supervision is effected. Therefore while there is no ban, international space law will impact on the authorisation of space advertising. Any proposed space advertisement that would, if carried out, violate international law ought not to be authorised under any domestic space law regime. Balsamello gives an example of this:

> Advertising that would so substantially clutter orbit that it would become
> impossible for other states to explore outer space would likely violate
> international law. (2009–10, p. 1785)

Where authorisation was issued in respect of such a project and the project proceeded
on that basis, the authorising state would be in breach of its international obligations
and arguably have committed an internationally wrongful act (ILC 2001, Art. 2). It
is therefore in a state's interests to ensure adequate supervision, not least because a
failure to do so would be a breach of the international space law with the potential
liability to make reparations.

With regard to the ownership of a space advertisement, this is unaffected by
presence in outer space but will be subject to the jurisdiction of the state of registry.
This latter jurisdictional aspect may be a factor in determining the appropriate
forum for a trademark infringement action.

National Law and Regulation with Regard to Space Advertising

To date, only the US has explicitly addressed space advertising in its national
space law. Whether other states will follow suit remains to be seen. US law on this
point will be considered as will the position in other states in the absence of a ban.

The US Approach

The US has put in place a ban on the licensing by it of all obtrusive advertising (as
defined above). Its law provides:

> Notwithstanding the provisions of this chapter or any other provision of law, the
> Secretary [of Transportation] may not, for the launch of a payload containing
> any material to be used for the purposes of obtrusive space advertising:
>
> (1) issue or transfer a license under this chapter; or
> (2) waive the license requirements of this chapter. (49 USC §70109a(a))

Non-obtrusive commercial space advertising as noted above is exempt and
includes 'advertising on (1) commercial space transportation vehicles; (2) space
infrastructure payloads; (3) space launch facilities; and (4) launch support facilities'
(49 USC §70109a(c)). By way of example, images of *SpaceShipTwo* show it in
bearing the 'Virgin Galactic' livery (Virgin Galactic 2015). Similarly, *SpaceX*'s
logo appears on its *Falcon 9* (SpaceX 2015). This approach is also reflected in
state practice. The NASA insignia has been authorised for use on apparel and
personal property items used by NASA employees in the performance of their
duties (14 CFR §1221.110(a)(4)) as well as spacecraft (14 CFR §1221.110(a)(4)).
The approach adopted in the US Code has been the subject of both criticism and

support. Huebert and Block argue in favour of the repeal of §70109a in light of free commercial speech and private property rights (2006, pp. 7–8). Wiley, discussing space advertising prior to the introduction of §70109a, favoured regulation of advertising (1995, p. 566) although his co-author, Tomlinson, favoured a complete ban, noting the difficulties with promulgating content-based restrictions in light of the protection afforded to free speech under the First Amendment of the US Constitution (1995, pp. 564–5).

Other Space-faring Nations

As no other state has legislative restriction on space advertising explicitly, obtrusive or otherwise, for other states the question of whether or not to permit space advertising will be have to be answered on a case-by-case basis in accordance with the criteria applicable within the context of their own national licensing regimes. This decision will be made in the context of the state's own legislative and regulatory framework against the backdrop of its own hierarchy of rights.

The legal basis of rights derives much, although not exclusive, protection from instruments within national law systems, such as an applicable Constitution. The balance struck amongst the rights themselves and between rights and duties is variable across national systems. Further, even well-accepted rights are not unlimited in law. They may be proportionately delimited for a number of legitimate governmental aims. In addition, other rights recognised in the system may act as counterweights. The regulation of the form and content of advertising varies across national systems too as does the view of the consumer and the prevalence of paternalism. In the absence of international legal definitions, this renders authorisation of space advertising at a national level problematic. For instance, national bans on obtrusive advertising will necessarily be territorially limited to applicants under its own licensing regime with the possibility of extra-territorial application to its own nationals elsewhere. Therefore a national ban *per se* will not guarantee citizens of that state a firmament free of obtrusive advertising. This may be addressed by formulating international law on the issue (cf. Balsamello 2009–10, pp. 1800–1806) including the adoption of an outright ban or, alternatively, criteria and standards or by self-regulation in the form of an international code. Additionally, there is the option of co-regulation combining both legislative and self-regulatory elements. In light of the supervisory provisions of the OST, some direct state oversight of space advertising by nationals is preferable to a purely self-regulating system.

In terms of non-obtrusive advertising, as noted above, state practice evidences no particular difficulty with the use of logos, branding on astronauts or space objects or even using space stations for shooting advertisements. Agencies' own marks may have protection as trademarks, for example 'JAXA' is a registered trademark in the law of Japan (Conditions, cl. 5). CNES is also registered as a trademark and appears on launch vehicles and may appear on space suits and space stations (Justia). DLR is also registered (Justia). These trademarks and logos then appear on uniforms of astronauts and on space objects. This supports the view that state practice with regard to non-obtrusive advertising both of the states' own entities and of private corporate entities is non-problematic in international and national law, a view apparently shared by the IAU (2001, p. 4).

Challenges for the Regulation of Space Advertising

Non-Obtrusive Advertising

State practice demonstrates clearly that non-obtrusive advertising is not intrinsically problematic or prohibited by any international or national law. However, it does not follow that there are no legislative or regulatory measures applicable. Even if a state licenses an object bearing non-obtrusive logos or slogans, the advertisement itself remains open to challenge if it infringes trademarks or other intellectual property. Similarly the regulation of trademarks may act to prohibit or revoke certain logos. For example, in US law, trademarks may be revoked if disparaging (see, for example, *Blackhorse & Ors v Pro-Football Inc.* 2014). Further, there is no reason in principle why the content of the advertisement would be excluded from content-based regulation or legislation. In this way, laws of different kinds in the national forum may have a bearing on permissible space advertising, in regulating content including revocation of trademark protection.

Obtrusive Advertising

Obtrusive advertising poses greater challenges. At an international level, concerns arise from its potential to interfere with the rights of other states in astronomical observation and environmental concerns. Content regulation also poses a challenge. One of the central arguments relied upon to justify obtrusive advertising is freedom of speech (see Huebert and Block 2006, p. 8).

Freedom of Commercial Speech

Freedom of speech or expression is widely recognised both in national law systems (First Amendment of the US Constitution, Art. 40.6.1(i) of the Irish Constitution 1937) and internationally (Art. 10 of the European Convention on Human Rights). This right is generally accepted as extending to commercial speech (see for example *Bigelow v Virginia* 1975, p. 821, *Central Hudson Gas & Elec. Corp. v. Pub. Serv. Comm'n* 1980, p. 563, *Zauderer v. Office of Disciplinary Counsel* 1985, p. 651; *Germany v Parliament* 2006, p. 11671 and Rome et al. 1985, p. 42). Advertising as a form of speech may constitute purely commercial speech or may stray into social advocacy and political advertising (for example, *Valentine v Chrestensen* 1942). Different national laws may weigh the value of commercial speech differently. Obscene material may have no protection at all (for example the US: *Miller v California* 1973).

However, the right of free commercial speech is not unlimited. The source of the limitations will again be found in the domestic legal order. Limitations may be expressed and include legitimate governmental aims and other counter-veiling rights. In Ireland, freedom of expression is expressly limited – it cannot 'be used to undermine public order or morality or the authority of the state' (Bunreacht na hÉireann, 1937, Art. 40.6.1). The weighting given to counter-veiling interests varies. For example, complete bans in tobacco advertising have been upheld in the EC, notwithstanding the recognition of commercial speech because of the legitimate aim of government with regard to public health. It is unlikely that the same could be effected in the US due to the weighting given to free speech in that legal system (Flanagan 2011). Other legitimate aims include the protection of consumers, the protection of children, the protection of public morals and the security of state (insofar as an advertisement may constitute an incitement to violence, riot or civil disorder). The right to free commercial expression must also be assessed in the light of a state's duty to comply with its international law obligations, which itself is a legitimate aim. Advertising may also attract legitimate aims. Advertising's informative function is beneficial to consumers and, as an activity, it has an economic value. As noted by Stigler, advertising is 'an immensely powerful instrument for the elimination of ignorance' (1961, p. 220). Advertising aids consumers in perceiving real or artificial differences between products/services (Pearce et al. 1971, p. 3.11). A consumer's interest in the free flow of commercial information has been recognised judicially (for example, in the US see *Virginia Pharmacy Board v Virginia Citizens Consumer Council* 1976, p. 764). It is the role of the state to balance these aims, insofar as they conflict. Proportionate restrictions on rights including prohibitions on space advertising may be justified by that balance.

Although an advertiser has freedom of speech, there is no right to be heard by the targets of advertising. While rights of audience are protected, this is in the context of civil or criminal proceedings. Freedom of commercial speech is not and ought not to be equated with a general right to be heard by one's target market. The right to free commercial expression is assessed against a matrix of other rights, some which are held by the very targets of the proposed advertising, including the right not to communicate, a right to privacy and property rights. To date, consumers do have and exercise the freedom to deny receipt of marketing communications. This may be done by simply choosing not to read the advertising section of the paper or by placing a 'no junk mail' sign on their letterbox. The exercise of this freedom by consumers is in direct conflict with the communicative aim of advertising. There is a question as to whether consumers will be able to choose *not* to read a space advertisement. Insofar as an avoidance of such an advertisement may be effected by closing the blinds and drawing the curtains, to be compelled to engage in this behaviour does not appear to vindicate private property rights.

The right to private property includes the right to the use and enjoyment of that land. For this reason, there is a qualitative difference between viewing billboards on a public highway and viewing a space billboard projected overhead while on one's own property. The issue lies not with the destruction of a view or prospect (Halsbury 2010, pp. 118–19) but that the light intrusion by way of increases in lux values may constitute a nuisance, that is, an interference with the use and enjoyment of property (*Fleming v Rathdown School Trust* 1993; *Blower v Suffolk County Council* 1994; *Bank of New Zealand v Greenwood* 1984; *Amphitheaters v Portland Meadows* 1948; Halsbury 2010, p. 157; O'Connell 1998). Increases in lux values at night-time can prove disruptive to circadian rhythms even at low levels (Fonken et al. 2013; Shuboni 2010). The use and enjoyment of land may also include use for amateur astronomy, which may be inferred by an obtrusive space advertisement. Obstruction of a view may amount to a public nuisance (for example, *Campbell v Paddington Corporation* 1911).

Whether or not a restriction on obtrusive space advertising is an impermissible restriction on freedom of commercial speech will have to be assessed within the national order and/or any supranational regime, for example the ECJ or European Court of Human Rights and in the context of the balance of rights in that regime. Further in supranational regimes, restrictions may well be found to fall within a state's margin of appreciation.

Astronomical Observations

The net issue is whether the commercial interest inherent in a space advertisement outweighs international or national interest in astronomical observations, which is not without a commercial aspect in itself. Some states have recognised dark-sky reserves. The Kerry International Dark-Sky Reserve in Ireland covers an area of approximately 700km² (White 2014). It is the first Gold Tier reserve in the Northern Hemisphere and there is an anticipated commercial benefit to the area in terms in the rise in astrotourism as a result (White 2014). The IAU (International Astronomical Union 2001, p. 5) notes that the brightness of fast-moving objects comparable to the brightness of Venus may damage the ultra-sensitive detector systems used on large telescopes which could necessitate protection by separate monitoring of the field for such objects. Any object comparable in brightness to the Moon will 'generate so much scattered light in the Earth's atmosphere that observations of all faint objects become impossible', and while space observatories would be immune to some of this pollution, the IAU notes that they are 'so costly and specialized that the future of astronomy cannot be based on space observatories alone' (2001, p. 5). In the case of an object illuminating an entire dark hemisphere of the Earth, the IAU states that 'all night-time astronomy suffers in proportion to the brightness of the illumination' (2001, p. 5). This would appear to be such a disproportionate interference in the right of use that it ought to be prohibited by states. The commercial benefit to an advertiser of a project intended to provide entire illumination of a dark hemisphere without any provision for deflecting unwanted illumination from dark-sky reserves or observatories cannot outweigh the interest in astronomical observations both within the licensing state and globally and the commercial interests in astrotourism. The benefit appears localised to one economy while the cost is global.

Environmental Concerns: Space Debris

All space objects generate space debris. Space advertising is no different. It is presumed that the object generating the debris has a purpose that outweighs the environmental consequences such as scientific experimentation, refuelling the ISS or remote sensing. In the case of space advertising, there are two concerns: first, whether that presumption is appropriate in the context of a space object whose sole purpose is to advertise and, secondly, whether the nature of space advertising generates a greater degree of risk of proliferations. On this second point, the IAU comments:

> In fact most space advertising is likely to greatly outlast the enterprise that launched it, unless end-of-mission deorbiting procedures are required and implemented. Moreover, because space objects used for advertising purposes need to be very large, they also present a large cross-section to impacts of existing space debris, resulting in the creation of even more such debris. (2001, p. 3)

For states without explicit bans, each project would require a case-by-case analysis, including consideration of the impact to existing debris, the creation of debris, compliance with any applicable debris mitigation guidelines and any proposed end-of-life measures. Liability for component parts of space objects will lie on the launching state for harm on an absolute basis to the surface of Earth or aircraft in flight or on a fault basis to other space objects (Liability Convention 1972, Arts II and III). While the launching state may be able to recoup any damages paid out from the licensee, this is only if that party is still extant.

Aesthetics, Transnational Effect and Content-based Concerns

As Shakespeare commented, '[b]eauty is bought by judgement of the eye, not utter'd by base sale of chapmen's tongues' (*Love's Labours Lost* 1588, II, i), and being so subjective, what may pass muster of one nation's aesthetic judgement may be sorely lacking for another. This inherent subjectivity renders the aesthetic assessment of advertising a challenge. As matters stand, with the exception of the US, it falls to the licensing regime of a single state to consider any aesthetic issues and national and transnational nuisance arising from obtrusive advertising.

Aside from aesthetics, indecency, incitement to hatred, riot and/or violent disorder, offensiveness (for example, where dehumanising, derogatory or discriminatory), graphic violent or adult content and misleading, fraudulent or deceptive advertising may all constitute variably defined grounds for restricting content. Consumer protection of vulnerable persons, such as children, may be grounds for restricting advertising of certain products (for example sweets, fast foods and so on) that do not offend any of these elements. If obtrusive advertising is permitted, the question is one of assessing whose and what, if any, content-based regulation or restriction is to be applied. There is also a deeper question of whether it is right or appropriate for the content standards in one country to be applied, without any further debate or discussion, to an advertisement that will be exposed to the citizens of another who have had no direct or indirect say in the formulation of those standards by way of their own legislative or self-regulating authorities.

Conclusion

There are some difficulties occasioned in defining 'space advertising' that flow in part from the lack of concrete definition of 'outer space' or indeed 'air space' in the *corpus iuris spatialis* and in international air law, respectively. However, the making of commercial representation for the purpose of promoting sales of goods and services in outer space is an activity which is not in and of itself subject to a ban in international space law. In national law, only the US has sought to address the issue and has distinguished obtrusive and non-obtrusive advertising: a definitional distinction that has been endorsed by the IAU.

As a space activity, space advertising will be subject to supervision by states in order to ensure compliance with the provisions of the Outer Space Treaty, which in turn provides for compliance with general international law norms, including environmental principles. This is effected by national space law regimes.

Non-obtrusive advertising is not banned internationally or nationally and state practice appears to evidence no difficulties with its occurrence. In the event that the advertisement is non-obtrusive and permitted, the content will not be excluded from the application of law affecting such content, such as laws protecting intellectual property.

The licensing of obtrusive space advertising poses far greater challenges, not least of which is the balance to be struck between different interests. States must have regard to the rights of other states and ensure that the proposed project complies within international law which will include the use of space by states to make astronomical observations. The impact of the project on the proliferation of space debris is also pertinent. Advertising that would violate international law should not be authorised. In addition, states will be tasked with balancing interests arising at national level including its own legitimate aims and the rights of its other citizens. As the balance to be struck will reflect national hierarchies of rights and duties, it may well be the case that the balance will be different for each state.

A complete national ban on obtrusive advertising even with extra-territorial effect to nationals outside of the jurisdiction is no guarantee of clear skies. Further, if obtrusive space advertising is permitted and transboundary display is intended or anticipated (and may well be inescapable), there is the possibility of conflict arising between variable content-based standards between the authorising state and the states into which the advertisement is displayed. As such, it would be preferable that the matter be considered at international level where there is a need for discussion, including the consideration of an outright ban in law or its regulation by the establishment of criteria and standards whose establishment although problematic is not insurmountable.

States have a window of opportunity to promulgate law and/or regulation in respect of obtrusive space advertising at this time, before it becomes a question of taking reactive measures. It is to be hoped that they fully exploit that opportunity and continue to extend the existing regime of cooperation.

References

Amphitheaters v Portland Meadows 184 Or. 336; 198 P.2d 847.

Balsamello, F.J. 2009–10, 'When You Wish Upon a Falling Billboard: Advertising in the Age of Space Tourism', *The Georgetown Law Journal*, 98: 1769–822.

Bank of New Zealand v Greenwood [1984] 1 N.Z.L.R. 525.

Belingheri, M. 2006, 'A Policy and Legal Framework for Commercial Utilisation' in Von der Dunk, F. and Brus, M. (eds), *The International Space Station Commercial Utilisation from A European Legal Perspective*. Leiden: Martinus Nijhoff Publishers, pp. 33–46.

Bigelow v Virginia 421 U.S. 809 (1975).

Blackhorse, Briggs-Cloud, Glover Pappan and Tsotigh v Pro-Football Inc., Decision of the Trademark Trial and Appeal Board, 18 June 2014, Cancellation No. 92046185, viewed 18 March 2015, http://ttabvue.uspto.gov/ttabvue/ v?pno=92046185&pty=CAN&eno=199.

Blower v Suffolk County Council [1994] 2 E.G.L.R. 204, 67 P. & C.R. 228.

Bunreacht na hÉireann/Constitution of Ireland 1937 as amended, Government Publications, Dublin, Ireland.

Campbell v Paddington Corporation [1911] 1 K.B. 869.

Case C-380/03 *Germany v Parliament* [2006] ECR I-11573.

Central Hudson Gas & Elec. Corp. v. Pub. Serv. Comm'n, 447 U.S. 557 (1980).

Cheng, B. 1983, 'The Legal Status of Outer Space and Relevant Issues: Delimitation of Outer Space and Definition of Peaceful Use', *Journal of Space Law*, 11: 89–105.

Chicago Convention 1944: Convention on International Civil Aviation, 61 Stat. 1180, 15 UNTS 295. Entered into force 6 April 1947.

Christol, C.Q. 1992, 'Legal Aspects of Aerospace Planes' in Cheng, C-J. (ed.), *The Highways of Air and Outer Space over Asia*. New York: Springer, pp. 77–91.

Code of Federal Regulations, Title 14, Chapter 1221, s.110, viewed 18 March 2015, https://www.law.cornell.edu/cfr/text/14/1221.110.

Constitution of the United States of America as amended, viewed 18 March 2015, http://www.law.cornell.edu/constitution/first_amendment.

Convention for the Protection of Industrial Property, 828 UNTS 305. Entered into force 26 April 1970.

COPUOS Legal Sub-Committee 1964, *Summary Records of the 29th to 37th Meetings held at the Palais des Nations*, Geneva from 9 to March 1974 UN Doc. A/AC.105/C.2/SR.29–37, viewed 18 March 2015, http://www.unoosa.org/pdf/transcripts/legal/AC105_C2_SR029–037E.pdf.

Diederiks-Verschoor, I.P.H. 2008, *An Introduction to Space Law*, 3rd ed., Kluwer Law International, Alphen aan den Riji, The Netherlands.

Directive 2006/114/EC of the European Parliament and of the Council of the 12th December 2006 concerning misleading and comparative advertising [2006] O.J. L 376/21, codified version viewed 18 March 2015, http://eur-lex.europa.eu/LexUriServ/LexUriServ.do?uri=CELEX:32006L0114:EN:NOT.

ESA, 'ESA and Trademarks' viewed on 18 March 2015, http://www.esa.int/About_Us/Industry/Intellectual_Property_Rights/ESA_and_trademarks.

Flanagan, S. 2011, 'Commercial Free Speech in the United States and the European Union: Why Comprehensive Tobacco Advertising Bans Work in Europe, but Fail in the United States' *Suffolk U.L. Rev.*, 44, p. 211.

Fleming v Rathdown School Trust, Unreported, High Court, Denham, J., 21 March 1993.

Fonken, L.K., Aubrecht, T.G., Meléndez-Fernández, O.H., Weil, Z.M. and Nelson, R.J. 2013, 'Dim Light at Night Disrupts Molecular Circadian Rhythms and Affects Metabolism', *Journal of Biological Rhythms*, 28(4): 262–71, viewed 18 March 2015, http://www.ncbi.nlm.nih.gov/pmc/articles/PMC4033305.

Goedhart, R.F.A. 1996, *The Never-Ending Dispute: Delimitation of Air Space and Outer Space*, Editions Frontières, Gif-sur-Yvette Cedex, France.

Halsbury's Laws of England 2010, 5th ed., Mackay of Clashfern (ed.), LexisNexis, London, 78.

Harwood, W. 2000, 'Zvezda Module Finally Launched to Space Station', *Spaceflight Now*, July 12, viewed 18 March 2015, http://spaceflightnow.com/station/zvezda/000712launch.

Huebert, J.H. and Block, W. 2006, 'In Defense of Advertising in Space', in Jorgenson, C. (ed), *Proceedings of the 49th Colloquium on the Law of Outer Space*, International Institute of Space Law, Valencia, 5.15, pp. 1–11, viewed 11 June 2014, http://jhhuebert.com/articles.

ICC 2011, *Consolidated Code of Advertising and Marketing Practice*, International Chamber of Commerce, viewed 18 March 2015, http://www.codescentre.com/media/2083/660%20consolidated%20icc%20code_2011_final%20with%20covers.pdf.

ILC 2001, 'Draft Articles on the Responsibilities of States for Internationally Wrongful acts', *Yearbook of the International Law Commission*, vol. II, Part two.

International Astronomical Union 2001, 'Obtrusive Space Advertising and Astronomical Research', Background Paper, UN Doc. A/AC.105/777, viewed 10 June 2014, http://www.oosa.unvienna.org/pdf/reports/ac105/AC105_777E. pdf.

JAXA, 'Conditions of Material Usage', viewed 18 March 2015, http://jda.jaxa.jp/en/service.php.

Justia, 'CNES – Trademark Details', viewed 18 March 2015, https://trademarks.justia.com/791/32/cnes-79132430.html.

Justia, 'DLR – Trademark Details', viewed 18 March 2015, http://trademarks.justia.com/753/59/dlr-75359917.html.

Lambin, J.J. 1976, *Advertising, Competition and Market Conduct in Oligopoly over Time*. Oxford: North-Holland Publishing Company.

Liability Convention 1972, Convention on the International Liability of Damage Caused by Space Objects 1972, 24 UST 2389; TIAS 7762; 961 UNTS 187; ILM (1971):1; [1972] Irish Treaty Series No.7. Entered into force 1 September 1972.

Lyall F and Larson PB 2009, *Space Law: A Treatise*. Farnham: Ashgate.

Miller v California 413 U.S. 15 (1973).

Moon Agreement, 1979: Agreement Governing the Activities on the Moon and Other Celestial Bodies 1979, 18 ILM 1434; 1363 UNTS 3. Entered into force July 1984.

Moon Publicity Corporation 2009, Shadow Shaping Technology, viewed 18 March 2015, http://www.moonpublicity.com.

National Aeronautics and Space Act 1958, Public Law No. 111–314, 124 Stat. 3328 as amended (previously Public Law No. 85–568, 72 Stat. 426) viewed 18 March 2014, http://www.nasa.gov/offices/ogc/about/space_act1.html.

O'Connell, M. 1998, 'Remedies for Light Intrusion in Irish Law after *Fleming v Rathdown School Trust*', *Irish Planning and Environmental Law Journal*, 5(2): 43–7.

Outer Space Treaty, 1967: Convention on the Exploration and Use by States of Outer Space including the Moon and other Celestial Bodies 18 UST 2410; TIAS 6347; 610 UNTS 205; [1968] Irish Treaty Series No. 7. Entered into force 10 October 1967.

Paris Convention 1919: Convention relating to the Regulation of Aerial Navigation, 11 LNTS 174; 1 International Legislation 339 (No longer in force).

Pearce, M., Cunningham, S.M. and Miler, A. 1971, *Appraising the Economic and Social Affects of Advertising*, Staff Report. Boston, MA: Marketing Science Institute.

Registration Convention, 1975: Convention on the Registration of Objects Launched into Outer Space 1975, 28 UST 695; TIAS 8480; 1023 UNTS 15. Entered into force 15 September 1976.

Rescue Agreement, 1968, Agreement on the Rescue of Astronauts, the Return of Astronauts and the Return of Objects Launched into Outer Space, 1968 7 ILM 149; 672 UNTS 119 (1968). Entered into force 3 December 1968.

Rome, E.P. and Williams, R. 1985, *Corporate and Commercial Free Speech: First Amendment Protection of Expression in Business*. New York: Prager.

Shakespeare, W. 1588, *Love's Labour Lost*, viewed 18 March 2015, http://shakespeare.mit.edu/lll/full.html.

Shuboni, Y.L.D. 2010, 'Night Time Dim Light Exposure Alters the Responses of the Circadian System', *Neuroscience*, 170(4): 1172–8.

Space Activities Act 1998 No. 123 of 1998 as amended by the Statute Law Revision Act 2013 (No. 103 of 2013) and the Space Activities Amendment Act 2002 (No. 100 of 2002) consolidated version viewed 18 March 2015, http://www.comlaw.gov.au/Details/C2013C00462.

Space Advertising Prohibition Act (1993) H.R. 2599, 103rd Cong. (Bill proposed but not passed).

Space Affairs Act 1993, No. 84 of 1993 viewed 18 March 2015, http://www.saflii.org/za/legis/num_act/saa1993113.

SpaceX 2015, 'Falcon 9', viewed 18 March 2015, http://www.spacex.com/falcon9.

Stigler, G.J. 1961, 'The Economics of Information', *The Journal of Political Economy*, 69(4): 213–25, viewed 27 June 2014, JSTOR Arts & Science Archive Collection.

Tomlinson, D.E. and Wiley, R.L. 1994–95, 'People Do Read Large Ads: The Law of Advertising from Outer Space', *Federal Communications Law Journal*, 47: 535–69.

United Nations General Assembly 2001, Resolution A/RES/56/51, viewed 18 March 2015, http://www.unoosa.org/pdf/gares/ARES_56_51E.pdf.

United States Code, Title 49, Chapter 701, viewed 18 March 2015, http://www.gpo.gov/fdsys/pkg/USCODE-2009-title49/html/USCODE-2009-title49-subtitleIX-chap701.htm.

Valentine v Chrestensen 316 U.S. 52 (1942) rev'd 122 F. 2d 511 (2d Cir. 1942).

Virgin Galactic 2015, 'Our Vehicles', viewed 18 March 2015, http://www.virgingalactic.com/human-spaceflight/our-vehicles.

Virginia Pharmacy Board v Virginia Citizens Consumer Council 425 US 748 (1976).

Von der Dunk, F. 2005, 'The Sky is the Limit – But where does it End? New Developments on the Issue of Delimitation of Outer Space', in the International Institute of Space Law, *Proceedings of the 48th Colloquium on the Law of Outer Space*, IISL, Fukuoka, published by the American Institute of Aeronautics and Astronautics, Virginia, pp. 84–94.

Von der Dunk, F. and Brus, M. (eds) 2006, *The International Space Station Commercial Utilisation from A European Legal Perspective*. Leiden: Martinus Nijhoff Publishers.

White, Albert 2014, 'Kerry Dark Sky Reserve Announced', posted 28 January, viewed 18 March 2015, http://www.darksky.i.e./kerry-dark-sky-reserve-announced/#more-436.

Zauderer v. Office of Disciplinary Counsel, 471 U.S. 626 (1985).

Chapter 9

Space Tourism: Risks and Solutions

Angie Bukley, Robert Frize, and Veronica La Regina

Space tourism is becoming more and more an interesting and attractive enterprise, not only for the space community but also for the aviation sector, given that the number of airline passengers continues to increase and the airways are becoming ever-more crowded. Thus, there is a trend in public opinion towards seeing space tourism not only as entertainment, but also as a resource providing the added benefit of access to alternative airspace routes. Such suborbital, or point-to-point suborbital routes, would offer shorter flying times and provide opportunities for technology creation and innovation. There are other potential benefits including opportunities for technology creation, innovation and verification; as well as new possibilities to conduct a broad range of scientific and educational research experiments in microgravity.

Regardless of these beneficial opportunities, there are still numerous concerns with significant implications associated with this new enterprise. The development of suborbital vehicles and ultimate implementation of space tourism raises issues including technical maturity, medical requirements, commercial viability and emerging business models. In addition, there are economic and political challenges, as well as regulatory concerns (van Pelt 2005; Jakhu et al. 2011). Addressing the full scope of this plethora of issues warrants a systematic and complete approach, shared by all stakeholders.

Space tourism is not science fiction anymore. It is the next logical step in the evolution of the commercial flight market. We are on the verge of opening the space frontier to more and more people. In the not too distant future, the space tourist will be simply a passenger just like everyone else, travelling from one place to another for business or personal reasons. Soon the choice of transportation modes will include suborbital space vehicles.

This next logical step forward requires a comprehensive approach to reach a near-consensus among the many different stakeholders. The stakeholders directly represent the demand of space tourists and passengers and the supply that includes both space vehicle manufacturers and spaceflight providers. The overall set of stakeholders also indirectly includes insurance companies, brokers and underwriters as facilitators of the match between demand and supply; medical experts evaluating impacts on the overall human wellness of the spaceflight experience without any manipulation of under- and/or over-estimation; as well as policymakers and regulators whose responsibility it is to establish a fair legal framework balancing all conflicting interests among the stakeholders.

Motivated by this requirement to facilitate a comprehensive discussion among the various stakeholders, the International Institute of Space Commerce (IISC), based on The Isle of Man, took the initiative to organise a workshop jointly with AON International Space Brokers (ISB) and the International Space University (ISU). The workshop convened on the 1st of February 2013 in London. The venue was the Old Library of the Lloyd's Building. The workshop comprised two panels; one to identify and discuss risks associated with space tourism and the other to propose potential solutions. The panellists represented a broad range of stakeholders, including space vehicle providers, ticket buyers and sellers, as well as insurance companies and brokers, all of whom were focused on the fledgling space tourism industry. The primary goal of the workshop was to focus attention on risk identification and management with a focus on insurance for all aspects of space tourism. It was clear from the proceedings of the workshop that the space tourism debate continues as both interest and concern grows worldwide. Representatives of the workshops organising committee, comprising AON ISB, IISC and ISU, moderated discussions among the panellists and the public attendees.

The first panel provided a comprehensive overview of the risks arising from space tourism activities. Members of this panel included experts representing vehicle developers, entrepreneurial flight brokers, the medical profession, the insurance industry and an adventure tourist who has already purchased flights on a suborbital vehicle. The panellists addressed a number of risk-associated topics from the medical, technological, commercial and insurance industry point of view.

The second panel addressed potential solutions to such risks in terms of liability regime, licensing policy and insurance mechanisms. The panel of experts represented a space agency and insurance companies, and also included two space tourists. This diverse panel membership aimed to achieve a shared vision about topics and issues in order to arrive at a comprehensive policy view. These results have not been published elsewhere and comprise an interesting and in-depth view into the risks inherent to space tourism, as well as possible mitigation strategies.

There were two general themes that permeated the discussions of the day. One recurring theme was associated with the business and commercial aspects, and in particular those investing in, or apparently investing in space tourism companies and the insurers of these enterprises. There was much discussion focused on demand of spaceflight ticket buyers who have purchased their tickets up-front (that is, someone who is buying a ticket to ride on a vehicle that has not been built or tested yet) and the insurance brokers' supporting obligation to refund damages as transferred by spaceflight providers and manufacturers to these customers. The advanced ticket-buyer as a consumer in this case is playing a significantly different role if they buy a ticket before the first operational flight takes place *versus* the people who buy and/or reserve their tickets after the flight systems are fully operational. In the first case, the consumer is also providing a much needed cash advance to the spaceflight operator. Early consumers can be viewed as atypical investors because they are in a sense betting on the successful accomplishment of the technical challenge of human spaceflight. However, they are not proper investors because their tickets are not equity positions in the company (Ordanini et al. 2011). It is a simple payment for the ticket at the time the reservation is booked.

However, and at the same time, the purchase creates the illusion of an investor. S/he is surely a trustee in the challenge and the purchase serves as catalyst for further purchasers and investments. For this reason, the advanced space ticket purchasers are typically investors, passionate space scientists and visionary wealthy individuals who are willing to bet on the success of the industry. In this way, they accept the risk to lose their investment if the challenges are not met. Should the company not be able to fulfil their commitment, these individuals are investors and they lose it all. However, in the case that they are considered consumers, they would probably be provided refunds on their tickets by the seller or through some sort of travel insurance.

In the case of suborbital space tourism, the insurance company plays different roles at this stage in the pre-flight market. It provides normal business insurance for non-operational spaceflights or unsuccessful flights. The success of a spaceflight for these purposes in terms of business relies on three main points including technology, market size and the regulatory environment. The technology is getting safer and more reliable, overcoming design risks through merging aeronautical and aerospace products. The technical maturity of aerospace products is typically indicated by its technology readiness level (TRL). Technology readiness levels are a method by which the maturity of critical technology elements may be assessed in a standard way using technology readiness assessments. The TRL scale ranges from 1 to 9, with TRL-1 being basic principles observed and reported up to TRL-9 indicating that the actual system has been proven through successful mission operations (Mankins 1995). The technology maturity for the purposes of overcoming design risks needs to be between TRL-4 and TRL-7. In addition, research and development have resulted in proposals for three basically different approaches including vertical takeoff/vertical landing, horizontal takeoff/ horizontal landing and vertical takeoff/horizontal landing.

In parallel to the technical challenges facing the suborbital human spaceflight community, there are other contextual risks of regulation and reputation. The regulation concerns are facing literally a *legal vacuum* wherein solutions come only from analogy, extensive interpretation or new law. The first two are objects of a huge law doctrine reviewing the existing regulation for an adaptation to these cases (Kleiman et al. 2009; Masson-Zwaan and Freeland 2010). The last one is a claim by those who support the opinion of a stagnant legal framework since the 1950s and argues that as the space tourism industry grows in the next decade, several countries may establish loose regulatory regimes in an effort to attract private space groups. This 'flags of convenience problem' that is prolific in the shipping industry may lead to irreversible environmental damage, increased space debris and safety hazards to space tourists (Taghdiri 2013).

The in-depth discussions arising from this workshop, the conclusions drawn and recommendations put forward are typical outcomes of an IISC forum. The mission of the IISC, as a leading space policy think-tank providing an intellectual home for space industry and academia around the world, is to foster such a dialogue in the context of the challenges facing a dynamic space industry. The IISC supports the requirements of its shareholders, which include The Isle of the Man, with an entrepreneurial vocation for future challenges and value-added creation. The International Space University, physically located in Strasbourg (France), embraces the mission of building capacity for the space industry according to its 3-I philosophy providing an Interdisciplinary, Intercultural and International environment for educating and training space professionals and post-graduate students via its Master of Space Studies, the annual summer Space Studies Program and Executive Courses. The ISU provide for the IISC an extended network of space experts and resources at global level.

Panel 1: The Risks of Space Tourism

As mentioned already, the first panel addressed the risks associated with the business of and the participation in space tourism. The first discussion focused on the development of the vehicles and technologies required to realise suborbital human spaceflight. The discussions then turned to the business aspects from the point of view of a flight broker as well as an adventure tourist and investor in the business. The medical aspects and potential risks were then addressed and the panel wrapped up with a conversation about the risks to the insurance companies themselves.

The panellists participating in the risk identification panel were:

Angie Bukley, Moderator, International Space University
Christophe Chavagnac of EADS Astrium (now Airbus Defence and Space)
Bernard Comet, MEDES – Institut de Médecine et Physiologie Spatiales
Garrett Smith, Cosmica Spacelines
David Wade, Astrium Space Insurance Consortium
Per Wimmer, WimmerSpace.

The format of the panel was that each panellist delivered a brief statement about his/her topic or area of expertise and summarised the risks associated with that particular aspect of space tourism. Following the statements, the floor was opened to questions from the audience, which was then followed by a summary from the panel moderator. Each category of risk addressed in the workshops is summarised in the following sections.

Technology Risks

There are a number of different companies taking various approaches to the realisation of vehicles capable of taking humans on suborbital spaceflights. The concepts are different ranging from single vehicles that take off and land using conventional runways, like the XCOR Lynx, to the two-stage configuration embraced by Virgin Galactic in which the WhiteKnight2 carrier aircraft takes the SpaceShip2 to an altitude where it is released and its rocket engines then take it into the edge of space. Each concept manifests a different flight profile and imposes different g-loadings on the passengers and crew.

EADS Astrium, now called Airbus Defence and Space, is developing the Spaceplane for the suborbital market exclusively. Their role is as a vehicle developer and integrator only, delivering vehicles to the space tourism operators. Through their promotion of this vehicle proposal, Airbus is seeking the investment of billions of Euros to develop a safe and reliable platform to meet not only the needs of the suborbital space tourism companies, but also the broader market for executing research in microgravity, delivering small satellites to orbit, and eventually point-to-point suborbital commercial transportation. The Spaceplane will be very similar to an ordinary aircraft, about the size of a regular commercial jet. The vehicle will take off and land using conventional runways. It will be fuelled by natural gas and oxygen with reusable rocket engines. Mature technologies are being used in the development of the vehicle to mitigate design risks and produce a safe and reliable reusable suborbital space vehicle.

The propulsion systems used on these vehicles is viewed as a critical technology. Basically, these craft are rockets with wings. They are very similar to aircraft but are fuelled with highly volatile materials, thus increasing the risk and accompanying cost of insurance.

Brand Image and Reputational Risks

One of the main risks associated with both the vehicle providers and operators in the space tourism industry is that of *brand image*. Any accident, whether there are deaths or not, will harm the image of the company who has developed and built or operated the vehicle involved. This risk is tightly coupled to the issue of vehicle development risk, which is primarily that of merging aeronautical products with aerospace products. This risk is being addressed in various ways by the vehicle developers, ranging from the use of mature technologies to extensive test programs.

There are also opportunity risks resulting from so many individuals who have purchased tickets and are now anxiously awaiting their flights. Indeed, the dates of the first passenger flights for vehicles under development continues to move into the future as a result of the technology not being completely ready and, unfortunately, accidents.

Reputational risks must also be considered. There are the reputations of all of the companies involved, from the vehicle developer, to the operator, to the ticket brokers that must be considered. In particular, accidents that involve a death or deaths of paying customers will no doubt cast a pall on the space tourism business. Accidents are inevitable and how the space tourism companies deal with them will be a driver in the eventual success, or failure, of this new enterprise. It is imperative that the manufacturers, operators and ticket brokers have a detailed public communication and engagement plan for when such incidents occur. Determining liability in the event of an accident will be challenging, depending on the circumstances, and is a major source of risk for all concerned, particularly given the lack of a legal framework, which will be addressed in a subsequent section.

Business, Investment and Financial Risks

The overarching operational risk associated with the space tourism business model and the associated investment and financial risks was a recurring theme among the panellists. Going to space, even on suborbital flights, will not be a routine event for some considerable time and there is significant business risk involved. Entrepreneurs who invest in this enterprise stand to make large sums of money, or lose everything. The same can be said of any investor be they an angel investor, a bank or any entity who puts money on the table. Even the true size of the market is yet to be determined, with various surveys producing different results.

One of the major business risks for the vehicle and operating companies is how to obtain start-up capital, particularly given that there will be no guaranteed revenues until flights become more or less routine. Once the operators begin providing commercial flights, how are investors and financiers protected against the loss of revenue in the event of grounded vehicles? In the event of an accident, what protection is there for loss of revenue due to trip cancellations? From the customer's point of view, how are they protected if s/he has purchased a flight and for whatever reason, the flight is cancelled? If the flight was purchased through a ticket broker, what protection does s/he have? There are many unanswered questions and the financial risks are significant.

The nature and incidence of these risks differ among the manufacturers, operators and ticket brokers. Manufacturers are currently investing huge sums of money on the design, development, test and deployment of suborbital flight vehicles. Until the sale of these vehicles becomes routine, there is significant risk of lost investment. Operators have been accepting deposits from customers who have purchased tickets in advance of the development of the vehicles on which they will be flying. Should the vehicles not be delivered or perform as advertised, then the operators run the risk of losing significant sums of money on refunds, as do the ticket brokers.

On the positive side, there is tremendous potential for research opportunities on suborbital platforms. Both Virgin Galactic and XCOR have incorporated accommodations for scientific experiment payloads into their vehicle designs. Both have issued payload users guides, which are available to potential users upon request, and are actively seeking customers and marketing the flight opportunities as affordable, reliable and repeatable (Virgin Galactic 2015, XCOR Aerospace 2015). A successful business model is certain to include educational and research customers as well as leisure opportunities for customers. Operators now believe that the mix of business between tourism and research/educational customers is likely to be closer to 50/50, rather than the 80/20 split originally envisaged. In fact, space tourism could end up subsidising research, or vice versa, depending on how the market develops.

Finally, there is the risk of doing nothing. This risk applies primarily to Europe where there is little activity, relatively speaking, in terms of developing the space tourism industry. There seems to be a viable business opportunity that will be missed if no action is taken.

Political, Legal and Regulatory Risks

The regulatory framework for human suborbital spaceflight is just beginning to be formulated. Most of the efforts to date have been with the Federal Aviation Administration in the United States. There is currently no regulatory framework in Europe. There has also been little discussion of what will happen when things go wrong and there is an accident. Will all such vehicles be grounded? There is no clear answer. The regulatory risk is significant.

Export control is a major regulatory risk to the space tourism industry, particularly to those companies like Virgin Galactic and XCOR that are based in the United States. Because these suborbital tourism vehicles are being developed in the United States, they are subject to the strict export control regulations imposed by the International Traffic in Arms Regulations (ITAR). US companies run the risk that they may not be able to deploy their vehicles outside of the US. The proposed European Spaceplane will not be subject to such regulations and could be operated anywhere in the world, hence mitigating that particular risk and opening up a huge potential market. Their goal is to address this emerging market with a reliable reusable vehicle with no export control restrictions.

Politically, space tourism is often viewed as elitist, which has strong implications on policy and politics. Politicians are typically slow to embrace high-tech, high-risk activities. They also see support of space tourism enterprises as both benefitting and financing wealthy individuals. In the event of a fatal accident, politicians would be quick to distance themselves from any decisions that supported the risky activity and are, in fact, inclined to remain neutral or even speak out against such 'dangerous' endeavours.

Insurance is essential to the success of the industry and serves as an enabler. The two most discussed points were hull insurance and third party liability. Hull loss for human spacecraft is currently approximately one in 100 vehicles. This must improve to something like a minimum of one in 1,000 vehicles for the space tourism industry to survive. Research institutions have concerns about the cumulative risk exposure of their researchers on multiple flights. Similar concerns will exist for crewmembers. The hurdle for an acceptable level of risk for organisations asking their employees to make multiple flights is likely to be much higher at 1 in 10,000 or above. This is still a significantly higher risk level than the commercial air travel industry, at approximately 1 in one million.

As the market for suborbital and LEO flights develops, the governmental space agencies will also be eager to achieve further clarity on issues of liability.

Pilot responsibility is a significant concern to insurers. The associated third party losses might be mitigated by the fact that most spaceports are currently located in very rural areas of the world, but there is always the possibility that in the event of an accident, there could be third party damages. As well, spaceport operators need to be mindful of the risks that could fall back on them in case of accidents. And when there is an accident, there is the question of jurisdiction in the case of a lawsuit. Insurers must also bear in mind that insurance must be affordable to all concerned, or there will be no possibility for success of this industry.

Suborbital Spaceflight Participant Risks

Being among the first to participate in human suborbital flights indeed presents a potential risk to life and limb. Certainly, space tourism needs to be open to the public. Currently, parabolic flight for both researchers and tourists imposes only the minimum medical requirements needed to ensure that the participant will not experience any threatening medical issues. In the case of parabolic flights on aircraft, the parabolic manoeuvres can be stopped and the aircraft can in most cases quickly return to the airport.

Some level of basic fitness will be required for suborbital flight, though there are not yet any medical regulations, other than the recommendations published some recently by the FAA. This guidance is designed to identify individuals who have medical conditions that could result in an in-flight medical emergency or in-flight death, or could compromise in any other way the health and safety of any occupants onboard a commercial space vehicle.

Certainly, the medical requirements for suborbital flight will not be so stringent as those imposed on astronauts who spend days, weeks or months in space. Most suborbital flights will expose passengers to at most approximately 5 g during the launch and re-entry phases for short periods, and to only four to five minutes of microgravity. The negative effects of suborbital flight are likely to be primarily anxiety (excitement or nervousness before the flight) and motion sickness, characterised by nausea, headache and vomiting. There are medical remedies for this condition. Regardless, there are medical and physical risks to consider.

Panel 2: Possible Solutions

During the second panel, the expert panellists addressed potential solutions to some of the risks identified in the first panel in terms of liability regime, licensing policy and insurance mechanisms. The panel comprised a mix of insurance, legal, media and governmental representatives, namely:

David Wade, Atrium Space Insurance Consortium
Jenny Robers, AON
Nigel Henbest
Richard Crowther, UK Space Agency
Nick Hughes, Holman Fenwick.

The discussion was free-flowing and addressed a number of potential solutions, some of which were applicable to a number of the previously identified risks. In the summary below, we have attempted to categorise the solutions and observations in a number of broad categories.

Legal and Regulatory Environment

In terms of providing a benign regulatory environment for the space tourism industry to develop, the liability shields that have been put in place both at federal and state level in the US will give operators significant comfort over liability risks. However, some elements of the regulations, informed consent for example, are novel in their application to leisure activities and may be subject to rigorous legal test in the event of an accident.

We are seeing some mixed messages from the operators regarding regulatory regimes. On the one hand, they say they need a relatively lenient licensing regime in order to develop the industry during this evolutionary phase. On the other, they say they need the stricter regulation of a certification regime in order to attract significant investment for future development. The UK Space Agency has been working with the UK Civil Aviation Authority in considering a transitional framework that could move from licensing to certification. Indications are that EASA might lean towards a certification regime, bypassing the initial licensing phase.

Although not currently mandated by regulation, a robust flight test programme will undoubtedly be part of operators' risk mitigation package. Virgin Galactic was described as being likely to conduct at least 30 full test flights before commencing commercial operations. However, at the time of writing, indications are that the number of full test flights that they will conduct will be significantly fewer.

Hull Insurance

The availability and cost of hull insurance will be a strong function of the size of the market. The differing philosophies between the aviation and space insurance sectors will need to be reconciled, as what is developing now is a hybrid of aviation and space vehicles. That is, one vehicle that can be considered as an aircraft and a spacecraft. Clearly this is new territory.

In a similar manner to individual spaceflight participant cover, insurance coverage for operators in relation to hull insurance has been on a bespoke basis to date. Undoubtedly, it would be easier to obtain hull cover if operators have existing commercial relationships with the aviation hull market.

For both the hull and the liability markets, there is a question over the resilience of the market to multiple loss events in such a young business. There will certainly be a different approach for testing and operations. The knock-on financial consequences to the operators' business of hull loss must also be considered.

In other industries, insurance 'pools' have been created in order for businesses to effectively self-insure, but spread risks. At this stage, the industry is nowhere near large or homogenous enough to support such an approach, although it might be considered in the future. Similarly, captive insurers are a popular and effective risk management tool for large corporations, and a case can be made for their use in this industry.

Liability (Participant and Third Parties)

Whether it was deliberate or not, the terminology used in the US Regulations (Spaceflight Participant, 'SFP') is a less passive description than a simple 'passenger'. It could be taken as implying some element of participation in the process of spaceflight, rather than a purely commercial arrangement. Indeed, individuals who have flown commercially to the International Space Station have undergone intensive training to a level comparable with non-Russian Soyuz crewmembers. At the time of writing, it is unclear whether nominated SFPs on Virgin Galactic flights might have specific safety-related duties, for example ensuring that all SFPs are in their seats at the end of the period of microgravity. Could a participant, through either action or inaction, endanger a mission, with consequent third party liability exposure? It is possible that these issues might lead to some transfer of liability risk onto SFPs, for which they would be well advised to seek some risk mitigation.

For passenger and third party liability, there is uncertainty about whether the space market or the aviation market would be the appropriate source for insurance cover. At the moment, capacity in the worldwide insurance market for high net worth individuals engaging in 'high risk' activities is limited to about USD25m. Clearly, this is not enough for a capacity flight on Space Ship Two with six potentially wealthy or high-profile passengers.

There has been a proliferation of liability 'shields' for commercial space travel in the US at both federal and state level, covering operators, manufactures and subcontractors. In the event of any catastrophe, lawyers for the affected parties are likely to attack at the weakest point of these shields.

In terms of managing reputational risks, loss of human life will be greatly more culturally unacceptable compared to property loss. Some commentators suggested that a substantial level of personal accident cover, whether encouraged by the operator, or even paid for by them, could reduce both operators' liability and reputational risk by dampening the propensity of affected participants to claim.

Informed Consent Regime

There are some parallels between the current approach to commercial spaceflight and the early days of aviation, particularly in relation to international flights, not only in the accident rates but also in its tolerance and approach to risk. US Regulations have been influenced by the US 'frontier spirit', as encapsulated in Congressman Rohrbacher's testimony that the 'industry is at the stage when it is the preserve of visionaries and daredevils and adventurers ... who will fly at their own risk [and] ... who do not expect and should not expect to be protected by the government' (FAA 2008). Other regions may not be so risk-tolerant, for example EASA has previously declared in favour of a full certification regime for space vehicles.

So far, the informed consent regime has raised more questions than answers, albeit in an environment when flight operations have not commenced and the regime has not yet been subject to the crucible of litigation. One of its major weaknesses is that it is virtually impossible to cover all relevant issues in 'informing' participants of the risks.

Solutions for Individuals

To date, insurance arrangements for individual SFPs have been bespoke, using the Lloyds market for cover.

At the moment, Virgin Galactic maintains that it is their customers' responsibility to arrange cover for any additional risks. However, it is clear that both Virgin and XCOR are focused on the engineering and technological challenges of getting their vehicles flight-ready – as the date for operational flights comes closer, the approach to this may change and we could conceivably see some 'bundled' cover as part of the ticket prices.

Clarifying and defining the criteria for 'mission success' in terms of the contract between the participant and the operator will be important for both managing participants' expectations and for protecting the operator against spurious claims.

Another source of risk, both to the operators and to their customers, is in the area of buyer's remorse – particularly in relation to non-achievement of the desired altitude necessary to define the flight as one to space. There is nothing in Virgin Galactic's contract regarding an 'altitude guarantee', and recent press comment from Mojave suggests initial flights may not be above the Karmann line, but rather to the lower 80-kilometre limit. XCOR, however, do provide this guarantee in their contract. For customers, the old advice of *caveat emptor* applies in relation to understanding exactly what is being purchased.

Medical Screening

Although the FAA have done some studies and released some guidelines regarding medical screening for SFPs, no regulations have been made. This issue is not on the UKSA's agenda either. Although information from operators (for example Virgin Galactic maintains that 95 per cent of their potential customers will experience no adverse effects from the microgravity aspect of the flight – with medication) suggests medical screening will not be a big issue, regulators may wish to impose more stringent hurdles in order to manage both third party and national liability exposure.

US vs. International Regulatory Framework

All regulators will want to see a sustainable industry, balancing safety concerns with providing operators with enough flexibility to develop new markets. There was a feeling that the development of 'flags of convenience' would not be desirable in the foreseeable future.

Conclusion

Many of the risks associated with the space tourism industry were identified during the course of the workshop. The risks fall broadly into the categories of technical, business, financial, political, legal, regulatory, personal (medical) and opportunity risks. Potential solutions have been identified. Clearly, strong partnerships among the vehicle developers, flight operators, ticket brokers, regulatory agencies and insurance companies must be forged to ensure that this forward-looking endeavour succeeds. There are few who travel regularly who would not be delighted at the opportunity to travel halfway around the world in a few hours. There are many who would welcome the opportunity to travel to the edge of space to enjoy the view of the Earth from such a vantage point. The potential for cutting edge research is huge. A way forward will be found.

References

FAA (2008) *Study on Informed Consent for Spaceflight Participants* Document Number: APT-CFA-230–0001–02F.

Jakhu R.S., Sgobba T. and Dempsey P.S. (2011) The Need for an Integrated Regulatory Regime for Aviation and Space: ICAO for Space? *Studies in Space Policy*, Vol. 7, Springer.

Kleiman M.J., Lamie J.K. and Carminati M.V. (2009) *The Laws of Spaceflight: A Guidebook for New Space Lawyers*. Chicago, IL: ABA Book Publishing.

Mankins J.C. (1995) *Technology Readiness Levels: A White Paper*. NASA Office of Space Access and Technology, Advanced Concepts Office.

Masson-Zwaan T. and Freeland S. (2010) Between Heaven and Earth: The Legal Challenges of Human Space Travel, *Acta Astronautica*, 66(11–12): 1597–607.

Ordanini A., Miceli L., Pizzetti M. and Parasuraman A. (2011) Crowd-funding: Transforming customers into investors through innovative service platforms, *Journal of Service Management*, 22(4): 443–70.

Taghdiri A. (2013) Flags of convenience and the commercial spaceflight industry: The inadequacy of current international law to address the opportune registration of space vehicles in the flag states. 19 *B.U. J. Sci. & Tech. L.* 405.

van Pelt M. (2005) *Space Tourism: Adventures in Earth Orbit and Beyond.* New York: Praxis Publishing.

Virgin Galactic (2015) *Research*, viewed 13 March 2015, http://staging.virgingalactic.com/research.

XCOR Aerospace (2015) *Payload Mission Capabilities*, viewed 13 March 2015, http://www.xcor.com/xynxpayloads.

PART III
Asteroid Mining and
The Space Environment

Chapter 10

Asteroid Mining, Integrity and Containment

Tony Milligan

There is every reason to believe that, at some point in the not too distant future, decades rather than centuries, serious attempts will be made to mine asteroids. In what follows I will suggest (and to some extent argue) that we have reasons for containment of the impact of such mining, reasons for containing terrestrial impact and, more controversially, its off-world impact. Such mining could help to open up a broader sphere of human activity, ultimately inclusive of modest settlement and space stations beyond Low Earth Orbit. The goal is, at present, out of reach but closer than we might imagine. Back in the 1990s, NASA was still looking at asteroids from a considerable distance, with the Galileo spacecraft photographing the asteroid 951 Gaspra on its way elsewhere (to Jupiter). A decade further on and the first spacecraft, NEAR Shoemaker, was able to land, after a cautious 230 orbits around 433 Eros. Less than five years later, in 2005, the Japanese space agency JAXA, was able to land a probe on 25143 Itokawa and return an, admittedly nominal, geological sample. Again admittedly, the exercise was primarily a way to test ion drives for future deep-space missions, but incidental targets can become game changers and JAXA already have a second probe planned with enhanced capabilities and more ambitious sampling goals. More recently, in 2012, the Dawn spacecraft ended several months in orbit around the giant asteroid, Vesta, and more recently still, in December 2012, the Chinese probe Chang'e 2 flew within 3.2 kilometres of 4179 Toutatis. Efforts are ongoing, successful within limits, and the variety of launch states is symptomatic of unease about being left behind.

The rationale for moving on to more ambitious goals is straightforward and goes far beyond political prestige. Asteroids can do a great deal to us and for us. With regard to what they can do *to us* (Earth impacts), the more we know, the better placed we may be to protect the planet (Arnould 2011, pp. 91–118). In terms of what they can do *for us*, mining is attractive by virtue of a combination of push and pull factors. The main push factor is mineral depletion here on Earth. We may have a good half-millennium of lithium still to go, but even something so basic as copper could become difficult to extract by the middle of the century and gold may become hard to access even sooner (Moyer 2010, pp. 59–60). The main pull factor is what asteroids are made of. Depending upon the type, they are rich in water and/ or volatiles and/or minerals. Water here should not be dismissed as second best. It is important not only for life-support and radiation shielding but because it can be cracked apart into hydrogen and oxygen for fuel. A Mars mission might run a lot more smoothly if the fuel for the journey did not need to be forced out of the Earth's deep gravity well. (Much the same goes for the return.) But not everyone is interested in breaking new ground elsewhere and that is where the minerals come in, particularly the platinum group metals such as osmium, iridium, palladium and platinum itself. Given the scarcity and value of the latter, the promise of asteroid mining is not just one of profitability but of super-wealth. Unlike other activities in space which may be easy to enthuse about but hard to justify, asteroid mining could serve terrestrial needs and interests.

The prospect of such mining does, however, introduce two familiar concerns, one economic, the other ethical, and both (simultaneously) political. The economic concern is that a sudden influx of raw materials could be economically destabilising. If the mining is carried out as a private sector operation then the agents who are involved in decision-making may not be concerned with socio-economic responsibility. And here, I do not suggest that we should buy into the image of the private space sector as destabilising cowboy rather than homesteader, but rather that any venture which requires a truly massive initial outlay will come with heavy pressures from investors to deliver big results while resources are still limited. What is in play is not a parody of the private, but the tragedy of the commons. While it may be better for everyone, better all round, if the market is not suddenly flooded, if this is going to happen anyway then it may seem better to be among those who open the gates rather than among those who go down in the flood.

The prevailing wisdom about this sort of danger, set out in the classic study of mining off-world (see John L. Lewis, *Mining the Sky*, 1996), is that supplies should only be fed onto terrestrial markets under some system of regulation or restraint (Lewis 1996, p. 114). Given the problems of self-policing in the private sector (witness the interesting approach to regulation adopted by the banking sector), we may require, from the outset, at least some state or multi-state regulation as a means of ensuring that everyone is playing safely and by some approximation to the same rules.

The other, and more directly ethical, concern is that undue political sway can go hand in hand with concentrations of wealth and that the latter can contribute further to distributive injustice. This is part of the broader concern, expressed by Alan Marshall back in the 1990s, that 'the development of even more resources is not likely to provide the necessities of most of the world's people. New resources contribute to the consumptive wants of the wealthy, not to the needs of the populous poor' (Marshall 1995, p. 42). This was and remains an oversimplification. What happens when new resources enter the system depends upon the prevailing economic conditions. However, Schwartz may well be right to press the point in a more qualified way and to affirm the 'strong possibility that asteroid mining and lunar mining would only exacerbate existing inequalities' (Schwartz 2014). This is, we might suspect, what Marshall had in mind all along.

The problems of super-wealth should not, however, be a concern only for those who are interested in social critique. They should also concern those who wish to keep the market as open as possible in the face of known tendencies towards monopoly. We are aware, from altogether too much experience, that market competition has winners and losers and that real markets do not operate in any optimal, competition-preserving manner. This is one of the driving considerations behind the familiar sci-fi scenario in which 'the company', variously representing capitalism, monopoly, unscrupulous free market agents or simply the 'big guy', comes to exercise undue influence and control over the lives of citizens and employees (much the same in the worst-case scenario). Some containment measures, to restrict terrestrial impact, at least until we can see which risks are genuine and which are phantoms, may be in order.

Viability

Talk about the *need* for a regulative system will, however, be moot if asteroid mining is a goal too far. Perhaps I have been too quick above to suggest otherwise simply on the basis of extrapolation (we are getting closer therefore we will surely get there). Greater caution about the future may be warranted. After all, the most ambitious exercise completed so far, the JAXA sampling mission, encountered all sorts of near-fatal problems before the ship finally limped home on two out of an initial four ion engines with a geological sample of around 100 particles, each of less than 0.001 millimetres length, so small that careful confirmation of origin was required. Yet this was a truly remarkable achievement, the first ever sample return from an asteroid. The difficulties and many ways in which it could have gone wrong may be an indication of just how difficult it will be to set up any manner of regular, scaled-up, mining operation. Even so, some reasonably well-funded organisations have set their sights upon this goal, not just NASA but also private-sector players: Planetary Resources and Deep Space Industries.

Of the two, the better-known is Planetary Resources, set up in 2010, headed by Chris Lewicki (flight director for NASA's Spirit and Opportunity landings and mission manager for the Phoenix lander) and with the involvement of Peter Diamandis, who has a habit of making difficult things happen (Dubbs and Paat-Dahlstrom 2011, pp. 167–79). Their plan is based around resource extraction for return with small dispensable prospector craft ('Fireflies') checking out likely candidate asteroids and then larger craft ('Dragonflies') being sent to carry out actual extraction. Deep Space Industries is a rather different operation set up in 2013 with some interest in extraction and return but with the larger ultimate aim of mining asteroids in order to service an emerging off-world economy. This is not a short-term investment.

The difficulties facing both, and any other would-be entrepreneurial prospectors, are not merely logistical. They are also legal. Space is currently regarded as a commons. Under existing Space Law, nobody gets to fence-off zones, planets, asteroids or planetoids for their exclusive use. In a well-worn phrase, space is the 'common heritage of mankind', always assuming that nobody else is out there in any region where we might be able to operate (Milligan 2011). Asteroid mining by the private sector will require both continuity of access and control over access. This could generate some awkward problems if an asteroid is parked in some accessible location by a company which has no property rights, licensing agreement or protection (Cooper 2003). Without a suitable regulative regime, there may be nothing to prevent competitors from arriving to mine once all the hard work has been done. The alternative to regulation is to work within in the context of celestial anarchy and/or resort to main force, the destructiveness of which in space should not recommend it as a preferred option.

Additionally, there are matters of liability which will need to be settled before anyone starts to alter asteroid trajectories and before anyone generates the free-floating debris that will almost certainly result from mining. Here, we should bear in mind the type of asteroids which will be of the most direct interest to the private sector: those with minerals and volatiles, that is, precisely the asteroids which are most likely to do serious damage to anything they hit and most also to survive a plunge through the Earth's atmosphere. By contrast, fragments from C-type asteroids with a good deal of water-ice content might cause a good deal of damage in space, but they are more likely to burn up if they hit the Earth's atmosphere.

To solve the logistical problems *and* to secure the relevant regulatory regime, the private sector will probably have to do what it has already been doing in other areas (such as resupply for the International Space Station), that is, it will need to piggy-back upon work by NASA and by the other national and international space agencies. President Obama's 2010 announcement that NASA itself should attempt a manned mission to capture and park an asteroid by 2025 may bolster the belief that such a mission will be possible but we may be sceptical about this too, albeit for different reasons. President Obama will be, conveniently, out of office when it comes time to deliver. Even so, NASA does have ambitions to try and realise the plan. Its budget for 2014 included funding to explore the possibility of setting a high-strength bag around a smallish asteroid (7–10 metres in diameter) then stabilising (de-tumbling) it and towing it away into a suitable lunar orbit. (Nobody thinks it's a smart idea to put asteroids into orbit around the Earth.) Manned missions might then be sent to the asteroid without any of the difficulties involved in an actual lunar landing. But even if all this were to take place within the specified timescale, the target (for obvious safety reasons) is a C-type asteroid. This means that it will not involve capture of the type of asteroid that would be the mainstay of commercial mining for return. Even so, it might serve as a proof of concept and could bring further investment into private sector operations. Overall, the proposed timescale for asteroid capture may be wildly over-optimistic, and the obstacles facing Planetary Resources, Deep Space Industries and NASA itself, may have been under-estimated or kept private, but the obstacles also look surmountable, perhaps even by the mid-century. Given this, ethical questioning of the legitimacy of asteroid mining is not moot.

The Focus of Ethical Concern

Like space tourism and, to some extent, the now defunct Shuttle Programme, space mining comes with the familiar ethical problems of risk (for participants and in the shape of debris), but it also introduces further problems which are continuous with those posed by terrestrial mining. The first is resource-depletion of a sort which raises issues of justice. What we use will not be there for the future use of others: other less-technologically equipped nations and future generations. This concern is not silenced by pointing out that we are hardly likely to deplete the asteroid belt given the number of objects that it contains. Resource depletion is not about what there is but about what can be accessed. It is no good depleting all that can be reached and then pointing to what remains at an impossible distance. Given that we are yet to set foot on Mars, the targeting of asteroids anytime soon will have to take the form of targeting those asteroids whose trajectories bring them towards us. This is a much smaller resource than we might imagine. There are currently around 10,000 known near-Earth asteroids. When John S. Lewis wrote enthusiastically about our future mining of the asteroids, back in the mid-1990s, there were only around 335. That was not much to go around, for all of humanity, for all of the human futures. Issues of fair access and distribution can easily be overlooked as they have been with our terrestrial use of fossil fuels. This should not, however, be treated as a point which is automatically hostile to space development. Rather, it may generate an ethical reason for at least modest Mars settlement in the interests of securing greater access to what sits beyond Mars but before Jupiter. Indeed, this looks like rather a better justification for Mars settlement than the idea that we might use the red planet to back-up our biosphere. If we can reach and establish infrastructure on Mars then future generations and other nations which are equipped with the relevant technological capabilities will have a very good chance of mining directly in the asteroid belt. We will have left more than 'as much and as good'. (A formula from Locke which works in this context but which I am far from wedded to.)

The second ethical problem is of a deeper sort and concerns the shaping of our identity. We may worry about mining off-world just as we worry about terrestrial mining because it informs our understanding of the world in which we are embedded. Suppose we ask 'What sort of people do we want to be?' One answer to this is 'The kind of people who use the world around us *simply* as a resource'. This is the kind of answer which many of us find deeply unattractive and in some way cut off from the reality of our own embeddedness in the world: *it* is not *out there* but rather *we* are *part of it*. This was Heidegger's concern about terrestrial mining and it connects up with related charges, such as a charge of hubris and aesthetic insensitivity, sometimes levelled against over-enthusiastic support for terraforming (Heidegger 1993; Sparrow 1999). This kind of objection, however formulated, may strike hard-headed supporters of mining as rather too philosophical, but we should also perhaps consider the likely political context of any human future off-world. Charles Cockell has pointed out the extreme vulnerability and dependence of future agents in space, factors which historically have generated a tendency towards authoritarianism. (The reproduction of dependency has been the dominant means of reproducing feudalism, tribute-based systems and wage-labour itself.) Whoever controls the air supply and infrastructure could control the people. Two contrasting attitudes towards the space environment mesh with this danger in very different ways. One is *assimilating into the local space environment* and identifying with it as home. The other is *being at war with the environment*. The latter is more likely to engender authoritarian control as wars invariably do. (Central control of resources, extraordinary measures for security and so on.) The former takes matters off a war footing but is simultaneously in tension with the idea that we can do *whatever* we like to and with our surroundings for *whatever* reason strikes us as important (Cockell 2013, pp. 19–20).

The third ethical problem is in some ways more general. It is the problem of destruction as the price of extraction. While this may be terrestrially unavoidable, up to a point, it may also be acceptable only up to a point. The current controversies over fracking are, again *arguably*, symptomatic of this. However, while we can readily see why terrestrial fracking might well be damaging in ways which warrant caution and perhaps opposition, we may wonder exactly what sort of *damage* could possibly be caused off-world. Asteroids are not, after all, ecosystems. They do not support us or anything else. With exceptions in the larger cases, to the best of our knowledge they are unlikely to harbour life. Perhaps a planetoid such as Ceres, with a thick mantle of water-ice, might conceivably do so, but it is out in the asteroid belt which makes it not, for the time being, an immediate issue. The familiar, or at least dominant, considerations which support planetary protection in space (preservation of scientific resources and any possible life forms) do not therefore seem to apply.

I want to suggest that (or concede that), with some possible exceptions, this is probably true. There simply is no good argument for *direct* ethical concern about damage to asteroids or about damage to most asteroids. But there may be indirect grounds, concerns about the possible knock-on effects of asteroid mining, concerns about what it could integrate with or lead to. For example, through the extraction of water and volatiles for fuel, such mining could become integrated with destructive activities on the surface of larger bodies such as the Moon or perhaps Mars. (It would certainly put the latter closer to our reach.) The force of this *could* is not purely speculative. Containment issues of a parallel sort have already been encountered here on the Earth. Think, for example, about the pressures to drill oil wells in previously protected locations in the US, even inside national parks, as a response to concerns about the security of supplies from the Middle East. Once the technology to *go further* and to move into protected areas is in place, protection in the face of corporate influence may be difficult to secure. And here, containment issues concerning what happens off-world overlap with containment issues concerning adverse terrestrial impact.

Planetary Integrity

Even so, worries about containment of off-world impact will be moot if there simply is no *deep* reason to uphold planetary protection (or protection of some of the larger sub-planetary bodies such as Phobos, Vesta and Ceres). And here, it is not simply size that matters but something else, something which is harder to pin down and is *not* captured by the familiar grounds for protection set out in COSPAR interpretations of Space Law. Although the COSPAR Panel on Planetary Protection has tentatively been considering additional grounds for protection (Ehrenfreund, Hertzfeld and Howells 2013), I want to suggest that, ultimately, an appeal to the scientific value of studying pristine environments and the importance of avoiding contamination where there may be indigenous life will not do enough work to protect all that needs to be protected (if only protected *up to a point*). What I am suggesting is that we need grounds for protection of a more robust sort and this will require us to think in terms of the importance of places and geographical features as warranting stewardship or otherwise having importance in their own right. But this is easier to propose than to justify. It is open to charges of sentimentality and/or anthropomorphism, the projection of value onto that which is *just there*.

Part of our difficulty in coming to terms with the standing of (apparently) lifeless bodies such as Mars is, of course, bound up with a historic sense of disappointment. We wanted to find canals on Mars, we wanted to find arabesque architecture and silk-clad life-forms. We wanted to find what a certain kind of science fiction has led us to expect from a truly rewarding encounter with what is other-worldly. We have come to want what isn't there and as a result we see these places in terms of what they lack rather than what they have, in terms of their desolation rather than their uniqueness and even magnificence. However, the problem goes deeper than the psychology of disappointment. It is, rather, conceptual and stems from a narrowness of understanding which represents reciprocity and rights as the heart of ethical discourse (Midgley 1983). Taking rights as basic is a way of picturing ethics which automatically excludes the non-sentient, but the exclusion is built into the picture rather than deduced from some more fundamental and neutral set of considerations.

We may then ask whether or not this is a good way of picturing what ethics is and what it does or, more specifically, whether or not it is a good way to understand the scope of ethics *in this particular context*. There are, I will suggest, some reasons to think not. Some of these reasons have nothing directly to do with space ethics. They concern the importance of maintaining a rich repertoire of ethical concepts and especially of concepts which relate to the virtues and vice, that is, to concepts such as justice, courage, practical wisdom, humility and hubris. If ethics is to connect up with what it is to be human, then there is a strong case for embracing some manner of normative pluralism which gives us a fuller picture of our many and varied ways of valuing. When we then move onto off-world issues, such normative pluralism allows us to ask whether it is hubris to imagine that we can do whatever we like with other worlds rather than, for example, asking whether or not Mars has rights (McKay 1990). For the sake of clarity: it doesn't. The background thought here is that when we shift from everyday talk about what matters into some sort of ethical theory, we can send familiar ethical considerations into exile but we may not be able to keep them there.

So, for example, we may declare ourselves to be the most fervent champions of the view that nothing inanimate or non-sentient matters in its own right (Smith 2009). But then we come up against the actual implications of this and a sense returns that somehow other things do matter. Brian Aldiss gives the example of Ayer's Rock in *White Mars* (1999) in order to make just this point. This surely is something that we *ought not* to damage for trivial reasons and, for Aldiss, the point is a precursor to affirming more generally that 'Planets are environments with their own integrity' (Aldiss and Penrose 2000, p. 323). Here we might imagine that what is in play is *only* the cultural significance of these objects. So, for example, we shouldn't damage Ayer's Rock because of the people to whom, and the human traditions within which, it has been and continues to be important. That, no doubt is an important consideration. We should no more damage such a site than we should damage the Sphinx or the Pyramids or Stonehenge. But this is not obviously exhaustive of our legitimate reasons for restraint. An appeal to cultural significance may capture a great deal but it still seems to miss something. To get a sense of what is still missing we can run a classic environmental thought experiment, the Last Man Experiment: imagine the last surviving human as someone in a position to wantonly destroy all manner of non-sentient things with his final actions (Sylvan 1973). Nobody else would be harmed in any straightforward manner. Many, and perhaps most of us, have the strong intuition that such wanton destruction would be very wrong, worse than vandalism.

What matters here also does not seem to be the question of whether or not something is an artefact or has a history of human care and construction. Blowing up Mt Everest would be just as wrong as blowing up the Sphinx, or at least wrong in some of the same respects. This is, of course, an incomplete story, a very incomplete story. But many of our ethical stories (and stories of other sorts) are just as incomplete. Yet it may still be more persuasive than rival and more complete stories which jar radically with our understanding of what it is to lead a good human life by proposing that we can reduce our attitude towards significant non-sentient objects down to a manner of strict instrumentalism. It is also a story which we can begin to develop in more detail by building in the appropriate sort of conceptual repertoire.

This is where the concept of integrity, rather than rights or interests, enters the story. By appealing to integrity, Aldiss echoes the approach of Holmes Rolston who points to the practice of *naming* as a rough indication of the difference between objects that have integrity and those which do not (Rolston 1986). Here we might think of those numbers we put in front of asteroid names as qualifiers of the latter. We might also compare the limited and repetitive structural features of asteroids with some of the more dramatic features of the Martian surface:

Olympus Mons, the greatest vulcano in the solar system, and the Vallis Marineris, which could contain the Grand Canyon many times. These places are integral to what Mars is. It is a world which, admittedly, has no interests, in the sense that we have interests, but it has a history of its own, a past which individuates it as different from all other places, and does so in ways which most well-informed agents would (arguably) tend to respond to as salient in decision-making. (Salient to forms of care which they would not, for example, typically have in relation to stone quarries.) To possess integrity in this sense is, in part, to have historically generated features which we can respect or fail to respect through our actions. By contrast with most asteroids, even Ceres tends to be named properly as an, in practice, recognition that something here is different.

This may, of course, be dismissed as a cautiously stated mysticism. If we are in the business of appealing to the authors of science fiction as authoritative voices then Kim Stanley Robinson (who rejects any such idea of the moral standing of planets) may be set against Brian Aldiss (Robinson 2009). And admittedly, I do not present a 'necessary and sufficient conditions account' of integrity but something far more provisional, an attempt to awaken the sense that there is something here to be taken account of and that a failure to do so might rest upon or encourage a curtailment of our appreciation of what it is to be a creature of our sort (Milligan 2014). Although provisional, this approach equips us to ask a more pertinent set of questions and here, as a persuasive move, the right kind of question may have more force than any available assertion. Rather than asking 'Does Mars have Rights?' it might make more sense to ask 'Would you want your children to be the kind of people who would happily level Olympus Mons in order to build the first Martian supermarket or the kind of people who might feel deeply that this ought not to be done?'

Conclusion

What I have set out is not a form of wholesale scepticism about transforming other worlds, or about mining or about establishing a human presence elsewhere. I am cautiously supportive of all three. Protection can, at least sometimes, be combined with use. What is set out above concerns, rather, the ethical sensibilities that we may need to take with us and how these, together with our regulative practices, can be shaped by some of the earliest decisions that we have to take about property rights, resource access and off-world entitlements. In a sense, what ultimately concerns me is not what we do in the 2020s but rather the shaping of a culture for space exploration and possibly settlement (Harris, pp. 159–70). At least some of the decisive, culture-shaping, decisions may be taken in relation to near Earth objects and asteroids in particular.

To reinforce the point that this is *not* a generalised form of scepticism about reaching out into space, I want to set out three important qualifications to any claim of integrity in relation to the Moon, Mars and the other planets and perhaps some planetoids. Firstly, integrity gives us reasons for action but there can be other, countervailing considerations such as the extending of life which also do so. It doesn't even, automatically, rule out planetary mining. The Aldiss formulations lean a little in this direction but Rolston's formulations do not. What integrity does is give us a reason to reject, without qualification, what is utterly unconstrained exploitation and wanton damage. As a rider, it is also not obvious what the precise criteria for planetary damage should be. Presumably they should resemble clauses for a 'land ethic' in the sense that they should approach damage in a holistic manner, rather than focused upon the standing of separate, individual items within the landscape (York 2005, pp. 72–3). Indeed, the language of 'integrity' suggests, from the outset, the influence of the land ethic and the idea of a structured or integrated whole rather than the importance of every rock and crevice.

Secondly, there may well be a difference between planets and asteroids which might license a far freer hand with the latter if we can be reasonably sure that there will not be any knock-on effects, or integration with damage elsewhere. However, if asteroids were used for water extraction in order to support an indefensibly destructive project on the lunar or Martian surface then the regulation of asteroid mining might serve as an indirect means of constraining other, more directly worrying, practices. Even so, in the absence of integrity, with the appropriateness of numbering rather than naming, there is a case for a freer hand with some exceptions. There may be a case for regarding at least some asteroids, such as those captured by a planet's gravity (perhaps including Phobos and Deimos), as systemically related to the planet in question. That being the case, if the planet is judged to have integrity of the relevant sort, there may then be grounds for regarding the asteroid as covered by the same judgement. (This could be slightly awkward for supporters of space-elevators which might have to be constructed in the path of a captured asteroid but this again is a consideration for more distant times.)

Finally, there may be contexts in which we are required to make a direct trade-off between mining asteroids and mining larger bodies with complex histories, structure and all that goes to make up integrity. In such a case we should (all other things being equal) favour the mining of asteroids. An example of mining which poses this dilemma is the mining of Helium-3. It is scarce on the Earth, important for nuclear fusion and present in both lunar and asteroid regolith. However, the lunar concentration tends to be far greater (albeit varying considerably from location to location) because asteroids do not retain their ejecta nearly so well as the Moon. As a result of their weaker gravitational pull, their regolith will be less mature. We do not yet have the relevant samples to compare but there is a strong suspicion that far less Helium-3 is likely to have been captured. Even if, as a result of this, the Moon is a best logistical option for mining, we should still favour mining sufficiently rich Helium-3 rich asteroids *in the interests of containment* (Milligan 2013). And so an acceptance of the integrity of larger bodies simultaneously strengthens the case for the regulation of asteroid mining (to secure containment of both sorts) *and* to strengthen the case for a *suitably regulated* exploitation of asteroids where trade-offs do have to be made.

References

Aldiss, B. and Penrose, R. 2000, *White Mars*. London: Warner Books.

Arnould, J. 2011, *Icarus' Second Chance: The Basis and Perspectives of Space Ethics*. New York and Vienna: Springer.

Cockell, C.S. 2013, *Extra-Terrestrial Liberty*, Edinburgh: Shoving Leopard.

Cooper, L.A. 2003, 'Encouraging space exploration through a new application of space property rights', *Space Policy*, 19(2): 111–18.

Dubbs, C. and Paat-Dahlstrom, E. 2011, *Realizing Tomorrow: The Path to Private Spaceflight*. Nebraska: University of Nebraska Press.

Ehrenfreund, P., Hertzfeld, H. and Howells, K. 2013, *COSPAR Workshop on Developing a Responsible Regime for Celestial Bodies*, Washington, Space Policy Institute.

Harris, P.R. 2009, *Space Enterprise: Living and Working Offworld in the 21st Century*, Chichester: Springer.

Heidegger, M. 1993, 'The Question Concerning Technology', in D. Krell (ed.), *Martin Heidegger: Basic Writings*. San Francisco; HarperCollins, pp. 307–42.

Marshall, A. 1995, 'Development and Imperialism in Space', *Space Policy*, 11(1): 41–52.

McKay, C. 1990, 'Does Mars Have Rights?' in D. McNaughton (ed.), *Moral Expertise*. London and New York, Routledge, pp. 184–97.

Midgley, M. 1983, 'Duties Concerning Islands', *Encounter*, 60(2): 36–43.

Milligan, T. 2014, *Nobody Owns the Moon: The Ethics of Space Exploitation*, Jefferson, NC: McFarland.

Milligan, T. 2013, 'Scratching the Surface: The Ethics of Mining Helium-3', *Proceedings of the 8th International Academy of Astronautics Symposium on the Future of Space Exploration*, July 2013, Turin, Italy.

Milligan, T. 2011, 'Property Rights and the Duty to Extend Human Life', *Space Policy*, 27(4): 190–193.

Moyer, M. 2010, 'How Much is Left?' *Scientific American*, 303(3): 56–63.

Robinson, K.S. 2009, *Red Mars*. London: HarperVoyager.

Rolston, H. 1986, 'The Preservation of Natural Value in the Solar System', in *Environmental Ethics and the Solar System*, E.C. Hargrove (ed.), San Francisco, CA: Sierra Club Books, pp. 140–82.

Schwartz, J.S.J. 2014, 'Prioritizing Scientific Exploration: A Comparison of the Ethical Justifications for Space Development and Space Science', *Space Policy*, 30(4): 202–8.

Smith, K.C. 2009, 'The trouble with intrinsic value: An ethical primer for astrobiology', in C. Bertka (ed.), *Exploring the Origin, Extent, and Future of Life: Philosophical, Ethical, and Theological Perspectives*. Cambridge: Cambridge University Press, pp. 261–80.

Sparrow, R. 1999, 'The Ethics of Terraforming', *Environmental Ethics*, 21(3): 227–45.

Sylvan, R. 1973, 'Is There a Need for a New, an Environmental Ethic?' in A. Light and H. Rolston III (eds), *Environmental Ethics: An Anthology*. Oxford, Blackwell, 2003, pp. 47–52.

York, R. 2005, 'Towards a Martian Land Ethic', *Human Ecology Review*, 12(1): 72–3.

Chapter 11

Three Ethical Perspectives on Asteroid Mining

Daniel Pilchman

Asteroids are a vast natural resource, the mining of which promises abundant wealth for space prospectors and an improved quality of life and products for consumers. These economic incentives make it likely that companies and entrepreneurs will pursue the excavation of valuable materials from near-Earth asteroids in the near future. However likely this possibility, little work has been done on the ethics of private asteroid mining. This chapter creates inroads into the question as to whether asteroid mining should be conducted. I present three views. Though independently plausible, reflection on the first two leads to a more moderate third view that asteroid mining is morally permissible if, but only if, it is conducted within a regulatory framework that manages inherent risks.

The first view, the strong prohibition on asteroid mining, claims that asteroid mining is impermissible, regardless of method or management. Two basic arguments support this claim. The first is that asteroid mining should be prohibited because asteroids themselves have the right not to be disturbed. The second is that asteroid mining should be prohibited because of the impact if has on human lives.

The second view endorses a radical permission for asteroid mining by responding to each of these objections. First, because asteroids are non-living entities, they do not have protective rights. Second, because asteroid mining is consistent with virtue, it does not inhibit the cultivation of admirable personality traits. Third, asteroid mining does not run afoul of Lockean property rights. Finally, because asteroid mining does not necessarily imply the creation of economic inequalities, we cannot completely reject mining operations on that basis.

Finally, I develop a moderate approach between the two extremes, based on the considerations raised in their discussion. Space mining is morally permissible only if there are effective moral and legal regulations that manage the associated risks. One such risk is the chance of exacerbating economic inequality on Earth. This is particularly problematic for the case of asteroid mining because high initial costs exclude poor would-be miners.

The Current State of Asteroid Mining

Last year, Planetary Resources – one of the most outspoken advocates for private space prospecting – successfully crowd-sourced over $1.5m to fund a public space telescope: people were struck by the apparent feasibility of and the company's nonchalance about such an audacious undertaking. While itself interesting, this project was largely proposed to generate interest and publicity for their larger goal to 'bring the Solar System within humanity's economic sphere of influence' (Planetary Resources 2013). This is a relatively small project compared to Planetary Resources' broader ambitions, but it represents a very real step in a paradigm shift away from thinking about space as inaccessible and inert to thinking about it as an available resource.

In simplest terms, asteroid mining is the extraction of valuable materials from large masses in space. While this may be done by public or private agencies (for example, governments, corporations, private citizens of extreme wealth), following the theme of this collection, I will focus on the case of private asteroid mining. This focus excludes governments, which I will not discuss, but also specifies a motive. Private space prospectors are, for the most part, motivated by the economic opportunity that asteroid mining represents. Once resources have been extracted and suitably refined, they can be sold on markets to the benefit of those whose capital (and labour) investments have made the venture possible. I will assume that this is a more or less accurate description of the phenomenon to be discussed: the extraction of valuable materials from large extraterrestrial objects by private entities for financial profit.

Asteroid mining is not currently practiced, but a combination of technological advances, available capital, terrestrial resource scarcity and popular interest has spurred on a new and growing set of projects to realise this idea out of science fiction. According to Planetary Resources, there are nearly 1,500 near-Earth asteroids of sufficient size and accessibility to make them viable candidate destinations for mining missions. Because of the trajectory of their orbits and their relatively small size, many are actually more accessible than the Moon. The main attractions for asteroid prospectors are water and platinum group metals. Water is most valuable as a rocket fuel that can be accessed by vehicles already in space, since all fuels currently have to be carried into space by enormous and expensive rockets. Platinum group metals have various uses, but are potentially available on asteroids in amounts that rival or even exceed the deposits on Earth. Perhaps even more importantly, it is estimated that these deposits are distributed more evenly throughout asteroids. This makes these valuable resources far easier to extract than from Earth, where they exist only near the core.

Posing the Moral Question

The idea of private asteroid mining resonates with a number of other contentious contemporary moral problems. On one hand, asteroid mining is a form of resource extraction. Other forms of resource extraction, notably hydraulic fracturing or 'fracking', have come under moral criticism for their adverse impact on the environment and on human life (Mooney 2011). On the other hand, extraterrestrial prospecting is a form of *Original Appropriation*, akin to the settlement of unoccupied territory. Such appropriation has been of interest in political philosophy now for centuries, largely due to John Locke's (1980, chapter 5) theory expounded in the second treatise.

Each of these analogous cases – fracking and appropriation – poses a different moral question. If we think of asteroid mining as primarily a problem about appropriation, then the moral question to pose is what I will call *methodological*. A methodological question is about *how* something ought to be done. Questions about the ethics of raising a child are like this, since they are about how children ought to be raised rather than *whether* children ought to be raised (Bornstein 2002). The methodological question about asteroid mining, therefore, is about how asteroid mining ought to be done. This will ideally offer guidance about how much of an asteroid, or how many asteroids, a space prospector may claim as one's own, about the conditions of ownership, and about appropriate standards for conducting a mining operation in space.

If we think of asteroid mining as primarily a problem akin to fracking, then the moral question to pose is what I will call *fundamental*. A fundamental question is about whether a practice should be permitted at all. Questions about the ethics of abortion tend to be fundamental questions, since many have argued either that abortion should never be permitted or that it should be permissible in special cases or left to the discretion of the mother (Thomson 1971; Marquis 1989). These fundamental arguments tend not to be about *how* abortions ought to be conducted, but try to give decisive reason to permit or abolish the practice altogether. The fundamental question about asteroid mining, therefore, is about whether asteroid mining should be conducted at all.

Because so little work has been done on the ethics of asteroid mining, we must still discover whether the methodological or the fundamental question is the most relevant to the current context. Of course, these are not mutually exclusive. We can, for example, ask moral questions both about whether *and* about how fracking should be done. The same, it seems, is true of asteroid mining. But methodological questions tend to be downstream from fundamental questions. Ethicists do not toil on the question of how best to commit a murder, one hopes, since we understand that there is a decisive objection to committing murder in the first instance. Methodological questions are only relevant after it has been affirmed that the practice in question is permissible. To focus only on how asteroid mining ought to be done presumes that we have already settled that that practice is permissible, which, given the nascent state of the field, is overly presumptuous in my judgement.

The Strong Prohibition: Rocks and Rights

Let us begin, therefore, with the fundamental question: Is it permissible for private companies to extract resources from asteroids for profit? Because the relevance of the methodological question is contingent on there *not* being fundamental arguments against asteroid mining, we should focus first on what those fundamental arguments might be. While there are surely more arguments than the few that I will here consider, these can be helpfully divided into at least two categories: nature-regarding arguments and human-regarding arguments. Nature-regarding arguments begin from the assumption that natural phenomena, including asteroids and what are commonly called 'natural resources', are worthy of moral concern in themselves.[1] Human-regarding arguments begin from the assumption that humans are worthy of moral concern, and moral restrictions on the treatment of natural phenomena are derived from this. Most arguments from the history of moral philosophy fall into the latter category, but both camps have offered illuminating ideas.

One prominent nature-regarding argument was promoted by W. Murray Hunt (1980, p. 62, quoting Warnock 1971, p. 148 and James 1897, p. 195) when he wrote:

> ... if merely 'being alive' is 'the condition of having a claim to be considered, by rational agents to whom moral principles apply', why should not 'being in existence' be such a condition as well? Here one is reminded of William James' well-known argument – though James' concern is limited to the 'demands' (interests?) of 'creatures' – 'Take any demand, however slight, which any creature, however weak, may make. Ought it not, for its own sake, be satisfied?'

There is much to criticise in this statement. Hunt is, for example, untroubled by talk of the 'claims' of non-living objects, while at the same time expresses confusion about James' talk of creatures' demands. He also overlooks clear examples of destruction that are obviously morally permissible, if not even necessary to an object's functioning. We destroy food when we eat it, though it is certainly not good, even for the food itself, that it be left uneaten and allowed to 'go bad'.

---

1   The distinction between nature-regarding and human-regarding arguments is very similar to the distinction between eco-centric and human-centric arguments. We should think of eco-centric arguments as a species of nature-regarding arguments, since not every natural phenomenon (as is clear in the case of asteroids) is obviously a part of some ecosystem. This fact excludes, for example, Aldo Leopold's land ethic.

Despite these obvious criticisms, the charitable reader can still find the following provocative syllogism at the heart of Hunt's essay: living things are worthy of moral concern; All distinctions between living and non-living things are morally arbitrary; if one group of objects is worthy of moral concern, and if that group is distinguishable from a second group only by morally arbitrary facts, then the second group is also worthy of moral concern; therefore, non-living things are worthy of moral concern.

Hunt's argument, thus articulated, is a valid one, and his strategy is promising. He begins from an initially plausible and widely held belief that, when all else is equal, life ought to be preserved. At least, we can interpret him this way. His proposal, on the basis of intuitive examples, is that what we apparently value about life is not life itself, but existence. Therefore, the common distinction we draw between living and non-living things is morally arbitrary. Instead, we should draw the line of moral concern at existence such that it includes non-living things.[2]

However valid, there is significant reason to doubt the soundness of Hunt's view. It is not obvious that all people, or even all philosophers, agree that all living things are worthy of moral concern.[3] Some think that what matters is rationality. Others think it is sentience. It is open to objection as to the extent that his argument relies on agreement about this point. Second, it is not obvious that the difference between living and non-living things is morally arbitrary. His assumption appears to be that the philosophers he is most interested in engaging with agree that there is no reason to prefer rationality or sentience over life as the basis of moral considerability, and *to these* philosophers he wants to suggest that there is no reason to prefer life over existence. Finally, even assuming that Hunt has shown that there is no more reason to use life as the necessary criterion for moral considerability than existence, he has not shown that there is more reason to use existence than life. At best, the matter is unsettled. This, however, will not suffice for someone who wants to defend the rights of non-living objects like asteroids.

Though unsound, his argument is instructive for the case of asteroid mining not because of its intrinsic plausibility, but because it is a clear example of what a nature-centric fundamental argument would have to look like. First, it would have to explain how asteroids could be worthy of moral concern independently from their usefulness to humans. Another example of such an argument is Aldo Leopold's land ethic (1986). Second, and unlike Leopold, the argument cannot make reference to an asteroid's role within an ecosystem. It has none. But the

---

2   Hunt's actual thesis is somewhat weaker than this. He writes that his point is merely that drawing a moral line at life is no more or less arbitrary than drawing at existence. Rather than offer a conclusive argument for one side or the other, he merely shifts the burden of proof back onto the shoulders of those who argue that there is something special about being alive. Another interpretation is that Hunt is only arguing that *if* we value living things in themselves, then we must also value existing things in themselves.

3   Hunt explicitly addresses this point, though he seems not to offer much of a response (see Hunt 1980, p. 62).

problems with Hunt's view will likely be problems for any of nature-regarding view. If nothing else, Hunt's argument demonstrates the obstacles that any nature-regarding and fundamental argument will have to overcome to justify the prohibition of asteroid mining.

The Strong Prohibition: Human-Regarding Arguments

Human-regarding arguments promise a way around the problems that haunt the nature-regarding approach. Because so much of the history of moral philosophy has focused on human life, the number of arguments available here is extensive. The challenge with human-regarding arguments is that asteroid mining is poised to deliver massive benefits to humankind in the form of cheaper fuels and valuable materials without forcing humans to bear the costs of environmental degradation that have hitherto been part and parcel with resource extraction. On its face at least, asteroid mining will be good for people. Given these obvious and substantial benefits, paired with the limited benefits asteroids afford humans currently, human-regarding fundamental arguments start out at a disadvantage since they cannot leverage the powerful utilitarian calculi so frequently used in environmental ethics. But there are other ways to resist asteroid mining besides utilitarianism. I will here focus on the three that stand out as particularly helpful to the case of asteroid mining – the virtue argument, the *Original Appropriation* argument and the *Egalitarian Argument*.

The *Virtue Argument* claims that asteroid mining is inconsistent with human flourishing and that by engaging in such a practice, we are actually impairing our own abilities to live good human lives.[4] Thomas Hill (1983, p. 215) summarises this point when he writes:

> I want to ask, 'What sort of person would want to do what they propose?' The point is not to skirt the issue with an ad hominem, but to raise a different moral question, for even if there is no convincing way to show that the destructive acts are wrong (independently of human and animal use and enjoyment), we may find that the willingness to indulge in them reflects the absence of human traits that we admire and regard morally important.

Hill is specifically talking about the destruction of terrestrial phenomena for use as resources, but his argument could be generalised to extraterrestrial phenomena like asteroids as well. Robert Sparrow (1999, pp. 232–3) expresses such a generalised view in his illuminating discussion about terraforming planets. The best people, the argument goes, are the ones who approach asteroids and other celestial objects with a sense of awe, reverence, respect and care. In order to flourish, and as a

---

4   Homes Rolston III has been a particularly forceful voice in environmental virtue ethics (see especially Rolston 2005, pp. 65–6, included in Sandler and Cafaro 2005).

part of flourishing, we should (and should not fail to) cultivate those dispositions and realise them in our actions. Mining asteroids not only fails to instantiate such virtuous dispositions, it allows monetary profits to reinforce non-virtuous ones such that they are more likely to become part of one's habituated persona. This argument amounts to a decisive objection against asteroid mining. Because mining encourages non-virtuous dispositions and because it is indicative of a lack of virtue otherwise, it ought not to be done.

What is unique about the virtue argument is that it claims that the wrong of asteroid mining is a kind of self-harm. Both the *Original Appropriation* and egalitarian arguments will focus on how asteroid mining might be a failure to make good on the moral treatment that people owe to each other. They are other-orientated in the sense that other persons are the loci of the moral concerns that motivate the ultimate moral judgement. The virtue argument is self-orientated while not falling into a form of simple egoism. This could help to explain the normativity of the prohibition on asteroid mining – that is, why someone who was not already altruistically disposed but who stood to profit from asteroid mining might heed the prohibition – and so avoid familiar problems about the difficulty of getting people to comply with moral commandments.

The *Original Appropriation Argument* claims that asteroid mining would violate moral principles about how agents claim property. Asteroids are currently unowned parts of what is often called 'the commons'. Mining is a kind of appropriation whereby agents gain property rights over asteroids, or at least over parts of them. Traditionally, property rights include the right to choose how property will be used and to transfer ownership to others, often in exchange for payment of some kind. Because asteroids are currently unowned, their appropriation is 'original'. Famously, John Locke (1980) advanced three criteria for justifiable *Original Appropriation*: (1) the labour criterion; (2) the no worsening criterion; and (3) the spoilage criterion. According to the labour criterion, an agent must mix his labour with an unowned object in order to appropriate it. This can be as simple as picking an apple from a wild tree to something as labour-intensive as ploughing a field to sow crops.[5] According to the no worsening criterion, a person may appropriate only so much form the commons that they leave 'enough and as good' for others. Thus a wanderer may claim a handful of apples off a wild tree, but not every apple on the tree, since that would leave everyone else without. According to the spoilage condition, a person may only appropriate so much such that what is appropriated will not spoil or go to waste under his care. Thus a person may only claim as many apples as he can actually eat before they rot, even if taking more would still leave as much and as good for others.

The *Original Appropriation* argument alleges that asteroid miners will necessarily run afoul of one of these conditions. Since mining is clearly labour-intensive, even if remotely done by machines, the practice seems to satisfy the labour condition. Since mined materials are both non-perishable and currently

---

5   The labour condition has been notably commented on in Nozick (1975, pp. 175–82).

subject to significant market demand, it seems unlikely that they would (or could) spoil in any relevant sense. So if asteroid mining fails to meet one of Locke's criteria for just appropriation, it must be the no worsening condition. How might this be?

At the moment, asteroid mining is something that is even remotely possible only for very wealthy corporations. Planetary Resources, for example, is backed by a number of the richest and most risk-tolerant people on our planet. And it needs to be, because the opportunity presented by asteroid mining is only available to those who can make the astronomical initial capital investment. The fact that this initial investment is so large makes space prospecting prohibitively expensive for most people, and so means that they will not even have the opportunity to be part of the appropriation process. Competition for mineable resources, if any there be, will be between only a few very wealthy groups, and these groups will have a natural incentive to extract the mineable resources to the point that future mining operations could not be profitable (that is, not leave enough for others) before others can join in. We could prevent this by introducing regulations that, for example, limit the amount that prospectors may extract. Without such special regulation, rationally self-interested prospectors will have be incentivised to take as much as they can, leaving as little as possible for others, thus violating the no worsening criterion.

This, it seems to me, is too quick. The mere fact of unequal access to markets does not, on its face, imply that resources will necessarily be extracted to the point that not enough remains to make mining economically profitable for others, though certainly there would be economic incentive to extract as much as possible as rapidly as possible. So while it may be an over-reach to say that socio-economic stratification of access to natural resources *will* result in space prospectors not leaving enough and as good for others, this is certainly a serious *risk* of an unregulated system of asteroid mining. While this risk might not even be realised, the mere fact that a practice exposes people to risk suffices to ground a decisive objection to unregulated asteroid mining.

Why might someone accept that the risk of violating one of the criteria, rather than violation itself, suffices to ground an argument against the practice? Consider an analogy with Russian roulette. When one aims the gun at the other's head and pulls the trigger, s/he is exposing the other to risk. If the target was unlucky, and there was in fact a bullet in the chamber, then certainly the person who pulled the trigger has done something wrong. They have killed a person for no good reason. But what about the other five possible outcomes, when no bullet was in the chamber and no harm was actually done? It seems clear that even these cases are wrong, simply because the person was exposed to serious risk of being wronged.

It is not obvious that the fact that access to asteroids depends heavily on one's pre-existing wealth will necessarily result in the violation of any of Locke's criteria. This fact does imply, however, that without regulation, those who are not currently wealthy enough to mine asteroids themselves, or even to join a group that is sufficiently wealthy to do so, are at risk of there not being enough left for them. As in the case of Russian roulette, exposure to serious risk of being wronged is itself a kind of wrong, and so ought to be prohibited. Because asteroid mining exposes the insufficiently wealthy masses to the risk of being left with no opportunity to enrich themselves through space prospecting, asteroid mining ought to be prohibited.

The *Egalitarian Argument* similarly claims that unregulated asteroid mining would exacerbate already problematic levels of economic inequality. Asteroid mining represents the possibility of expanding one's own wealth significantly, but, as discussed, this possibility is only available to those who are already extremely wealthy. Without regulation, like taxes on mining operations to pay for public services that improve the lot of the worse off in society, the practice of asteroid mining threatens to further concentrate wealth in the hands of the very few.

Such unequal concentration of wealth is objectionable for many reasons. First, because a human's self-esteem is sensitive to his/her relative worth with respect to others, inequality actually undermines this important part of human well-being. Self-esteem, the conviction that one is worthy of respect, is an important part of living any good human life. By improving the lot of the wealthiest, even without reducing the *absolute* well-being of the worst off, unregulated space mining would actually worsen the lives of the poorest by widening the income gap and thus diminishing their sense of relative worth. Second, such inequality fails Rawls's original position test. Rawls (2005, pp. 72–80) argues that practices that introduce inequalities can only be justified by the fact that they benefit the worst off better than any available alterative version of that practice. However, unregulated asteroid mining appears only to stand to benefit those wealthy few who can engage in it. It does not benefit the worst off. Because inequality is morally objectionable, and because asteroid mining introduces and exacerbates inequality, asteroid mining ought to be prohibited.

Defending Permission

Four fundamental arguments have been advanced for the claim that asteroid mining is morally impermissible. The practice: (1) violates an asteroid's right to moral consideration; (2) is incompatible with human flourishing; (3) violates moral standards for *Original Appropriation;* and (4) exacerbates economic inequality. Anyone who claims that asteroid mining is morally permissible will have to respond to each of these objections, as well as others that I have not here discussed. How might one so respond?

To the claim that asteroids are the bearers of rights to moral consideration, and that humans have correlative duties to respect those rights, two objections may be raised. First, it is not obvious in the first instance that asteroids do have rights. According to the two predominant views in rights theory (Hart 1955; Feinberg and Narveson 1970; Raz 1984), an entity can only be the bearer of rights if they have interests or if they are able to make choices. Asteroids can do neither of these things. Hunt argues that there is no morally relevant difference between living and non-living entities, but the fact that living things can intelligibly be ascribed interests seems to be precisely the kind of difference for which he asks. Second, it is not obvious what an asteroid's right to moral consideration would actually amount to in terms of respectful action? Is it disrespectful to climb a mountain? To pick up a seashell? To eat a cupcake? It is not even clear how one ought to think about these cases. Perhaps this is merely evidence of how far corrupted my moral sensibilities have become, but it also might be evidence that talk of the rights of non-living things is a category mistake.

To the claim that asteroid mining is incompatible with human flourishing, we might again wonder whether the practice really does conflict with being virtuous people. The concern, recall, was that space prospectors view the universe as a resource to be used for profit rather than with a sense of awe and reverence. But one might think that asteroid mining actually represents one of the greatest opportunities for human flourishing in history. Not only does asteroid mining promise wealth, which is essential for the instantiation of virtues like generosity and magnificence, it is a chance for humans to be creative, inventive and explorative. The inherent risks occasion bravery. The ambitious scale of the project makes it an opportunity to achieve glory.[6] These are all human virtues, arguably constitutive of the best human life. Not only is asteroid mining compatible with flourishing, it creates a new way for humans to achieve it.

To the claims that asteroid mining will wrong people, either by exposing them to risks of immoral exclusion from opportunities because of failures to meet standards for appropriation or by exacerbating inequality, the defender of asteroid mining can argue that these wrongs are not necessary consequences of asteroid mining. Certainly these are possible consequences, but with proper regulation, asteroid mining can be conducted without causing serious exposure to risk or expansion of inequality. As suggested earlier, to address the risk that space prospectors will not leave enough for others, governments or other terrestrial regulatory agencies might introduce caps on how much material can be extracted. Alternatively, regulators might allow prospectors to mine more than their fair share, but tax mined resources beyond some threshold. Tax revenues could be used to compensate non-miners for the opportunity costs forced on them by over-extraction. Such taxes could also alleviate the problems of inequality. James Schwartz (2015, pp. 69–89) has recently advanced similar ideas, relying specifically on a Rawlsian framework. While asteroid mining has its moral perils, these are evitable with well-designed regulations.

---

6   Someone like Sparrow (1999, pp. 232–9) might argue that glory should not be included in this list because seeking glory is a form of hubris. But seeking glory is not, in itself, a form of hubris. Olympic athletes exemplify this. By mining asteroids, humans are not seeking to supplant the gods. Even if we exclude glory from the list of virtues promised, asteroid mining still appears to be an opportunity for human flourishing. My gratitude to an anonymous commentator for persuading me of the importance of this point.

Conclusion

If we accept these responses to the fundamental arguments against asteroid mining, then we will have made room to ask the methodological question: How should asteroid mining be done? How must it be done to be morally permissible? Initially, the methodological question appeared to be about technology and instrumentation. Which kinds of tools should be used? Should mining be done remotely or should humans be sent to asteroids to do the work? Which materials should be the focus of mining operations? These may yet be important moral questions for reasons that are not presently obvious. But the previous responses to the fundamental arguments against asteroid mining suggest that in order for it to be permissible, we must adopt regulatory policies that will control the broader problems of excessive appropriation and inequality.

Moreover, this discussion can be generalised so as to be instructive beyond the particular problems of excessive appropriation and inequality. There are other ways that an economic practice can be morally problematic besides these. For example, the sudden and large influx of valuable materials from these new sources might destabilise existing markets and increase the risks of economic crises. The greater availability of these materials might decrease the value of terrestrially mined resources, which can result in worker displacement due to layoffs as mining companies tighten their belts. Not only is this an egalitarian issue, it becomes an issue about ensuring that all people live above some humanitarian minimum. Asteroid mining could represent a seismic shift in certain markets, and this exposes people to a variety of risks. If it is to be above moral reproach, we have an obligation to create regulations to ensure that these risks are not realised and to make sure that when these risks eventually are realised, people are justly compensated for these extra burdens. Moreover, space prospectors have an obligation to comply with these extra burdens, on pain of the moral impermissibility of the practice of asteroid mining altogether.

This discussion suggests how the continued study of the ethics of asteroid mining might proceed. There seems, in my opinion, to be nothing particularly objectionable about asteroid mining in principle. It represents not only an opportunity to vastly increase the collective wealth of humankind, but also an alternative to mining practices that are demonstrably destroying living ecosystems. It is a chance for us to invent, explore and test the boundaries of possibility. But it comes with various risks and potential harms. Excessive appropriation by private organisations and the consequent exacerbation of current economic inequalities are two examples of what is almost certainly a much longer list. If asteroid mining is to be morally permissible, these 'negative externalities' must be managed. I have suggested that government regulation is one promising way that such morally problematic implications might be addressed.[7] The task for moral philosophers going forward, then, is to identify other such externalities, to argue why they make

---

7   I borrow this language from Kumm (2013).

the practice of asteroid mining morally problematic, and to propose regulatory regimes for their management.

References

Bornstein, M.H. 2002, *Handbook of Parenting*, 2nd ed., vol. 5. Mahwah, NJ: Lawrence Earlbaum Associates.

Feinberg, J. and Narveson, J. 1970, 'The nature and value of rights', *The Journal of Value Inquiry*, 4(4): 243–60.

Hart, H.L.A. 1955, 'Are there any natural rights?', *The Philosophical Review*, 64(2): 175–91.

Hill, T.E. and Center for Environmental Philosophy, The University of North Texas, 1983, 'Ideals of human excellence and preserving natural environments', *Environmental Ethics*, 5(3): 211–24.

Hunt, W.M. 1980, 'Are mere things morally considerable?', *Environmental Ethics*, 2(1): 59–65.

James, W. 1897, *The Will to Believe and Other Essays in Popular Philosophy*. New York: Longmans Green and Co.

Kumm, M. 2013, 'Constitutionalism and the cosmopolitan state', *New York University Public Law and Legal Theory Working Papers*, available at: http://lsr.nellco.org/nyu_plltwp/423.

Leopold, A. 1986, *A Sand County Almanac*. New York: Ballantine Books.

Locke, J. 1980, *Second Treatise of Government*, 1st ed. Indianapolis, IN: Hackett Pub Co.

Marquis, D. 1989, 'Why abortion is immoral', *The Journal of Philosophy*, 86(4): 183–202.

Mooney, C. 2011, 'The truth about fracking', *Scientific American*, 305(5): 80–85.

Nozick, R. 1975, *Anarchy, State, and Utopia*, 2nd ed. New York: Basic Books.

Planetary Resources 2013, 'Planetary resources surpasses US $1.5 million to launch world's first crowdfunded space telescope', *Planetary Resources*, 1 July 1, viewed 16 June 2014, http://www.planetaryresources.com/2013/07/planetary-resources-surpasses-us-1–5-million-to-launch-worlds-first-crowdfunded-space-telescope.

Rawls, J. 2005, *A Theory of Justice: Original Edition*. Cambridge, MA: Belknap Press of Harvard University Press.

Raz, J. 1984, 'On the nature of rights', *Mind*, 93(370): 194–214.

Rolston III, H. 2005, 'Environmental virtue ethics: half the truth but dangerous as a whole', in R. Sandler and P. Cafaro (eds), *Environmental Virtue Ethics*, Lanham, MD: Rowman & Littlefield.

Sandler, R. and Cafaro P. (eds) 2005, *Environmental Virtue Ethics*, Lanham, MD: Rowman & Littlefield.

Schwartz, J. 2015, 'Fairness as a moral grounding for space policy', in C. Cockrell, (ed.), *The Meaning of Liberty Beyond Earth*. Switzerland: Springer.

Sparrow, R. 1999, 'The ethics of terraforming', *Environmental Ethics*, 21(3): 227–45.

Thomson, J.J. 1971, 'A defense of abortion', *Philosophy & Public Affairs*, 1(1): 47–66.

Warnock, G.J. 1971, *Object of Morality*. London: Methuen Young Books.

Chapter 12

Exploring the Heavens and the Heritage of Mankind

Robert Seddon

Selene, divine daughter of Hyperion, lover of Endymion the shepherd, has faded into the realm of poetry. Readers of this book, hoping for scholarly insight into the morals of lunar mining and other uses of advanced technology in space, are perhaps unlikely even by modern standards to worship the gods of ancient Greece. The Moon that can be mined is plainly a rock. Yet while Selene offers nothing to the technology that lets humans explore the Moon, our ethics may have to accommodate her memory.

A powerful moral ideal in the modern world is that of conserving cultural heritage. National and international legal regimes have developed doctrines concerning 'cultural property': 'objects that embody or express or evoke the culture [of some group]; principally archaeological, ethnographic and historical objects, works of art and architecture, but the category can be expanded to include almost anything made or changed by man' (Merryman 1990, p. 513). A United Nations organisation now oversees a World Heritage List intended to name sites of 'outstanding universal value' to the entire human race (UNESCO n.d.).

What counts as whose heritage, and how rival claims should be resolved, is the subject of a burgeoning literature created by legal scholars, anthropologists and archaeologists, and increasingly by moral philosophers. After all, it 'would be naïve to suppose that where items of cultural heritage hold different significances for different people, any disagreements should be readily resolvable given a modicum of mutual understanding and goodwill' (Scarre and Coningham 2013, p. 8). Journeys into space will not escape these different significances, for human cultures have been finding meaning in the night sky since before the dawn of recorded history. 'Celestial bodies have been named, used to navigate, track the seasons and tell stories. The Moon features in stories created by cultures from Australia to the Arctic. Every culture from prehistoric times can rightfully claim the Moon as a part of its cultural heritage' (O'Leary 2006).

The practical question, the point of intersection between space ethics and heritage ethics, is this: what moral constraints, if any, are placed upon what explorers of space may do by the long involvement with space of terrestrial human cultures? In recent work on the ethics of lunar mining, Tony Milligan has suggested that the cultural significance of the Moon gives us reason not to treat it as a mere resource (Milligan 2013; see also his contribution to the present volume).

This claim draws on prior developments in space law: the Moon and its natural resources are designated by an international treaty (albeit one which no major spacepower has signed or ratified) as 'the common heritage of mankind' (United Nations 1979), in language akin to that which underpins the World Heritage List. (Here I am glossing over technicalities concerning what overlap exists between 'cultural' and 'natural' heritage. The crucial point seems to have been more that the Moon is common heritage than that it is naturally occurring.)

Much of the existing literature on heritage in space is concerned with the physical traces of exploration after it has taken place, and how to secure their preservation as a collection of historic sites or places of archaeological interest. This literature is sufficiently developed for a Master's thesis in space law to have been written with its focus on protection of the Apollo 11 landing site (DiPaolo 2013). Archaeologists have been notably vigorous in seeking protection for space heritage of this sort: a World Archaeological Congress Space Heritage Task Force was formed to manage sites and objects related to the history of space exploration, including 'satellites and so-called space junk in orbit round Earth; spacecraft and space debris in orbit around other bodies in the Solar System; [and] landing and crash sites on the Moon, Mars, Venus, a small selection of asteroids and soon some of the moons of the outer planets' (World Archaeological Congress n.d.; see also Campbell n.d.; Darrin and O'Leary 2010; Spennemann 2004).

However, I say little about this kind of cultural heritage in this chapter, since I take it that it is not the *ethical* features of this sort of heritage site which render it so unconventional. Once it is agreed that the Apollo 11 landing site qualifies as an archaeological site, moral arguments for its importance as either American or human cultural heritage can draw on the moral vocabulary already employed with respect to terrestrial archaeology (although there will be certain differences: for example, when it comes to determining who is morally responsible for ensuring the conservation of sites). The idea that the entire Moon, or perhaps even a smaller celestial body such as an asteroid, may qualify as heritage is not so easily brought within the scope of the ethics of cultural heritage as familiarly construed.

In what follows I set out to explore what potential exists to extend our thinking about the ethics of cultural heritage and apply it to the special case of space. Against a backdrop of the various roles which celestial objects have played and continue to play in human cultures, in the next section I move to questions of whose culture is under discussion: are heavenly bodies part of a shared cultural heritage, of 'the common heritage of mankind', or should we entertain a more pluralistic view, recalling that different cultures have developed quite different accounts of the heavens and their contents? In the subsequent section I discuss a further dilemma: given that, for most of human history, our encounters with space have been from a wholly terrestrial standpoint, is it truly celestial objects which might count as our cultural heritage, or just the way they look from Earth?

Next I move to another related question: much of what space has contributed to human cultures comes in the forms of long-lived mythology and the 'softer' (that is, less scientifically grounded) kind of modern science fiction. Given that it is precisely an adhesion to scientific plausibility that makes space exploration possible, when we consider space as cultural heritage may we, or indeed should we, give priority to those construals of space which accord with what scientific cultures have come to consider realistic? Here I make the conciliatory suggestion that whether we aim at boundless and soaring imagination, at grounded science or indeed at religious devotion or aesthetic delight or any other response, space has significance for us as an intellectual resource that fosters all these responses. On this basis I conclude by drawing on the idea of stewardship as it has developed within archaeological ethics, and consequently by suggesting that explorers of space should conduct themselves also as stewards of it.

Popular Culture and Pioneering Colonists

Many things in space were unknown to humans in antiquity, but more recent discoveries have been making their way into cultures beyond the world of astronomy. If you have played the Asteroids arcade game, or recall the asteroid belt in *The Empire Strikes Back* or remember the asteroid Adonis from Hergé's *Explorers on the Moon*, then you have seen that asteroids have found roles to play in popular culture. Now they are being investigated as candidates for mining (Planetary Resources n.d.; Deep Space Industries n.d.).

Though their status as a source of inspiration to the arts and the entertainment industries is plain enough, it is harder to say whether their contributions to our culture mean that asteroids, or any particular asteroid, should be counted as anyone's cultural heritage in any significant sense. If everything that contributes to human culture qualifies as part of the cultural heritage of our species, then it becomes difficult to think of things which are not someone's and perhaps everyone's cultural heritage. This is not a conclusion that should be rejected out of hand; but if the notion of cultural heritage is going to inform our ethics then we shall need some means of working out just when the contribution which something has made to a culture entails moral constraints on what we may do with it.

Unsurprisingly, this problem is not new to the literature of heritage ethics. Often a related question is formed around conceptions of value or importance: when does the value which an object holds for some culture mean that it ought to be in the possession of representatives of that culture, and nobody else? (see for example Thompson 2003; Young 2007). This leads to further questions about how value is to be measured, and what kinds of value (aesthetic, religious, historic and so on) are relevant.

I take it that where space is concerned we will typically not be concerned with the value which any of the heavenly bodies may hold just for any one terrestrial culture in particular. Of course, different cultures feature different interpretations of the sky, originating from different locations on the Earth's surface. Even where there is agreement, for example, that the Moon is a divinity, Selene of the ancient Hellenic traditions is not Tsukuyomi of Japan's Shinto faith. However, since every human culture has developed under Earth's skies, none is in a strong position to make special and overriding claims on space exclusively for itself.

It is true, of course, that some cultures have absorbed more than others from the scientific and technological investigation of space. The examples of asteroid-related popular culture which I gave above represent a manifestly western background, unevenly reflected in the interests and experiences of people and peoples across the globe. A case might therefore be made that space is disproportionately the heritage of peoples that have sought to venture into it, with the former participants of the 'space race' leading the pack. (The peoples in whose scriptural heritage the Tower of Babel features might have a claim of greater antiquity, but that endeavour, so the story goes, met with less success than more modern space programmes.)

However, whilst richer nations have always had the technological advantage in investigating space (though there are nowadays more countries than before for which space exploration is viable), it would be excessive to infer that space looms consistently larger in the wealthier national cultures of the 'developed world'. Lebanon had an active space programme in the 1960s (Hooper 2013); and individuals who lack engineering resources still have one of the universal features of human culture, the power to invent and tell stories. 'Reading science fiction as a commentary on modernization', writes M. Elizabeth Ginway, 'one can begin to grasp the adaptation of science fiction, the quintessential First World genre, to Third World cultures' (2005, p. 467). Jonathan Dotse links science fiction to 'the rise of a completely different mindset from the ones that has dominated the developing world until very recently; a growing recognition among [the] youth of the immense potential for science and technology to induce tangible social change' (2012). If science fiction and the genre's long engagement with space exploration have their natural home in any region, others are catching up fast and making contributions of their own.

In consequence, I think that when we ask whether there is cultural heritage in space, having in mind naturally occurring objects rather than the remnants of past exploration, what we are asking about is going to concern the 'common heritage of mankind', and only that.

What, though, about the cultures which might develop amongst a community living away from Earth? Thus far only small groups of astronauts have ever done so, and only for limited portions of their lives. Much of what we would like to see done in space is better done by robots, controlled remotely from Earth. However, if a permanent colony is ever established elsewhere in the Solar System, given time it will develop a distinctive culture of its own. Quite how distinctive that is will depend in part upon the strength of the colony's communication links with Earth, and particularly on how long it takes before anyone is able to make a return journey; the Mars One project plans for one-way emigration (Mars One n.d.) (and its feasibility has been called into question nonetheless (Devlin 2015)).

Colonists of Mars would develop a vastly more intimate involvement with their new planet than anyone left on Earth would have with it. It would inform their common identity as Martian colonists, a society of people whose lives centred on the challenges and possibilities of life on Mars. At some point, when colonies had become long established and their members numerous, it would probably seem plausible that Mars was more their cultural heritage than anyone's on Earth, the antiquity of the latter population's claim notwithstanding. (Should intelligent beings turn out to be dwelling in the bowels of the planet, their claim will of course be best of all.)

In our present situation, however, no such colonies exist. Any pioneers landing on Mars will be landing on a planet which, if it is anybody's cultural heritage, is the heritage of our species in general. Can we say much about the cultural 'importance' or 'value' of Mars in comparison with that of, say, asteroid 11384 Sartre? In practice we may not need or wish to; even if we do think that both relevantly qualify as heritage, we may nonetheless think that Martian planetary mining and asteroid mining pose moral questions significantly distinct from one another. Trying to bring everything astronomers have ever glimpsed together under a unified scheme of moral priorities might prove a vexing task for anybody seeking practical guidance. If cultural heritage is to prove a useful idea when considering our moral obligations involving heavenly bodies, its use may have to be of a somewhat different sort.

Seeing Lunar Seas

Is it celestial bodies themselves that enter into our cultural heritage, or their appearances when observed from Earth? When we deal with terrestrial heritage, such a question does not normally arise: if an item of heritage exists physically in the first place (as some do not, such as languages, songs or artistic motifs), then its appearance will be of interest, especially if the item is held to be of aesthetic merit, but the material object which *has* that appearance is what is said to be the item of heritage. Even landscapes, not easily delineated, are not reduced to the vistas they offer us. Terrestrial landscapes, however, tend to be more often and easily walked over than those of other worlds.

Humans have been looking up at the sky for millennia, but we have had a very limited view of what is out there, and our myths (and science fictional imaginaries) are products of this history of limitation. With the naked eye we see a Moon which waxes and wanes, and in the dark lunar seas we perceive pareidolia which vary with culture: the Man in the Moon for Westerners, a rabbit in parts of Asia. Everything else is a tiny light if we can make it out at all.

Over the past few centuries, what astronomers can see has been hugely enhanced through technological progress. Much of this development, including human beings' first visit to the Moon, has happened within living memory. Like our distant ancestors, we can look up and see the Man in the Moon; unlike them, we can also examine photographs taken from the lunar surface.

Suppose we think that the Moon is part of our cultural heritage as human beings. We also think that the Moon is a large, rocky spheroid, a place which humans have visited. We seem to be getting no closer to the Man in the Moon who, according to Tolkien, Stayed Up Too Late. If anything, we are pushing him into some other corner of our minds. Yet he, as part of popular folklore, is a rather more obvious candidate for consideration as cultural heritage than distant rocks tend to be.

Here is a possible lesson: when it comes to cultural heritage, treating the Moon as an object can be a conceptual error. We are interested in what terrestrial cultures have made of space, and what they have made of it has drawn upon what little has been visibly apparent. This is plain when we consider constellations, which have the forms they do only when viewed from our direction. What celestial bodies truly are is, for cultural heritage, irrelevant.

If correct, this might prove a liberating thought. It would take a tremendous amount of mining to make even the Moon, our nearest neighbour and the largest object in the night sky, look noticeably different when viewed from Earth. In fact, the most obvious moral constraint to result from this account of space as heritage would be on 'light pollution', the way in which all but the brightest stars are obscured by the numerous electric lights of modern settlements, so that in many places we are left with something brighter and yet drabber than our ancestors' skies. Since this volume is concerned with the *exploration* of space, however, I do not develop this theme further.

There are reasons, nonetheless, to take the opposite view that it is not just appearances but objects that feature in our celestial heritage. In the first place there is our construal of perception. We ordinarily feel free to say (and without sophisticated philosophical justification) that we saw a rabbit this morning, or whatever it was we saw, without having to specify that what we saw was the left side of a rabbit, and anyway it might conceivably have been the left side of a hare at that distance. It would be consistent with ordinary practice not to insist that our ancestors, seeing one side of the Moon at a great distance, therefore were talking merely about something else, the *appearance* of the Moon, when they came up with Selene and the lunar rabbit and the rest. Certainly they were calling it the Moon before anyone had much knowledge of lunar geography to attach to the name (or its equivalent in other languages).

There is also the fact that there is no short history of humans seeing heavenly bodies as places. Lucian of Samosata, writing in the second century AD, has his heroes lifted by a whirlwind onto the surface of the Moon: its inhabitants are warring with those of the Sun over colonisation of the Morning Star. Thinking of the Moon as a place above the Earth, with a surface upon which people might walk, does not appear to have unduly taxed the brains of Lucian's readers. It might therefore seem arbitrary to say that they knew the Moon only from its appearance, when they and we have both been able to look up and see it as a physical place.

An Intellectual Resource

Let us tentatively grant, then, that celestial bodies, and not just their sublunary appearances, can be part of human cultural heritage. The complication persists that human cultural heritage includes an awful lot of notions *about* celestial bodies, some inconsistent with others. Besides the obvious incompatibility of the Moon as a rock and as a charioteering goddess, there are subtler differences. For example: once telescopes were developed which granted a somewhat detailed view of lunar geography (unavailable to Lucian when he wrote his satire), disagreement promptly raged among men of science concerning whether our Moon, or other moons and planets of our solar system, might support alien life (Dick 1982; Crowe 1986). No less a figure than Johannes Kepler seems to have favoured the doctrine of lunar inhabitation; to protect their readers from its seduction, Giovanni Battista Riccioli and Francesco Maria Grimaldi wrote at the top of their lunar map of 1651 that 'neither do men inhabit the Moon, nor do souls migrate there'. History has vindicated Riccioli and Grimaldi, but both pro- and anti-Selenite doctrines belong to the tangled history of human thought. In this respect, cultural heritage is insensitive to truth: our culture has transmitted to us both the Moon-landing footage of 1969 and the conspiracy theory that it was faked, and both are thereby included in the culture which we have inherited.

Must our ethics take stock of *everything* that has ever been popularly imagined about space, regardless of the plausibility or compatibility of all these notions? We know that explorers of space will be working within the concepts and conventions of modern science roughly as we know it; no-one who attempted anything radically different has yet succeeded in becoming an explorer of space. Is our ethical reasoning supposed to take account of, for the purposes of moral judgement, even ideas which our practical circumstances otherwise compel our reason to reject?

The tension is a little reminiscent of one surrounding some heritage objects of a conventional sort, concerning how the meanings which people have attributed to an object, and the uses to which it has at one time or another been put, should influence the manner in which it is acquired and exhibited by a museum. The manner of display can emphasise scientific concerns, teaching visitors about an object's historical provenance and how it serves as evidence of the past; or it can favour artistry over artefact, encouraging visitors to appreciate the exhibit as an object of open-ended aesthetic judgement.

Perhaps fortunately, however, there is not much we can do to exhibit space to our liking. It is implacably *there*, looming above us, and tricky to conceal entirely even from the naked human eye. Still, the comparison with museum display offers one advantage: it suggests a path towards reformulating our question about the permissible roles of unscientific ideas in the cultural heritage of a space-faring species.

My suggestion is that we construe space as an intellectual resource, or the objects within it as intellectual resources which together arouse and sometimes satisfy our curiosity about space. Through this characterisation we can encapsulate the various ways in which space has informed and inspired the human intellect and the ideas which pass among us, from the most systematic of the sciences to the freest of space opera. More useful than that, once we have the category of a *resource* available to us, it becomes easier to see how the various cultural roles which space can play might complement each other in our ethics. For example, instead of seeing the Moon as a site *either* of extraterrestrial inhabitation *or* of lifelessnesss, and consequently inferring that because the latter view is empirically true, the former must be a defective and discredited and therefore barely relevant aspect of our heritage, we can instead see the Moon as a stimulating part of a vigorous history of scientific debate, and more broadly of human intellectual curiosity.

Space furnishes us with many kinds of intellectual material. The hard scientific measurements of astronomy are one sort; science fiction converts them into another. Religious contemplations are a third, whether the sky seems full of gods and mythic figures or whether it is held to reveal the majesty of one supreme Creator. 'Bright star, would I were steadfast as thou art' is a line in which space offers us both a moral example and at the same time a contribution to a poetic oeuvre. (Keats was but one of innumerable poets and lyricists who have taken inspiration from the heavens; applying a criterion of popular familiarity might make *Twinkle, Twinkle, Little Star* a stronger example still.) People almost invariably know their own star signs regardless of what they believe about the operations of destiny or character. Rising stars hurtle meteorically towards success in their careers, financial black holes appear in companies' accounts and nothing is ever rocket science. Space is so quintessentially a part of human experience that it gave rise to the very word, which recalls the *quinta essentia*, the fifth element of Aristotelian metaphysics, once thought to be the stuff of which the heavenly bodies were composed. Space is a resource upon which our minds, and hence our cultures, have long been drawing.

This does leave us still some way from arriving at practical advice for those wondering how to mine the surface of an intellectual resource in a morally responsible fashion. For the business (in fact, the industry) of space exploration, it is no doubt interesting or even moving that so much of what we are is inspired by space; but this observation falls short of moral force. We have the foundations of an understanding of why celestial objects might be worthy of careful treatment, but in just what ways we might be morally obliged to treat them with care remains a further question. The concluding section of this chapter will not go all the way to tracing out a handy list of moral guidelines for explorers of space. It will, however, highlight another potentially illuminating idea which we can draw from the terrestrial literature on heritage and its ethics.

Stewards of the Sky?

'In recent years the principle of stewardship according to which archaeologists are stewards of the past has become the epicentre of criticisms of archaeological ethics. Stewardship, however, has shaped the ethical concerns of archaeologists by raising awareness of ethical issues related to archaeological practice' (Pantazatos 2010, p. 96). Stewardship has not furnished archaeological ethics with an exhaustive conceptual toolkit, any more than it has the environmental ethicists who have sought to make use of ideas about stewardship of the natural world in either religious or secular contexts. It probably will not confer one upon us when we want to know about our moral responsibilities towards heavenly bodies *qua* intellectual resources; but it offers us a starting point.

In archaeological ethics, stewardship evokes the power not of a possessor, but of one holding goods in trust for others. In this model the goods at stake are those of disinterested scientific knowledge about the past; archaeological sites are repositories of such knowledge, and their preservation and proper excavation is vital if it is to be brought to light. Archaeologists, whose expertise enables them to bring this about, therefore find themselves with the responsibilities of custodianship. Archaeological sites are a resource, not merely economically but intellectually: investigated with the proper care and insight, they yield material for human thought from which everyone may benefit.

In the previous section I suggested that we should consider space, too, to be an intellectual resource. Resources, however, are often appropriated and made into sources of private benefit. Resource management is not, in itself, the foundation of a moral calling. It is here that the idea of cultural heritage becomes significant: whilst the mineral resources in space may be open to construal as virgin territory, the cultures of the Earth have ancient involvement with the intellectual resources of space. How then should explorers of space comport themselves? A possibility nicely in keeping with the moral practices of Earthbound work connected to cultural heritage is that they should take cues from the professional ethics of archaeologists, and seek to comport themselves as the careful stewards of an intellectual resource, accountable to those in whose cultures that resource looms large.

Stewardship is not a flawless, unobjectionable and universally acclaimed moral principle or framework, even for archaeologists; in some respects it was the arbitrary choice of a professional committee (Wylie 2005). I do not intend, in endorsing it in this chapter, to foreclose or discourage further debate. Perhaps my suggestion will be lampooned in centuries to come (if not wholly forgotten) as the small-minded doctrine of a man who wanted to extend to the exploration of the whole majestic cosmos a moral ideal developed by people who keep their eyes downward as they dig for human artefacts: the parochial recommendation of a philosopher who would never have advocated ethics with such limited horizons if he had ever had the chance to see a tiny Earth glinting distantly in the skies of Mars.

Still, every journey must start somewhere, including the forays of a space-faring species into youthful regions of moral philosophy. Stewardship of intellectual resources is one concept through which explorers of space might be able to reflect upon their moral purposes alongside their technological and economic objectives. Their accomplishments, after all, have great potential to enrich human culture with new knowledge, new stories and new ambitions. Cultural heritage need not be always and only a moral constraint on action: it is also through cultural interchange, and through ideas about 'the common heritage of mankind', that we have been able to affirm our shared humanity, in which explorers of space and even eventual colonists of Mars will also participate.

Stewardship as an ethical concept, even allowing for this archaeological inspiration, does not necessarily limit explorers of space to the role of disinterested scholars, any more than 'stewards of the Earth' are forbidden from cultivating it for their own gain. It implies not a duty to leave things just as they are, but a duty to preserve information and avoid thoughtless, wasteful destruction. Since space is part of the heritage of every human culture, stewardship also suggests a responsibility to manage this intellectual resource for the cultural benefit of the whole species, regardless of where a space-faring organisation may be incorporated, under which national laws it may operate and who benefits economically from its operations.

Conclusion

The further from our native planet we cast our minds and send our probes, the more hubristic it may seem to speak of all this as 'our' cultural heritage: to speak of all these worlds as ours (even Europa) when our exploration of space has so far been so local. If I had chosen to use the language of 'cultural property', that accusation would be hard to rebut. However, 'cultural heritage', like the natural resources which are so indispensable to life, can connote something upon which we depend as well as something to which we may have a claim. Through our cultures we shape what we are, and we and our cultures have been shaped by the conditions of existence here in our place within the Milky Way. If there ever does turn out to be other intelligent life somewhere out there, space probably offers enough cultural heritage to share.

References

Campbell, J.B. n.d., *Space Exploration and Space Heritage*, viewed 22 May 2014, http://explorationheritagespace.com/research/space-exploration-and-space-heritage.

Crowe, M.J. 1986, *The Extraterrestrial Life Debate 1750–1900: The Idea of a Plurality of Worlds from Kant to Lowell*. Cambridge: Cambridge University Press.

Darrin, A. and O'Leary, B.L. (eds) 2010, *Handbook of Space Engineering, Archaeology, and Heritage*. Boca Raton, FL: CRC Press.

Deep Space Industries n.d., *Abundance from Asteroids*, DSI, viewed 22 May 2014, http://deepspaceindustries.com/asteroids.

Devlin, H. 2015, 'Mars One plan to colonise red planet unrealistic, says leading supporter', *Guardian*, 23 February, viewed 18 March 2015, http://www.theguardian.com/science/2015/feb/23/mars-one-plan-colonise-red-planet-unrealistic-leading-supporter.

Dick, S.J. 1982, *Plurality of Worlds: The Origins of the Extraterrestrial Life Debate from Democritus to Kant*. Cambridge and New York: Cambridge University Press.

DiPaolo, A.J. 2013, 'Space law and the protection of cultural heritage: the uncertain fate of humanity's heritage in space', Master's thesis, McGill University, viewed 22 May 2014, http://digitool.library.mcgill.ca/webclient/StreamGate?folder_id=0&dvs=1400792830353~390.

Dotse, J. 2012, 'Developing world: Beyond the frontiers of science fiction', *IEETblog*, web log post, 11 February, viewed 23 May 2014, http://ieet.org/index.php/IEET/more/dotse20120210.

Ginway, M.E. 2005, 'A working model for analyzing third world science fiction: The case of Brazil', in *Science Fiction Studies*, 32(3): 467–94.

Hooper, R. 2013, *Lebanon's Forgotten Space Programme*, BBC, viewed 23 May 2014, http://www.bbc.co.uk/news/magazine-24735423.

Mars One n.d., *Humankind on Mars*, Mars One, viewed 24 May 2014, http://www.mars-one.com/mission/humankind-on-mars.

Merryman, J.H. 1990, '"Protection" of the cultural "heritage"?', *American Journal of Comparative Law*, 38, supplement 'U.S. law in an era of democratization', pp. 513–22.

Milligan, T. 2013, 'Scratching the surface: The ethics of helium-3 extraction', in Giancarlo Genta (ed.), *Proceedings of the 8th IAA Symposium on the Future of Space Exploration: Towards the Stars*, International Academy of Astronautics, Torino, Italy.

O'Leary, B.L. 2006, 'The cultural heritage of space, the Moon and other celestial bodies', in *Antiquity*, 80(3070), online-only project gallery viewed 22 May 2014, http://antiquity.ac.uk/ProjGall/oleary.

Pantazatos, A. 2010, 'Does diaspora test the limits of stewardship? Stewardship and the ethics of care', *Museum International*, 62(1–2): 96–9.

Planetary Resources n.d., *Asteroids Are the Best Real Estate in the Solar System*, Planetary Resources, Bellevue, Washington, viewed 22 May 2014, http://www.planetaryresources.com/asteroids.

Scarre, G.F. and Coningham, R. 2013, 'Introduction', in R. Coningham and G.F. Scarre (eds), *Appropriating the Past: Philosophical Perspectives on the Practice of Archaeology*. Cambridge: Cambridge University Press.

Spennemann, D.H.R. 2004, 'The ethics of treading on Neil Armstrong's footprints', *Space Policy*, 20(4): 279–90.

Thompson, J. 2003, 'Cultural property, restitution and value', *Journal of Applied Philosophy*, 20(3): 251–62.

UNESCO n.d., *World Heritage List*, UNESCO World Heritage Centre, Paris, viewed 20 May 2014, http://whc.unesco.org/en/list.

United Nations 1979, General Assembly resolution 34/68, *Agreement Governing the Activities of States on the Moon and Other Celestial Bodies*, viewed 22 May 2014, http://www.oosa.unvienna.org/oosa/SpaceLaw/moon.html.

World Archaeological Congress, n.d. *Terms of Reference for the Space Heritage Task Force*, WAC, viewed 22 May 2014, http://www.worldarchaeologicalcongress.org/site/active_spac.php.

Wylie, A. 2005, 'The promise and perils of an ethic of stewardship', in L. Meskell and P. Pels (eds), *Embedding Ethics*. Oxford and New York: Berg.

Young, J.O. 2007, 'Cultures and cultural property', *Journal of Applied Philosophy*, 24(2): 111–24.

Chapter 13

Terraforming, Vandalism and Virtue Ethics

Robert Sparrow

'Terraforming' is hypothetical climatic and geo-physical engineering of other planets on a grand scale, with the aim of turning the so-called 'barren' planets in our (or for that matter another) solar system into habitable Earth-like ecosystems. Although terraforming sounds like an idea from science fiction (where it indeed has appeared), it has been seriously proposed as a future project for the human race (Fogg 1995).[1] With such a technology we could colonise the solar system and perhaps eventually others, moulding them in an image of our own making. In this chapter I will consider the ethics of terraforming through the lens of an 'agent-based' virtue ethics.[2] I will argue that advocacy of – and any attempt at – terraforming is likely to demonstrate two significant character flaws in agents: an insensitivity to beauty; and, hubris, an excessive pride or faith in our own abilities in the course of transcending the proper limits of human activities.

The most promising planet in our solar system as a candidate for terraforming is Mars. There is a flourishing scientific literature on the feasibility of terraforming Mars (Beech 2009; Briggs 1986; Fogg 1995, pp. 13–24, 490–95; Haynes 1990; McKay 1990; Rolston 1986; Todd 2006), in which a number of mechanisms for terraforming Mars have been suggested. Mars is blessed (for the purposes of terraforming) with polar ice caps and a layer of perma-frost beneath the planet's surface, both of which contain water along with other frozen gases. The beginnings of an atmosphere could be created simply by melting these, either with fusion reactors, space-based solar-powered lasers or collector mirrors or by spreading a thin layer of soot across the ice caps so that they absorb the Sun's heat. This would create an atmosphere of water, carbon dioxide and other gases. Such an atmosphere will almost certainly initially be extremely poisonous. Other processes that might be used to produce an atmosphere include the introduction of genetically engineered organisms whose life chemistry would free gases existing in common compounds on the planet's surface. Once an atmosphere exists, we could modify it using genetically engineered micro-organisms designed to convert existing gases and compounds into oxygen, carbon dioxide and water. Over time and with extensive human intervention this program might create seas

---

1 What is perhaps the most well-known treatment of the science and ethics of terraforming in science-fiction occurs in the course of Kim Stanley Robinson's 'Mars trilogy' originally published by Bantam.

2 Much of the argument below first appeared in Sparrow (1999).

and eventually an Earth-like and (hopefully) breathable atmosphere. Throughout this process we would attempt to adjust the planet's surface temperature by intentionally manufacturing a greenhouse effect to heat it up or by placing large sheets of molecular thickness mirroring in orbit around the planet to cool it down. Once conditions are suitable we could introduce (again genetically modified) plants and animals capable of surviving in the existing conditions and eventually create a working ecosystem, which in turn might support human life. The whole process (Fogg 1995) is supposed to take a number of centuries but at the end of that period ... voilà! A new garden of Eden!

If it could be done, terraforming Mars would create a new home for billions of happy human beings for centuries to come. No matter how high the initial cost of the project, our assessment of the consequences, be it in terms of utility or some other calculation, will turn out to be massively positive once we take the benefit for future generations into account. We should get down to it.

Of course the face of Mars would be totally and irreversibly transformed by this process. I want here to describe briefly what would be lost in the change and outline a few other assumptions in order to establish and clarify the example. To develop the argument that interests me, I shall assume that Mars currently sustains no life. Thus I assume that terraforming Mars will not affect any living thing, will cause no suffering and violate no rights that other life forms might possess. Rights or utility-based arguments will therefore provide us with no reasons as to why we should not go ahead with the project.

Despite the absence of any living systems, there are still extremely complex inorganic systems on Mars. Mars has a unique geography and complex chemical and physical systems operating over thousands of years. It may be the 'dead planet', but when compared to other planetoids, such as our Moon for instance, it is an exceedingly lively place. Mars possesses an (albeit thin) atmosphere and its polar ice caps contain water. It has seasons and a climatic history. Winds and occasionally dust storms blow across its surface. These climatic and atmospheric processes exist in a dynamic and intricate relation with each other, with past geological processes and with the physical landscape. They shape the planet and the planet in turn shapes them. Their operations over the millennia have produced many features of striking natural beauty and vast scale. Amongst these are a volcano, Olympus Mons, which rises 29 kilometres from the planet's surface, spectacular dunes systems and 'desert' canyon systems three times deeper than the Grand Canyon.

Note, however, that although Mars has many features of great beauty, any aesthetic or interest-based accounts of why we might preserve these features, that proceed from the assumption that they have value because of the pleasure they provide to human witnesses, are likely to fail. The vistas of Mars have no such value because, being on Mars, we are unable to appreciate their beauty. There is no chance that more than a few human lives will be enriched or changed by taking a walk in the Martian desert and being awed into ethical reflection. The value of the beauties of Mars in terms of the pleasures or benefits they provide for human beings are therefore minimal. It is also the case that Mars would probably possess many beautiful and unique features *after* terraforming that human beings (or future happy Martians) *could* appreciate as they strolled across the surface of Mars. Of course, these would be completely different to those that exist today and the aesthetic experiences that they might provide would be the result of the destruction of the existing features.

To summarise: in terraforming Mars we would be drastically altering the character of a whole planet, a unique environment, which includes complex inorganic systems and possesses many features of striking natural beauty. Finally, of course, it must be pointed out that colonisation (and thus terraforming) other worlds is by no means necessary for the survival of the human race. No matter the scale of environmental destruction we wreak on the Earth or the population pressure we experience, for the foreseeable future it will always be easier to 'terraform' the Earth, so that we may survive here, than to modify other planets. To terraform Mars is a choice. We could choose not to do it and remain here and experience a reasonable quality of life.

So, what are the ethics of this project? As I have described the example (and deliberately so), there are no good arguments based in the interests of humans or even other living organisms for not terraforming Mars. The only thing stopping us from radically reshaping Mars – and in doing so destroying the character of a whole planet – is lack of technical know-how. If this is true, I believe it reveals a shocking moral bankruptcy at the heart of our attitude towards the environment. It suggests that we have no obligations to the world around us itself, to approach it with a certain humility or respect, but only to the organisms that live in it. Are there, then, *any* ethical considerations that might give us cause to resist terraforming?

An Agent-based Virtue Ethics

I believe that a significant set of reasons regarding projects such as terraforming can be found in the realm of virtue ethics. Virtue ethics (Aristotle 1976; Baron 1985; Foot 1978; MacIntyre 1984; McDowell 1978, 1979; Slote 1990, 1992; Solomon 1988) directs our concern to the character of ethical agents. It asks us to pay attention to the virtues and vices that we display through our actions. The particular virtue ethics I wish to develop here draws on a distinction made by Slote (1995) in a paper published in *Midwestern Studies in Philosophy*. In that paper Slote (1995, pp. 83–4) distinguishes between two varieties of virtue ethics, which he calls 'agent-focused' and 'agent-based' ethics.

'Agent-focused' virtue ethics are the familiar ethics of Aristotle and most contemporary virtue ethicists. These ethics hold that, if we wish to act rightly, rather than attempting to develop a theory of the good or of what makes an action right, we should cultivate the virtues. Only the virtuous agent will reliably be able to know what to do in a morally ambiguous world. However, despite the attention paid to virtue by these theorists, it is not an action's nature as a virtuous action that makes it right. For an 'agent-focused' virtue ethics (McDowell 1979, pp. 330–34; Slote 1995, pp. 83–4) the 'right maker' remains in the world. The rightness or wrongness of an action is independent of the character of the actor and instead is presumably a function of states in affairs in the world or perhaps of some unspecifiable set of duties or obligations. The reference to the character of the agent is made necessary by the epistemology of moral evaluation. Only the virtuous person can perceive what the correct thing to do is in a morally complex situation. So if we wish to act rightly in a particular instance, we should follow the example of the virtuous person and, if we wish to act rightly throughout our lives, we ourselves should cultivate the virtues. The acts that we perform, however, will be acts of independent worth and would retain their value even if we had performed them out of different motives.

However, as Slote points out, a different and more radical virtue ethics is also possible, which holds that actions are actually made right or wrong by the fact that they demonstrate a virtuous (or vicious) character. For an 'agent-based' virtue ethics, virtue is actually constitutive of right action. Rather than virtue allowing us to perceive the right action, which is made right by some complex set of facts about the world, right actions are right *because* they are virtuous. On this understanding, the 'right maker' for a given action (Slote 1995, pp. 83–4) is simply the character of the agent.[3] Agent-based virtue ethics seem implausible at first, I think, because we tend to believe that, for instance, we call people cruel who commit a certain type of action. Most of us feel that our intuitions about actions come first (Elliot 1989, p. 199; Louden 1984) and that it is the ethical status of the actions that determines the character of the actor. However, there seems no reason why we cannot reverse the normal priority of intuitions and hold that the facts that we can be most sure about are the goodness or otherwise of character and motives and that our belief that, for instance, increasing the happiness of others is good, stems from the fact that this is the sort of activity that benevolent people, whom we admire, engage in. In fact the epistemology of virtue suggests that this is the case. It is much easier to point out those who are cruel or benevolent in a community than it is to provide a description of what counts as a cruel or benevolent act. How then can we insist that it is the morality of the acts that has the priority in determining who is virtuous and who not? Instead we should admit, as agent-based ethics hold, that it is the virtuous (or vicious) character of the actor that makes the act virtuous (or vicious). For Slote (1992, pp. 93–6, 159–68; 1995, pp. 86–7), once we have recognised that there is no necessary reason why our intuitions about the ethics of actions should be seen as fundamental, we are free to recast all our ethical judgements about actions in terms of judgements about the character of agents.

The ethics I develop in what follows is intended to be agent-based. At first sight, an agent-based virtue ethics looks like an extremely odd choice upon which to base conclusions in environmental ethics. Because it seeks to found all its

---

3   The existence of this distinction is not always recognised in discussions of virtue ethics, which fact seems to be responsible for some of the confusion in the area.

ethical claims in claims about the light in which certain actions reveal the character of human beings, such an ethics seems to be paradigmatically anthropocentric. However, given the example as I have set it up, it is hard to see where else we could found an ethics. I have already ruled out claims based in the sufferings or rights of other living things. The only other source of obligation on us (Haynes 1990; McKay 1990; Rolston 1986) might be hypothetical and mysterious intrinsic value that complex inorganic systems are sometimes said to possess. Given the many problems that beset claims about intrinsic value (Rollins 1995, pp. 50–60), the virtue ethical approach is at least worth a try.

The advantage of an agent-based virtue ethics over the more familiar and less ambitious agent-focused ethics is that, in theory, an agent-based approach avoids the need for *any* account of the value of complex inorganic systems. An agent-focused ethics still seems to require some account of the value of such systems, or why it might be wrong to alter them, which is available independently of its claims that a virtuous person would not do so. Although the only way to tell that it is wrong to act in a certain way towards the non-living environment is that a virtuous person would not do it, the reason why the virtuous person would not act that way is because it is in fact wrong to do so (even if it is difficult to specify why). Thus an agent-focused ethics seems to let claims about the moral status of inorganic systems in via the back door. By making the intuitions about the virtues fundamental, an agent-based ethics avoids this difficulty.[4]

Furthermore, an agent-based ethics need not be as human-centred as it first appears. Although it must focus on the character of the human agent, some strong environmental conclusions may follow from an agent-based ethics if it is possible to show that a failure to respond to the environment in certain ways constitutes a vice or that certain sorts of responses are virtuous. These virtues (and vices) need not serve human ends. Even familiar virtues, such as kindness, which do contribute towards human happiness in an obvious fashion, often require that we respond in certain ways to circumstances around us and in this way may place demands upon us which are independent of human interests. For instance, as Slote (1995, pp. 86–7) suggests, kindness may require us to be kind to animals as well as people. The anthropocentrism of virtue ethics therefore need only consist in the fact that its claims are claims upon human beings. However this is a feature of any ethics.

Using an agent-based virtue ethics, I shall argue that terraforming reveals in us two serious defects of character. Firstly, it would demonstrate us to be suffering from an ethically significant aesthetic insensitivity. We would become 'cosmic vandals'. Secondly, it would involve us in the sin of hubris. We show ourselves to be suffering from an excessive pride that blinds us to our own place in the world. In attempting to shape another planet to our ends, we are seeking to become 'as gods'. I shall deal with each of these claims in turn.

---

4 Although no account of the value of complex inorganic systems is required by an agent-based approach, we will see below that such an approach does make possible a certain account of their value.

An Aesthetic Insensitivity

The first vice that, I believe, terraforming would demonstrate in us is a reprehensible aesthetic insensitivity – on a massive scale. Destroying the unique natural landscape of an entire planet to turn it to our own purposes reveals us to be vandals and brutes. For Sagoff (1974), it shows that we lead impoverished lives, being unable to respond appropriately to the beauty that is in the world around us.[5] The argument (Elliot 1989; Hill 1983; Passmore 1975, p. 263) that the destruction of natural environments may reveal in us a problematic aesthetic insensitivity has been made before. What I wish to emphasise in my account, however, is that the virtue ethics I am applying allows that a vice may be demonstrated simply because of the character it reveals in the agent and regardless of any considerations of the consequences it may have.

There are two arguments that suggest that an aesthetic insensitivity is a vice that may render the destruction (or neglect) of beauty wrong simply in itself.

First, the act of destroying beauty is itself reprehensible independently of any consequences that may flow from it. Even if the beauty destroyed would replace itself, it would still be wrong to destroy it precisely because doing so demonstrates an aesthetic insensitivity. This is best illustrated by use of an example. Consider a person who goes hiking in the Snowy Mountains early one morning and discovers, by the edge of a cutting, a stunning array of icicles, a thing of great beauty, formed when the creek, which ran over the cutting at that point, froze over. Let us stipulate that this display is formed anew every night and occasionally disappears completely by the end of the day and, furthermore, that the hiker knows this. We also know that no-one else will be hiking that path that day. Isn't it still the case that if the hiker destroys the icicles, they have demonstrated a significant defect of character and lessened themselves as a person in doing so? The person who casually runs a stick across them, thus destroying them for no reason but a petty act of will, demonstrates an insensitivity to their beauty, which is gross and disturbing. Their destruction of the icicles suggests that they have not seen them clearly. If they had truly seen and comprehended their beauty, they could not have destroyed them. The fact that they were destroyed is not important here, except in that it points to the insensitivity of the vandal. What is significant is the blindness they have displayed to beauty even though no-one else may suffer from its loss. This blindness is a failing on their part. It is a vice.

---

5   Sagoff (1974) is critical of arguments that we should value nature for its beauty. The real reason we should preserve natural environments, he argues, is out of respect for other, less mundane, aesthetic qualities such as 'majesty', 'fierceness', 'power', 'integrity' and the like. The arguments below are also intended to work for aesthetic qualities of this sort. In terraforming Mars, we are likely to display a morally reprehensible blindness to these aesthetic properties of Mars as well. For reasons of parsimony, however, I will refer to those aesthetic qualities, which we consider it deplorable to be insensitive to, simply as 'beauty'.

The second way in which we may demonstrate a troubling insensitivity to beauty, although without destroying it, is by using it to our own purposes, which make no reference to its beauty. Again I will illustrate this by use of an example. Take the case of someone who finds an original Van Gogh – another 'Sunflowers', on hardboard – in the musty attic of their new house. This painting is an object of great – nay extraordinary – beauty. However, our hypothetical discoverer merely glances at it, puts it aside and later turns it upside down and places it on top of a crate in order to make a table on which they can store tins of paint. Let us suppose that doing so does not damage the painting in any way. It is merely being used for a purpose other than that for which it was created. Let us further suppose that, because no-one knew of the existence of this painting, nobody suffers any loss by virtue of its use in this fashion. However, again, a person who acts in this way demonstrates that they are blind to the beauty of the world around them. The way in which they see the object is not the way they should see it. It neglects what any normal person would recognise as the most significant property of the painting – its beauty. This failure to recognise beauty is deplorable.

In each of these examples, although the presence (and neglect) of beauty is necessary to demonstrate the existence of the vice, it is not the fact that beauty is destroyed or neglected that is the source of our condemnation. It is not the consequences of the action that are significant. They are, in each case, benign. Instead, it is the character flaw itself that invites our disapproval. It is true that bad consequences may flow from the vice, such as, for instance, the fact that we would lead impoverished lives if we could not see the beauty around us, but that is not the reason we should avoid the vice. To be insensitive to beauty is deplorable simply in itself, regardless of the consequences that follow from it.[6]

This account of the vice of aesthetic insensitivity would be most powerful if we possessed an objectivist account of beauty. It would then require that we be sensitive even to systems which we do not find in the first instance to be beautiful but which (we recognise) fit some objective description of beauty. However, as Willard (1980, pp. 295–7) maintains, the account would still work with a response-dependent or inter-subjective account of beauty, in which case we would only be required to respond to those systems that normal (or appropriately qualified) observers recognise as beautiful. In either case, the role played by beauty illustrates my earlier claim that an agent-based ethics need not be as human-centred as one might think. In order to avoid demonstrating a vice, we are required to respond to

---

6   We can easily imagine a case where an aesthetically insensitive person benefited from their blindness to beauty and also a case where others profit as well. Perhaps a janitor is employed to burn a series of extremely beautiful and also controversial religious paintings which, if they are not destroyed, will continue to provoke destructive riots in the community. The janitor's lack of aesthetic sensibility makes it possible for him/her to do this with ease where a normal individual would suffer greatly or even be unable to complete the task. Despite the benefits that all concerned reap from the janitor's failure to be moved by beauty, we would still say that it is deplorable.

features of the world around us which are independent of our own interests. If an objectivist account of beauty (Slote 1992, Chapter 10) can be provided then we are required to respond to facts about the world which make no reference to facts about humans at all.[7]

The Sin of Hubris

The other vice which terraforming might involve us in is the sin of hubris. Hubris is a vice, discussed in classical Greek literature and mythology, which is popularly thought to involve 'excessive pride before the gods' (Fischer 1992).[8] For Hill (1983, pp. 216–22) and Reinhardt (1982), it occurs when men (sic) wilfully ignore their limits and seek to become as the gods.[9] Hubris is traditionally punished by disaster. The excess of pride is the undoing of those who possess it and they are put in their place, usually roughly. The paradigmatic example of hubris (Ovid 1916, pp. 407–67, 1929, pp. 67–118), on this understanding, is given in the legend of Icarus, who flew too close to the sun in the attempt to reach heaven and lost his son as a result.

Planetary engineering strikes me as a good candidate for the sort of project which would demonstrate hubris. We would be playing God. This sentiment is never far from the literature. The rhetoric of terraforming is quite self-consciously a rhetoric of transformation and transcendence. Terraforming is not just another project but a project that would make us 'world-makers' (Fogg 1995, p. xi; Haynes 1990).[10] It would mark the next stage of human destiny and the beginning of conquest of space.

---

7   Slote's argument that a virtue ethics can support generalised imperatives analogous to deontic moral prohibitions suggests that, if it is a vice to be blind to beauty, this requirement may even take the form of a deontic imperative.

8   In fact, this is a popular *misunderstanding* of the historical notion of *hybris* (Fischer 1992). Despite the fact that the popular understanding does not accurately represent the original Greek notion, I am going to continue to make use of the popular concept of hubris as described above because it encapsulates the idea of a certain sort of excessive pride or arrogance which is recognisably a vice and is my interest here.

9   Hill argues that certain actions in relation to the environment may demonstrate a failure to appreciate our proper place in the universe, which he in turn links with the absence of a proper humility or a failure to possess a particular kind of self-acceptance. My account here is in sympathy with his, but emphasises the deplorable aspects of the active desire to transform the environment in certain ways.

10   Fogg himself names the desires to transform worlds as *hubris*. The subtitle to Haynes' essay – 'Playing God on Mars' – is in reference to concerns which he suggests were immediately raised when he broached the subject of terraforming at a NASA committee meeting in 1967. Obviously some of the advocates of terraforming are acutely conscious of the grand scale of their ambitions.

What about someone who denies that there are any limits on human activity? Someone who holds that there are no Gods, no-one to challenge, and that human beings can and should forge a glorious destiny. It is obviously unsatisfactory to rely on religious claims about the proper place of humanity. For the argument to be convincing in modern circumstances we must be able to give a non-theistic account of hubris.

There are two strategies we may pursue to develop such an account.

The first and the easiest is to focus on the character and phenomenology of the vice of hubris. It is to give a description of hubris as an attitude and to show that the project of terraforming is both the result of and a source of such attitudes. As noted above, the proponents of terraforming often seem to demonstrate an attitude which is a good *prima facie* candidate for hubris. Classically, hubris involves glorying in one's own powers, a false optimism about them and a haste to put them to the test. A lack of self-knowledge and self-reflection is also characteristic of hubris, as is a dismissive attitude toward both critics and past failures. All of these traits are sometimes evidenced in the discussion of terraforming. The project attracts interest simply because it *is* so dramatic and because of the proof it could provide of the supremacy of the human spirit and our engineering skill. This enthusiasm for terraforming looks particularly damning in the light of past technological disasters on Earth. There is little self-reflection going on in the debate about terraforming (Briggs 1986; Fogg 1995; Haynes 1990; McKay 1990; Rolston 1986), which is largely a technical debate about feasibility and methods and which allows little room for questions about why we would want to engage in such a project.[11]

So the attitudes surrounding and driving terraforming seem to fit the phenomenology of hubris. However, this strategy will not, I suspect, prove effective against an entirely serious (including morally serious) and reflective advocate of terraforming who denies that any of the above attitudes are involved and who challenges the conservative and parochial consequences of the critique. Although the attitudes described above are all, as a matter of contingent fact, demonstrated by current advocates of terraforming, it remains to be argued that they are always likely to be so. In order to meet objections of this type, we need to try to show that the sin of hubris involves a reference to certain sorts of projects. The above attitudes are all part of the burning desire to transgress our limits. We need to give some account of our limits and to show that terraforming is outside them.

The second strategy is thus to try and formulate a (non-theistic) account of humanity's place in the cosmos and of appropriate limits to human activities,

---

11   There is admittedly, at various points in the debate, recognition that the project raises difficult issues in environmental philosophy. There is some debate over whether or not it is a project we should undertake. However, what is lacking is reflection on why we might want to undertake it. Schwartz (2013) is a notable recent exception to this general rule.

in order to show that projects which transgress these demonstrate hubris.[12] It is important to understand that this argument is attempting to show that seeking to transcend certain limits demonstrates hubris and is therefore wrong rather than attempting to show why seeking to transcend certain limits is wrong and therefore demonstrates hubris. It is intended to remain within an agent-based framework. We need an account of our limits in order to better show when people are trying to overcome them. However, the fact that trying to do so is wrong is solely a function of whether it demonstrates hubris or not, which will also depend on any other number of things besides.[13]

How do we distinguish these limits? Again it seems to me that there are two ways we might seek some guide to the limits of proper human action.

The first moves indirectly towards an account of our limits by focusing on the nature of our actions and arguing that certain features are characteristic of projects which seek to transcend our proper limits. There is often a significant relation between our actions and the projects they are part of. In the case of hubris, acts of hubris are usually large, dramatic and unprecedented acts. They are usually punished by disaster. The pride and the fall go hand in hand. The possibility of disaster then, of failure which would bring us low, operates as a sign of hubris. Terraforming certainly involves the possibility of catastrophic failure. Given the scale of the project and the amount of energy involved, failures are likely to be disastrous. Instead of a habitable planet, we may produce one with a poisonous atmosphere or without water or lashed by continual typhoons. Indeed, given the amount of resources and human effort which would need to be dedicated to terraforming anything other than complete success would be a disaster. Note that it is the possibility of disaster rather than its probability which is important here. I am not arguing that the risks are too great or that the costs of failure would be too high. Instead the possibility of a catastrophic failure which would reveal our ambitions as arrogant and futile acts as an indication that the project is one which oversteps the limits of our wisdom and abilities.

Secondly, we might attempt more directly to flesh out the idea of our own proper human place. We could try to gain a sense of possible limits to the ambitions which are appropriate to human beings. When considering terraforming, because the limit we are considering here is the physical limit of being confined to a single planet, it seems fair to invoke the metaphor of 'our proper place' in a spatial sense. However, this metaphor (Hill 1983, pp. 216–20; Reinhardt 1982) can also be

---

12   This project is, I believe, an important one even outside of the context of the current argument. It seems to me that any complete ethics would provide an account of what it is to lose our humanity and why this has often been thought to be one of the greatest disasters which can befall a moral agent. There are some desires such as the desire to become immortal or to be as gods which, if we were to realise them, would involve the loss of our humanity. We need some account of why such projects are monstrous.

13   As I will argue below, at the very least it depends on the history of the agent and the context of her actions.

understood more generally to pose the question of our proper place in the scheme of things or the limits of the sphere of human activity.[14] To say that some location or area is 'our proper place' is not an empty thought. It implies a certain relation of appropriateness in our presence there. A proper place is one in which one can flourish without too much of a struggle. It is one that we can live in and sustain. It is a place in which one 'fits' and does not appear uncomfortable or 'out of place'.

It is *prima facie* implausible to suggest that Mars is our proper place. The vast amount of effort required for us to sustain a presence there, even to the point of entirely transforming the planet, indicates that it is not a natural environment for us. Our presence there would be analogous to that of a penguin in the Sahara or a rabbit underwater. If we have to wear space suits to visit and to completely remodel it in order to stay, then it's simply not our place. Another way to try to understand our 'proper place' is by relating it to the idea of a home. It seems natural to say of most creatures, at least as individuals and perhaps as species, that they have a home. This is a place which nurtures them, in which they grow up, reproduce and which offers them some semblance of safety. It is difficult to say of human beings collectively, who have colonised all reaches of the globe, where our 'home' is. However, 'Earth' looks like a plausible answer. Planets seem to have a certain status as possible homes for creatures because of their nature as whole self-contained systems on which life can evolve. The relation between the idea of a 'home' and the idea of our proper place that I am suggesting is an ethical one. Our proper place is at home until we have shown that we are mature enough to leave it. Whether or not people are ready to leave home depends on how well they live at home and how they look after that home. On this test, the human species does not look well qualified to start moving out to other planets. We must show that we are capable of looking after our current 'home' before we could claim to have any place on another. For the moment, at least, our proper place is on Earth and the desire to colonise other planets is indicative of hubris.

These arguments are explicitly parochial. They hold that human beings are limited creatures, whose ambitions should not seek to escape these limits and with a proper place in the natural world.[15] However, note that even denying that human

---

14   Hill discusses what might be involved in appreciation of our 'place in the universe'. His discussion links it to a certain sort of humility. While suggestive, Hill's treatment of the issue is obviously not sufficient for my purposes. If our 'proper place' is defined by reference to humility (or the absence of hubris), then my argument that to seek to transcend it demonstrates hubris will be circular. Reinhardt's meditations on the attitude that it is appropriate for us to take towards nature are less obviously so and are useful in this regard. My argument here rests on the hope that it will be possible to give an account of our proper place which is conceptually independent of intuitions about hubris (or humility).

15   I am not sure how to argue further with someone who denies this absolutely, in the sense of denying that there should be any limits on human activity or that humans have any 'place' in the world. Indeed denying this simply looks to me like an expression of hubris. So it may be in fact that the intuition about hubris is foundational – which should not surprise us in an agent-based ethics.

beings have any fixed or proper place in the universe is not necessarily to deny that we have a proper place at the moment. It may be that humans have ultimately no fixed place in the universe, that it is in our nature to explore, wander and alter our environment. Yet this is not to say that we cannot fix our place at a given time. History and context are important here. One can grow into a place, or show that one's place has become too small or (more likely) that one is not suited to occupy one's current place. Given the current state of this planet's ecosystem and the responsibility that human beings bear for this, I think one would be hard pressed to argue that we are morally fit to assume control over another. Until we heal the Earth we have no claim to any further space.

Finally, notice that hubris is a paradigmatic example of an agent-based vice. If we think poorly of someone who demonstrates hubris it is solely because of what they have revealed about their character. Although, as I have argued, the risk of disaster plays some role in determining what sorts of actions demonstrate hubris, the *actual* consequences flowing from these actions are not relevant to our assessment. Indeed there may be no ill consequences resulting from hubris. Those who commit hubris may 'get away with it' and their projects succeed.[16] Nonetheless we may still deplore the character they have demonstrated.

Some Further Reflections

The arguments above, because they proceed via our character, still fall short of justifying a total injunction on terraforming. Rather they suggest that we examine ourselves and how the project reflects on our character before we undertake it. I have tried to show that terraforming is likely to reflect poorly on our character because it would involve blindness to beauty and an excessive faith in our own judgements and abilities. The nature of the project is such that the onus is on those who wish to engage in it that they do not display these vices. However, it remains possible that the project might be undertaken with a different motivation and character. If, for instance, terraforming was a project undertaken with genuine reluctance, in full knowledge of what was being destroyed, because no alternative existed for the survival of the human race, then it would not demonstrate hubris – because hubris involves an enthusiasm for its projects. If it was the case (Briggs 1986) that those involved were fully aware of the beauty that they were destroying and demonstrated genuine regret over the fact, then terraforming might not involve blindness to beauty either.[17]

---

16   It is true that it is internal to the popular concept of hubris that those who commit it are often punished with disaster by the gods. However, such punishment befalls us because hubris is a vice. It is not a vice because we are punished for it.

17   Interestingly, in this regard, Briggs draws a distinction between terraforming Mars and Venus on the grounds that he thinks that Mars is beautiful whereas Venus is not. He also

Note also that when we make assessments about character, we ordinarily take history and context into account. When a parent who has a long history of acts of kindness acts seems to act cruelly towards her child on a particular occasion, we may reassess our judgement of her actions in the light of her history and conclude that this act may well also be a kind one, although we do not yet understand why.[18] Virtues and vices develop and are displayed over extended periods of time, as well as in particular instances. In some cases, our knowledge of an agent's history will give us reason to alter our judgement about an instance. In others, our knowledge of their history will only confirm that they are acting deplorably on this occasion.

What this suggests is that the history of our relation to our current planet is relevant to an assessment of the ethics of terraforming another. If we have been insensitive to the beauty of inorganic features of our own planet, then it is likely that we may be equally insensitive in our designs on another. If we are suffering the consequences of our hubris on Earth (environmental disaster), then it is unlikely that we have left that hubris behind when we desire to terraform Mars. On the other hand, if we can demonstrate a reformed character in our attitude towards the Earth, then perhaps one day we can look to inhabiting other planets without being convicted of these vices.

A Response to Schwartz

James Schwartz (2011; 2013) has criticised these arguments after a version of them first appeared in *Environmental Ethics* (Sparrow 1999). He argues that I fail to establish that terraforming is morally impermissible and suggests that both my claims about the vice of aesthetic insensitivity and the nature of hubris are beset by crucial errors. I believe Schwartz's objections primarily stem from misunderstanding both the nature of my argument and its details. Nevertheless, I think the way in which he has misunderstood my argument itself highlights some of the methodological difficulties involved in evaluating claims about agent-based virtue ethics. Correspondingly, a brief response in this context may assist the reader in understanding the argument I *have* made.

Before I respond to the detail of his criticisms, I must observe that, for the most part, Schwartz is tilting at windmills in so far as he represents me as trying to argue that terraforming is *morally prohibited*. As is made clear in the preceding section, this is a stronger claim than that for which I have argued here (or in the original paper). On an agent-based account, whether or not terraforming is morally

---

believes that if terraforming Mars would release water and in doing so return Mars to an earlier and arguably more beautiful state, then this fact might justify it in the case of Mars.

18   Of course we may also judge, because her action is of the sort that others notorious for their cruelty engage in, that she is demonstrating a vice in this case. However, in either case our judgement moves from our assessment of the character to our assessment of the action.

permissible will depend upon the character of those who are attempting it. While I have offered some reasons to believe that a desire to terraform Mars (or other planets) will usually be vicious, especially while our relation to our own planet remains so vexed, I've also conceded that it is possible to imagine circumstances where this need not be the case. If Schwartz (2011) succeeds, then, in showing that terraforming would be morally permissible were it done with appropriate care and humility or (perhaps) to avoid an urgent threat of species extinction, this would not threaten my thesis that the desire to terraform will usually risk significant vices.

Schwartz's first criticism targets my claim that terraforming need demonstrate an aesthetic insensitivity on the basis that (he holds) it relies upon an idea of objective beauty that is no more plausible than the notion of 'intrinsic value' that I wish to abjure (Schwartz 2013, p. 23). Again, this is misrepresentation of my argument. While it is true that I believe that the argument about aesthetic insensitivity would be *most* powerful if we were able to rely upon a claim about Mars being objectively beautiful, as I explicitly state above, the argument would still work with a response-dependent or inter-subjective account of beauty. Schwartz thinks I need a notion of objective beauty to avoid the possibility that we might simply 'decide' that Mars is not beautiful. However, I cannot see that we would be less inclined to describe someone as suffering from a blindness to beauty when they decide to reject a long-standing consensus about the beauty of some object if we thought that aesthetic judgements should be evaluated (for example) with reference to the assessments of an appropriately situated and qualified community rather than with reference to the objective facts. What matters is that Mars is beautiful (and awe-inspiring and majestic ... and so on) rather than the particular philosophical account we give of the nature of aesthetic judgements or properties.

Schwartz is also critical of both my attempts to explain why terraforming would most likely demonstrate hubris.

He objects that terraforming does not risk catastrophic failure because a failure to produce a breathable atmosphere (for instance) need not be viewed as a catastrophe given that Mars's atmosphere is already poisonous and that we might gain valuable scientific knowledge in the attempt. This strikes me as an attempt to make a silk purse out of a sow's ear, if ever there was one! If humans were to spend 500 years and untold trillions of dollars in the attempt to produce a breathable atmosphere on Mars, failure to achieve this goal would, I submit, be a catastrophe. The fact that we might have learned something along the way would not alter this.

Schwartz's criticisms of my attempts to provide a non-theistic account of humanity's 'proper place', which might support the intuition that terraforming involves the desire to transcend appropriate limits on human activities, are more compelling. Schwartz points out that the various criteria I put forward for distinguishing our 'home' or 'proper place' would also imply that large portions of the Earth are not appropriate places for human beings to settle. Yet a place may be one's home without one being able to live in every part of it: I can't, for instance, live in the oven or chimney of the house that is my home. Similarly, things may have a proper place that it is appropriate to characterise with a description that includes some areas that are in fact hostile to them in some circumstances. Moreover, when it comes to the question of whether terraforming other planets would involve us in transgressing our proper limits, it is the home or place of human beings considered collectively or as the species *Homo sapiens* that is at issue rather than the home or place of individual humans. It still seems plausible to me to insist that 'Earth' is the proper place of, and a home for, human beings in a way that Mars is not.[19]

It must be admitted however that Schwartz's line of objections is one that my attempt to found substantive claims about the morality of terraforming in an agent-based account invites. I have argued that terraforming is wrong because – and in so far – it would involve those advocating or doing it in morally significant vices. To put this strongly: it is the aesthetic insensitivity and/or hubris, which I have suggested it would involve, that makes it wrong. However, in order to substantiate the claim that terraforming is likely to involve these vices, I have had to tell a story about terraforming that makes reference to the nature of the project and its relation to concepts like 'beauty', 'home' and 'our proper place'. It's understandable, then, that Schwartz contests this story and objects that it need not involve such vices. Indeed, while I have suggested that it is more likely to than he argues, I've also conceded this possibility. Yet more fundamentally, this is, in some sense – as I have also indicated – to locate the argument in the wrong place: on an agent-based account the character of the agent is supposed to determine the ethics of the action rather than the action of the character of the agent. Precisely how to draw conclusions from – or argue about – truths about character, which are prior to claims about actions, remains one of the key challenges in applying agent-based ethics to practical dilemmas. Schwartz's arguments highlight the extent of this challenge, even if – as I hope is the case – they do not unsettle my conclusions in this particular instance.

Conclusion

When it comes to the ethics of our interactions with complex inorganic systems, then, our actions towards them should be governed by reflection on how those actions reveal our character. We should pay heed to the sort of creatures we demonstrate ourselves to be through our actions – even when our actions affect no living things. We should cultivate virtues and avoid vices in our relation to the

---

19   Schwartz (2011) also argues that the presence of human beings in low Earth orbit, on the International Space Station, demonstrates that our proper place can expand to include space. Nevertheless, there is an enormous distance (if you will forgive the pun) between 'our' presence on the International Space Station and Mars being (or becoming) our proper place.

natural world.[20] I have argued that there are two vices in particular that we may demonstrate when we act to terraform other planets – an insensitivity or blindness to beauty and hubris, an excessive pride or faith in our own abilities – which motivate us to try to transcend our proper limits. When we contemplate radically reshaping the surfaces and atmospheres of other planets, we should pause to reflect on whether we reveal ourselves to be blind to their beauty in doing so or to be suffering from hubris.[21]

Finally, as I suggested earlier, the agent-based virtue ethics that I have developed here makes possible a further account of the value of complex inorganic systems, such as the other planets in our solar system. They have value by virtue of the character traits that they can expose in us. They are a sort of moral touchstone. We should treasure them because they allow us to demonstrate certain virtues and vices and thus potentially allow us to become better people. While this reason to preserve such systems is a consequence of my agent-based account, it is itself not a reason within that account. This value that complex systems have is not, at least initially, the reason why we should not destroy them. We should not do this where it would be deplorable to do so and its being so is not a function of the fact that such systems allow us to demonstrate the virtues. However, this fact may provide a further instrumental and explicitly anthropocentric reason for preserving them.[22]

References

Aristotle 1976, *The Nicomachean Ethics*, translated by J.A.K. Thomson, Penguin Books Ltd, Harmondsworth, original work published in 1953.
Baron, M. 1985, 'Varieties of Ethics of Virtue', *American Philosophical Quarterly*, 22(1): 47–53.

---

20   I have focused on vices in this chapter because my concern has been to show why we should not engage in certain sorts of projects. However, it will also be true that for each of the vices I have discussed, there will be a corresponding virtue. We should aim to cultivate within ourselves an appreciation of the beauty of the world around us and, in place of hubris, we should seek to instil in ourselves a humility in the face of the natural world and a sense of our own limited place within it. The existence of such virtues explains why we may perceive activities such as bushwalking or gardening to be admirable, as well as why we find much to admire in the attitude of some indigenous cultures towards the world around them. Schwartz (2011; 2013) points out, quite correctly, that the exploration of space, which offers many opportunities for intense aesthetic experiences as well as for reflection on our place in the universe, may also help us to cultivate and exercise these virtues.

21   In an earlier version of this chapter (Sparrow 1999), I argued that the construction of tourist resorts in wilderness areas and the development and use of recombinant DNA technologies might involve us in both these vices.

22   I would like to thank Mark Huba for his able assistance in preparing this chapter for publication.

Beech, M. 2009, *Terraforming: The Creating of Habitable Worlds*. New York: Springer.

Briggs, G. 1986, 'The exploration and utilization of the planets', in E. Hargrove (ed.), *Beyond Spaceship Earth*. San Francisco, CA: Sierra Club Books.

Elliot, R. 1989, 'Environmental degradation, vandalism and the aesthetic object argument', *Australasian Journal of Philosophy*, 67(2): 191–204.

Elliot, R. 1995, 'Faking nature', in R. Elliot (ed.), *Environmental Ethics*. New York: Oxford University Press.

Fischer, N.R.E. 1992, *Hybris: A Study in the Values of Honour and Shame in Ancient Greece*. Warminster: Aris & Phillips.

Fogg, M. 1995, *Terraforming: Engineering Planetary Environments*. Warrendale, PA: SAE International,

Foot, P. 1978, *Virtue and Vices and Other Essays in Moral Philosophy*. Berkeley and Los Angeles: University of California Press.

Haynes, R.H. 1990, 'Ecce Ecopoiesis: playing God on Mars', in D. MacNiven (ed.), *Moral Expertise: Studies in Practical and Professional Ethics*. London: Routledge.

Hearne, V. 1986, *Adam's Task: Calling Animals by Name*. New York: Alfred A. Knopf.

Hill, T. 1983, 'Ideals of human excellence and preserving natural environments', *Environmental Ethics*, 5: 211–24.

Louden, R. 1984, 'On some vices of virtue ethics', *American Philosophical Quarterly*, 21(3): 227–36.

MacIntyre, A. 1984, *After Virtue*. Notre Dame, IN: University of Notre Dame Press.

McDowell, J. 1978, 'Are moral requirements hypothetical imperatives?', *Proceedings of the Aristotelian Society*, LII, supplementary volume, pp. 13–29.

McDowell, J. 1979, 'Virtues and reasons', *The Monist*, 62(3): 331–54.

McKay, C.P. 1990, 'Does Mars have rights? An approach to environmental ethics of planetary engineering', in D. MacNiven (ed.), *Moral Expertise: Studies in Practical and Professional Ethics*. London: Routledge.

McKibben, B. 1989, *The End of Nature*. New York: Random House.

Ovid 1929, *The Art of Love, and Other Poems*, translated by J.H. Mozley. Cambridge, MA: Harvard University Press.

Ovid, 1916, *Metamorphoses*, translated by F.J. Miller. Cambridge, MA: Harvard University Press.

Passmore, J. 1975, 'Attitudes to nature', in R.S. Peters (ed.), *Nature and Conduct*. London: Macmillan.

Passmore, J. 1974, *Man's Responsibility for Nature*. London: Duckworth.

Reinhardt, L. 1982, 'Some gaps in moral space: reflections on forests and feelings', in D.S. Mannion, M.A. McRobbie and R. Routley (eds), *Environmental Philosophy*, Department of Philosophy, Research School of Social Sciences, Australian National University, Monograph Series, Canberra.

Rollin, B. 1995, *The Frankenstein Syndrome: Ethical and Social Issues in the Genetic Engineering of Animals*. New York: Cambridge University Press.

Rolston, H. 1986, 'The preservation of natural value in the solar system', in E. Hargrove (ed.), *Beyond Spaceship Earth*. San Francisco, CA: Sierra Club Books.

Sagoff, M. 1974, 'On preserving the natural environment', *Yale Law Journal*, 84(2): 205–67.

Schwartz, J.S.J. 2013, 'On the moral permissibility of terraforming', *Ethics and the Environment*, 18(2): 1–31.

Schwartz, J.S.J. 2011, 'Our Moral Obligation to Support Space Exploration', *Ethics and the Environment*, 33(1): 67–88.

Slote, M. 1992, *From Morality to Virtue*. Oxford: Oxford University Press.

Slote, M. 1990, *Goods and Virtues*. Oxford: Oxford University Press.

Solomon, D. 1988, 'Internal objections to virtue ethics', *Midwest Studies in Philosophy*, 13(1): 428–41.

Sparrow, R. 1999, 'The ethics of terraforming', *Environmental Ethics*, 21(3): 227–45.

Todd, P. 2006, 'Planetary biology and terraforming', *Gravitational and Space Biology*, 19(2): 79–84.

Tudge, C. 1993, *The Engineer in the Garden*. London: Jonathan Cape.

Willard, L.D. 1980, 'On preserving nature's aesthetic features', *Ethics*, 2(4): 291–310.

PART IV
Space Weapons

Chapter 14

Seizing the High Ground? The Dubious Utility of Space Weapons

Armin Krishnan

Since the beginning of the modern space age, American space warriors have consistently claimed that outer space represents the new military high ground and that it was imperative to seize control of outer space in order to gain a military advantage in future conflicts on Earth and in space. Early spacewar advocate General Thomas Dresser White reformulated the airpower doctrine into a new space power doctrine: 'Whoever has the capability to control the air is in a position to exert control over the land and seas beneath. I feel that in the future whoever has the capability to control space will likewise possess the capability to exert control of the surface of the Earth …' (Stares 1985, p. 48). This sentiment was echoed more than 40 years later in Space Command's *Vision for 2020* (1998) and in the even more hawkish Space Commission Report (2001). The latter document bluntly declared a need to develop space weapons. It stated: 'It is also possible to project power through and from space in response to events anywhere in the world. Unlike weapons from aircraft, land forces or ships, space missions initiated from Earth or space could be carried out with little transit, information or weather delay. Having this capability would give the U.S. a much stronger deterrent and, in a conflict, an extraordinary military advantage' (US Space Commission 2001, p. 33).

Space war theorists have drawn persuasive comparisons of space warfare with aerial warfare and naval warfare to support the argument that outer space is destined to become not only *a* new battle ground, but potentially *the* decisive domain of war that will dominate all other major domains of warfare (land, sea, air and cyberspace). The US seems to be determined to weaponise space in the pursuit of military advantage and global domination. The George W. Bush administration took some concrete steps to make space wars a reality when they quit the Antiballistic Missile (ABM) Treaty in 2002, which had become an impediment to American efforts of space weaponisation, while also reviving Reagan-era missile defence and directed energy weapons programs. The successful Chinese test of an ASAT weapon in 2007 and the US subsequently shooting down a failing satellite with a missile one year later seemed to confirm that there is an ongoing arms race in outer space and that we are now on the verge of a new age of space wars with Low Earth Orbit (LEO) quickly becoming a major battlefield or a 'global no-fly zone' (Dolman 2010, p. 4).

Although it is notable that at least the US, Russia, China and India have demonstrated a potential ASAT capability over the years, none of them has up to now deployed operational ASAT weapons or has shown much enthusiasm for placing *offensive* weapons in space. As a matter of fact, Russia and China have even proposed an international treaty for the Prevention of an Arms Race in Outer Space in 2008 with a clear prohibition of 'weapons in outer space', which has been repeatedly rejected by the US government (Moore 2008, pp. XVIII–XIX). It is argued in this chapter that despite the mostly American space war rhetoric, there is in reality little benefit of either fighting *in* space or *from* space. Fighting in space is likely to produce space debris that becomes also a danger to own space assets. In addition, it would be an act of war to interfere with space assets of another nation and thus could result in a nuclear response by the attacked nation. Fighting from space to attack targets on Earth is much more expensive and can deliver far less force than is possible through terrestrial-based weapons. These have been the main reasons why space weaponisation has not occurred even almost 60 years after the first satellites started orbiting Earth. There are few indications that space wars would become any more tenable in the future than they are now. However, certain institutional and private actors in the US have a great stake in space warfare and they have been keeping the idea alive regardless of the very obvious negative diplomatic, military, and environmental consequences that could result from space weaponisation.

Defining Space Weapons

The definition of the term 'space weapon' matters greatly with respect to the assessment of whether we have already crossed the line to deploying space weapons and whether there is already an ongoing space arms race. Although there is currently no commonly accepted definition of a 'space weapon', it is generally understood that 'space weapons' are weapons that are either based in outer space or that can reach into space (basically ASAT weapons). Outer space begins at an altitude of about 52 miles above the Earth's surface, which is the lowest point at which an object could maintain an orbit (Dolman 2010, p. 115). Therefore, suborbital weapons that stay below 52 miles or fall back to Earth before reaching a stable orbit, such as ICBMs, hypersonic cruise vehicles, suborbital space planes or high altitude airships, should not be considered to be space weapons although they are sometimes included in discussions of space warfare.

For greater analytical clarity, many space warfare analysts distinguish the notion of the *militarisation of space* from the *weaponisation of space*, in which militarisation of space is a continuum with weaponisation representing the upper range of the spectrum (Mueller 2003, p. 3). Space has been militarised in the sense of becoming a medium for military operations since the early 1960s when the first military Earth observation and communications satellites were deployed. The overall roles, capabilities and usage of space assets have continuously grown ever since. The 1991 Gulf War is usually credited with having been the first 'space war', as the US and its allies relied on no fewer than 60 satellites for reconnaissance, communications, navigation, early warning and weather monitoring (Anson and Cummings 1991, p. 45). Since 1999 the US military has also used satellite-guided bombs and cruise missiles, which have greatly improved the precision of conventional bombing. It is thus debatable whether the hypothetical line from space militarisation to space weaponisation has already been crossed (Dolman et al. 2006, pp. 11–12). However, space weaponisation, especially the idea of placing weapons in space, remains a diplomatically extremely sensitive matter since it violates a perceived fundamental taboo expressed in the Outer Space Treaty. The treaty clearly prohibits basing 'nuclear weapons and any other kinds of weapons of mass destruction' in space and urges all signatories to use outer space 'for the benefit of all peoples' and for 'peaceful purposes' only (United Nations 1967, Art. IV and Preamble). However, not all space weapons are equally threatening or equally unacceptable.

Space weapons can be distinguished according to a set of criteria that help determine the 'space weapon-ness' of a space weapon: 1) where they are based (Earth-basing or space-basing or pop-up); 2) what its primary intended targets are (location or type); 3) what kind of weapon mechanism they use (KE, DE, nuclear, electronic and so on); 4) whether they can achieve a 'soft kill' (disabling effect) or a 'hard kill' (physical destruction); 5) whether they are likely to cause collateral or environmental damage (space debris); and 6) what their main military utility would be (defensive or offensive posture) (Mueller 2003, p. 5). The least threatening space weapon would be therefore a terrestrial-based defensive weapon directed merely against the offensive weapons of an adversary (for example a ballistic missile defence (BMD) system), while the most threatening and thus least acceptable space weapon would be a permanently orbiting space-to-terrestrial weapon that can cause massive physical destruction on Earth (a first-strike weapon). The following section will look at the main types of existing or proposed space weapons.

Terrestrial-based BMD/ASAT

Any terrestrial BMD that can reach into space with an interceptor missile or a laser has at least a latent ASAT capability. The first BMD weapons that could be also used against satellites were interceptor missiles with a nuclear warhead that could be detonated in the vicinity of an incoming missile or a satellite. The US deployed such systems in the 1960s, including the Nike Zeus, Spartan and Sprint missiles, while the Soviets developed the similar Galosh and Gazelle missiles. Deployment of these systems was later severely restricted by the 1972 ABM Treaty. However, in the 1980s both superpowers tested aircraft-based ASAT systems that could attack satellites in LEO. The US conducted five ASAT tests in 1984 and 1985 with the ASM-135 system fired from at a steep angle from a F-15 jet and the Soviets tested the 'Kontakt' system fired from a MiG-31D in 1984. Both the US and the Soviet airborne ASAT systems were cancelled in the late 1980s (Weeden

2008). The US has several ground-based BMD systems that can destroy satellites in LEO. Up to now only a few nations could shoot down satellites from Earth with interceptor missiles, but they include the US adversaries China, Iran and North Korea (Zenko 2014, p. 1).

Alternatively, it is possible to attack satellites with a ground-based laser to either temporarily blind them (imaging satellites are particularly vulnerable) or to destroy them. The US blinded one of its satellites with a laser from the ground in 1997 and is developing a ground-based laser as an ASAT weapon (Broad 2006). The Chinese have at least on one occasion directed a dazzling laser at an American satellite (Moore 2008, p. 50). However, it seems unlikely that ground-based laser could do any serious damage to a satellite in orbit (Butt 2009, p. 20). Finally, the communications (uplink and downlink) of satellites can be electronically jammed from Earth, which is a low cost method of (temporarily) disabling satellites that are in reach of even unsophisticated adversaries (Ackerman 2005) or satellites could be disabled through cyber warfare (Bowcott 2013).

Space-based BMD

SDI explored several possibilities for a space-based BMD system, none of which was ever deployed. One system was called 'brilliant pebbles', which would have utilised a large number of interceptor satellites in orbit that could destroy incoming missiles by manoeuvring towards them and colliding with them. The original planning envisioned 4,600 'pebbles' in orbit, which would have been sufficient to overload any Soviet ASAT capability (Yenne 2005, p. 325). A more ambitious and expensive system was the space-based laser (SBL) that could shoot down multiple ICBMs in rapid succession. Its main advantage would be that it could engage ICBMs in the boost stage when they are still slow, far away from the defender's territory, and before they could disperse decoys or submunitions. Like the brilliant pebbles, the SBL did also face enormous engineering challenges, but unlike the brilliant pebbles, the program survived the Cold War. The BMDO awarded in 1998 a contract to develop a Space-Based Laser Readiness Demonstrator, which envisioned a constellation of 12 to 24 SBLs of a size of 17.5 tonnes each, using a chemical laser that could kill incoming missiles in bursts of 1 to 10 seconds with retargeting in less than 0.5 seconds (Rogers 2001, p. 82). The program was cancelled in 2002 because of cost overruns and the technological complexity of the project.

Space-based ASAT

There are numerous ways how a satellite could destroy or disable another satellite, ranging from explosion (nuclear and non-nuclear), collision, kinetic energy (KE) projectiles, directed energy weapons (DEW), non-nuclear EMP (HERF), signal jamming and so on. The simplest and cheapest method is the use of 'space mines' that are placed in a nearby orbit to the target satellite and that can be triggered when the other satellite is close. However, co-orbital space mines forfeit the element of surprise (Collins 1989, p. 58). Having satellites in a different orbit makes it more challenging to manoeuvre them in a position where they can attack another satellite. The Soviets have first successfully tested a 'killer satellite' that could manoeuvre towards a target satellite and destroy it through explosion in 1968 and they managed to have an operational system by 1978, which was later abandoned (Zak 2013). The US also developed a number of concepts for killer satellites, but never deployed any. Most valuable would be a space-based ASAT that could disable or destroy a satellite without causing space debris. In 2013 the Chinese demonstrated that they can do that: they manoeuvred a satellite towards another satellite and captured it with a robotic arm (David 2013). Research on space-based ASAT weapons has been ongoing since the 1950s and they could be easily deployed by a number of countries very soon if there was sufficient political will to do so.

Orbital Bomber

The Nazi engineer Eugen Sänger envisioned already in the mid-1930s a suborbital bomber codenamed Silverbird that could exit the atmosphere and reach the United States in series of bounces where it would gain very high altitude and drop again. The US Air Force (USAF) has been fascinated by this idea and has since the 1950s attempted to build an orbital bomber that could reach any point in the world in a few hours. Based on Sänger's 'skip-glide'-design, the USAF decided to develop a space plane codenamed Dyna-Soar or X-20 in 1958. The Soviets had a similar project called MiG-105. Even more ambitious was the Air Force's idea to build a 250-tonne space plane that could fly on Earth *and* to the Moon (Yenne 2005, p. 145). Although several projects of this kind were cancelled because they lacked a clear purpose or were too ambitious, the USAF has never given up on the idea of a space plane or common aero vehicle (CAV). In 2010 it first tested the X-37 unmanned space shuttle that rides to space on an Atlas V booster and that can manoeuvre in LEO, deorbit and land like a plane. However, the X-37 is most likely not any sort of weapon, but rather a sensor platform that can manoeuvre in orbit more easily than satellites (Hsu 2010). Other nations have also declared the goal of building a space plane. For example, Britain wants to test a space plane by 2020 and China and Russia have made similar announcements.

Orbital Bombardment

Placing weapons in orbit for bombing targets on Earth seems like a straightforward idea right out of a James Bond movie. One could launch a devastating attack on a country within minutes or threaten immediate destruction if demands are not met. These benefits in mind, the Soviets developed the Fractional Orbital Bombardment System (FOBS) that would have enabled them to place targetable nuclear warheads in orbit over the US or to attack the US in a fractional orbit from the South coming over the South Pole (Yenne 2005, p. 66). Realising the massive destabilising effect of space-based nuclear weapons, both sides agreed in the Outer Space Treaty not to place nuclear weapons in space. This unfortunately left the door open to orbital kinetic bombardment platforms. RAND suggested already in the 1950s to place bundles of hypervelocity rods made out of a dense material (tungsten or depleted uranium) in orbit that could be dropped from space on terrestrial targets that they would destroy through kinetic impact alone. A 20-foot long and one-foot wide tungsten rod dropped from GEO could reach a speed of Mach 10 and produce a truly devastating effect comparable to a low-yield nuclear weapon, but without the radiation. Furthermore, the rods could penetrate deep into the ground to destroy underground bunkers. The USAF indicated in its 2003 *Transformation Flight Plan* document that it seeks the capability 'to strike ground targets anywhere in the world from space' and explicitly mentions 'hypervelocity rod bundles' (US Air Force 2003, p. D-7), but it does not seem that there would be any funding for such a program.

The Questionable Military Utility of Space Weapons

Without doubt, first steps have been taken in the direction of weaponising space since the beginning of the space age and space wars have become more technologically feasible in recent years. It has been possible for a long time to fight in space and from space. At the same time, there is little reason to believe that occupying the ultimate high ground could result in the kind of decisive advantage that space warriors claim. It would thus be unreasonable for the US to invest very substantial amounts of money (possibly trillions) into defensive or offensive space warfare capabilities.

The Vulnerability of Space Assets

The general problem in space warfare is that space assets of any kind will always be very vulnerable. Outer space is an extremely dangerous environment and there is no terrain where one could hide. All satellites orbiting Earth are generally visible from Earth through optical means and they can be easily tracked by radar. They move on predictable trajectories and they have only a very limited ability to manoeuvre – most satellites cannot change their orbit by themselves and those that can carry only limited amounts of fuel. Space launches that place satellites in orbit cannot be hidden. Even stealth satellites invisible to radar can in principle be discovered through optical means and an analysis of open source information like the fabled 'Misty' that was discovered by a hobby astronomer in the early 1990s shortly after its launch (Paglen 2010, p. 119).

Any nation with a space launch capability could destroy satellites by placing some objects in their orbital path that would collide with them at high speed. At an orbiting speed of 17,000 mph even a bag of nails could literally shred a fragile object like a satellite. One could also deny others the use of their space assets by attack from the ground with lasers or electronic jammers or by attacking ground control stations. Space-based offensive ASAT weapons are not necessary to deny others the use of space. Space-based defensive ASAT weapons like 'bodyguard'-satellites that could pre-emptively attack enemy spaceborne ASATs are not likely to make space assets significantly more secure in view of the great range of ASAT attack options (Butt 2008).

Of course, any space-based offensive weapon that can attack terrestrial targets would be particularly hard to hide because of its necessary size and the need to conduct highly visible weapons tests in space. A 'rod of God' platform or SBL could not be deployed covertly. Despite some greater possibilities for hardening due to size, it would be still difficult to defend since adversaries might opt to take it out with a nuclear missile. Its mere existence would be unacceptable to great powers that could be targeted by such a space weapon, namely Russia and China, and would create strong incentives for them to attack it pre-emptively before it becomes operational or during a crisis.

Environmental Hazards of the Weaponisation of Space

Space warfare would create several environmental hazards that could impact on humanity's ability to use space and could cause environmental damage to the Earth. First of all, space weaponisation would make it necessary to transport even more and much bigger satellites with hazardous materials on board into space. Any accident during a space launch could turn into an environmental disaster. Most worrying is the use of nuclear materials and nuclear reactors in satellites and spaceborne weapons. A report to Congress suggests that nuclear reactors are 'the only known long-lived, compact source able to supply military space forces with electric power' (Collins 1989, p. 108). Several military satellites containing nuclear materials have uncontrollably deorbited in the past. For example, the Soviet Cosmos 954 satellite crashed in Canada in 1978 and the materials had to be recovered and the site decontaminated (Richelson 2009, pp. 48–68). A failing US satellite was shot down by the US Navy in 2008 to prevent the highly toxic hydrazine tank to crash on Earth.

Space weaponisation would encourage placing many more satellites into an already very crowded circumterrestrial space, which would make accidents much more likely. There are over 1,100 active satellites in orbit (half of which are in LEO) and over 2,000 inactive satellites that have become space junk, plus 23,000 smaller pieces of space junk that are tracked by NASA and about 170 million pieces of debris that are too small to be catalogued and tracked (Slann 2013). In 2009 an American Iridium satellite collided with the Russian Cosmos 2251 satellite, producing over 1,600 additional fragments (Wang 2010, p. 87). The 2007 Chinese ASAT test has reportedly produced 3,000 fragments, some of which are going to orbit Earth for 500 years and threaten other satellites in LEO (Talent 2007). Up to now there are few available methods to clear growing amounts of space debris. Even if satellites could be destroyed without fragmenting them, it would still increase the amount of space junk since they would stay in orbit and would need to be replaced by additional satellites. Many critics of space warfare therefore fear that space war could massively compound the problem of space debris, making outer space effectively unusable for humanity. Mankind would be entombed on Earth. Fighting in space, especially in the crowded circumterrestrial space, would create huge problems for everybody, including the nations that employ ASATs.

High Cost and Engineering Challenges

One of the biggest obstacles to any kind of space weapon is the extremely high cost of launching anything into space, especially when it comes to basing any large multi-tonne weapons platform in space. It costs in average about $20,000 to transport 1 kg into LEO using booster rockets. As long as rockets are used for space launches it will be very difficult to reduce space transportation costs substantially (Coopersmith 2011, pp. 77–8). A weapons platform in space would most likely cost billions of dollars in space transportation costs alone. The weapons platform would need to carry sufficient amounts of ammunition, be it chemicals for a laser or KE projectiles for a hit-to-kill weapon. Rearming the platform after usage would be expensive. At least a dozen weapons platforms in space would be needed for coverage to avoid the problem of having to manoeuvre a weapons platform in orbit to reach a good firing position on a particular target. The American Physical Society even estimated that for a space-based BMD system, 1,600 space-based interceptors weighing a tonne each would be necessary for global coverage (Hitchens and Samson 2004, p. 24). This could be worth it if space-basing weapons would offer unique capabilities that are far beyond terrestrial-based systems. This does not seem to be the case. Space-based weapons offer relatively little 'bang for the buck'.

The best argument for space-based weapons would be their utility for BMD. However, critics have pointed at various issues with the whole idea of BMD, regardless of whether it was a space-based or terrestrial system. This includes the possibility of overloading any defensive system through a massive attack, the decoy problem, the enormous speed and precision required for any BMD system to work, not to speak of the possibility that there are many alternative ways for an adversary to deliver payloads, including cruise missiles or the literal nuclear bomb in a suitcase (Graybosch 1988, p. 55). BMDs would hurt crisis stability, encourage adversaries to respond with building more offensive weapons and could result in an illusion of invulnerability (Kavka 1985, p. 686). Furthermore, spaceborne BMD would create incentives for adversaries to develop ASAT capabilities to attack such systems or spaceborne C^3I systems needed to make BMDs function, which undermines the idea that BDM can enhance deterrence or even limit damage in a major attack (Graybosch 1988, pp. 53–7). Analysts have also pointed out that any chemical laser would consume vast amounts of chemicals and that this could make such a weapon impractical for space-basing (Spacy 2003, p. 164). It is already difficult to put a chemical laser on a Boeing 747 that can carry 100,000 pounds in payload, but there is not even a rocket that could launch a 40-tonne SBL into orbit. Precise targeting from space can be an issue due to the movement generated by the laser system itself (O'Hanlon 2004, p. 79). The use of kinetic kill vehicles fired from a space weapons stations against an incoming missile in the boost stage as an alternative to an SBL would make no sense since they would need hours to reach their targets (Weeden 2008).

In theory, an SBL might be effective for engaging a range of terrestrial targets, including military bases, chemical manufacturing plants or refineries (Rogers 2001, p. 76). However, William Spacy argues '[t]he inherent "hardness" of most militarily significant surface targets coupled with the difficulty of maintaining the integrity of the laser beam as it transits the atmosphere makes destroying them with an orbital laser problematic' (Spacy 2003, p. 167). While 'rods from God' seem to be a more promising idea than a space-based chemical laser, critics have pointed out the numerous practical problems that need to be overcome to make such a system work. The physicist Richard Garwin argues that rods made out of even the hardest material would liquefy at impact speeds above 1 km/s, which means they would need to be slowed down in flight through a rocket engine and that they 'could only deliver one ninth the destructive energy per gram as a conventional bomb' (Garwin 2003, p. 4). Deeply buried targets may not be as vulnerable to a 'rods from God'-attack than previously believed. Many countries have the capability of constructing tunnels several hundred feet deep. To penetrate such tunnels the rods would need to be too big to be practical (Spacy 2003, p. 203).

A space plane might offer greater advantages than the space-basing of weapons: 1) it can reach any point on Earth within hours; 2) it could be used as a responsive temporary and manoeuvrable sensor platform in orbit, for example replacing space capabilities lost in an attack; 3) it could interfere with enemy satellites in a way that does not cause debris, for example capturing them; and 4) it could deliver payloads from space to any location with great precision. However, some key problems with respect to an orbital bomber have not yet been solved. First of all, the system would most likely have to reach orbit with a rocket, which makes it by definition very expensive to use. For example, the cost of lifting the unmanned X-37 into space on an Atlas V booster costs at least $100 million per launch (Hsu 2010). The space plane would only be able to carry a very limited amount of payload or troops (1,000 to 2,000 pounds). Once it deorbited it could not by itself reach the orbit again, which means that it could not easily return home and might be therefore in the context of many scenarios not actually reusable. An orbital bomber would also run into the same problems as conventional ICBMs: nations with an early warning system could easily detect the space plane launch/ re-entry, but they have no way of knowing whether it carries a nuclear warhead or what its intended target is. Furthermore, it makes little sense to base troops in outer space or celestial bodies like the Moon as rapid response forces for earthly emergencies. The costs of sustaining human life under hostile conditions of outer space for even a short period of time are far too high to contemplate 'Starship Trooper'-inspired orbital landings.

Terrestrial Alternatives and Responsive Access to Space

Despite some obvious advantages of satellites such as global coverage and low maintenance costs, there is actually little that can only be done from space and not from Earth. High-altitude airships and drones could function as low cost alternatives to satellites, providing communications, reconnaissance, surveillance, navigation and targeting services. Manoeuvrable airships could climb above 100,000 feet and cover areas up to 200 km (Jamison et al. 2005, p. 5). Future solar-powered UAVs could remain in the air for months and could be suitable at serving as mobile communications hubs. Private companies like Facebook are already looking into utilising solar-powered drones or high-altitude balloons for providing Internet connectivity to developing countries (Metz 2014). In some ways, unmanned airships, balloons and drones have greater military utility than satellites, especially for the types of intrastate low-intensity conflicts that will remain the focus of western militaries in the foreseeable future. They are also much cheaper and offer greater flexibility. They can be easily moved to any geographic area of interest, they can be more cheaply replaced if lost and are not subject to orbital mechanics.

Operating in suborbital space may be in the end much more interesting for modern militaries than outer space. For example, unmanned suborbital hypersonic cruise vehicles could strike any point on Earth within an hour – there is no need to completely leave the atmosphere. Dominating suborbital space could provide opportunities for space control/space superiority, including the control of the weather and the Earth's atmosphere. The USAF can already conduct global bombing missions with its ageing bomber fleet and can rely on stealth rather than on a capability of instant attack from space, which would be in any case extraordinarily expensive and highly destabilising. Over time modern militaries can also systematically reduce their dependency on space systems by switching to suborbital or unmanned airborne and terrestrial systems, which can help them to reduce their vulnerabilities to space warfare and also their overall costs.

In addition, it is likely that it will become much cheaper to transport small payloads of up to a few hundred kilograms into LEO using new and revolutionary methods. One technology that has been under development for some time is a 'space gun' that could shoot up to 500 kg of payload into orbit at a cost of only $250 per pound (Elahi 2010). Another possibility is an 'orbital airship' that could reach the most upper layer of the atmosphere through lighter-than-air flight and cross into space using rockets. In other words, a cheaper and more responsive access to space vastly diminishes any advantage anybody could gain from attacking satellites in LEO since they could be easily replaced and since there would be terrestrial alternatives as back-up.

Conclusion

Considering the enormous problems and challenges that result from any attempt of turning outer space into a battleground and the few real tangible benefits, one has to wonder why the US military even entertains the idea of doing so. The answer to this riddle may be twofold: firstly, there is the sentiment that a space arms race may be beneficial for humanity in the long run because it could jump-start human space exploration after 40 years of neglect, and, secondly, it would create a bonanza for the aerospace industries, while massively elevating the prestige and importance of space forces.

On the face of it, the progress in human space exploration has been greatly disappointing. Despite the ambitious plans of the 1950s and 1960s, there is still no human outpost on Mars and not even a base on the much closer moon. In fact, the last manned Moon landing took place in 1972, more than 40 years ago. The earliest projected dates for any manned mission to either the Moon or Mars are the 2030s and 2040s. Under these conditions it would be only in the later part of the twenty-first century before humanity could even start colonising the solar system, unless there was enough political will to divert enormous wealth and resources towards the conquest of space to reach the stars earlier. In the absence of a superpower competition that made the Apollo landings possible, it is unlikely that such resources could be made available. A new space race could be a solution to break the political deadlock and could be hugely beneficial for mankind in the long run. Space war theorist Everett Dolman also argues that a US empire based on space domination would be more benign and far less threatening than one that relies on forward-based land forces (Dolman 2010).

But far more important than these idealistic views of space weaponisation is the fact that it would greatly benefit particular institutional and private stakeholders, namely the USAF and the military-industrial complex (MIC). Carl Builder has argued that the USAF had lost its direction when it quietly abandoned airpower theory in favour of protecting the factional interests of the institution, sacrificing the unifying ends (the concept of airpower) for the factionalised means (aircraft, missiles, space) (Builder 1994, p. 34). The USAF has now come to embrace space warfare because it represents for them a final frontier and a chance to replace the old airpower doctrine that wrongly assumed that command of the air was strategically decisive with a similarly flawed space power doctrine that could reunify the splintered organisation. Since space warfare would necessitate directing more resources to the USAF, it would diminish the relative prestige and influence of the other service branches. John Arquilla suggests: '[t]he U.S. military is drawn, like Icarus, ever higher. Yet, if it became capable of waging war in space, the results would be as catastrophic as they were for Icarus when he flew too close to the sun' (Arquilla 2006).

The biggest winners, however, would be the aerospace industries that could earn trillions by developing extraordinarily expensive space weapons, transporting them into space and operating them. Since there are only limited possibilities for the space industry to expand their commercial business – demand for commercial satellite launches remains stable and there will not be much demand for other purposes such as space tourism for the time being – the prospect of space weaponisation looks like a great long-term business opportunity, especially with looming defence budget cuts. It is thus no surprise that the MIC and its closely connected think-tanks portray space weaponisation as being inevitable and promote the idea that space warfare capabilities are somehow needed. Bruce Deblois has expressed the concern that '[t]oday we find ourselves in a situation with an absence of clear top-down policy guidance on space weapons, and in such a case, military doctrine can build an inertia of its own, and impact – or even become – the default policy' (Deblois 2003, p. 35). Unfortunately, this could result in the waste of great wealth on a needless space arms race and make disastrous and unnecessary space wars more likely.

References

Ackerman, R.K. 2005, 'Space vulnerabilities threaten U.S. edge in battle', *Signal Magazine*, June, viewed 16 May 2014, http://www.afcea.org/content/?q=node/973.

Adams, E. 2004, 'Rods from God', *Popular Science*, 1 June, viewed 10 May 2014, http://www.popsci.com/scitech/article/2004-06/rods-god.

Anson, P. and Cummings, D. 1991, 'The First Space War: The Contribution of Satellites to the Gulf War', *The RUSI Journal*, 136(4): 45–53.

Arquilla, J. 2006, 'Rods from God', *SF Gate*, 12 March, viewed 5 May 2014, http://www.sfgate.com/opinion/article/RODS-FROM-GOD-Imagine-a-bundle-of-telephone-2539690.php#page-1.

Bowcott, O. 2013, 'Outer space demilitarisation agreement threatened by new technologies', *The Guardian*, 11 September, viewed 23 April 2014, http://www.theguardian.com/science/2013/sep/11/outer-space-demilitarisation-weapons-technologies.

Brewin, B. 2013, 'Pentagon's 2014 budget continues its focus on Asia', *NextGov.com*, 14 April, viewed 16 May 2014, http://www.nextgov.com/defense/2013/04/pentagon-2014-budget-request-includes-47-billion-cyberspace-operations/62406.

Broad, W.J. 2006, 'Administration researches laser weapon', *The New York Times*, 3 May, viewed 16 May 2014, p. A22.

Builder, C.H. 1994, *The Icarus Syndrome: The Role of Air Power Theory in the Evolution and Fate of the U.S. Air Force*. New Brunswick, NJ: Transaction Publishers.

Butt, Y. 2008, 'Can space weapons protect U.S. satellites?', *Bulletin of the Atomic Scientists*, 22 July, viewed 16 May 2014, http://thebulletin.org/can-space-weapons-protect-us-satellites.

Butt, Y. 2009, 'Effects of Chinese laser ranging on imaging satellites', *Science & Global Security*, 17(1): 20–35.

Collins, J.M. 1989, *Military Space Forces: The Next 50 Years*. Washington, DC: Pergamon-Brassey's.

Coopersmith, J. 2011, 'The costs of reaching orbit: Ground-based launch systems', *Space Policy*, 27: 77–80.

David, L. 2013, 'China's satellites have experts guessing about space program's intentions', *Huffington Post*, 11 September, viewed 16 May 2014, http://www.huffingtonpost.com/2013/09/11/china-satellite-mystery_n_3901540.html.

DeBlois, B.M. 2003, 'The advent of space weapons', *Astropolitics*, 1(1): 20–53.

DeBlois, B.M., Garwin, R.L., Kemp, R.S. and Marwell, J.C. 2004, 'Space weapons: Crossing the U.S. rubicon', *International Security*, 29(2): 50–84.

Dolman, E.C. 2001, *Astropolitik: Classical Geopolitics in the Space Age*. London: Frank Cass.

Dolman, E.C. 2010, 'The case for weapons in space: A geopolitical assessment', *American Political Science Association Meeting*, Washington, DC, viewed 16 May 2014, http://papers.ssrn.com/sol3/papers.cfm?abstract_id=1676919.

Dolman, E.C., Hays, P., Mueller and K.B. 2006, 'Towards a U.S. grand strategy in space', *George C. Marshall Institute*, Washington Roundtable on Science & Public Policy, Washington, DC, viewed 16 May 2014, http://marshall.org/events/toward-a-u-s-grand-strategy-in-space.

Elahi, A. 2010, 'A cannon for shooting supplies into space', *Popular Mechanics*, 15 January, viewed 22 April 2014, http://www.popsci.com/technology/article/2010-01/cannon-shooting-supplies-space.

Garwin, R. 2003, 'Space weapons: Not yet!', *Pugwash Workshop on Non-Weaponizing Space*, 22–24 May, viewed 10 May 2014, http://www.fas.org/rlg/030522-space.pdf.

Graybosch, A.J. 1988, 'The ethics of space-based ballistic missile defense', *The Monist*, 71(1): 45–58.

Hitchens, T. and Samson, V. (2004), 'Space-based interceptors: still not a good idea', *Georgetown Journal of International Affairs*, 5(2): 21–9.

Hitchens, T., Katz-Hyman, M. and Lewis, J. 2006, 'U.S. space weapons: big intentions, little focus', *Nonproliferation Review*, 13(1): 35–56.

Hsu, J. 2010, 'Air Force's new X-37B space plane likely an orbital spy', *Space.com*, 19 May, viewed 10 May 2014, http://www.space.com/8450-air-force-37b-space-plane-orbital-spy.html.

Jamison, L., Sommer, J.S. and Porche III, I.R. 2005, *High-altitude Airships for the Future Force Army*. Santa Monica, CA: RAND.

Kavka, J.S. 1985, 'Space war ethics', *Ethics*, 95(3): 673–91.

Metz, C. 2014, 'Facebook will build drones and satellites to beam Internet around the world', *Wired*, 27 March, viewed 5 May 2014, http://www.wired.com/2014/03/facebook-drones.

Moore, M. 2008, *Twilight War: The Folly of U.S. Space Dominance*. Oakland, CA: The Independent Institute.

Mueller, K.P. 2003, 'Totem and taboo: Depolarizing the space weaponization debate', in Logsdon, J.M. and Adams, G., *Space Weapons: Are the Needed?* Washington, DC: George Washington University, pp. 1–49.

O'Hanlon, M. 2004, *Neither Star Wars Nor Sanctuary: Constraining the Military Uses of Space*. Washington, DC: Brookings Institution Press.

Paglen, T. 2010, *Blank Spots on the Map: The Dark Geography of the Pentagon's Secret World*. New York: New American Library.

Preston, B., Johnson, D.J., Edwards, S.J.A., Miller, M. and Shipbaugh, C. 2002, *Space Weapons, Earth Wars*. Santa Monica, CA: RAND.

Richelson, J. 2009, *Defusing Armageddon: Inside NEST, America's Secret Nuclear Bomb Squad*. New York: W.W. Norton & Co.

Rogers, P. 2001, 'Towards an ideal weapon? Military and political implications of the airborne and spaceborne lasers', *Defense Analysis*, 17(1): 73–87.

Slann, Phillip A. 2013, 'Space debris and the need for space traffic control', *Space Policy*, 30: 40–42.

Spacy, W.A. 2003, 'Assessing the military utility of space-based weapons', in Logsdon, J.M. and Adams, G. (eds), *Space Weapons: Are They Needed?*, Washington, DC: George Washington University, pp. 157–237.

Stares, P.B. 1985, *The Militarization of Space: U.S. Policy, 1945–1984*. New York: Cornell University Press.

Steinberg, A. 2012, 'Weapons in space: The need to protect space assets', *Astropolitics*, 10(3): 48–67.

Talent, D.L. 2007, 'An assessment of the impact of the January 2007 Chinese ASAT test on the LEO environment', Advanced Maui Optical and Space Surveillance Technologies Conference, viewed 13 May 2014, http://www.amostech.com/TechnicalPapers/2007/Poster/Talent.pdf.

United Nations 1967, *Treaty on Principles Governing the Activities of States in the Exploration and Use of Outer Space, Including the Moon and Other Celestial Bodies*, United Nations Office for Outer Space Affairs, viewed 16 May 2014, http://www.unoosa.org/oosa/SpaceLaw/outerspt.html.

US Air Force 2003, *The U.S. Air Force Transformation Flight Plan*, Future Concepts and Transformation Division, viewed 16 May 2014, http://www.au.af.mil/au/awc/awcgate/af/af_trans_flightplan_nov03.pdf.

US Space Command 1998, *Vision for 2020*, Peterson AFB, CO, viewed 16 May 2014, http://www.fas.org/spp/military/docops/usspac/visbook.pdf.

US Space Commission 2001, *Report of the Commission to Assess United States National Security Space Management and Organization*, Washington, DC, viewed 16 May 2014, http://www.dod.gov/pubs/space20010111.html.

Wang, T. 2010, 'Analysis of the debris from the collision of the Cosmos 2251 and the Iridium 33 satellites', *Science & Global Security*, 18(2): 87–118.

Weeden, B. 2008, 'The fallacy of space-based interceptors for boost-phase missile defense', *The Space Review*, 15 September, viewed 16 May 2014, http://www.thespacereview.com/article/1212/1.

Yenne, B. 2005, *Secret Weapons of the Cold War: From the H-bomb to SDI*. New York: Berkley Books.

Zak, A. 2013, 'The hidden history of the Soviet satellite killer', *Popular Mechanics*, 1 November, viewed 16 May 2014, http://www.popularmechanics. com/technology/military/satellites/the-hidden-history-of-the-soviet-satellite-killer-16108970.

Zenko, M. 2014, 'Dangerous space incidents', Council on Foreign Relations, Contingency Planning Memorandum 21, viewed 16 May 2014, http://www. cfr.org/space/dangerous-space-incidents/p32790.

Chapter 15
Militarising Space: Weapons in Orbit[1]

Matthew Beard

Talk of the militarisation of outer space tends to evoke images from science fiction: Grand Moff Tarkin of the Death Star ordering the destruction of Alderaan in *Star Wars*; 'Orbital Defense Platforms' in the videogame series *Halo*; or modified World War II fighters destroying a Dalek battleship on *Doctor Who*. Indeed, President Ronald Reagan's proposed 'Strategic Defense Initiative' was dubbed 'Star Wars' by its critics. However, despite the fictional basis of most peoples' images of a militarised outer space, the existence of weapons that deploy from, into or amongst outer space is a continuing possibility.

This chapter will distinguish the different types of space weapons that are possible if the move to militarise space were to occur, and explore the ways in which these newly proposed weapons are similar to, and differ from, more familiar types of weapons. I will also explore what is motivating states to consider the militarisation of space. This will allow us to answer the question of whether space-based warfare would be a category shift from existing modes of warfare, or merely an extension of existing warfare into a new domain. I will argue that warfare in outer space, at least in the form currently proposed, is more similar than different from existing types of warfare and can therefore be explained by existing moral frameworks, such as Just War Theory. The chief challenges explored will be questions of sovereignty, and the possible legitimacy of targeting dual-use infrastructure in space.

Included in the exploration of the type of weapons with which we are concerned, I will explore the relevant principles and treaties in international law that bear on our discussion. Most significant will be the 1967 *Outer Space Treaty* and the 2006 *Space Preservation Treaty*. From these, in conjunction with more general principles of military ethics found in the ethical framework known as Just War Theory, we will be able to establish some general ethical limits on the militarisation of outer space. Finally, I will conclude by offering some suggestions of what I believe to be legal and ethical manifestations of space weaponry.

---

1   I would like to thank the comments of one anonymous reviewer, whose feedback on this chapter helped me to clarify some important details.

Just War Theory

It will be worthwhile to begin by briefly introducing Just War Theory as the prevailing ethical framework within the moral philosophical literature for addressing the ethics of war. Just War Theory has traditionally divided the morality of war into different conditions and categories. The major categories are: *jus ad bello* – when resorting to war is a morally legitimate option; *jus in bello* – the morally correct way in which wars should be fought; and the more recent *jus post bellum* – the morally appropriate way to end war and transition to peace (Orend 2007). Although *jus post bellum* is a question of growing importance (and discussion), this thesis is concerned primarily with *ad bellum* and *in bello* matters, and so my discussion of JWT is limited to these two categories.

Jus ad bellum concerns the moral questions that need to be addressed before war can be engaged in at all. Traditionally, this is seen to be the domain of the political leadership and senior military command. *Jus ad bellum* is commonly divided into six principles (Orend 2007):

- Just cause: wars may only be fought in response to an actual injustice that has occurred. Responding in defence of oneself or another against aggression.
- Right intention: the just cause must not only be present, but be the motivating condition for engaging in war. It is not justifiable to be motivated to go to war for political or economic reasons, even if a just cause is used as a pretext.
- Proportionality: the hypothetical state of affairs post-war must be morally preferable to the state of affairs that would come about if war was not declared (considering, for instance, civilian casualties, destruction of property and economic harms).
- Legitimate authority: wars must only be engaged in when authorised by those to whom the political community has granted the power to do so.
- Last resort: war must not be engaged in until all other reasonable options have been exhausted.
- Probability of success: unless there is some likelihood of the military engagement being successful, war ought not to be engaged in (as it would mean that all the harmful consequences of war had knowingly been for nothing).

Jus in bello focuses on the way that military agents are permitted to conduct themselves once war has commenced. There are two overarching principles of *jus in bello* that will be relevant to our discussion here:

- Discrimination: only other combatants may be intentionally targeted by lethal force. Noncombatants may not be the targets of attack (although certain attacks may harm noncombatants as a side-effect and still be morally permissible, under certain conditions);

- Proportionality: the harmful effects of any particular attack cannot outweigh the good that an attack achieves. For instance, cutting off the water supply to a populated town to root out a single insurgent would be a disproportionate strategy.

This is a sufficient introduction to Just War Theory as I will be discussing it here. It is my position that these principles are sufficient to address the ethical questions that arise from the possible migration of war into outer space.

Space-Based Weapons

If science fiction is anything to go by, the future of space weapons will consist in beam weapons; more specifically, lasers. However, for the moment, the type of weapons we are likely to see in space will be of a kind with which current militaries are already familiar; that is, missiles and kinetic weapons. In fact, some such weapons already exist; for instance, in 2007, China successfully tested an anti-satellite missile that destroyed one of its own decommissioned weather satellites (Spencer 2007). The United States, similarly, have proposed the 'Rods from God' program, which is explained by John Arquilla:

> To picture what these God rods might look like, think of a bundle of insulated metal telephone poles, dropped from an exquisitely calculated orbital location and reaching a speed of Mach 10 (over 7,000 mph) by the time they hit Earth. (Arquilla 2006)

These two examples demonstrate two different types of space weapons: the Chinese anti-satellite (ASAT) weapon is an example of an Earth-to-space weapon aimed at eliminating objects already placed in outer space (such as, for instance, satellites). Importantly, we should understand *why* nations might be interested in possessing or developing Earth-to-space weapons. Here the first clue should be in considering the type of objects that tend to be sent into space: satellites. The United States' Union of Concerned Scientists estimates that there are over 1,000 operational satellites orbiting Earth, of which 7 per cent are for military surveillance (Union of Concerned Scientists 2013). This means a high likelihood that a state's behaviour – particularly that of a large state – is being monitored by others. The development of ASAT technology helps to reduce the likelihood of spy satellites both by actually destroying them if they are discovered, and because of the deterrent threat posed simply by the existence of ASAT capabilities.

A more insidious motivation for the development of ASAT weaponry concerns the 59 per cent of satellites estimated to be used for communication, and the 8 per cent used for navigation (Union of Concerned Scientists 2013). The destruction of a selection of these satellites could amount to a crippling blow on the functioning of communities all around the world, including diminishing the ability of military and government agencies to communicate efficiently in times of emergency. Indeed, it is this scenario that Lt Col Michael E. Baum described as a second Pearl Harbour in his article 'Defiling the Altar: The Weaponization of Space'. In that article, Baum described a fictional full-scale attack the Chinese on US military facilities, including ASAT attacks that had:

> destroyed or damaged the satellite reception stations at Headquarters North American Aerospace Defense Command (NORAD), the Jet Propulsion Laboratory (JPL), Headquarters Space Command (SPACECOM), Headquarters European Command (EUCOM), Atlantic Command (LANTCOM), Headquarters Pacific Command (PACOM), and Fort Belvoir Virginia. The destruction of these downlink centers virtually crippled the ability of the Joint Warning Indications Center (JWIC) to monitor the crisis area. The Chinese certainly had taken Sun Tzu to heart and had studied both the strengths and weaknesses of the US forces. (Baum 1994)

In this vein, attacks on *satellites* which aim to undermine the functioning of a target nation's civilian and/or military populations seem to differ very little from the newly developing area of war known as cyberwar, which as Randall Dipert explains, 'belong to a large genus of all kinds of attacks on information systems' (Dipert 2010, p. 386). Elsewhere, I have defined cyberwar as 'the use of computer software and technology by one nation to attack the governmental or civilian information systems of another nation' (Beard 2013, p. 2). The only difference, it seems, between an attack like the one suggested by Baum, and the DDOS attacks originating from Russia that crippled Estonia for some days in 2007 is the manner in which the different attacks would be carried out: either by *physically* crippling the satellite in question, or by *digitally* stopping the signal from the satellite.

A second category of space weapons are those referred to by the 'Rods from God' proposal: space-to-Earth weapons. These weapons consist largely in implementing the immense kinetic energy developed as an object falls from space in some aggressive manner. The most obvious use, according to Arquilla, is 'to be able to "take out" a rogue nation's deep underground facilities, where illicit nuclear weapons development might be going on' (Arquilla 2006). The implementation would consist simply in placing a guidance computer on a large object – the most common proposal is a long tungsten rod – which would then orbit around the planet until needed, at which point it would fall out of orbit at a guided trajectory until crashing into the Earth with 'enough kinetic power to destroy even the deepest known facilities – many hundreds of feet beneath the Earth's surface' (Arquilla 2006).

At first sight, the use of space-to-Earth weapons appears simply as an extension of the type of 'bunker-buster' bombs that have been employed by various militaries since World War II. The difference here is simply the depth at which orbital kinetic weapons are able to penetrate. However, orbital weapons also possess a second substantial advantage over their terrestrial-bound equivalents:

speed of deployment. By placing the weapons in space, on satellites, these rods could be positioned and deployed within minutes, meaning that the introduction of these weapons would grant its holder almost guaranteed first-strike capability; effectively placing every nation on Earth within the targeting scope. Thus, a dual-use of orbital kinetic weapons is that they become the practical and moral (even if not legal) equivalent of stationing sea-to-ground missile-equipped submarines in international waters on the edge of a nation's sovereign territory, *just in case* that nation commits an offense worthy of attack. Thus, even if the motivations for developing orbital kinetic weapons are limited only to the ability to strike at dangerous facilities deep within the Earth's crust, the practical reality is that the same technology presents a real and present danger to any other state on the planet.

It is also worth noting that, in conjunction with the rapid deployment of orbital kinetic weapons, their reliance on kinetic energy means that they should be categorised as 'fire and forget' missiles, that is, missiles which require no further guidance after being launched. This means, however, that they cannot be redirected in the case that a mistake is made, the situation changes or the targeting was incorrect. This is not unique amongst missiles – many missiles, especially heat-seeking and homing ones, are fire and forget missiles – but given the Rods from God are capable of causing 'an explosion the same magnitude of that of an Earth-penetrating nuclear weapon, but with no radioactive fallout' (Anzera 2005). One would hope that such devastating force could be called off in the event of a mistake or change in situation.

Finally, a third form of space weapons are those deployed from space against other targets in space. This form of weaponry has garnered less interest that the other two forms, perhaps due to the inherent difficulties with firing an effective weapon in space. However, one would anticipate that if logistical difficulties could be overcome, such weapons could be employed in a similar way to ASAT weapons: as a way of destroying unmanned (or, for that matter, manned) objects in space. Significantly, however, space-to-space weapons also serve more immediate self-defensive functions; they could potentially be employed to destroy, for instance, a meteor on a collision course. Thus, they avail themselves to a form of justification which is not as immediately applicable to Earth-to-space weapons.

In this way, space-to-space weapons are also analogous to contemporary forms of weaponry. Their justification by way of self-defensive (by comparison with ASATs) draws comparison to the contemporary debate regarding drone pilots' justifications for the killings they perform. As Michael Walzer notes in his exploration of the moral status of soldiers, '[t]hey [enemy soldiers] can try to kill me, and I can try to kill them' (Walzer 1977, p. 36). What justifies the killings is the fact that all people, soldiers included, possess the right to self-defence (Rodin 2002, p. 35). As such, those who kill whilst not defending themselves must utilise other justifications for their killing. Drone pilots are one such example, as they experience no risk in the killings they employ, which constitutes a serious moral challenge on the legitimacy of their enterprise (Galliott 2015, pp. 165–85). This helps us to understand that similar justifications to those of individual soldiers might be available to individual spacecraft, provided that the purpose for those weapons is defensive. It also serves to demonstrate that Earth-to-space weapons must either be shown to be self-defensive in some other sense, or avail themselves of a different kind of justification.

What's Special About Space?

In each of the three types of space weapons discussed above, I suggested some ways in which existing problems and debates in military ethics can inform new debates regarding space weapons. Noticing the analogies between space weapons and terrestrial weapons begs the question, however, as to whether there is anything unique regarding space as a military domain. Perhaps the most compelling argument for space as a unique military domain is that, as the Outer Space Treaty notes, 'outer space is not subject to national appropriation by claim of sovereignty, by means of use or occupation, or by any other means' (United Nations 1967). The fact that states cannot claim sovereignty over a particular region means that states can permissibly station weapons within immediate striking distance of other states without violating the letter of the law with regard to state sovereignty.

To fully appreciate the challenge posed to sovereignty, it is worth taking some time to understand how it operates within customary interstate relations. Sovereignty is an ideal that is enshrined in international law and Just War Theory by way of two rights that are afforded to every state: political sovereignty and territorial integrity (Walzer 1977, p. 53). These rights emerge, as Brian Orend notes, from 'the human rights of individuals' (Orend 2007, p. 33). Because individuals have rights, for instance, to freedom of choice and expression and security, the states that individuals inhabit are afforded the rights necessary to defend individual rights. As such, the international community affords states sovereignty 'from foreign control and coercion' (Walzer 1977, p. 89). Both of these are potentially challenged by the existence of readily deployed, freely roving weapons in space.[2]

Note that the most pressing challenge to sovereignty is posed by space-to-Earth weapons. This is largely for the reasons described above: they are long range, rapidly deployable and hugely devastating. However, we should also note that similar challenges to sovereignty emerge from the destruction of communication and navigation satellites by space-to-space or Earth-to-space weapons. However, the challenges posed by attacks on satellites are, as was noted above, in many ways akin to cyberattacks and do not designate anything unique about space-based warfare, save that communication assets remain vulnerable targets. Space-to-Earth weapons, on the other hand, *do* designate something of

---

2   They are also challenged, in a different way, by the existence of spy satellites monitoring activities from within another nation. However, although questions of the ethics of espionage are both important and topical, they are beyond the scope of this chapter.

particular significance about space, that being that space is not owned by anybody, and therefore any object in space is free to move unimpeded around the Earth (or anywhere else, for that matter). This could mean a substantial shift in terms of the use of military deployments as political bargaining chips or coercive threats in international relations.

Consider the following hypothetical: following a series of escalating tensions between Japan and China surrounding ownership of the Senkaku and Diaoyu Islands in the East China Sea, the Chinese position warships in Japanese territorial waters. In response the United States intervenes on the side of Japan, positioning orbital weapons above China as a means of encouraging the withdrawal of Chinese warships from Japanese waters. Eventually, Japan asks the United Nations to order sanctions on the Chinese incursion, whilst China requests the United States be sanctioned for violating its sovereignty through the use of military coercion.

The case is intentionally messy and disputed. However, we might ask whether it is reasonable to see Japan and China as the only nations to have made threats on the sovereignty of other states in this case. Given that an orbital kinetic weapon is as quickly deployable, and presents an equally immediate threat, it seems that there is no categorical difference between stationing warships within the territorial waters of another nation, and stationing kinetic orbital weapons above another nation. Practically speaking, both represent equally imminent threats to the territorial integrity and political sovereignty of the victim state. My point here is not to suggest current international laws forbidding sovereign ownership of outer space are bad laws. The Earth's continual rotation both around its own axis and around the sun mean that any claims to sovereignty over a particular segment of outer space on behalf of a state would be incredibly nitpicky and confusing at best. However, I do want to suggest that the presence of quickly deployable weapons in outer space, *especially* if stationed near to another nation, but even if stationed above their home nations, represent threats to sovereignty that should be prohibited by the law, and which ought certainly to be forbidden by a moral theory such as Just War Theory.

One might reasonably ask why, *prima facie*, Just War Theory ought to reject orbital kinetic space-to-Earth weapons on the mere basis that they represent challenges to sovereignty. After all, so too do Intercontinential Ballistic Missiles (ICBMs), armed drones and indeed any weapon that has the ability to cross the borders of another country. What makes space-to-Earth weapons so special? Here, my response is in two parts. First, *there is nothing that makes space weapons, by their very nature, unique*: they are not unique in their challenges to sovereignty, as the use of ICBMs, CIA use of armed drones or the stationing of warships on the high seas (which are also free from sovereign claims) (United Nations 1982, Article 89) also pose similar challenges with regard to weapons that can be quickly deployed, and are thus threatening. Notably though (with the possible exception of warships on the high seas), ICBMs and targeted drone strikes by the CIA are violations of at least international law (United Nations 2002; 2013), whilst the use of militarised space weapons may not be. However, if Just War Theory ought to reject such weapons, it is not solely because of the threat to sovereignty, it is also because of the ability of such weapons to cause widespread and indiscriminate damage to noncombatant populations.

Indeed, whether or not space-to-Earth weapons are permitted by international law or not is contested because proposed space-to-Earth weapons are of an incredibly destructive scope. Indeed, the proposed Rods from God are expected to create an explosion similar to that of a nuclear warhead. Although the Outer Space Treaty forbids placing 'in orbit around the Earth any objects carrying nuclear weapons or any other kinds of weapons of mass destruction' (United Nations 1967, Article IV), no explicit definition of weapons of mass destruction exists in international law, and the most common usage refers to nuclear, biological and chemical weapons, none of which describes kinetic orbital weapons. In this vein, again, the difficulty is with regard to the *destructiveness* of the weapon coupled with the challenges posed to sovereignty, not its status as being housed in outer space.

I want now to deal briefly with a second argument against the militarisation of space, which I will call the romantic argument. The romantic argument is as follows:

> Humanity's exploration into outer space is an occasion on which humanity faces the opportunity to co-operate, and present itself as a unified whole. Thus, any moves into outer space that aim solely at the advancement of national, rather than global, interests, besmirch the nobility of humanity's expansion into outer space and the possibilities it offers for the common good of humanity.

Indeed, an argument very similar to this lies as the rationale for the UN Committee on the Peaceful Uses of Outer Space. That Committee was born of the UN General Assembly.

- *Recognising* the common interest of mankind as a whole in furthering the peaceful use of outer space;,
- *Believing* that the exploration and use of outer space should be only for the betterment of mankind and to the benefit of states irrespective of the stage of their economic or scientific development;
- *Desiring* to avoid the extension of present national rivalries into this new field;
- *Recognising* the great importance of international cooperation in the exploration and exploitation of outer space for peaceful purposes;
- *Noting* the continuing programmes of scientific cooperation in the exploration of outer space being undertaken by the international scientific community;
- *Believing also* that the United Nations should promote international cooperation in the peaceful uses of outer space (United Nations 1959).

The romantic argument holds that what distinguishes outer space from other domains is that space is an environment in which the players (or potential players) are global, not national. As such, global interests should be advanced and self-interested nationalism discouraged with regard to space expansion. This sits in contrast to, for instance, a speech by the United States ambassador to the UN Conference on Disarmament, in which he noted that 'peaceful exploration and use of space obviously does not rule out activities in pursuit of national security goals' (ACRONYM 2002).

On the surface, the romantic argument appears to be based on restricting humanity's violent tendencies to within the atmosphere, seeing no need for further expansion of war. And indeed, these are noble and worthwhile goals, but they alone do not constitute a knock-down moral argument against the militarisation of space. What might be more compelling, albeit somewhat unorthodox, is an argument based in political governance and expediency. If we allow either for the possibility of alien life forms somewhere in the universe, or for the possibility of humanity's expansion to other planets in the future, then we will soon face questions as to whether nation states are the best mechanisms by which to conduct interplanetary dialogue and cooperation. And if, as Locke claimed, one of the chief functions of government is to regulate individuals' rights to common resources, (Locke 2010, Sec. 27–36), then it is reasonable to think that the expansion of humanity into outer space will also require the formation of governments that are larger than nation states in order to regulate the common resources of the planet by comparison to other planets, as is in the 'the common interest of all countries' (ACRONYM 2002).

This argument is one of analogy: just as nationally bound regions (such as the state of NSW in Australia) do not involve themselves in matters of international importance, neither should nations involve themselves in interplanetary affairs. Thus, the regulation, expansion, exploration and militarisation of outer space should be done by a globally representative body, with shared resources from all nations. It seems then, that the romantic argument is not romantic at all, but grounded in bureaucratic efficiency! I should also note that I have not offered this argument because I necessarily believe it is true, but it is a view worth remembering as I enter into the final area of discussion: morally legitimate uses of space weapons.

Justifications for Space Weapons

What I have argued thus far has suggested problematic elements in the use of space-to-Earth weapons, at least of the kind described by the 'Rods from God' program. I also noted how there might be analogies between different areas of military ethics, such as cyberwar, unmanned warfare and challenges to state sovereignty, and new areas of debate in the ethics of space weaponisation. In this final section I will argue that what has been discussed thus far indicates that the justifications for space weapons will, like other weapons, be subject to the principles of *jus ad bellum* and *jus in bello* as they are explained in Just War Theory. I will return again to discussing each of the three categories of space weapons in turn. It is important to emphasise that the use of space weapons, just like any other weapons, is also subject to broader moral principles of Just War Theory, most significantly the *in bello* requirements of discrimination and proportion.

Recalling Baum's 'second Pearl Harbour', Earth-to-space weapons, particularly ASATs, are at their most devastating when they destroy communications and intelligence infrastructure in conjunction with a conventional military attack (as are their terrestrial equivalent, cyberweapons). At first sight, this does not seem particularly difficult, morally speaking, especially given that modern militaries often employ dedicated satellites for their communications. Thus, a nation pursuing a just cause could permissibly destroy enemy communication satellites to expedite a less bloody victory. Complexities arise, however, when and if civilian satellites are targeted (either to further cripple the nation, or because they serve a dual-use purpose). At this point, one needs to be careful to adhere to the *jus in bello* requirements of discrimination and proportion, which regulate who are legitimate targets of military attacks, and how much damage it is just to ensure in pursuing a particular military goal respectively. It may be justifiable that civilian infrastructure be damaged as a foreseen side-effect of a discriminate attack (if, for instance, communications are destablised). This is similarly true in cases where a civilian satellite is destroyed as an unintended side-effect of destroying a military one (because of debris, or some other accident): the principles that govern these cases are those of discrimination and proportion – so long as the civilian damage is proportional to the military gain and is unintended and unavoidable, then unpleasant as it might be, the attack can be morally justifiable.

If, however, one chooses to target a civilian communications satellite for the purposes of destabilising society, restricting free movement and facing further pressure on the host nation's government personnel, this appears to fail the discrimination principle which designates noncombatants as immune from intentional military attack. In this case, although the noncombatants have not been *directly* targeted vis-à-vis aimed at down a targeting scope, civilian suffering has still been brought about to serve one's end of achieving victory. As Richard de George notes, reflecting on the future of weapons development:

> The more advanced technologically a society is, the more it is dependent on the technology it has developed and uses routinely for all the necessities of life, from providing water and electricity, to communications and transportation. Consider a city like New York. To deprive it of electricity would be to paralyze it. And if all the circuits were burned out and had to be replaced, the task would be enormous. Add to that the destruction of the communications systems, the transportation system, and all the private and business computers. The city would stop functioning except on the most primitive level, and hence the effect on innocent civilians would be devastating. (de George 2007, p. 308)

What de George alludes to is the fact that discrimination extends beyond refraining from intentionally killing civilians; rather, it requires a military force to avoid inflicting suffering on civilian populations as a strategy for expediting victory. This is evidently not the case in strikes on civilian communications satellites, and thus using ASATs in this way should be strictly prohibited.

A second use of ASATs that can be justified is in destroying spy satellites that are conducting espionage on a nation. Just as intelligence agents captured conducting espionage subject themselves to criminal prosecution, spy satellites are subjected to the risk of being destroyed. Nor can a nation seek to claim damages for the destruction of a satellite which is conducting intelligence observations on another nation; it is within a nation's right to be subjected to wholesale, widespread spying of the type that satellites are capable of. This argument extends, of course, even more clearly to weaponised satellites equipped with space-to-Earth weapons.

Space-to-Earth weapons are more difficult to justify because of the potential for widespread damage and thus the difficulty they too face in adhering to the discrimination principle. It is very rare that a weapon which causes a nuclear-scale explosion could be used without threatening to kill large numbers of noncombatants. In addition to this, the fact that these weapons can be deployed anywhere around the world almost immediately represents an imminent threat to the sovereignty of every other nation. Thus, space-to-Earth weapons that have global remit and overwhelming payloads should be avoided. However, this is not to suggest that all space-to-Earth weapons must always be prohibited; there may still be room for more limited uses of such weapons in ways that do not violate sovereignty or the discrimination principle. Here the work of Paul Ramsey on limited nuclear warfare is relevant.

Paul Ramsey held that any weapon whose payload was so large as to inevitably kill noncombatants cannot claim to be *unintentionally* killing noncombatants, and that therefore such weapons always violate the principle of discrimination:

> I say simply that any weapon whose every use must be for the purpose of directly killing noncombatants as a means of attaining some supposed good and incidentally hitting some military target is a weapon whose every use would be wholly immoral. (Ramsey 1961, pp. 345–6)

However, he did not believe that *all* nuclear weapons fit this category. Rather, he claimed that 'counter-force nuclear war [i.e. war directed against the warmaking capacities of an enemy] is the upper limit of rational, politically purposive military action' (Reichberg, Syse and Begby 2006, p. 616). Nuclear weapons of a certain type *might* be permissible if the circumstances were right. These circumstances require the targeting only of military assets, and that nuclear usage be in defence of one's own territory or another's. Here Ramsey sets up his unique claim: that there is nothing specific about nuclear technology that renders it inherently immoral. It is rather a coincidence of design and military need that the technology which has been developed is of a kind which is destructive on so large a scale. However, according to Ramsey this need not be the case, we could have nuclear weaponry of a much more limited kind. Similarly, it might be conceivable that limited space-to-Earth weapons, which were not so rapidly deployed, and delivered more controlled payloads, might be justifiable in the future. For now, orbital kinetic energy weapons like the 'Rods from God' ought to be categorised as weapons of mass destruction, and therefore prohibited from being placed in space.

Finally, and briefly, the romantic argument provides one possible justification not only for space-to-space weapons, but also the continued development of Earth-to-space weapons; that being the continuing possibility that our planet is not currently, nor will always be, the only inhabited by life forms capable of organised military attack. As such, military groups on Earth would be morally justified (at least in principle, although one may question the prudence of such an exercise) to develop space-to-space and Earth-to-space weapons that will allow the planet to defend itself from any assailant that may arrive from outer space. Such weapons would also be justified if intended to be deployed against a large comet threatening the Earth (as has been the premise of several science fiction films), or if, in future times, humanity has colonised other planets, each of which is governed by an independent political system. In such cases, planetary defensive weapons would be no less justifiable than are national defensive weapons in our current political system.

Conclusion

This chapter has begun, perhaps several years too early, to inquire into the applicability of the Just War Theory to questions of the militarisation of outer space. I believe that the principles of Just War Theory can serve to adequately police the ethical questions that arise with regard to the weaponisation of space – especially given that none of the questions that arise are *sui generis* applicable to outer space, but rather emerge similarly in other aspects of military ethics. However, we should continue to discourage the use of space for rapidly deployable, large-scale weapons, and seek to be conservative in our attitude to space. For the moment, this should consist largely in defensive placement of Earth-to-space weapons.

References

Anzera, Giuseppe 2005, 'Star Wars: Empires strike back', *Asia Times*, 18 August, viewed 30 December 2013, http://www.atimes.com/atimes/Front_Page/ GH18Aa01.html.
Arquilla, John 2006, 'Rods from God', *SF Gate*, 12 March, viewed 28 December 2013, http://www.sfgate.com/opinion/article/RODS-FROM-GOD-Imagine-a-bundle-of-telephone-2539690.php.

Baum, Michael E. 1994, 'Defiling the Altar: The Weaponization of Space', *Airpower Journal*, 8(1): 52–62.

Beard, Matthew 2013, 'Cyberwar and Just War Theory', *Journal of Applied Ethics & Philosophy*, 5: 1–12.

Galliott, Jai 2015, *Military Robots: Mapping the Moral Landscape*. Farnham: Ashgate.

George, Richard 2007, 'Non-Combatant Immunity in An Age of High Tech Warfare' in Steven Lee (ed.) *Intervention Terrorism, and Torture: Contemporary Challengers to Just War Theory*. Dordrecht: Springer.

Javits, Ambassador Eric M. 2002, 'US Speech on Outer Space, May 28', *The Acronym Institute for Disarmament Documentation*, viewed 1 December 2013, http://www.acronym.org.uk/docs/0205/doc17.htm.

Locke, John 2010, *Second Treatise on Government*, Project Gutenberg, viewed 31 November 2013, http://www.gutenberg.org.

Orend, Brian 2006, *The Morality of War*. Toronto: Broadview Press.

Ramsey, Paul 2005, *War and the Christian Conscience*, 1961 in Arthur F. Holmes (ed.), *War and Christian Ethics*, 2nd Edition. Michigan: Baker Academic.

Reichberg, Gregory M., Syse, Henrik and Begby, Endre 2006, *The Ethics of War: Classic and Contemporary Readings*. Victoria: Blackwell Publishing.

Rodin, David 2002, *War and Self Defence*. Oxford: Oxford University Press.

Spencer, Richard 2007, 'Chinese missile destroys satellite in space', *The Telegraph*, 19 January, viewed 28 December 2013, http://www.telegraph.co.uk/news/worldnews/1539948/Chinese-missile-destroys-satellite-in-space.html.

Union of Concerned Scientists 2013, 'UCS Satellite Database', viewed 28 December 2013, http://www.ucsusa.org/nuclear_weapons_and_global_security/space_weapons/technical_issues/ucs-satellite-database.html.

United Nations Press Briefing 2013, 'Human Rights While Countering Terrorism', 25 October, viewed 30 December 2013, http://www.un.org/News/briefings/docs/2013/131025_Terrorism.doc.htm.

United Nations 2002, 'International Code of Conduct against Ballistic Missile Proliferation', viewed 30 December 2013, http://www.armscontrol.org/documents/icoc.

United Nations 1982, 'United Nations Convention on the Law of the Sea', viewed 30 December 2013, http://www.un.org/depts/los/convention_agreements/texts/unclos/unclos_e.pdf.

Walzer, Michael 1977, *Just and Unjust Wars*, 3rd Edition. New York: Basic Books.

Chapter 16

Artificial Intelligence and Space Robotics: Questions of Responsibility[1]

Jai Galliott

Ongoing human missions to the International Space Station have crews working with extra-vehicular robots and supporting semi-autonomous systems onboard the spacecraft and in mission control. With future exploration missions, these human-robot partnerships will evolve and humans will gradually be removed from the control loop and replaced with artificially intelligent systems. Indeed, terrestrial unmanned systems with weak forms of artificial intelligence developed largely in the military domain are now seeing civilian and science applications, with robots of varying degrees of autonomy already at work for NASA and the space agency acknowledging that these systems will become more pervasive in its future (NASA 2010), further blurring the line between operator and supervisor. The United States Air Force has also tested the X-37B unmanned spacecraft in extended orbit, suggesting that space will become increasingly militarised. The purpose of this chapter is to demonstrate that while artificial intelligence certainly exacerbates some traditional problems and may cause us to rethink who we ought to hold morally responsible for some crimes carried out in space, our standard conceptions of responsibility are capable of dealing with what some allege is a 'responsibility gap', involving the inability to identify an appropriate locus of responsibility when these systems are used in a highly autonomous mode. This chapter begins by exploring conditions under which responsibility is typically attributed to humans and how these responsibility requirements are challenged, highlighted by examples involving semi-autonomous military systems. Following this is an examination of Sparrow's notion of the 'responsibility gap' as it pertains to the potential deployment of highly autonomous weapons systems. It is argued that we can reach a solution by shifting to a forward-looking and functional sense of responsibility, which incorporates institutional agents and ensures that the human role in both engineering and releasing these systems is never overlooked.

---

1   This article is updated and adapted version of a chapter derived from: *Military Robots: Mapping the Moral Landscape*. Farnham: Ashgate. Copyright 2015. All rights reserved.

Challenges to Responsibility Attribution in Technologically Enabled Missions

Moral responsibility, whether in war or space operations, is about actions, omissions and their consequences. To be held responsible in accord with Fischer and Ravizza's (1998) landmark account – which is based on the idea of guidance control and that the mechanism that issues the relevant behaviour must be the agent's own and be responsive to reasons – actors must not be 'deceived or ignorant' about what they are doing and ought to have control over their behaviour in a 'suitable sense' (Fischer and Ravizza 1998). Put more specifically, this means that an agent should only be considered morally responsible if they intentionally make a free and informed causal contribution to the act in question, meaning that they must be aware of the relevant facts and consequences of their actions, have arrived at the decision to act independently and were able to take alternative actions based on their knowledge of the facts. If these conditions are met, we can usually establish a link between the responsible subject and person or object affected, either retrospectively or prospectively (the latter will be the focus of the final section). However, technologically enabled missions present various challenges for these standard accounts of moral responsibility. For the sake of a complete exposition and refutation of the idea that, the responsibility gap presents an insurmountable threat, it is necessary to take a closer look at how semi-autonomous technologies can complicate responsibility attribution through lessons learned in the military domain, which may one day be extended to space if international treaty mechanisms fail or are circumvented.

There are many barriers to responsibility attribution in the military domain and many are so closely interrelated that it makes providing a clear and lucid discussion quite problematic. The most important for present purposes is associated with the subject's causal contribution to the action in question. According to the above referred-to account, for an agent to be held responsible, they must have exerted due influence on the resulting event. What is 'due' will be subject to further reflection in the remaining sections, but there is little to be gained from blaming someone or something for an unfortunate event about which they/it legitimately had no other choice or over which they/it had no control. That acknowledged, the employment of modern warfighting technologies based on complex computing and information technologies can lead us to lose our grasp of who is responsible, because it obscures the causal connections between an agent's actions and the eventual consequences. When utilising complex technologies, tracing the sequence of events that led to a particular event usually leads in a great number of directions (Noorman 2012). The great majority of technological mishaps are the product of multifaceted mistakes commonly involving a wide range of persons, not limited to end users, engineers and technicians. For those looking from the outside in, it can be very difficult – and some might say impossible – to identify contributing agents. This difficulty in identifying contributing agents is Dennis Thompson's (1987) so-called 'problem of many hands'. This problem should not be confused with the 'responsibility gap' that will soon be addressed, because it is not as deflationary and falls short of the complete abdication of responsibility.

Added to the problem of many hands is the physical distance that warfighting technologies often create between agents and the consequences or outcomes of their actions. This further blurs the causal connection between action and event. Batya Friedman (1990) earlier noted this effect in an educational setting which encourages young people to become responsible members of the electronic information community. The challenge has been reinvigorated with the development and deployment of autonomous systems in the military setting and the employment of distanced drone operators. It is these war-making agents that now need to be encouraged to play a responsible role in network-centric operating environments. Unmanned systems technologies – more than any other material technology – extend the reach of military activity through both time and space. While enabling a state's military force to defend itself over a greater range may be praiseworthy, this remoteness can also act to disassociate them from the harm that they cause. When someone uses an unmanned aircraft operated from a control station on the ground in the US to conduct military operations in the Middle East, the operator might not be fully aware of how the system and its munitions will affect the local people and may not experience or fully appreciate the true consequences of their actions (Waelbers 2009). This has a direct bearing on their comprehension of the significance of their actions and has a mediating role when it comes to considering the extent to which they are responsible.

This mediation of responsibility has much to do with the fact that unmanned systems and the sensors that they carry can actively shape how moral agents perceive and experience the world at large, which further impacts upon the conditions for imposing moral responsibility. In order to make the appropriate decisions which are sanctioned by Just War Theory, a moral agent must be capable of fully considering and deliberating about the consequences of their actions, understanding the relevant risks and benefits they will have and to whom they will apply. This, in turn, calls for them to have adequate knowledge of the relevant facts. While McMahan (2009) and others have offered accounts, it remains unclear what epistemic thresholds ought to apply here, but what is generally accepted is that it is unfair to hold someone responsible for something they could not have known about or reasonably anticipated. The capability of unmanned systems and other intelligence-gathering technologies is importantly relevant, because in some respects they assist the relevant users in deliberating on the appropriate course of action by helping them capture, collate and analyse information and data (Zuboff 1985). In their sales demonstrations to the military, for example, representatives of the drone industry typically argue that their piece of military hardware will grant them the opportunity to see 'beyond the next hill' in the field and 'around the next block' in congested urban environments, enabling them to acquire information that they would not otherwise have access to without incurring significantly greater risk (US DoD 1999). This may well be true with respect to some systems, and these would allow operators greater reflection on the consequences of their tactical decisions. However, with the technical, geographical and operational limits discussed elsewhere (Galliott 2015, 2012, 2012/13), there are many respects in which these systems preclude one from gaining a view of the 'bigger picture' and may alter an operator's resulting action/s, perhaps limiting responsibility.

Many intelligent military systems have such complex processes that they get in the way of assessing the validity and relevance of the information they produce or help assess and, as such, they can actually prevent a user from making the appropriate decision within an operational context and therefore have a direct impact on their level of responsibility. A consequence of this complexity is that people have the aforementioned tendency to rely either too much or not enough on automated systems like those we increasingly find embedded into unmanned aircraft or their control systems, especially when in the time-critical and dynamic situations which are characteristic of modern warfare (Cummings 2004). The U.S.S. Vincennes most shockingly illustrated this during its deployment to the Persian Gulf amid a gun battle with Iranian small boats. Although this warship was armed with an Aegis Combat System, which is arguably one of the most complex and automated naval weapons system of its time (it can automatically track and target incoming projectiles and enemy aircraft), the U.S.S. Vincennes misidentified an Iranian airliner as an F-14 fighter jet and fired upon it, killing nearly 300 people (Gray 1997). Post-accident reporting and analysis discovered that overconfidence in the abilities of the system, coupled with a poor human-machine interface, prevented those aboard the ship from intervening to avoid the tragedy. Despite the fact that disconfirming evidence was available from nearby vessels as to the nature of the aircraft, it was still mischaracterised as a hostile fighter descending and approaching them at great speed. In the resulting investigation, a junior officer remarked that 'we called her Robocruiser ... she always seemed to have a picture and ... [always] seemed to be telling people to get on or off the link as though her picture was better' (Rogers and Rogers 1992). The officer's impression was that the semi-autonomous system provided reliable information that was otherwise unobtainable. In this case, at least, such a belief was incorrect. The system had not provided otherwise unobtainable information, but rather misleading information. It is therefore questionable whether the war-making agent has a more comprehensive understanding of the relevant state of affairs because of the employment of advanced military technology or whether her/his understanding and knowledge are less accurate (Manders-Huits 2006). That is, it is unclear whether the attribution of moral responsibility is enhanced or threatened. The view advanced here is that, even though there may be an aggregate increase in the amount of information that is accessible, there is a morally relevant decrease in understanding which single piece of information ought to influence autonomy of action and the resulting decision-making, even when the bulk of information is clear and accurate. The implication is that operators of sophisticated systems might be held to high standards of responsibility on the basis that they had access to a great deal of relevant information when, in fact, the provision of this information may have clouded their judgement, meaning that they are less responsible.

It must also be added that advanced technologies may exert a certain level of influence over their users in a way that might be unclear or even immeasurable (Manders-Huits 2006). This sort of control is not implicit in the technology itself, but rather exerted through the design process and the way in which alternative moral options are presented for human action. Semi-autonomous military technologies help to centralise and increase control over multiple operations, reducing costs and supposedly increasing efficiency. However, there is a limit to how much control a human being can exert and, in reality, this 'increased control' can only be achieved by outsourcing some low-level decisions to computerised processes and leaving the human to make a choice from a more limited range of actions. In other words, some technologies are designed with the explicit aim of making humans behave in certain ways, further mediating the imposition of responsibility. However, note that we are still a long way from saying that we cannot attribute responsibility in such cases.

The Alleged Responsibility Gap Associated with Autonomous Systems

In the previous section, we saw how developments in autonomous systems technology have led to a partial loss of influence on the part of operators or users and hold broader implications for the attribution of moral responsibility more generally, namely by limiting the operator's responsibility and perhaps causing us to consider the redistribution of the remaining share of responsibility. In the following section of this chapter, we shall see how many of the problems described above are only being exacerbated as unmanned systems become more computerised. These problems and others come together in highly automated missions to create a problem that Sparrow and others see as significantly more serious than any of those already discussed, posing what is supposedly an insurmountable threat to the attribution of responsibility. As a final step towards fully understanding and refuting the nature and implications of this problem, it will be necessary to discuss the arguments drawn on by Sparrow, but namely those originally put forward by Andreas Matthias (2004).

Matthias (2004) argues that the further we progress along the autonomy continuum, the closer we are to undermining society's centuries-old effort to establish rule systems in order to attribute responsibility. He says that with non-autonomous systems, it is relatively safe to take the use of a machine to signal that the operator has read the user manual and assumes responsibility for its use, except in cases where the machine fails to operate with the predefined limits (Matthias 2004). Thus, the user has control and is responsible for the actions and events that come from the normal operation of the system, but if it explodes or does something which was not stated in the manual when it should have been, we ought to blame the manufacturer. We know from the preceding discussion that when machines capable of being ever so slightly autonomous are introduced, because of the rigidity and limited nature of non-autonomous systems, moral responsibility is complicated. Indeed, the agent responsible for operating this machine loses an element of control over the system. What happens if we progress further? Matthias (2004) argues that if a NASA technician was operating a semi-autonomous space vehicle and the vehicle falls into a crater between inputs because of long response times, we should not consider the technician responsible. Task-autonomous unmanned systems create a buffer between agent and system as well as another buffer between action and event, giving their operators the potential ability to increase their workload by operating multiple drones, but at the cost of understanding and situational awareness. The locus of responsibility categorically shifts away from the operator. However, the real problems arise when it comes to intelligent machines which are capable of adapting and learning new skills. That is, robotic systems for which unpredictability in their operations is a feature rather than a computer glitch or technical failure (Millar and Kerr 2012). Matthias (2004) asks us to imagine how we would impose moral responsibility if we were to revisit the space vehicle case and stipulate that it will not be remotely controlled from Earth, but rather have its own integrated navigation and control system, capable of storing data in its internal memory, forming representations and taking action from these. It should, therefore, be able to record video imagery and estimate the difficulty of crossing any familiar terrain. He asks, in this revised case, whom we should hold responsible if the vehicle were to once again fall into the crater?

Sparrow (2007) subsequently takes up this question. He has us imagine that a drone, directed by sophisticated artificial intelligence, bombs a platoon of enemy soldiers who have indicated their intent to surrender. Who should we hold morally responsible for a particular event when relevant decisions are made by an autonomous system without a human operator? The reader's first intuition is probably to say that the responsibility for any crimes or violations rests with the developer of the system. However, Sparrow (2007) objects to this by relying on the user manual analogy. This analogy says that this would be unfair if it is a declared system limitation that the machine may not performed as desired in some percentage of cases. If this is the case, he suggests it may be the responsibility of the user (since s/he is assumed to have read the manual). Secondly, he says that to hold the programmers or manufacturer responsible for the actions of their creation, once it is turned on and made autonomous, would be analogous to 'holding parents responsible for the action of their children once they have left their care' (Sparrow 2007). Sparrow assumes this is wrong and that it naturally leads us to consider holding the commanding officer responsible. Yet again, he views this as unfair and thinks that to do so calls into question the nature of our 'smart' systems. If the machines start to make their own decisions, he suggests that there will come a point at which we cannot hold the commanding officer responsible for anything troubling that may unfold (Sparrow 2007). It will be argued in the next section that Sparrow is mistaken about the assumed wrongness of sharing responsibility and that we are not yet at the tipping point he describes.

The final possible locus of responsibility under Sparrow's account, however, is the machine itself. Moral responsibility is typically attributed to moral agents and, at least in the Anglo-American philosophical tradition, moral agency has been reserved for human beings. The reason being that unlike the majority of animals, rational human beings are seen as able to freely deliberate about the consequences of their actions and choose to act in one way or other, meaning that they are originators of *morally significant* actions. Although some people tend to anthropomorphise robots and notable philosophers like Dennett (1997) and Sullins (2006) have argued that they could be classed as moral agents, Sparrow argues that they should not and objects to the idea that they could have the kind of capacities that make human beings moral agents. He argues that it is unlikely that they will ever have the mental states, common sense, emotion or expressivity equivalent to those of humans, and that, if they do develop these things, it would undermine the whole point of utilising robots instead of human beings (Sparrow 2007). According to the argument, they would hold a moral status equivalent to that of human beings. But this is disputable, as it could be argued that while artificial moral agents may be worthy of moral consideration, they would still hold different status to biological moral agents by virtue of some natural/artificial distinction that gives greater weight to means of creation. Even if robots do not acquire human-level moral status, lower levels of machine autonomy may be sufficient for us to hold robots responsible. However, Sparrow (2007) holds that no robot can be held responsible because they cannot suffer. This presupposes that suffering is a requirement for responsibility, a presupposition not supported by any conventional responsibility framework that might govern war or space, but we will return to this point after having summarised the alleged problem.

For Sparrow, like Matthias before him, we have reached or are about to reach an important impasse. We already have many machines in development and a limited number of those, which are in use, are task-autonomous and can decide on a course of action in some limited scenarios without any human input. Going forward, all indications point to there being machines with rules for action which are not fixed by their manufacturers during the production process and which are open to be changed by the machine itself during its operation. That is, these machines will be capable of learning from their surroundings and experiences. Conventionally, there are several loci of responsibility for the actions of a machine, but both Matthias (2004) and Sparrow (2007) argue that these robots will bring about a class of actions for which nobody is responsible, because no individual or group has sufficient control of these systems. These cases constitute Matthias's 'responsibility gap'. At first blush, it might seem that this is basically the problem of many hands – the classical problem described earlier but with new relevance to the emergence of unmanned systems and the prospect of fully autonomous weapons systems. But to assume this would be mistaken. The argument advanced by Matthias and Sparrow is not that we cannot identify who is responsible, but simply that nobody is responsible. Sparrow would likely argue that if there is any problem identifying the relevant persons, it is because they do not exist. In his article on corporate responsibility, Philip Petitt (2007) refers to the matter described as the 'problem of no hands'. This is a slight but important twist on Thompson's more familiar 'problem of many hands', as described earlier and characterised by the widespread relinquishment of moral responsibility.

The problem that proponents of the responsibility gap put forward is fairly straightforward, though certainly not indisputable. However, to differentiate his argument from Matthias's, Sparrow (2007) suggests that we might better conceptualise his dilemma if we consider a case in warfare where the waters are somewhat muddied: the use of child soldiers. This analogy is outlined because it will be useful in problematising Sparrow's argument, though the similarity between child and machine learning is not as great as Sparrow indicates. He says that like robots, one of the many reasons why it is unethical to utilise children in combat is that it places decisions about the use of force in the hands of agents that cannot be held responsible for them. According to him, child soldiers lack full moral autonomy, but they are clearly autonomous in some respect and 'certainly much more autonomous than any existing robot' (Sparrow 2007, p. 73). He goes on to say that while they are not capable of understanding the full moral dimensions of what they do, they possess sufficient autonomy to ensure that those who order them into action do not or cannot control them, presenting problems for any effort to hold those who give the orders exclusively personally responsible for the child soldiers' actions (Sparrow 2007). The idea Sparrow advances is that there is a conceptual space in which children and robots are sufficiently autonomous to make the full attribution of responsibility to an adult or conventional moral agent problematic, but not autonomous enough to be held fully responsible themselves. Sparrow argues that his opponents try to close this space by stipulating that the relevant entities hold more or less responsibility than they should and thus fit within one of the polar boundaries, but that this does not adequately or fairly resolve the problem. The next section will propose that we can actually handle this problem by moving to a more collective, pragmatic and forward-looking notion of shared responsibility.

Toward a Revised Notion of Responsibility

Having explored some of the challenges that semi-autonomous systems pose for responsibility attribution and described the dilemma over responsibility for autonomous unmanned systems, the need for a revised notion of responsibility should be clear. But to clarify, the arguments of both Matthias and Sparrow hinge on three basic premises. The first is that programmers, manufacturers, commanding officers and the like may not be able to foresee what an autonomous robot, capable of learning, will do in the highly complex and dynamic environments such as war or space. The second is that either independently of or related to the fact that none of these agents are able to exert full control over the development or subsequent deployment of these systems, harm to others may eventually occur. The third is that an agent can only be held responsible for these harms if they have control in the sense that they have an awareness of the facts surrounding the action that leads to the harm and are able to freely manipulate the relevant causal chains based on these facts. The conclusion stipulates that since this is not the case as it pertains to programmers, manufacturers or commanding officers, there is some sort of moral void created by the deployment of these systems, one that cannot be bridged by our traditional concepts of responsibility. While the problem is clear, it is not obvious that the overall conclusion can be accepted at face value or that any individual premise is correct. There are a number of points at which the alleged responsibility gap can be overcome, or, at least, a number of premises that can be called into question in order to cast doubt over the supposed insurmountability of the problem at hand.

In discussing the nature of this alleged responsibility gap and showing its inadequacy as a justification for a moratorium on autonomous systems, it is important to point out that the scope of the conditions for imposing responsibility have been overstretched or considered in too wide a frame. As will soon be shown with reference to the idea of shared responsibility, it is not impossible to impose responsibility in situations in which no individual has total control over the function of an autonomous system. Both Matthias and Sparrow go too far in suggesting that programmers, manufacturers or commanding officers are freed from any form of responsibility because they do not have total control over the operation or manufacture of unmanned systems. An appeal to common sense should reveal that it is absurd and potentially dangerous to identify the failings of multiple individuals in their development and deployment and then deny their moral responsibility (Gotterbarn 2001). To do so is to deny an opportunity for the rectification of past, present and future wrongs. As opposed to what might be stipulated by strict liability law, such a strong sense of control is not necessary for the imposition of some degree of moral responsibility. The relevant programmers, designers, manufacturers and commanding officers are all responsible to some degree or extent. Take Sparrow's claim that to hold the programmer of a dynamic learning machine responsible for its actions would be analogous to holding a parent responsible for the actions of their child once they are out of their care. While there are limits to any such analogy because of the varied learning mechanisms employed by child and machine, he seems to ignore the fact that parents are at least partially responsible for preparing their children for that moment when they leave their care and become independent. In much the same way, the developers of unmanned systems hold significant responsibility for ensuring that their robots can operate as desired once given independence, something that is still a long way off in the majority of cases. Also, take the case of the commanding officer and continue with the parenting analogy. When a parent is teaching their child how to drive, for instance, the parent places the child in an area where s/he can learn the necessary skills without risking her/his own safety or that of anyone else. Similarly, the commanding officer of an autonomous system has a responsibility to ensure that the system has been thoroughly prototype tested or is placed in an appropriate learning or test bed environment until such time that it performs at least as well as a manned system or until the chance of any serious harm occurring is so tiny that we can deal with it via the 'functional morality' described later on, which recognises that engineers and manufacturers will often choose to release intelligent machines with remnant unpredictability and that reprogramming for minor errors can assume the place of punishment.

The machine's path to full autonomy is a long (if not impossible) one and the child warrior analogy points to this. Machines will not just 'wake up' as is depicted in films about human-hating 'terminators'. Indeed, there is simply no way in which someone could deliberately create such an entity without a collective effort on the scale of the Manhattan project. The general lesson to be drawn from this is that all of the involved agents and any others associated with the use of unmanned systems (including the user in the case of semi-autonomous systems) retain a share of responsibility, even though they may claim that they were not in complete or absolute control. It would be foolhardy, or even dangerous, to conclude from the observation that responsibility is obscured by the use of unmanned weaponry that nobody is, or ought to have been, held to account and that it is impossible to deal with the case of autonomous systems. On the contrary (and as others have argued in relation to informatics more generally, see: Manders-Huits 2006) we are at such an important junction in the development of unmanned systems that we have reason to adjust and refine our conception of moral responsibility and to leave behind the idea that the imposition of moral responsibility relies on agents having full control over all aspects of the design or deployment of advanced robotics. This is because these systems are so complex that few of the design-, development- or deployment-related decisions are made on an individual basis. Why concentrate on the intentions and actions of humans alone in our moral evaluation of these systems when no human exerts full control over the relevant outcomes? We need to move away from the largely insufficient notion of individual responsibility, upon which we typically rely, and move towards a more complex notion of collective responsibility, which has the means and scope to include nonhuman action. That is, it must be a holistic approach which is capable of acknowledging the contribution of various human agents, systems and organisations or institutions. The need to update our moral values and associated notions of responsibility will become more important as the technology develops, the risks increase and the number of potential responsibility-related problems accumulate.

It is worth noting that others, foreseeing the difficulties that we are now facing with the development of things like intelligent autonomous robots, have already thought about calls for change in the way we think of responsibility. For instance, both Daniel Dennett (1973) and Peter Strawson (1974) have long held that we should conceive of moral responsibility as less of an individual duty and more of a role that is actively defined by pragmatic group norms. This argument in endorsed here, primarily because more classical accounts raise endless questions concerning free will and intentionality that cannot be easily resolved (if at all) from a practical perspective aimed at achieving results here and now. This sort of practical account has the benefit of allowing nonhuman entities, such as complex socio-technical systems and the corporations that manufacture them, to be answerable for the harms to which they often cause or contribute. It seems to require that we think in terms of a continuum of agency between non-moral and full moral agents, with the sort of robots we are concerned with here falling just short of the latter. This pragmatic (or functional) approach also allows for the fact that agency develops over time and shifts the focus to the future appropriate behaviour of complex systems, with moral responsibility being more a matter of rational and socially efficient policy that is largely outcomes-focused. We should view moral responsibility as a mechanism used by society to defend public spaces and maintain a state of relative harmony, generated under the contract by the power transferred from the individuals to the state. The end of this responsibility mechanism is, therefore, to prevent any further injury being done to society and to prevent others from committing similar offences. While it might be useful to punish violators of the social contract, it is not strictly necessary, nor is it necessarily the best approach to preventing harm in all scenarios. As Jeroen van den Hoven and Gert-Jan Lokhorst (2012) have argued, treatment is in many cases an equally effective option for the prevention of harm and one that we can apply to nonhuman agents in different forms, whether it is psychological counselling in humans or re-engineering or reprogramming in the case of robots. This is important because it means that there is sufficient conceptual room between 'operational morality and genuine moral agency' to hold responsible or, in Floridi's language, hold morally accountable, artificial agents which are able to perform some task and assess its outcome (Wallach and Allen 2009; Floridi and Sancers 2004).

Scholars in the autonomous systems debate seem to have become fixated on a backward-looking (retrospective) sense of responsibility, perhaps because even engineers and programmers have tended to adopt a malpractice model focused on the allocation of blame for harmful incidents. However, an effective and efficient responsibility mechanism that remedies the supposed gap should not only be about holding someone responsible only when something goes wrong. Therefore, this backward-looking sense of responsibility must be differentiated from forward-looking (prospective) responsibility, a notion that focuses more on capacity to effect change than blameworthiness or similar (Gotterbarn 2001). That is, at some point, we must stop thinking purely about past failures to take proper care and think about the reciprocal responsibility to take due care in future action. This is because in debates about real-world problems such as the deployment of increasingly autonomous systems, we will also want our conception of responsibility to deal with *potential* problems. To this end, we can impose forward-looking or prospective responsibility to perform actions from now on, primarily in order to prevent undesirable consequences or to ensure a particular state of affairs obtains more effectively and efficiently than through the alternative means of backward-looking models. It establishes a general obligation on the part of all those involved in the design, manufacture and use of unmanned systems to give regard to future harms. Admittedly, as Seamus Miller (2008) has pointed out in the case of computing, it is difficult to reach any solid conclusion on how far into the future they are required to foresee. That said, two things are clear: first, if the recent troubles plaguing unmanned systems are any indicator, agents have reasonable grounds to expect the unexpected. Second, once truly autonomous systems are developed and deployed, no amount of policy-making will stop their spread.

For the latter reason in particular, we have to think more carefully about where the majority of the forward-looking responsibility falls. In discussing the claim that wealthy countries must do more than comparatively poor countries to combat climate change and making use of Kant, James Garvey (2008) argues that in much the same way that 'ought implies can', 'can implies ought' in a range of other circumstances where the financial or political means behind the 'can' have contributed to the problem that ought to be corrected or mitigated. This seems also to hold true in the responsibility debate with which we are engaged. Generally speaking, the more power an agent has and the greater the resources at their disposal – whether intellectual, economic or otherwise – the more obliged s/he is to take reasonable action when problems arise. Jessica Fahlquist (2008) has proposed a specific approach to identifying the extent of a person's obligation in relation to environmental protection based on varied levels of capacity to contribute to social causes; and given that power to enact change varies within the military and military-industrial complex to much the same extent as in the environmental world (and with some convergence), there is little reason why this should not be applied to the drone debate and extended to cover the manufacturers of unmanned systems as well as the governments that regulate them. The companies of the military-industrial and space complex are in a unique position, and have it well within in their power, to anticipate risks of harm and injury and theorise about the possible consequences of developing learning systems. The costs of doing so after the fact are great and many. Moreover, manufacturers are best positioned to create opportunities for engineers to do what is right without fear of reprimand, whether that would be going ahead as planned, designing in certain limitations in the system or simply refusing to undertake certain projects. It therefore seems reasonable to impose forward-looking responsibility upon them. However, we know that profit can sometimes trump morality, so concerned parties should also seek to share forward-looking responsibility and ascribe some degree of responsibility to the governments which oversee these manufacturers and set the regulatory framework for the development and deployment of their product, should manufacturers fail to self-regulate and establish appropriate industry standards.

Note that, while it may seem that the point advanced in this chapter is pitched against any prohibition on the development and subsequent use of these systems in space, this is only partly true. It is not at all obvious that scholars need to make the very bold claim that nobody can be held responsible for the use of intelligent robots that fall between having operational autonomy and genuine moral autonomy. It seems that many other agents are sufficiently responsible and that, through embracing an instrumental approach toward backward-looking responsibility and combining it with a forward-looking account of responsibility put forward earlier, it is possible to distribute responsibility fairly. It may also be that some of the relevant agents, namely governments, may reach the conclusion that artificial intelligence should not be used in either the military or space domains. That is, while states have a contractual obligation to effectively and efficiently protect the citizens who grant them power, it may turn out that this would mean avoiding the use of unmanned systems in some circumstances. In fact, as unlikely as it seems, time may prove that autonomous systems pose such a problem that it warrants making a concerted effort to form an international treaty or a new Geneva Convention banning their use in all but very particular cases. However, this is not yet clear and in light of the features of the revised account of responsibility advocated here, there seems to be no intrinsic responsibility gap that warrants a prohibition of the use of autonomous systems, at least not without reference to some of their other problems, be they technical or ethical.

Critics are likely to argue that any account which allocates too much responsibility to organisational or governmental actors will erode the sense of personal responsibility that individuals feel and will not thus have the desired effect of improving the attainment of good outcomes. What will happen, they may ask, if individual parties to collective atrocities are excused from the responsibilities that they would otherwise have under traditional notions of responsibility? There are a few ways to respond to this worry. The first consists in stressing that individuals are not in fact freed or excused from responsibility according to either the backward-looking or the forward-looking model. Individual agents will still be held causally responsible for their part in any harmful events under the functional/pragmatic account. They will also be encouraged to ensure that systems are designed, developed, tested and used in the desired way through the imposition of forward-looking responsibility. The second way to respond is to reaffirm that, because individual agents are the core units of any social system, it would obviously be ideal if they were to gradually begin to embrace the right values and do the right thing, but allow that, in some circumstances, it is fairer or more effective to distribute the burden of action between individuals, institutions and governments. This is due to the fact that, in the short to medium term, it must be recognised that both human and nonhuman agents will make mistakes that will lead to violations of the law. As a consequence, the greatest share of responsibility must be ascribed to the most capable agents in the relevant scenario. In trying to highlight the oversimplified analysis of duties in rights-based theories, Henry Shue (1988) suggests that in some circumstances we must look beyond individuals and distribute responsibility to institutions in the most effective and efficient fashion relative to the time we have as well as the nature and severity of the problem. For it is indeed institutions, such as judicial systems and police forces, upon which the duty to provide physical security ultimately falls. In fact, it seems best to impose much of the forward-looking responsibility to the government or its relevant standards departments, just because the government is best placed to ensure that systems are designed to rule out or reduce the impact of such mistakes or that measures are put in place to do the same thing. Again, it must be stressed that this does not mean that individual agents or corporations with the relevant capabilities and resources are excused from efforts to achieve the desired effects or their share of responsibility, but merely that governmental agents ought to take greater efforts.

Conclusion

This chapter began by demonstrating that technology generates a number of barriers to attribution of responsibility, from distancing users from their sense of responsibility to obscuring causal chains, making it more difficult to identify where a moral fault lies. In the third, it was outlined how these issues and others come together in the case of highly autonomous systems to create what some allege is a 'responsibility gap', or a class of actions for which nobody/nothing is supposedly responsible. The final section laid the foundations for a theory of responsibility, which revolves around the idea that action and responsibility can be distributed amongst human and nonhuman agents or some combination thereof. More work is needed to reveal exactly what this new theory of responsibility will look like and to determine its precise implications, but if nothing else, this chapter has hopefully demonstrated that while ascribing responsibility in the case of autonomous systems is more complex and troubling than in the case of semi- and non-autonomous systems, it is not yet an insurmountable problem.

References

Cummings, M.L. 2004, *Automation Bias in Intelligent Time Critical Decision Support Systems*. Paper presented at the AIAA 1st Intelligent Systems Technical Conference, Chicago.
Dennett, D.D. 1973, Mechanism and Responsibility, in T. Honderich (ed.), *Essays on Freedom of Action*. Boston, MA: Routledge and Keegan Paul.
Dennett, D.D. 1997, When HAL Kills, Who's to Blame? Computer Ethics, in D.G. Stork (ed.), *HAL's Legacy: 2001's Computer as a Dream and Reality*. Cambridge, MA: MIT Press.
Fahlquist, J.N. 2008, Moral Responsibility for Environmental Problems – Individual or Institutional? *Journal of Agricultural and Environmental Ethics*, 22(2): 109–24. doi: 10.1007/s10806-008-9134-5.
Fischer, J.M., and Ravizza, M. 1998, *Responsibility and Control: A Theory of Moral Responsibility*. Cambridge: Cambridge University Press.
Floridi, L. and Sancers, J. 2004, The Foundationalist Debate in Computer Ethics, in R. Spinello and H. Tavani (eds), *Readings in CyberEthics* (pp. 81–95). Massachusetts: Jones and Bartlett.

Friedman, B. 1990, *Moral Responsibility and Computer Technology*. Paper presented at the Annual Meeting of the American Educational Research Association, Boston, MA.

Galliott, J. 2015, *Military Robots: Mapping the Moral Landscape*. Farnham: Ashgate.

Galliott, J.C. 2012, Uninhabited Systems and the Asymmetry Objection: A Response to Strawser. *Journal of Military Ethics*, 11(1): 58–66.

Galliott, J.C. 2012/13, Closing with Completeness: The Asymmetric Drone Warfare Debate. *Journal of Military Ethics*, 11(4): 353–6.

Garvey, J. 2008, *The Ethics of Climate Change: Right and Wrong in a Warning World*. Bloomsbury: New York.

Gotterbarn, D. 2001, Informatics and Professional Responsibility. *Science and Engineering Ethics*, 7(2): 221–30.

Gray, C.S. 1997, AI at War: The Aegis System in Combat, in D. Schuler (ed.), *Directions and Implications of Advanced Computing* (pp. 62–79). New York: Ablex.

Grossman, D. 1995, *On Killing: The Psychological Cost of Learning to Kill in War and Society*. Boston, MA: Little, Brown and Company.

Lokhorst, G-J. and van den Hoven, J. 2012, Responsibility for military robots, in P. Lin, K. Abney and G. Bekey (eds), *Robot Ethics: The Ethical and Social Implications of Robotics* (pp. 145–56). Cambridge, MA: MIT Press.

Manders-Huits, N. 2006, *Moral Responsibility and IT for Human Enhancement*. Paper presented at the Assocication for Computing Machinery Symposium on Applied Computing, Dijon.

Matthias, A. 2004, The Responsibility Gap: Ascribing Responsibility for the Actions of Learning Automata. *Ethics and Information Technology*, 6, 175–83.

McMahan, J. 2009, *Killing in War*. Oxford: Oxford University Press.

Millar, J. and Kerr, I. 2012, *Delegation, Relinquishment and Responsiibility: The Prospect of Expert Robots*. Paper presented at the We Robot, Coral Gables.

Miller, S. 2008, Collective Responsibility and Information and Communication Technology, in J. van den Hoven and J. Weckert (eds), *Information Technology and Moral Philosophy* (pp. 226–50). Cambridge: Cambridge University Press.

National Aeronautics and Space Administration 2012, Robotics, Tele-Robotics and Autonomous Systems Roadmap, viewed online 7 January 2015, http://www.nasa.gov/sites/default/files/501622main_TA04ID_rev6b_NRC_wTASR.pdf.

Noorman, M. 2012, Computing and Moral Responsibility. *Stanford Encyclopedia of Responsibility*, from http://plato.stanford.edu/archives/fall2012/entries/computing-responsibility.

Petitt, P. 2007, Responsibility Incorporated. *Ethics*, 117(2): 171–201.

Rogers, W. and Rogers, S. 1992, *Storm Center: The USS Vincennes and Iran Air Flight 655*. Annapolis: Naval Institute Press.

Shue, H. 1988, Mediating Duties. *Ethics*, 98(4): 687–704.

Sparrow, R. 2007, Killer robots. *Journal of Applied Philosophy*, 24(1): 62–77.

Strawson, P.F. 1974, Freedom and Resentment *Freedom and Resentment and Other Essays*. London: Methuen.

Sullins, J.P. 2006, When is a Robot a Moral Agent. *International Review of Information Ethics*, 14(2): 219–33.

Thompson, D. 1987, *Political Ethics and Public Office*. Cambridge, MA: Harvard University Press.

United States Department of Defense. 2009, *FY2009–2034 unmanned systems integrated roadmap*. Washington DC: Department of Defense.

Waelbers, K. 2009, Technological delegation: Responsibility for the unintended. *Science and Engineering Ethics*, 15(1): 51–68.

Wallach, W. and Allen, C. 2009, *Moral Machines: Teaching Robots Right from Wrong*. Oxford: Oxford University Press.

Zuboff, S. 1985, Automate/Informate: The Two Faces of Intelligent Technology. *Organizational Dynamics*, 14(2), 5–18.

PART V
Bioethics for Outer Space

Chapter 17

Space Medicine: The Bioethical and Legal Implications for Commercial Human Spaceflight

Sara Langston

Commercial human spaceflight inherently raises numerous medical, legal and ethical considerations with regard to the health and safety of civilian spaceflight participants (SFPs) and commercial crewmembers. Nascent and emerging space companies are currently proposing a diverse range of commercial orbital, suborbital and eventually point-to-point transportation services. Bioethical and ensuing legal issues therefore arise throughout the course of these activities including *preflight* medical screening, evaluation and training; medical services and emergency measures in transit to and from space; as well as tele-medicine and medical services that may be rendered while *in* space, and *post-flight* evaluations.

While US commercial launch regulations stipulate medical certification requirements for commercial pilots and crew, they do not include SFPs. Nor has any other supranational body or nation promulgated relevant regulations to date. Ultimately, the decision-making authority on fitness to fly currently remains in the hands of licensed commercial launch operators. This triggers a plethora of novel ethical and legal questions, such as:

- Whether physicians and medical facilities screening potential SFPs should be accredited or hold special aerospace medical knowledge and expertise.
- Defining the relationship between corporate screening physicians and commercial SFPs.
- Defining the physician's duty to disclose, and degree of disclosure, on potential health risks in order to allow for informed consent.
- Distinguishing and balancing health risks, caution and benefit in human spaceflight.
- Identifying risk-taking cultures and ethical implications where the novelty of spaceflight and associated health risk profiles are unknown or uncertain.

From a regulatory standpoint, s.50905(c)(2)-(3) of the *United States Code* restricts the Federal Aviation Administration's (FAA) licensing authority for commercial human spaceflight where health and safety measures involve vehicle design and operations, that is until 1 October 2015 or until a serious incident occurs. The legislative intent is to allow for the industry to mature without the stifling effect that overregulation can incur. The FAA has consequently worked alongside stakeholders in drafting the *Recommended Practices for Human Space Flight Occupant Safety* (Recommended Practices), released in August 2014 (FAA 2014). The purpose of the document is to incorporate standards garnered from the history of human spaceflight that can be applied to most human spaceflight system concepts (Commercial Space Transportation Advisory Committee [COMSTAC] 2013).

The scope of the Recommended Practices, however, remains limited to *launch* and *re-entry* activities – the FAA's limited sphere of jurisdiction. The document therefore does not address long duration flights (beyond two weeks in orbit) and other related non-Earth orbital spaceflight activities (FAA 2014). Consequently, there is room for further development on these relevant issues, whether through regulation or policy guidelines.

One of the main challenges of human spaceflight is known environmental hazards coupled with limited knowledge of the effects and risks of spaceflight on humans, presenting a unique challenge for the commercial space industry. Opening the passenger manifest to average individuals with reduced fitness profiles leads to high risk and uncertainty with regard to even just the main threats from space travel (acceleration forces, microgravity and radiation). This chapter will address spaceflight risks, review current legal and ethical parameters for clinicians and physicians in providing medical care to SFPs and discuss novel bioethical and legal considerations for the new commercial space industry and society.

Medical, Legal and Ethical Issues

The space environment inherently presents a hazardous environment to human life and it is widely accepted that spaceflight remains an inherently dangerous activity. Health and medical concerns are also dependent on the type of space activity, to include suborbital space transportation, orbital flight, long-duration missions and voyages and ultimately extraterrestrial settlement. Consequently, the implications for commercial operators, physicians and spaceflight participants (SFPs) are far-reaching. In analysing the current and future issues for commercial human spaceflight an interdisciplinary approach is necessary to fully understand the myriad of medical, legal and ethical considerations. Pertinent questions here include: What are the roles and responsibilities of the space medical profession? What flexible legal solutions exist? And what new ethical considerations are raised by commercial human spaceflight?

A new space transportation industry inevitably means an increase in space access for the general public, researchers and tourists in the near future. Opening spaceflight to civilian populations brings new issues to the fore in areas where health, medicine, risk/safety analysis and laws currently lack certainty. As a result, human spaceflight activities present challenges to the medical, legal and public policy communities equally, with these questions and issues often being intertwined.

For contextual purposes, it may be helpful to perceive the stage of growth for this space era as reflecting civil aviation in the 1950s – perhaps more functional than luxurious. Unlike aviation, however, the reality of human spaceflight inherently incurs extraordinary risks to passengers and crew alike. And unlike aviation, which is deemed 'common carriage', commercial spaceflight is still perceived as an activity akin to an extreme sport and the SFPs bear the brunt of the risk under the US liability waiver scheme.[1] Medical, bioethical and legal implications, therefore, inevitably arise in convolution requiring careful consideration.

Physician/Clinician Responsibilities

'Space medicine' is a broad term used to encompass both medical support and the monitoring of astronauts' health in space, as well as medical evaluation, health and related training requirements on Earth concerning space activities. Thus, it can be seen as part operational medicine, part medical research as well as training and education (Wilke et al. 1999, p. 581). In addition, 'space surgery' relates to 'surgery in support of space exploration' (Grenon et al. 2012a, p. 11). Cumulatively, space medicine pertains to the duties and normative ethics for medical professionals in the field of space.

Standardisation

No regulations or performance standards on space medicine and bioethical procedures for screening physicians or commercial SFPs currently exist (Langston 2011, p. 384). In fact, space tourism companies, like Virgin Galactic, intend to limit medical exclusions for potential customers (Virgin Galactic 2014), thus making access to space available to a wider public. The FAA's Recommended Practices is intentionally silent on medical criteria for determining the acceptable health status of commercial SFPs stating '[SFPs] should be free to make decisions about their own individual risk' (FAA 2014, p. 7). In 2013, the FAA reasoned '[t]here is little clear statistical evidence on the actual impact of space flight on the health of an occupant with pre-existing conditions. Medical screening of space flight participants is included as a practice to inform them of risks and to ensure they will not be a danger to other occupants' (FAA 2013, p. 8). Thus, a regime of informed disclosure is favoured over regulation.

Naturally, it is in the best interests of the commercial launch operator to employ or appoint qualified physicians with aerospace knowledge and experience to

---

1   The US Congress currently excludes commercial space transportation from the scope of common carriage law, along with the traditional legal duties for common carriers and passenger rights (Boehlert 2004).

conduct medical screening and evaluations for SFPs. The Recommended Practices merely stipulates that '[w]ithin 12 months of flight, each space flight participant should consult with a physician, trained or experienced in aerospace medicine, to ascertain their medical risks of space flight' (FAA 2014, p. 46). What qualifies as sufficient 'training' and 'experience' is not defined, neither is the consultation a legal obligation under US law. It is foreseeable that an SFP could request his/her own physician to perform the medical evaluation, in concert with any stipulations issued by the licensed operator. The concern here is that this could potentially result in medical forum shopping or inadequate disclosure.

Analogously, States Parties to the International Space Station (ISS) Agreement promulgated the *Medical Standards and Certification Procedures for Spaceflight Participants* in 2002 with the advent of space tourists to the *ISS* (Grenon et al. 2012a, p. 85). However, this document is specific to the intergovernmental space station and therefore is not binding on the FAA or relevant to all types of commercial spaceflight activities. Subsequently, on 31 March 2003 the FAA issued an informational memorandum on *Guidance for Medical Screening of Commercial Aerospace Passengers* (FAA 2003). This document was updated in 2006 and iterates general nonbinding guidance, similar to the *ISS* standards, for commercial suborbital and orbital spaceflight company passenger selection (Antuñano et al. 2008).

As a result, international medical professionals have suggested that medical screening and training centres develop standardised tests and procedures for SFPs on a global level (Kluge et al. 2013, p. 192). This would serve to facilitate the training process with all necessary equipment at specific centres, and allow for assessment and medical data to be mutually shared with the licensed launch operator to further facilitate the selection of appropriate SFP candidates (ibid.). While this standardisation proposal would streamline the medical evaluation process, effectuate communication and medical data exchange and minimise international and domestic discrepancies, it would be legally and ethically essential to maintain patient confidentiality and privacy protections at all times – both for data collected on the ground and while in space. This is an issue that has yet to be thoroughly addressed in commercial space.

Moreover, different spaceflight plans incur diverse medical implications and risk factors for consideration. The impact of orbital spaceflight on human health is inherently more severe than that of suborbital spaceflight, for instance. Both the US and Russia have traditionally applied stringent medical and fitness evaluations and training for orbital flights for astronauts and space tourists. Case in point, in 2006, Russia forfeited the seat of space tourist and Japanese businessman, Daisuke Enomoto, to the *ISS* because of an ongoing minor health issue – a kidney stone (*Enomoto v Space Adventures Ltd (2009)* 624 F.Supp.2d 443; Langston 2011, p. 385). While this does not ordinarily endanger a human life on Earth, Russian doctors were unwilling to stake their interests and allow Enomoto to fly to the *ISS*. Enomoto's seat was subsequently allocated to the next healthy individual in line. The Recommended Practices, likewise, advises commercial operators to screen for identifiable infectious and communicable diseases prior to multi-day orbital flights that could interfere with flight (FAA 2014, p. 46), but establishing such procedures is voluntary.

Acquiring health data post-flight would also contribute to our understanding of the space environment on human physiology and mental health although this is not necessitated in the Recommended Practices or under US law. Practitioners, however, recommend that medical screenings and evaluations be conducted post-flight for upcoming suborbital flights to ensure the overall health of the SFP and acquire data on any potential or actual health implications (Kluge et al. 2013, p. 192). In future point-to-point space transportation, subsequent screenings will require cooperation and collaboration between spaceport authorities (national/international), companies and physicians as well as compatible medical standards and procedures. Again, this argues for medical standardisation and data exchange while triggering the need to safeguard ethical duties in doctor-patient confidentiality and data protection laws.

Professional and Ethical Duties

The Code of Medical Ethics inescapably makes a physician responsible to his/her patient not to an employer or third party (for example the launch operator) interested in widening its customer base. The American Medical Association's *Principles of Medical Ethics*, for instance, establishes the physician's ethical duties towards his/her patients in compliance with the law (American Medical Association [AMA] 2001). A corporate screening physician therefore owes the same professional duties of care and confidentiality to an SFP that he/she does to any other patient. Thus, conflicts of interest or physician loyalty issues ought not to arise in regard to medical evaluations of SFPs.

Physicians should likewise be assertive towards their own practice. A licensed operator and/or medical screening physician should ensure adequate malpractice and liability insurance for space-related evaluations. This is particularly relevant given the uncertain nature of the personal liability waivers (Langston 2011, p. 389) and the breadth of known hazards and undetermined medical implications and health risks involved in spaceflight (Grenon et al. 2012a).

Medical Research and Spaceflight Participants

Ethical concerns are inevitably triggered with regard to medical research and experimentation on astronauts. As governmental employees, astronauts are legally civil servants working in a hazardous occupation where risk to life and health are acknowledged. Medical research for knowledge acquisition is one valuable function provided by astronaut research participants (Institute of Medicine [IOM] 2014a, p. 85). Conversely, commercial crews and SFPs do not fall under the same rubric and bioethical safeguards as official astronauts. Thus bioethical concerns may be heightened here due to the lack of administrative oversight.

For instance, pharmaceutical testing on astronauts is necessary to learn how drugs metabolise differently in space. This knowledge is essential for planning longer duration space missions as well as beneficial for applications on Earth. NASA's senior bioethicist, Paul Root Wolpe (2013), has raised some pertinent ethical questions in this regard, such as:

- Is it ethical to use astronauts as human test subjects to discover metabolic reactions of medications in different microgravity environments?
- More specifically, is it ethical to test drugs on a perfectly healthy individual in space or one who would not ordinarily require the treatment?
- If so, how are the medications or treatments to be prioritised and selected from the numerous testable drug options?

These basic bioethical questions are also pertinent to the commercial spaceflight industry and SFPs, not just to national space agencies.

To date, space tourists to the *ISS* have obtained sponsorships by conducting medical and scientific experiments in space (Young 2005; European Space Agency [ESA] 2006). With the advent of commercial suborbital flights and orbital flights, it is foreseeable that SFPs may acquire similar corporate sponsorships by becoming human research subjects for pharmaceutical drug companies. While international and national ethics and legal policy exist on the use of participants (humans and animals) for medical research, supervision and compliance remains unclear here for the private commercial sector concerning SFPs.

Forward-looking ethical discussions should therefore incorporate social justice concerns in space science and research. For instance, extending lessons learned from medical events on Earth, consideration should be given to safeguarding individuals from any unethical pharmaceutical and scientific research practices in the near future. Likewise, ethically progressive pharmaceutical research in space should promote the selection of potentially beneficial drugs for global populations, not just treatments pertaining to first world health issues.

Medical Insurance Companies

Allianz Global Assistance (Allianz) is the first insurance company to offer personal and corporate insurance for commercial SFPs. The scope of coverage includes commercial SFPs (tourists and scientific researchers) and spaceliners (launch operators). In a 2011 Press Release, Allianz stated its intention to actively engage with the spaceflight process and accompany SFPs from the first preparatory phase of spaceflight until their return (Allianz 2011). Allianz also intends to provide 'medical assistance solutions, as well as expert advice and personal services for space travellers' (ibid.). It is unclear exactly what role the insurance company seeks to play with regard to the screening and selection process or how contract terms may affect doctor-patient confidentiality, if at all.

Informed Consent

The US *Code of Federal Regulations* (CFR), Title 14, Part 460.45(a), requires that SFPs consent to the following communicated facts from the launch operator: '[t]hat there are hazards that are not known' and '[t]hat participation in space flight may result in death, serious injury, or total or partial loss of physical or mental function'. The SFP's consent to broad unknown risks, however, does not absolve the launch operator from all liability (Kleinman, Lamie and Carminati 2012, p. 109; Langston 2011, p. 387). Lack of knowledge on certain medical cases may increase the risk for the SFP, the liability of the physician and the liability of the launch operator.

Admittedly, limited medical knowledge on the effects of disease or pre-existing conditions in space is due to restricted experience. The physiological impact of microgravity, G-forces and heightened radiation exposure during the flight on a general population is unknown (Grenon et al. 2012a, p. 32). Medical implications may also arise from other preflight training or in-flight activities that may exacerbate some conditions (p. 86). Physicians therefore have a challenging task in providing SFPs with sufficient informed disclosure on pertinent medical impacts (actual or potential) involved in the launch, in space and re-entry stages that invoke health risks. Practitioners already acknowledge that while not all general physicians will have space medicine expertise, 'they will have to understand how [spaceflight] affects their patients' (Grenon et al., 2012b, p. 2) as commercial spaceflight becomes more common.

The Zero-G Corporation, which conducts parabolic flights to simulate various microgravity environments, has flown fit and less-than-fit individuals. Previous passengers include Stephen Hawking (who has motor neuron disease) in 2007 and other wheelchair-bound teenagers in 2008 accompanied by medical experts (Diamandis 2013). While these flights were a success, the relative physical ease of a parabolic experience does not necessarily provide a substantive basis for longer duration spaceflights and higher G-forces. Much remains to be learned on risk profiles for human spaceflight.

With regard to commercial orbital space stations ('hotels') proposed by companies like Virgin Galactic (Moskovitz 2013), Orbital Technologies (McKie 2011) and Bigelow Aerospace, commercial SFPs generally will face the same health risks as astronauts on the *ISS*, which may include cardiac, pulmonary and musculoskeletal system events (Grenon et al. 2012a, p. 82). Thus an individual with chronic illness or who requires certain medications is unlikely to be cleared for spaceflight (Kluge et al. 2013, p. 190). An alternative less-risky approach may be to first carefully study the effects of parabolic flights on these high-risk candidates.

Other analogous policies, such as the Joint Aviation Authorities (JAA) crew medical selection criteria, may be used as a basis for SFP medical screening, which includes a health questionnaire and evaluation to filter out 'no-go criteria' for spaceflight (p. 189). Although, the applicability of crew requirements to

SFPs and excludable health profiles by commercial spaceflight companies remain unclear. Significantly, however, individual health risks for susceptible or vulnerable individuals may extend beyond a question of medicine and consider the overarching safety and liability for all flight passengers and crew.

Similarly, high-risk factors may include advanced age. Former astronaut and Senator, John Glenn was the oldest person to fly and orbit in space, at 77 years old. NASA permitted this because it provided a unique opportunity to observe the effects of microgravity environments on an elderly person. The scientific knowledge garnered from this experiment was also intended to benefit geriatric research on Earth (Dunn 1998). Some of the health conditions studied were bone loss, muscle weakness and lack of balance, as these conditions are similarly experienced by astronauts in space as well as elderly people on Earth (ibid.). While John Glenn thrived on his experience, the risk that NASA took in allowing him to fly was high indeed. Glenn also required particular medical attention which may not be available to all SFPs. Ultimately, age and health may be inter-connected consideration factors where extreme activities, like spaceflight, are concerned.

Current regulations are silent on the question as to whether minors can fly as SFPs. This question triggers the requirements of informed consent, full disclosure and medical screening. But, can a minor give informed consent to engage in an extreme activity? The FAA currently interprets informed consent to imply age of majority (18 years old), although this is not stated in either the legislation or the regulations, leaving the questions open (FAA 2006, p. 75626).

US regulations require the launch operator to provide the SFP with full disclosure on flight safety risks and receive written informed consent from the SFP prior to engaging in suborbital spaceflight (14 CFR Part 460.45; Langston 2011, p. 390). The SFP must also be informed that the US government has not certified the safety of the flight and flight vehicle (51 USC s. 50905). While the regulations pertain more to technical safety disclosure than medical, the SFP is entitled to ask further questions and receive additional information (14 CFR Part 460.45(f)). This may include medical or physiological concerns.

It is uncertain, however, whether a minor would be capable of fully understanding the risks, both medical and safety, to provide the requisite informed consent. Adolescents generally lack the basic experience and biological maturity to understand and evaluate risk-benefit situations appropriately. This may be inferred from prior studies on adolescent risk-taking behaviours (IOM 2011a). As a question of law, minors generally lack the capacity to give legal consent and this would apply to any human spaceflight activity as well.

On the other hand, parents and guardians routinely consent to medical procedures that incur high levels of risk to a child. So can this right to consent to risk-taking on behalf of a minor be extended to include inherently dangerous activities for entertainment? We may anticipate future scenarios here where families may desire to engage in suborbital space tourism activities together, or where point-to-point space transportation becomes a reality or even where commercial competitions or organisations, like Make-A-Wish Foundation, may seek to fulfil an individual's dream of spaceflight.

The underlying issue here is, to what extent can parents/guardians provide consent for a minor to engage in extreme and dangerous activities? Domestic laws or public policies may indicate risk-caution tendencies, although distinctions may exist between risky medical procedures and extreme sports. With extreme sports, such as sky diving, a participant is usually required to be at least 18 years of age. However, this is not always the case. Many companies legally allow a minor to participate in dangerous activities, like bungee jumping, where a parent or guardian signs the consent and liability waiver form on his/her behalf.

Consequently, the answer to whether children can engage in human spaceflight is ultimately dependent on societal leanings with regard to children, risk and public policy. No specific legal rationale would prohibit physicians, parents or guardians from consenting to a minor engaging in a suborbital flight, for instance. It is unlikely, however, that this issue will be addressed until the industry demonstrates successful operations. Therefore, the issue of informed consent and minor SFPs remains open for regulatory/policy clarification.

If the law and licensing authorities are to permit minors to fly on suborbital flights, additional factors to consider may include: what health and age restrictions are appropriate for spaceflight or whether size and weight would be a more appropriate parameter; what structural and safety accommodations may be necessary onboard the space vehicle; and what additional crew and standards may be required, if any, to ensure safety and emergency procedures can be adequately discharged towards minors.

Training Requirements

As health and safety are inextricably intertwined, US regulations mandate that the launch operator provide SFPs with preflight training on safety and emergency measures (14 CFR Part 460.51).[2] But these very basic requirements lack specificity. It remains to be seen exactly what training practices and procedures licensed launch operators will employ for SFPs. Medical practitioners have also suggested that appropriate (customised) training may alleviate certain health concerns (Kluge et al. 2013, p. 189).

For now, Virgin Galactic has announced their training program will consist of three days' instruction at the spaceport that will include preflight briefings, basic emergency response training, parabolic flights and exercise techniques in preparation for experiencing G-force and microgravity environments (Virgin Galactic 2014). XCOR Aerospace, in concert with RocketShip Tours, has stated a similar four-day training and screening program for suborbital SFP candidates

---

2 14 CFR Part 460.51 provides 'An operator must train each space flight participant before flight on how to respond to emergency situations, including smoke, fire, loss of cabin pressure, and emergency exit'.

(Cruise Everything 2012; XCOR 2009). XCOR even offers cancellation insurance given its $95,000 ticket cost (ibid.). On the other hand, Bigelow Aerospace offers astronaut training for orbital flights and space station life as part of its prospective space station lease enterprise (Bigelow Aerospace 2014).[3]

Additional Bioethical Implications

As commercial spaceflight presents novel human activities, additional questions of related bioethics and law are raised concerning SPF selection and human spaceflight. The following present a sampling of potential future issues.

Scientific Observation: Children and Spaceflight

The question of scientific and medical preflight and post-flight screenings with adult participants for the purpose of data collection may be satisfied by applying ethically established protocols, procedures and obtaining informed consent. When it comes to studies utilising child participants, these ethical concerns are heightened. Human spaceflight screenings and evaluations are no exception. A lack of scientific and medical information on spaceflight implies that at some point healthy children will become space pioneers if we are to obtain any significant medical data on the physiological effects of spaceflight for this demographic. The quandary rests with whether this is morally permissible based on ethical principles.

Legal and Ethical Duties of SFPs

The Outer Space Treaty (OST 1967) stipulates only one requirement for individuals. Article V states that astronauts in space 'shall render all possible assistance' to other astronauts. This is the only personal duty required of astronauts under the international space law regime, and stems from traditional maritime principles and law of the sea. However, no uniform definition of 'astronaut' currently exists and US legislation governing SFPs is silent on this specific obligation. Thus it is uncertain whether commercial launch operators and SFPs will be included in this treaty provision.

The significance of distinguishing SFPs from astronauts under the treaty directly relates to implications of SFP health, safety and law. A legal duty to render assistance would exclude SFPs who are unwilling or unable to do so. For instance, Stephen Hawking would be unable to render assistance to another person on a suborbital flight even if cleared by a physician and launch operator. This also raises

---

3   Bigelow Aerospace advertises this '[t]raining will include qualification screening for mental and physical health, acclimation to physical forces including microgravity, operation of space station daily living systems, and mission specific training'.

additional liability issues for the SFPs and the launch operator as the personal liability waiver is not generally concluded between passengers. Any commercial astronaut with limited fitness and related restrictions may fail to comply with this international obligation. What then?

The underlying ethical question raised here is whether a moral duty to render possible assistance to other persons in space exists, regardless of whether one is an SFP or crewmember. This is also a question of public policy. If yes, it follows whether the 'Good Samaritan' Principle should also be extended to commercial human spaceflight and in-space activities to promote and protect prospective rescuers. The practical ethics and legal implications of this question have yet to be addressed.

Risk-taking, Culture and Ethics

In general, ethics is the study of what ought to be done. What *should* be done does not necessarily equate with what *can* be done. Space-related risks and decision-making invokes both cultural and ethical factors. The US and Russia, for instance, possess risk-taking cultures and histories, particularly with regard to spaceflight (Spennemann 2007, pp. 901–6). These nations also have greater technological capabilities, government sponsorship, the resources to take big risks and to transport humans into Earth orbit and more.

Independence and autonomy are also fundamental values in American history and culture, perhaps more so than any other culture, and this is particularly evident in the national space culture (Carminati 2014). Conversely, Australia may be deemed more risk adverse, especially concerning space, and therefore does not participate in human spaceflight missions. Does this imply that as a global society we should let individuals engage voluntarily in extremely hazardous activities in those countries and cultures that are more favourable to risk? If so, is it likewise morally permissible for adults to voluntarily participate for a one-way trip to Mars?

One position argues that we should allow people to take risks that they voluntarily subscribe to (Langston 2011, p. 390; Carminati 2014). A prime example can be seen in those who undertake to climb Mount Everest every year – a very high-risk activity with regular health implications and fatalities – or those who engage in orbital space tourism to the *ISS*. On the other hand, is there a moral duty to protect thrill-seekers from themselves? And if so, at what point does this duty apply and to what extent?

Legally, moreover, there is no significant distinction between one who voluntarily pays to engage in an extreme sport costing thousands of dollars and the average Jane or John Doe who wins a lottery trip to space. Both must provide voluntary and informed consent to partake in the activity. From a moral viewpoint, questions arise as to how ethical reasoning and justice may apply to these scenarios?

One of the precepts of a moral principle is its universal application. If a principle applies to one person, ethics dictates that it should apply to all (Taylor 1986, p. 46). Fairness and equity are principles applied in both law and ethics, and yet we see societal values with regard to risk-taking diverge between cultures. A person's right to individual risk assessment and decision-making is not universally held – a gap is distinctly visible between space-faring nations and non-space-faring nations. Which implies that risk is not purely a matter of individual autonomy but also social preference.

Paternalism is an applied ethical concept that allows a state to interfere with an individual's right to autonomy if it is in the individual's best interests (Dworkin 2014). There are varying degrees of paternalism that allow for less or more abrogation of personal autonomy. The overall question that deserves to be acknowledged here is to what extent can a regular person engage in an extreme and dangerous activity, like spaceflight? And what should be the ethical parameters for state involvement with regard to this autonomy? These ethics questions require consideration from philosophical, practical and interdisciplinary perspectives to develop a uniform bioethical approach to space encompassing the general public and civilian SFPs.

Ethical Decision-making Frameworks

In July 2014, the US Institute of Medicine released *Health Standards for Long Duration and Exploration Spaceflight: Ethics Principles, Responsibilities, and Decision Framework* (IOM 2014a). This report focuses on developing a decision-making framework for NASA's long-duration flight health guidelines, incorporating 'ethical issues raised by exposing astronauts to environments with uncertain and even unknown risks to their health, and excessive levels of known health risks' (IOM 2014a, p. ix). This is a worthy contribution in light of a relative dearth of industry applicable interdisciplinary literature and frameworks on bioethical issues, space and ethics.

Applying a practical approach, this multidisciplinary group of experts chose to adopt applied ethical principles to the recommended framework instead of debating various philosophical schools of thought. The result is a recommended list of six ethical responsibilities concerning astronaut health, related decision-making and implementation measures. The fundamental ethical principles applied in this framework include the established moral principles: to avoid harm, uphold beneficence, maintain a favourable balancing of risk and benefit, respect for autonomy, ensure fairness and recognise fidelity (IOM 2014a, p. 6).

The Institute of Medicine (IOM 2014b) summarised the ethical duties towards astronauts in providing guidance for decision-making as follows:

- Avoid harm by preventing harm, exercising caution and removing or mitigating harms that occur.
- Provide benefits to society.
- Seek a favourable and acceptable balance of risk of harm and potential for benefit.

- Respect autonomy by allowing individual astronauts to make voluntary decisions regarding participation in proposed missions.
- Ensure fair processes and provide equality of opportunity for mission participation and crew selection.
- Recognise fidelity and the individual sacrifices made for the benefit of society, as well as honour societal obligations in return by offering health care and protection for astronauts during a mission and over the course of their lifetimes.

These mid-level ethical principles may also find applications in commercial human spaceflight. The recommended framework itself, however, renders specific application to space agency medical and health procedures and official astronauts with distinct governmental implications. Nonetheless, this report is a valuable tool in unravelling the ethical issues and principles pertaining to human spaceflight.

Conclusion

Commercial spaceflight triggers convoluted questions of medicine, safety and law, much of which has yet to be defined. Despite the lack of specific regulatory requirements and medical uncertainties, screening physicians still have a legal duty to evaluate and inform SFPs on the actual and potential health risks inherent to spaceflight. These risks, however, may vary on a case-to-case basis considering less fit-to-fly individuals and the type of space activity concerned. Consequently, the scope of information to be provided and basis for candidate exclusion is unclear.

Questions raised for further consideration include: how much medical disclosure (general/specific information) suffices for compliance? And what are the professional and ethical implications towards patients where unknown health risks and impacts exist? What data collection procedures should be standardised and how are they to be widely and ethically implemented? And, what are appropriate ethical practices for commercial human space research? The inherent uncertainties in commercial space activities and space medicine require a balancing of factors. What is evident is that an ethics inclusive interdisciplinary approach and framework is necessary to address these concerns going forward.

References

Allianz 2011, 'Allianz Global Assistance and the International Space Transport Association (ISTA) partners in space tourism industry', Press Release, 14 November, viewed 1 July 2014, http://www.allianz-global-assistance.com/corporate/media/press-releases/Allianz-Global-Assistance-and-International-Space-Transport-Association-partners-in-space-tourism-industry.aspx.

American Medical Association 2001, *Principles of Medical Ethics*, viewed 1 July 2014, http://www.ama-assn.org/ama/pub/physician-resources/medical-ethics/code-medical-ethics/principles-medical-ethics.page?

Antuñano M., Baiseden D., Davis J., et al. 2008, *Guidance for Medical Screening of Commercial Aerospace Passengers*, Federal Aviation Administration, Technical Report Office of Aerospace Medicine, No., DOT-FAA-AM-06–1, Washington, DC.

Bigelow Aerospace 2014, *Training Astronauts*, viewed 1 July 2014, http://www.bigelowaerospace.com/training-astronauts.php.

Carminati M. 2014, '"Doctor, Doctor, Can I Go?" Medical Rules, Standards and Guidelines for Suborbital Space Space', *Space Safety Magazine*, 28 March, viewed 1 July 2014, http://www.spacesafetymagazine.com/doctor-doctor-medical-rules-standards-guidelines-suborbital-space/

Commercial Space Transportation Advisory Committee 2013, 'Public teleconference', *Federal Register*, 78(168), p. 53496.

Cruise Everything, *RocketShip Tours*, viewed 1 July 2014, http://www.cruiseeverything.com/rocket_ship_tours.

Diamandis P. 2013, 'Prof. Hawking goes weightless – the true story', Peter's Blog, web log post, 15 April, viewed 1 July 2014, http://www.diamandis.com/the-launch-pad/prof-hawking-goes-weightless-the-true-story/1726.

Dworkin G. 2014, 'Paternalism', in E. Zalta (ed.), *The Standford Encyclopedia of Philosophy*, viewed 1 July 2014, https://leibniz.stanford.edu/friends/members/view/paternalism.

Dunn M. 1998, 'John Glenn, floating medical laboratory', *The Sunday Gazette*, 1 November, p. A11.

Enomoto v. Space Adventures, Ltd, (2009) 624 F.Supp.2d 443.

European Space Agency 2006, *ESA Experiments with Spaceflight Participant Ansari to ISS*, 12 September 2006, viewed 1 July 2014, http://www.esa.int/Our_Activities/Human_Spaceflight/International_Space_Station/ESA_experiments_with_spaceflight_participant_Ansari_to_ISS.

Federal Aviation Administration 2003, *Information: Guidance for Medical Screening of Commercial Aerospace Passengers*, viewed 1 July 2014, http://www.faa.gov/about/office_org/headquarters_offices/ast/licenses_permits/media/passengers_03_final_memo_2atr04.pdf.

Federal Aviation Administration 2006, 'Human space flight requirements for crew and space flight participants', Federal Register, 71(241, p. 75616.

Federal Aviation Administration 2013, *Draft Established Practices for Human Space Flight Occupant Safety (7/31/2013), with Rationale (added 9/23/2013)*, Washington, DC.

Federal Aviation Administration 2014, *Recommended Practices for Human Space Flight Occupant Safety (7/27/2014)*, Washington, DC.

'Godspeed Again, John Glenn: At 77, You Still Have `Right Stuff', *Sun Sentinel*, 29 October 1998, viewed 1 July 2014, http://articles.sun-sentinel.com/1998–10–29/news/9810280103_1_glenn-s-flight-john-glenn-nasa.

Grenon S.M., Ball C., Kirkpatrick W., Saary J 2012a, *Surgery in Space*, Saarbrücken: Lambert Academic Publishing.

Grenon S.M., Saary J., Gray G., Vanderploeg J. and Hughes-Fulford M. 2012b, 'Can I take a space flight? Considerations for doctors', *British Medical Journal*, 345 no. e8124.

Institute of Medicine (IOM) 2011, *The Science of Adolescent Risk-taking: Workshop Report*, Institute of Medicine and National Research Council, Washington, DC.

Institute of Medicine (IOM) 2014a, *Health Standards for Long Duration and Exploration Spaceflight: Ethics Principles, Responsibilities, and Decision Framework*, Institute of Medicine, The National Academies Press, Washington, DC.

Institute of Medicine (IOM) 2014b, *NASA Should Use an Ethics Framework when Making Decisions about Health Standards for Long Duration and Exploration Spaceflights*, Press Release, 2 April, viewed 1 July 2014, http://www8. nationalacademies.org/onpinews/newsitem.aspx?RecordID=18576.

Kleinman M., Lamie J. and Carminati M. 2012, *The Laws of Spaceflight: A Guidebook for New Space Lawyers*, American Bar Association, Chicago, IL.

Kluge G., Stern C., Trammer M., Chaudhuri I., Tuschy P. and Gerzer R. 2013, *Commercial Suborbital Space Tourism – Proposal on Passenger's Medical Selection, Acta Astronautica*, 92: 187–92.

Langston S. 2011, 'Suborbital flights: A comparative analysis of national and international law', *Journal of Space Law*, 37(2): 299–392.

McKie R. 2011, 'Space hotel to give rich a thrill that's out of this world', *The Guardian*, 27 August, viewed 1 July 2014, http://www.theguardian.com/ science/ 2011/aug/27/space-hotel-rich-thrill-world.

Moskovitz C. 2013, 'Flights of fancy: Virgin galactic plans space hotels, day trips to the Moon', *Scientific American*, 7 October, viewed 1 July 2014, http://www. scientific american.com/article/virgin-galactic-space-hotels.

Statement of Rep. Boehlert 2004, *Congressional Record*, House of Representatives 4 March, 150(27), p. H836, Washington, DC.

Spennemann D. 2007, 'Extreme cultural tourism from Antarctica to the Moon', *Annals of Tourism Research*, 34(4): 898–918.

Taylor P. 1986, *Respect for Nature*, Princeton, NJ: Princeton University Press.

Title 51 United States Code s. 50905.

Title 14 Code of Federal Regulations Parts 460.45(a), 460.45(f), 460.51.

Treaty on Principles Governing the Activities of States in the Exploration and Use of Outer Space, Including the Moon and Other Celestial Bodies, 27 January 1967, 18 UST 2410, 610 UNTS 205.

Virgin Galactic 2014, *Overview*, viewed 1 July 2014, http://www.virgingalactic. com/overview/training.

Wilke D., Padeken D., Weber T. and Gerzer R. 1999 'Telemedicine for the International Space Station', *Acta Astronautica*, 44(7–12): 579–81.

Wolpe P. 2013, *Star Trek – The Ethics of Space Exploration*, online video, 29 May, viewed 1 July 2014, http://youtu.be/VmMS6rX11T8.

XCOR Aerospace 2009, 'XCOR participates in RocketShip tours Lynx Beta spaceflight Participant Qualification Program', *XCOR Newsletter*, 1(4), 14 September, viewed 1 July 2014 http://www.xcor.com/newsletters/090914/rocketship_tours_ participant_program.html.

Young K. 2005, 'Space tourist will experiment on himself', *New Scientist*, 29 September, viewed 1 July 2014, http://www.newscientist.com/article/dn8070-space-tourist-will-experiment-on himself.html #.U7Pmy43qe6Q.

Chapter 18

Enhancing Astronauts: The Ethical, Legal and Social Implications

Keith Abney and Patrick Lin[1]

Though it has been more than 40 years since the last person stepped foot on the Moon, we humans are again making plans to leave *terra firma* for other planets and moons. The surge of both public and commercial projects to explore outer space is the stuff of science fiction. These include: the US Department of Defense's 100-Year Starship Mission (100 Year Starship 2014); The Netherlands-based Mars One company to establish a Martian colony (Mars One 2014); Planetary Resources and Deep Space Industries for asteroid mining (Planetary Resources; Deep Space Industries 2014); several private spaceflight companies, for example, Virgin Galactic, Copenhagen Suborbitals, Airbus Defence and Space and others to promote tourism (Virgin Galactic 2014; Copenhagen Suborbitals 2014; Airbus Defense and Space 2014); and NASA's Mars 2020 Science Definition Team for a Mars mission to search for, and possibly return with, Martian life samples (NASA 2014a, 'Overview', para. 2).

The prospect of extended space travel seems to be getting closer, insofar as there are real investments, technological proofs of concept and other early steps in making it so. To that extent, it would be appropriate to begin considering the ethical challenges that may arise, given that space is one of the most hostile, distant and isolated environments for humans to inhabit and explore. These worries are far from unprecedented: US President Nixon had a speech ready, should the lunar return module fail, stranding astronauts Neil Armstrong and Edwin Aldrin on the Moon where they would die (Klein 2014). But such lifeboat-ethics questions are merely one of numerous new puzzles in the emerging field of astronaut bioethics.

'Lifeboat' Ethics and Other Dilemmas

If we are to send people, it must be for a very good reason – and with a realistic understanding that almost certainly we will lose lives. Astronauts and

---

1 The authors would like to thank Jordan Rowley and Erik Persson for their discussions in preparing this chapter and California Polytechnic State University, San Luis Obispo, for its support of our work. The statements expressed here are the authors alone and do not necessarily reflect the views of the aforementioned persons or organisations.

Cosmonauts have always understood this. Nevertheless, there has been and will
be no shortage of volunteers. (Sagan 1994, p. 119)

In 2025, suppose you are a crewmember on the first human spaceflight headed to
the red planet – on the Mars One spaceship, launched on schedule in late 2024 to
colonise Mars. Previous ships were already sent to build a basic habitat, and now
your ship is only five days away from landing. But something has gone terribly
wrong. Micrometeorites have pierced the hull and caused a slow leak; calculations
show there will not be enough oxygen for all four crewmembers to survive. Unless
one person stops breathing immediately, all four will asphyxiate before landing.
In fact, if you wait even one day before killing a crewmember, then at most two
members could survive.

   As the pilot and captain of the ship, what should you do? If you volunteer to
die, the mission and surviving crew would be forced to rely on the autopilot, which
is especially risky during the final, treacherous landing manoeuvres. If the ship's
doctor is to die, this would risk the future lives of the colonists. And choosing any
other crew member to die similarly sacrifices rare but essential skills, making it a
difficult dilemma in deciding who gets to stay on the proverbial lifeboat.

   But suppose this particular lifeboat dilemma could be avoided before launch.
Let's say that we could enhance astronauts' ability to breathe at low partial
pressures – for instance, with artificial red blood cells, or 'respirocytes', that act as
millions of microscopic oxygen tank (Freitas Jr 2002) – so there would be enough
oxygen for all to survive. Is this morally problematic? Consider another option to
enhance their ability to survive by placing astronauts into a low-temperature kind
of stasis, that is, 'suspended animation', during an oxygen crisis (Giles 2004). We
might readily accept that any external, technical fail-safe such as this would be a
godsend, indeed, morally required in such a situation – so what exactly (if anything)
would be morally troubling about making them internal to the astronauts?

   We can perhaps see a reasonable case for these or other enhancements as
ethical for astronauts to undergo. If so, they could help make a case to allow
human enhancements in other cases for the rest of us down here on Earth, such as
the athlete on anabolic steroids for a competitive edge, the student on modafinil to
study better or the military pilot on amphetamines to stay awake on long missions.
Likewise, if there are reasons why these or other cases may be questionable, that
may inform the ethics of astronaut enhancements.

   The kind of lifeboat scenario above for astronauts is not a mere fantasy; it
could easily become all too real in the near future. Humans, for the first time, are
beginning to extend space flight to destinations in which return to Earth is only
possible in time frames of months to years – if ever. The Moon astronauts faced
fearsome challenges and risks, but as Apollo 13 demonstrated, safe return to Earth
was still possible even if something goes wrong (Howell 2012). But for trips to
Mars and beyond, that might not be the case. In those travels, we encounter truly
novel circumstances – destinations more impossible of return than even Columbus
sailing off to the New World.

And such lifeboat scenarios will not cease upon a successful landing on Mars. The habitation modules of Mars One will be a fragile oasis of water and oxygen on a barren, desolate and profoundly inhospitable Martian soil, with temperatures averaging around minus 55 degrees Celsius (minus 67 Fahrenheit) in a desert world with almost no water and a thin, carbon-dioxide atmosphere. They will be subject to the whims of ultraviolet and other kinds of damaging radiation, solar and dust storms, meteorite strikes, physical injury, possible alien contamination and the other barely glimpsed vicissitudes of Martian living.

Given the extraordinary dangers, is it even ethical to recruit astronauts for a one-way trip to Mars – in all likelihood, a suicide mission? Or does that exploit a vulnerable population that has an overdeveloped sense of adventure or other psychological conditions? If a sustainable colony is the goal, is it ethical to have a baby in the harsh environment of outer space and other planets or moons, given the unknown effects of space radiation, unearthly gravity, social isolation and so on in child development? An enhancement drug (or disenhancement, depending on one's perspective) could be given to lower astronauts' libido, thus avoiding procreative behaviour.

Some have proposed to get avoid this dilemma by recruiting older, married couples for space travel, on the assumption that accidental or deliberate reproduction would not be possible after the woman has reached menopause (Tate 2014). The marriage requirement is meant to ensure stability in the relationship, though of course many marriages are anything but that. But this recruitment strategy also can raise ethical and legal concerns: Does deploying only older, married couples violate labour laws against discrimination based on gender, marital status or sexual orientation? If not, what does it tell us about the limitation of labour laws or the exigencies of certain human endeavours, such as science, business and war?

What Exactly is Astronaut Enhancement?

Arguments about the ethics of human enhancement run the gamut from those who see it as an illegitimate impulse towards a Promethean mastery and a hubristic quest to play God (Sandel 2008), to those who see enhancement as a moral necessity, just as or perhaps even more important than routine therapy, especially for children (for example, Savulescu 2001). But these discussions have all taken place against an assumption of a decidedly terrestrial framework, taking the current to near-term human condition here on Earth as a given, and arguing about what changes to that are morally permissible or not.

But in our very near future, the issues of human enhancement will move into the celestial sphere. We are at the dawn of a new space age, in which people for the first time will begin routinely going into near-Earth space, as tourists and workers, not just as elite government-trained astronauts or cosmonauts. And in what promises to be the most significant development, humans will leave the Earth as *colonists* – intending to settle on Mars (and eventually the Moon, Europa and beyond), and potentially never to return. As mentioned, the Mars One group has (probably overambitious) plans to begin such colonisation by 2025, and they have competition, and not merely from NASA. The founder of the private space launch company SpaceX, Elon Musk, has stated his intention to die on Mars – preferably not on impact! (Harris 2010)

To clarify our discussion, we need to define 'human enhancement', but this has been a notoriously challenging issue with no clear consensus among experts (Lin and Allhoff 2008). Nonetheless, it may still be useful to begin with this exercise, as inconclusive as it may be:

A popular understanding of enhancement is in its contrast to medical therapy, a widely accepted good (Lin and Allhoff 2008). Suppose, as a first approximation of a distinction between enhancements and therapy, that we attempt to use the distinction between natural and unnatural (or artificial) (for example, Allhoff et al. 2010; Lin et al. 2013). Some support for the natural-unnatural distinction as a proxy for the enhancements-nonenhancements distinction comes from certain aspects of our common word usage: medical treatments for the sick, moderate exercise and typical modes of education (such as the '3 Rs') are often deemed 'natural' activities, ones that have been species-typical throughout our recorded history. Insofar as many ethicists who use the distinction presume that what is natural is good, these activities are not seen to be morally problematic (Abney 2013).

In contrast, amphetamines that would enable us to fly jets for 48 hours straight without sleep, or other drugs that would give us the endurance of Siberian huskies, or enable us to cycle faster than any previous human up a French mountain, all seemingly serve as enhancements that take us beyond 'natural' limits of human functioning, and provide 'unnatural' abilities. Certainly, at least some of the common public revulsion over the use of steroids and other performance-enhancing drugs in sports also comes from the sense that the athletes are not content with developing their natural abilities and instead resort to unnatural enhancements. In these senses, then, enhancements are unnatural, artificial aids, and what is unnatural should evoke at least caution and scepticism, if not outright moral censure – or so the distinction would seem to imply.

But the natural-unnatural distinction, understood as above, collapses upon sustained reflection. In the sense above, some trees and rocks are 'natural', in that they exist independently of human agency or intervention, and an idealised science of them (such as botany or geology) could explain their causal roles and activities completely independently of any causal influences of humanity (Abney 1996, 2013). It is also true that many if not all of the things we consider artificial (such as houses and computers) are non-natural in this sense, as their existence depends on human manipulation of materials.

But many things that common usage terms 'natural' depend on external manipulation, such as a bird's nest or a beaver's dam. If we then retreat and stipulate that external manipulation means *only* human manipulation, then nothing created by – or even affected by – humans can be considered to be natural. Exercise, typical medical care and education are all in fact thoroughly *unnatural* on such an understanding. In other words, using a natural-versus-artificial distinction does not get us closer to understanding what human enhancement is, according to common usage; everything affected by human agency – including all therapeutic medical interventions – would then be artificial and an enhancement. And whatever one thinks about the ethics of enhancement, this definition of enhancement is impossibly broad; the idea that education and exercise, cancer surgery and taking penicillin for an infection are all *enhancements* is a farcical misuse of everyday terminology.

The key problem with any definition of enhancement is the apparent arbitrariness of the concept of 'normal' that is built into the therapy-enhancement distinction. But even if the distinction is arbitrary (Bostrom and Ord 2006), it may be that far more medical interventions termed 'treatment' are morally defensible (or a higher moral priority) than those termed 'enhancements'. For example, John Rawls' Difference Principle (1971, 2001) asserts that it is a matter of justice that social inequalities be arranged so that they help even the worst off. But an Aristotelian theory of justice as proportional equality, in which all just differences are based on and proportional to differences in merit, may find it harder to defend the moral priority of therapy over enhancement; instead, it seems one should get whatever medical interventions one merits, whether they be termed 'therapy' or 'enhancement'.

The genetic lottery (Bostrom 2008) further undermines the importance of the distinction: How could it be just that your therapy is covered whereas my enhancement is not, but the difference is due to our genetic endowments, which we do nothing to deserve and cannot possibly merit? Space bioethics reinforces questions, for astronauts may well differentially benefit (or 'be enhanced') from genetic treatments that would not be as helpful on Earth – such as increased resistance to cellular damage by radiation, or the ability to breathe at lower partial pressures of oxygen, or more efficient use of water by the body or any number of other conceivable changes. The key moral question would seem to be whether a medical intervention aids in human flourishing, whether or not one's genetic makeup (or physical environment on Earth or in space) would cause it to be classified as either therapy or enhancement.

The lifeboat example in the introduction helps us see the point, by revealing how enhancement could make a difference, for example by being able to breathe at lower partial pressures, or enabling hibernation, the dilemma could be avoided. Or if it couldn't help with survival, then at least drugs that enhance emotional control and other aspects of affect may enable one to accept death more easily – or kill without remorse. Should we have 'joy pills' or enhanced serotonin receptors to help astronauts deal with the boredom and possible depression of long-term spaceflight?

In the longer term, enhancements that more fundamentally change human nature could be entertained. For example, having an exoskeleton (like an insect or crab) would be useful to avoid lethal doses of cosmic rays during extended spaceflights. And developing the ability to photosynthesise could greatly reduce the need to carry all one's food along for the ride. Indeed, becoming a cybernetic organism that could meld one's body with the spaceship itself may enhance the repair and survivability of both ship and crew. With such enhancements, are there any moral limits, or should it be 'anything goes'? As our technical capabilities and our desire to go further and further into space progress, such questions will become ever more pressing.

There are further, related ethical issues that astronaut enhancement raises. For example, for one-way suicide missions, could enhancements change the actual nature of objective risk? If not, could they change the subjective nature of acceptable or unacceptable risk, so that people would be more accepting or less upset by heightened risks?

And what about the idea that enhancements ought to be reversible: If the astronauts wish to return to Earth, should we require that the enhancements be reversible? What if an enhancement for Mars (for example, a thinner bone structure that helps one in dealing with lower gravity more naturally without excess weight) would become a disenhancement upon return to Earth and its higher gravity; must these be reversible? Could enhancements for better mental functioning or observational powers undermine privacy rights? Is there a risk of changing the human species into something else, something more – or less – than human? Is changing the species 'bad', or is it prejudiced in our favour as racist and sexist views are?

Uncertainty and Risk

The mention of risk raises a fundamental problem for astronaut bioethics: How shall astronauts, their employers, regulators and state and commercial sponsors determine what constitutes an acceptable risk or not? As argued in the previous section, astronaut enhancement offers the promise of bettering the odds that we fulfil our objectives in space. But enhancement also poses risks, to individuals and even potentially our entire species.

For instance, how should we account for great uncertainty about bioethical risks and benefits of such space travel, including the risk on a long mission of microgravity and bone loss, or depleted oxygen or prolonged exposure to radiation? Who gets to determine that 'acceptable risk', and whether the statistically expected deaths (or other harms) of astronauts are worth it? Should each astronaut be allowed to assess risks for him- or herself; or do we need some objective or third party standard?

To help answer these and other questions, we need a method to determine what constitutes an ethically acceptable or unacceptable risk. In other social contexts (Abney, Lin and Mehlman 2013), all of the following have been defended as proper methods for determining that a risk is unacceptable:

Good-faith subjective standard: under this standard, it would be left up to each individual to determine whether an unacceptable risk exists. But the idiosyncrasies of human risk-aversion make this standard problematic, as it may simply lead to the most thrill-seeking risk-takers becoming the first deep space-faring astronauts, with little regard for any rational assessment of risks and benefits. There are related problems of autonomy: once committed to the project and following the orders of the space organisation's chain of command, can we trust individual subjects to defy authority when undue risk arises, especially when the authorities make clear their reasonable expectation that orders will be carried out? Further, what happens in a crew when some members subjectively disagree about the acceptability of the risk of some operation (say, a spacewalk to repair a communications antenna)?

The reasonable-person standard: an unacceptable risk might be simply what a fair, informed member of a relevant community believes to be an unacceptable risk. Can we substitute standard NASA regulations or some other basis for what a 'reasonable person' would think for the difficult-to-foresee vagaries of conditions of a manned spaceflight that lasts six months, rather than three days? Or what kind of judgement would we expect an isolated, stressed, cold, hungry and possibly psychologically disturbed astronaut to have: Would we trust them to accurately determine and act upon the assessed risk? Would they be better – or worse – than an 'ordinary' astronaut back in Mission Control in risk assessment? Would their isolation, boredom and other factors distort their judgement?

Objective standard: an unacceptable risk requires evidence and/or expert testimony about the reality of, and unacceptability of, the risk. But there is the 'first-generation problem' to consider: How do we understand that something is an unacceptable risk unless some first generation has already endured and suffered from it? For the first spacefarers to Mars, such a standard appears impossible; indeed, until we have a statistically significant number of such spaceflights, such a standard appears impossible to implement.

Existential Risk

> Since, in the long run, every planetary civilization will be endangered by impacts from space, every surviving civilization is obliged to become spacefaring-- not because of exploratory or romantic zeal, but for the most practical reason imaginable: staying alive … If our long-term survival is at stake, we have a basic responsibility to our species to venture to other worlds. (Sagan 1994, p. 371)

One additional consideration gaining credence in bioethics may justify enhancing astronauts in the attempts of Mars One and others to colonise Mars, even if success remains unlikely: the concept of existential risk, popularised by philosophers such as Nick Bostrom (2002), refers to a risk that, should it come to pass, would either annihilate Earth-originating intelligent life or permanently and drastically curtail its potential. Existential disasters would end human civilisation for all time to come. For utilitarians, existential risks are terribly important: doing what we can to mitigate even a small chance that humanity comes to an end may well be worth the cost. And for deontologists, the idea that 'one always has a moral obligation never to allow the extinction of all creatures capable of moral obligation' is at least a plausible *prima facie* (and perhaps absolute) duty; such a survival principle appears required for any viable ethics (Abney 2004).

There is increasing acceptance that we ought to take such worries seriously. For instance, the B612 Foundation (B612 2014) wants to track Earth-crossing asteroids and is soliciting funding for its 'Sentinel Mission', a space-based infrared survey mission to discover and catalogue 90 per cent of the asteroids larger than 140 metres in Earth's region of the solar system. If it turns up a killer asteroid that threatens life on Earth, then presumably that would be money well spent.

But suppose we discover such a killer asteroid too late, or fall prey to any of a number of the other potential calamities that could imperil human life on Earth. If Mars One astronauts could possibly succeed in creating a permanent, sustainable colony on Mars (as remote as that prospect appears), then humanity could nonetheless survive a cataclysm on Earth. Accordingly, existential-risk theorists hold that Mars One and other similar colonisation efforts could be worthwhile, even if the odds of success are minuscule. The costs of colonising space are far less than what would be lost if life on Earth were to be annihilated.

Once we have begun a permanent, sustainable civilisation on another planet (or Moon, or space station), then the end of human life on Earth, while a calamity, would no longer be the end of humanity. Colonising another planet may be the single greatest means available to us to mitigate existential risk. As such, even if Mars One bears the smallest possibility of success, our deontological survival principle or a utilitarian calculation of risk and benefit may well determine it is worth it. Eventually, it could become the difference between life and death, not for individuals, but for our species.

Nonetheless, mitigating existential risk does not allow us to ignore more mundane ethical concerns. For instance, under virtue ethics, we would unacceptably demonstrate a vicious character if we were concerned with either individual or collective survival at the cost of the other things that make life worth living. So, it still seems implausible that a remote existential risk justifies pushing ahead with space exploration in whatever manner we want. If it could, then it would also justify any implausible project to save the species, given the sheer number of lives at stake. Ethics and law are still important to observe in every step. However, such considerations lead to a final ethical puzzle.

But Can You Come Home Again?

Existential risk connects up with one of the most exciting aspects of space exploration and, indeed, a main focus of NASA: the search for alien life (Search for Extraterrestrial Intelligence 2014). But the search for alien life brings along its own puzzles in bioethics (construed broadly). For example, what moral status would alien life have? Would we be free to experiment upon it, or even keep it as a pet? And what safety precautions are morally mandated for dealing with any new discoveries?

One of the activities Martian explorers and colonists will assuredly engage in is the search for Martian microbes, in the hope that we will find a second source of life in the universe (though, as astrophysicists such as Paul Davies remind us, it may be that life on Earth actually began with microbes who hitched a ride from Mars) (Davies 2004). If the search for alien life on Mars fails, we will surely one day search for it in the deep oceans of Europa or Ganymede, or the petrochemical seas of Titan, and so on, until we find that we are not alone in the universe.

But the 'Great Silence' (Brin 1983) – the fact that, in all of human history, we have never found any incontrovertible evidence of life from anywhere else – raises questions about why that silence should be. Why have our probes not already found evidence of life? Various answers are possible: perhaps intelligent civilisations are scarce, or quickly move beyond using the kinds of communications we could overhear. Or perhaps the only life elsewhere is microbial; complex animals or intelligence have evolved only here on Earth. Or, perhaps, alien life is lethal and, whether microbial or not, kills any other life-forms with which it comes into contact. This places a different spin on existential risk: perhaps what will end humanity is our discovery of the first alien life-form! The Great Silence could exist because civilisations die out as they encounter alien life.

Such considerations raise a bioethical question normally encountered on Earth only in connection with pandemic flu and the like: What of astronauts and quarantine? Under what circumstances (if any) should we deny living astronauts the opportunity to return to Earth? Should off-Earth facilities (for example, on the ISS) and quarantine be used for scientific research on any newly discovered extraterrestrial life until safety has been established? After all, it may be that astronauts who undergo Mars-specific enhancements remain fine in that environment, but would spread communicable disease upon entry into the different environment of the Earth.

NASA's Office of Planetary Protection has protocols in place (NASA 2014b), but we may wonder if protocols focused on Moon and near-Earth exploration are prepared for what will happen if astronauts encounter novel Martian microbes, to say nothing of possible Europan sea creatures. And it remains unclear whether private businesses, such as Mars One, are legally obligated to follow NASA's protocols – especially if they are not based in the US. Suppose a sick astronaut on a private spaceflight wants to return to Earth – who would have the authority to forcibly stop him, even if we could? For that matter, how could we be sure we will even know, before it is too late, if an astronaut is infected?

In such circumstances, ethicists sometimes turn to something termed the 'precautionary principle'. Although variously formulated, here is a representative statement of a strong version of the precautionary principle from The Wingspread Conference of 1998 (Science and Environmental Health Network 1998 'The Wingspread Consensus Statement on the Precautionary Principle', para. 5): 'When an activity raises threats of harm to the environment or human health, precautionary measures should be taken even if some cause and effect relationships are not fully established scientifically'.

Space travel is a paradigm of an unknown risk, so perhaps precautionary reasoning is in order. Considerations of existential risk on Earth then seem to bid us to colonise new worlds, even if the odds of success are slight, in order to raise the odds of a long-term human future. But such considerations also seem to bid us beware of any attempt for such travellers in space to ever return to Earth, lest they harbour a pathogen that will end us all.

Perhaps Mars One has the right ethical approach after all: to boldly go where no man has gone before – and never return. Or like the Hotel California, perhaps Mars is someplace where you can check in any time you like; but we Earthlings need to make sure that you will never leave.

Conclusion

In the above, we have opened a window to only a fraction of the questions society will need to face in the push for space exploration, looking at bioethics primarily as the most pressing area of concern. But many other questions deserve further research as well. For example, enhancement, like most other increases in technical capacity, inevitably raises dual use issues: Could civilian enhancements have unacceptable dual uses as military weapons? Space is 'the ultimate high ground', and enhancements meant to help astronauts better function and survive in space would likewise be a boon to warfighters in space. Would military enhancements for space possibly contravene the Outer Space Treaty, the Biological and Chemical Weapons Conventions (Lin, Mehlman and Abney 2013), or other relevant international agreements, or otherwise be unethical?

There's much to think about before astronauts make another giant leap for humankind – from today's labour laws, to near-term bioethics questions, to justifications for space exploration in the first place, to more speculative scenarios if we were to find alien life. Current ethical frameworks, including bioethics and risk assessment, can help us here. But it could be that those frameworks need to be adapted for the exigencies of outer space, a unique context that they weren't designed to handle.

This isn't without precedent: human enhancement technologies in the military – such as engineering soldiers who don't need to sleep or eat, or have bionic parts and neural implants – also seem to be a special case that slips into the gaps (Lin, Mehlman and Abney 2013). As just one reason, current bioethical models don't consider the concept of military necessity, we recently argued. Likewise, exploration or frontier scenarios could challenge the usual ethical frameworks, especially in literally alien geographies.

The conversation also doesn't end with bioethics, though that's what we've focused on in the above. If space settlements come to pass, we'd likely also need institutions to govern them on site, since law enforcement and other Earthly systems won't have that far a reach (Lin 2006). And over time, humans raised in a Martian environment will become progressively less and less like Earth-bound humans, from physical differences due to lower gravity to the inevitable socio-cultural differences that their extreme isolation would only enhance. Every colony will eventually want its independence, history suggests, and for Martians, that independence may exist *de facto* from the very start.

Thus, we have a clean slate – a *tabula rasa* – in front of us to reinvent society, without being bogged down by legacy systems for property, economics, governance and so on. Where the Apollo and other historical missions were run by governments, much of those programs under a cloak of secrecy, the privatisation of space today means that we now have a responsibility to open the policy and ethics discussion to the global community. Outer space and the future of humanity don't belong to any one nation-state but to all of us.

References

100 Year Starship 2014, US Department of Defense, Washington, DC, viewed 7 March 2015, http://100yss.org.

Abney, K. 1996, 'What is natural?', *Contemporary Philosophy*, 18(5): 23–9.

Abney, K. 2004, 'Sustainability, Morality and Future Rights', *Moebius*, 2(2), viewed 7 March 2015, http://digitalcommons.calpoly.edu/moebius/vol2/iss2/7.

Abney, K. 2013, 'Problematizing the "Natural": The Internal/external Distinction and Technology', *Synesis: A Journal of Science, Technology, Ethics, and Policy*, 4, pp. T29–36, viewed 7 March 2015, http://www.synesisjournal.com/vol4_t/Abney_2013_T29–36.pdf.

Abney, K., Lin, P. and Mehlman, M. 2013, 'Military neuroenhancement and risk assessment', in J Giordano (ed.), *Neurotechnology in National Security: Practical Considerations, Neuroethical Concerns*. Boca Raton, FL: CRC Press.

Airbus Defence and Space (formerly European Aeronautic Defence and Space Company Astrium), Paris, France, viewed 7 March 2015, http://www.space-airbusds.com.

Allhoff, F., Lin, P., Moor, J. and Weckert, J. 2010, 'Ethics of human enhancement: 25 questions & answers', *Studies in .Ethics, Law and Technology*, 4(1), viewed 7 March 2015, http://www.human enhance.com/NSF_report.pdf.

B612 Foundation 2014, Menlo Park, California, viewed 7 March 2015, http://sentinelmission.org.

Bostrom, N. 2002, 'Existential Risks: Analyzing Human Extinction Scenarios and Related Hazards', *Journal of Evolution and Technology*, 9, viewed 7 March 2015, http://www.jetpress.org/volume9.

Bostrom, N. and Ord, T. 2006, 'The reversal test: Eliminating status quo bias in applied ethics', *Ethics*, 116(4): 656–79.

Bostrom, N. and Savulescu, J. 2008, 'Human Enhancement Ethics: The State of the Debate', in J. Savulescu and N. Bostrom (eds), *Human Enhancement*. Oxford: Oxford University Press.

Brin, G.D. 1983, 'The 'Great Silence': The Controversy Concerning Extraterrestrial Intelligent Life', *Quarterly Journal of the Royal Astronomical Society*, 24(3): 283–309, viewed 7 March 2015, http://articles.adsabs.harvard.edu/full/seri/QJRAS/0024//0000283.000.html.

Copenhagen Suborbitals 2014, Copenhagen, Denmark, viewed 7 March 2015, http://copsub.com.

Davies, P. 2004, 'Life (and Death) on Mars', *The New York Times*, 15 January, viewed 7 March 2015, http://www.nytimes.com/2004/01/15/opinion/life-and-death-on-mars.html.

Deep Space Industries 2014, McLean, Virginia, viewed 7 March 2015, http://deepspaceindustries.com.

Freitas Jr, R.A. 2002, *Respirocytes*, Kurzweil, viewed 7 March 2015, http://www.kurzweilai.net/respirocytes.

Giles, J. 2004, 'Could astronauts sleep their way to the stars?', *Nature News*, 3 August, viewed 7 March 2015, http://www.nature.com/news/2004/040802/full/news040802-8.html.

Harris, P. 2010, 'Elon Musk: "I'm planning to retire to Mars"', *The Guardian*, 31 July, viewed 7 March 2015, http://www.theguardian.com/technology/2010/aug/01/elon-musk-spacex-rocket-mars.

Howell, E. 2012, 'Apollo 13: Facts About NASA's Near-Disaster', *Space and NASA News*, 23 August, viewed 7 March 2015, http://www.space.com/17250-apollo-13-facts.html.

Klein, C. 2014, 'What If the Moon Landing Had Failed?', *History in the Headlines*, 16 July, viewed 7 March 2015, http://www.history.com/news/what-if-the-moon-landing-had-failed.

Lin, P. 2006, 'Space Ethics: Look Before Taking Another Leap for Mankind', *Astropolitics*, 4(3): 281–94, viewed 7 March 2015, http://ethics.calpoly.edu/nanoethics/paper042406.html.

Lin, P. and Allhoff, F. 2008, 'Against Unrestricted Human Enhancement', *Journal of Evolution and Technology*, 18(1): 35–41, viewed 7 March 2015, http://jetpress.org/v18/linallhoff.htm.

Lin, P., Mehlman, M. and Abney, K. 2013, *Enhanced Warfighters: Risk, Ethics, and Policy*, Greenwall foundation, California Polytechnic State University, San Luis Obispo and Case Western Reserve University, viewed 7 March 2015, http://ethics.calpoly.edu/Greenwall_report.pdf.

Mars One 2014, Netherlands, viewed 7 March 2015, http://www.mars-one.com.

National Aeronautics and Space Administration, 2014a, NASA, *Mars 2020, Mission Overview*, NASA Jet Propulsion Laboratory, viewed 7 March 2015, http://mars.jpl.nasa.gov/mars2020.

National Aeronautics and Space Administration, 2014b, NASA, *Office of Planetary Protection, Methods And Implementation*, viewed 7 March 2015, http://planetaryprotection.nasa.gov/methods.

Planetary Resources 2014, Seattle, viewed 7 March 2015, http://www.planetaryresources.com.

Rawls, J. 1971, *A Theory of Justice*. Cambridge, MA: Belknap Press.

Rawls, J. 2001, *Justice as Fairness*. Cambridge, MA: Belknap Press.

Sagan, C. 1994, *Pale Blue Dot: A Vision of the Human Future in Space*. New York: Random House.

Sandel, M. 2008, *The Case Against Perfection: Ethics in the Age of Genetic Engineering*. Cambridge, MA: Belknap Press of Harvard University Press.

Savulescu, J. 2001, 'Procreative Beneficence: Why We Should Select the Best Children', *Bioethics*, 15(5–6): 413–26.

Science and Environmental Health Network 1998, *Precautionary Principle*, viewed 7 March 2015, http://www.sehn.org/wing.html.

Search for Extraterrestrial Intelligence 2014, NASA, viewed 7 March 2015, http://www.seti.org/about-us.

Tate, K. 2014, 'Dennis Tito's 2021 Human Mars Flyby Mission Explained (Infographic)', *Space and NASA News*, 27 February, viewed 7 March 2015, http://www.space.com/19985-private-mars-mission-flyby-dennis-tito-infographic.html.

Virgin Galactic 2014, Las Cruces, New Mexico, viewed 7 March 2015, http://www.virgingalactic.com.

Chapter 19

Vulnerable Cargo: The Sacrifice of Animal Astronauts

Jane Johnson

Ordinarily when (human) research subjects are identified as vulnerable, special protections are triggered to ensure these subjects are not exploited. However in the case of much research with nonhuman animals (including space research), a greater good is generally considered to prevail which permits their use and exploitation, irrespective of their vulnerability. Although experiments on animal astronauts have a well-justified goal (to ensure harms to human astronauts are identified and minimised), the overall rationale for space research is not sufficient to warrant the sacrifice of animal astronauts.

This chapter begins by identifying those animals who have been the subjects of space research (animal astronauts), before outlining how these creatures are inherently, situationally and pathogenically vulnerable. Existing mechanisms for addressing the vulnerability of animal astronauts are discussed and shown to be wanting since they generate further pathogenic vulnerabilities and are ultimately overridden by a purported greater good for humans. Although taken in isolation this greater good seems plausible, viewed in light of the weak overall rationale for space research, its plausibility slips away.

Who are Animals Astronauts?

A wide variety of nonhuman animals have been used in experiments related to space research including cats, dogs, nonhuman primates, bears, rats, mice, hamsters, guinea pigs, pigs, rabbits, fish, amphibians and invertebrates. For some of these animals the term 'astronaut' seems more readily applicable than it does for others. For instance it seems clearly to apply to primates who can perform certain tasks, are of a certain size, can wear a space suit in a way similar to a human astronaut and so on. However, for the sake of simplicity and to avoid distracting discussions about the capacities of animals and what this means for how they ought to be regarded (questions over which there is no philosophical or ethical consensus), I will refer to all nonhuman animals who have participated in space research as 'animal astronauts'.

Animal astronauts have been involved in an enormous range of experiments related to national space programs in countries as diverse as the United States, the

Soviet Union, China, France, Japan and Iran. These experiments have included terrestrial ones as well as those undertaken within the Earth's atmosphere and in outer space.

The Vulnerability of Animal Astronauts

To make a case for the vulnerability of animal astronauts, I will be appealing to an account of the sources of vulnerability developed by Catriona Mackenzie, Wendy Rogers and Susan Dodds (henceforth *MRD*) (2012, 2014). Their account is, I argue, superior to other accounts in the literature for a number of reasons. Although the taxonomical framework they articulate is not intended to apply to nonhumans, I argue this framework can be deployed for these purposes, as will be shown below.

Well-recognised shortcomings in approaches to vulnerability are addressed by *MRD*. For instance, many accounts of vulnerability have restricted applicability and are simply concerned with, and tailored to suit, the context of research ethics; a more inclusive account which can capture how vulnerability functions in other settings is surely to be preferred, and the approach taken by *MRD* does just that. Another inadequacy common to approaches to vulnerability is a focus on one element of vulnerability, whereas *MRD*'s account is more comprehensive, capturing the many senses of vulnerability from what is sometimes referred to as 'ontological vulnerability' (the vulnerability that comes from mere existence), through the kind of contextual factors that may generate vulnerability, to how vulnerability can be enshrined and perpetuated within institutions. *MRD*'s account is also suggestive of remedies to meet the challenges generated by vulnerability.

MRD describe three conceptually distinct sources of vulnerability – inherent, situational and pathogenic, with the latter comprising a subset of situational. Though these categories are conceptually distinct, they overlap and are not exclusive. In the following paragraphs I will briefly articulate what is involved in each source of vulnerability and demonstrate how this source can be applied to describe the circumstances of animal astronauts.

For *MRD* 'inherent vulnerability' describes the ontological vulnerability of human beings, that is, our latent susceptibility to the conditions of our embodiment – to pain, suffering, illness and disease. Humans have basic survival needs which must be met as well as more complex emotional, psychological and social ones. Dependency on others to differing extents at different points of life (for instance, when we are young, ill, incapacitated and so on), is another feature of our inherent vulnerability. Inherent vulnerability can be moderated and assuaged, but it remains nonetheless an in-eliminable part of the human condition.

Clearly, as biological creatures animal astronauts share our inherent vulnerability. Just like us they have basic needs that must be met if they are to survive (for example for food, water, shelter), and there are more complex needs at play too, which vary across species. Depending on their particular circumstances

and background, these creatures will also have been dependent on human and/
or other animals to varying extents and at different stages of their lives. Thus
inherent vulnerability describes a kind of baseline vulnerability possessed by
animal astronauts.

The category of 'situational vulnerability', on the other hand, captures the way
individuals or groups can be made vulnerable by features of their circumstances
such as social, political, economic and environmental factors. For instance, any
person as inherently vulnerable could die of a gunshot wound. However, features
of an individual's situation (living in a war zone in the twenty-first century, being
a criminal in certain countries and so on) furnish conditions in which this inherent
vulnerability is more likely to be realised.

Inherent and situational vulnerabilities can be causally linked so that inherent
vulnerabilities can lead to situational ones and vice versa. For example, a case of
the former would be where a person's mental illness leads to unemployment and
poverty, while a case of the latter might involve the stress of unemployment and
poverty contributing to health problems.

Before outlining the specific situational vulnerabilities experienced by animal
astronauts it is worth observing that nonhuman animals in general can experience
a range of situational vulnerabilities unrelated to humans and their activities.
For instance, wild animals prey on other creatures so that certain species are
vulnerable to other species. There are also environmental factors that make animals
situationally vulnerable irrespective of whether they are in the wild or living with
humans, for example animals can be vulnerable to the impacts of bushfires, floods,
hurricanes and so on. Thus the situational vulnerability of nonhuman animals does
not relate exclusively to humans and their actions. However, the foundation of
the situational vulnerability of animal astronauts is their dependency on humans.
Humans have confined these creatures and created the conditions under which they
are reliant on people to meet all their needs. These animals would perish without
the ongoing intervention of humans, and humans can manipulate this situation
to their advantage. Bergwin and Coleman, for instance, describe instances where
chimpanzee astronauts were forced to perform various tasks in order to meet their
basic needs for food and water (1963).

The dependency described above functions either in a contingent way for tame
animals or in a more stable and permanent fashion for domesticated creatures.
Tame animals have been habituated to human contact such that prior to their
contact with humans they may have lived independently. It might also be possible
for these animals and their offspring to live an existence independent of humans
in the future. The bears and chimpanzees involved in space research, for instance,
fall into this category.[1]

---

1 Bergwin and Coleman proudly state how the chimpanzees used in early US space
research were 'carefully chosen "on location" in their native equatorial haunts', that is,
they were made situationally vulnerable in a specific kind of way by being captured and

It is much less clear that the kind of independence that might be possible for tame animals can be replicated in the case of domesticated creatures, for instance dogs and mice in research. Selective breeding for traits that serve a human purpose or goal drives domestication and perpetuates and enshrines the reliance of nonhuman animals on humans. The all-encompassing nature of this dependency makes these animals particularly vulnerable to harm at the hands of humans. Ani Satz, drawing on ideas from Martha Fineman's work, points to this link between dependency and the implications for animal vulnerability. 'Throughout their lives, domestic animals rely on humans to provide them nourishment, shelter, and other care. The permanent dependency of domestic animals is created and controlled by humans, rendering them uniquely vulnerable to exploitation. Domestic nonhuman animals are, for this reason, perhaps the most vulnerable of all sentient beings' (Satz 2009, p. 80).

Humans hold the power in this relationship of dependency. Commenting on this powerless of animals, Jean Harvey has suggested nonhuman animals therefore 'constitute a greatly oppressed group; consisting of some of the most vulnerable individuals in the world' (Harvey 2007, p. 31).

Against this backdrop of dependency, a significant source of situational vulnerability for animal astronauts has been environmental. Animal astronauts have been exposed to environmental hazards that it was unclear they would survive (for instance launch and the conditions of outer space) and for those animals engaged on unmanned flights, equipment failure in the isolated environment of space generally resulted in death. Some of the deaths of animal astronauts were also anticipated since animals were sent into space prior to the development of recovery techniques. For dogs, a species known for their intra- and interspecies sociality, the isolation of space represented an extremely hostile environment.

Given their dependence on humans in the research setting and the limited ways they have of resisting their use, the participation and compliance of nonhumans in experimentation can be regarded as effectively coerced. Nonetheless, on occasion there have been opportunities for animals to respond in ways that may moderate their experimental participation. One such case involved a monkey astronaut used in balloon flights. These flights crashed to the ground twice because a backup parachute failed to ease the landing. According to Bergwin and Coleman, '[o]n the second failure, [the animal handler] was nipped by the angry monkey, who by this time, had figured he'd had enough. Everyone agreed and he was excused from further flights' (1963, p. 82). No such accommodation was offered up to the Soviet dog Strelka. Confined in a small chamber intended to mimic flight conditions, Strelka 'found the close quarters not to her liking. She demonstrated her reaction by barking and repeated attempts to bite through the restraining leashes and free herself' (Bergwin and Coleman 1963, p. 97). Less dramatically the authors note

---

removed from their homes, disturbing both their own lives and that of their fellow creatures (1963, p. 65).

that chimpanzees in the US space program would be given 'time off' if they demonstrated signs of fatigue (1963, p. 65).

Situational vulnerability has as a subset what *MRD* label 'pathogenic' vulnerabilities. These arise either through personal or social relationships which are in some way morally dysfunctional (that is, involve discrimination, injustice, oppression and so on) or when efforts to address existent vulnerabilities have the unintended effect of exacerbating these vulnerabilities or generating new ones. An example of the former would be where women may be more likely than men to experience domestic violence due to discriminatory personal and societal attitudes toward their gender. A case of the latter would be where attempts to address indigenous disadvantage in Australia through the provision of welfare has arguably resulted in substance abuse, increased social problems and disempowering welfare dependence (Pearson 2004).

Relationships between humans and animal astronauts can be cast as pathogenic because of the frequently discriminatory attitudes and practices toward the latter by the former, recalling this is in a context where animals are highly dependent on humans. Again, as Satz argues about nonhumans in general, they 'have a history of powerlessness and discrimination, they are subject to stereotypes about their cognitive abilities and their capacity to suffer is undervalued, and their species status is irrelevant to their capacity to suffer and is immutable' (Satz 2009, p. 72).

Animal astronauts are not regarded as having the same value and standing as humans, hence they have been used in ways that would be unacceptable for their human counterparts. Explaining how chimpanzees could have electrodes implanted in their brain and body to monitor physical reactions to space, a NASA spokesperson explicitly stated 'You can't do that with a man' (Bergwin and Coleman 1963, p. 179). Due to a lack of available subjects, the experimental conditions they would be exposed to, and the kind of samples that would need to be extracted to understand the effects of flight on physiological systems, it has been claimed that such experiments 'cannot be performed using humans' (Sonnenfeld 2005a, p. 31). The supposed intellectual superiority of humans has been used to justify exposing animals to risks in order to progress space research. 'Since man is a higher form of life, rational, priceless and irreplaceable as an individual, it was only natural and right that he should turn to animals in his research toward getting man into space' (Bergwin and Coleman 1963, p.20). In using animals in this way, space research complies with the status quo – 'it has been traditional that animal precede man. And outward bound penetrations of space are no exception to this tradition. Man is priceless and irreplaceable' (Bergwin and Coleman 1963, p. 63). Certain research strategies are ruled out point blank in humans, but not animals. As Sonnenfeld states regarding infectious disease and tumour studies, '[f] or obvious reasons, such studies could not be carried out using humans' (2005a, p. 32). No argument therefore need be provided, since all humans are presumed to share this intuition about human superiority and its implications for the use of animals in space research.

Failing to acknowledge the value of animals permits sentient creatures to be used instrumentally, to be objectified and to be regarded as mere tools to achieve a particular purpose. As one of the veterinarians involved in the early US space program commented, the laboratory animal 'should be considered in the same light as any other tool or reagent used in research. It must be carefully controlled and as painstakingly calibrated and standardized as the most sensitive instrument' (Bergwin and Coleman 1963, p. 75). In spite of the time that has elapsed since this view was expressed, it is still one arguably held by many researchers, particularly with respect to certain kinds of animals like laboratory mice (Birke et al. 2007).

Responses to Vulnerability

Establishing the vulnerability of human subjects in research triggers attempts to ensure these subjects have their intrinsic value protected; that they are not exploited or their vulnerability further exacerbated. There are a variety of strategies that may be pursued to achieve this goal, for instance recruitment processes might be altered to avoid possible coercion, research protocols might be amended to be responsive to particular vulnerabilities, researchers might avoid recruiting individuals or groups perceived to vulnerable and so on. This response, however, generally does not apply when the vulnerability identified inheres in nonhuman animals. Robert Nozick captured well the difference between the ethical standards applied to humans as opposed to animals when he famously stated 'utilitarianism for animals, Kantianism for humans' (1974). In the case of animals in research this utilitarian response amounts to offering up limited protections to vulnerable animals (which in fact generate further pathogenic vulnerabilities), and proposing some greater good for humans which trumps the interests of animals.

Across many jurisdictions (including in the United States) the 3Rs developed by Russell and Burch – to Replace, Reduce and Refine animal use – are the basis on which the inherent and situational vulnerabilities of animals in research are addressed (1959). The goal of *Replacement* promotes the use of alternative non-sentient models when possible; *Reduction* involves using the minimum number of animals to achieve the aims of a research protocol; and *Refinement* concerns techniques which minimise pain and suffering. Whilst these may appear as laudable goals, in effect and perversely, they have contributed to the pathogenic vulnerability of animals in research. Therefore in addition to morally dysfunctional relationships contributing to the pathogenic vulnerability of animal astronauts (as discussed earlier), some of the mechanisms intended to protect them (such as the various codes for the Care and Use of Animals that NASA complies with) in conjunction with particular scientific ideals, contribute to further harms and entrench the use of particular animals in space research.

Rather than leading to the development of alternatives to animal use (thereby addressing animal vulnerability by removing animals from research), the goal of *Replacement* has come to be interpreted in governing codes like that adhered to by

NASA as replacing so-called 'higher' organisms (primates, dogs and so on) with 'lower' ones (such as rodents and fish). Although this might assuage certain public concerns about using creatures that look like us (primates) or that many people have as companion animals (dogs and cats), arguably little of real substance is achieved if one species of sentient creature is simply substituted for another.

The goal of *Reduction* harbours similar problems since it has driven the creation of increasingly standardised animals. To ensure the optimum number of animals are used (so not too few so as to compromise results and not too many so that research can still be regarded as legitimately reducing numbers used), rodents have been standardised and particular strains created (increasingly via genetic modification) to attempt to insure uniformity. NASA's new project to examine the long-term effects of microgravity, for instance, will use rodents created for the purposes of laboratory research, including genetically altered strains (Figliozzi 2014). Rodent models are developed to meet particular scientific ideals about controlling for variables and the repeatability of results, and can be tailored to address specific research questions through their genetic makeup. Another rationale behind rodent use is that their short life cycles enable the results of phenomena such as the effects of radiation to be observed more rapidly than in humans (Bergwin and Coleman 1963). Although fewer bespoke rodents might be used in a particular protocol than when compared to wild type rodents, this has not lead to a reduction in the overall numbers of animals used in research. In fact, the use of genetically modified organisms tracks greater animal use in research (Ghosh 2010).

A focus on *Refinement* also contributes to pathogenic vulnerability, since it has the effect of sidestepping deeper ethical questions about the routinised use of animals. A concern with *Refinement* at the expense of other considerations allows the status quo to be perpetuated, making it appear as though animal ethics is being addressed, whilst simultaneously ignoring more difficult questions about whether animal use is appropriate in research and about the sacrifice of animals in experimentation. Who would challenge the claim that the pain and suffering of animals ought to be minimised in research? Yet it is a mistake to be caught up in construing this to be the central ethical issue that somehow exhausts the ethical terrain. Describing how chimpanzees used in centrifugation experiments were 'sacrificed' (that is euthanised) in order to closely examine the injuries caused by G forces, Bergwin and Coleman state: '[i]t must be emphasized here that these animals did not suffer. They were handled under the provisions of humane standards set by the American Medical Association' (1963, p. 52). Again when referring to the euthanasia of bears in research as part of the space program, these authors reinforce that '[w]hen animals have to be sacrificed, it is done so according to the standards accepted as being humane. All such sacrifices are painless. The subjects do not suffer at all' (p. 55). However that the death is humane is surely not the central ethical issue, but that animals are used and then killed in order to secure data. Whilst a death involving pain and suffering ought to be avoided, focusing on this element of research distracts from questions about the instrumental life and death of animals in research.

It is also important to note that the type of harm *Refinement* addresses is primarily harm that is extrinsic to the goals of research. If animal needs (such as relieving pain or providing environmental enrichment) potentially compromise the goals of research, and the research goal is deemed sufficiently significant, then those needs will be regarded as expendable.

The 3Rs therefore fail to adequately address the vulnerability of animal astronauts and instead contribute to their pathogenic vulnerability. Further, and in a way that would be untenable for research on humans, a utilitarian 'greater good' for humans is often employed to override the interests and well-being of nonhuman animals in research. How does this play out when justifying animal use in space research?

From early in the space program, experimentation using animal astronauts was intended to address a number of questions crucial to the basic survival of biological creatures in space; the kind of physiological changes that might result from space flights; and the safety of space vehicles and equipment (Hoban-Higgins et al. 2005). Empowered with knowledge obtained from animal models, measures to deal with any problems which emerged could be designed and tested so that harm to humans would be minimised.

The fundamental problem of whether nonhuman animals (and by extrapolation humans) could survive away from the Earth drove the Montgolfier brothers back in 1793 to send a sheep, a duck and a rooster aloft in a balloon (Hoban-Higgins et al. 2005). From the late 1940s, rocket flights with nonhuman primates demonstrated it was possible for creatures phylogenetically close to humans to survive launch, flight and re-entry. Prior to experimentation with primates, there was some question over how human physiology might operate in space. It was unclear whether it would be possible to eat, sleep or perform various tasks in space. There were also worries that weightlessness might cause debilitating disorientation and nausea (Hoban-Higgins et al. 2005). Experiments which monitored the body function and performance of animals on various tasks satisfied scientists that not only would humans survive in space but, in spite of various physical and psychological challenges, they would be able to successfully perform the tasks essential to space travel.

With a baseline of survivability and functionality established, scientists looked to test the viability of living in space for longer periods. Scientists from the US and the Soviet Union sent primates on extended missions to determine whether prolonged exposure to microgravity would lead to deterioration in skeletal muscle and bone and orthostatic hypotension. Results showed it was possible for these creatures to adapt to microgravity and then readapt to life on Earth. The data acquired from these experiments provided invaluable insight into the physiological and behavioural changes resulting from extended exposure to microgravity, and helped identify risks and develop countermeasures to the adverse impacts of space travel (Hoban-Higgins et al. 2005).

For its success, the space program also required the development of safe equipment, including for retrieval of space capsules carrying biological cargo.

This involved solving technical problems including dealing with the heat of re-entry and capsule recovery. Many animal astronauts (including the Soviet dog Laika) died prior to the development of this technology.

Thus the program of experimentation using animal astronauts was and is justified on the basis that it attempts to ensure that harms to human astronauts (both short and long term) are identified and minimised. The greater good at stake in animal research is the health and well-being of humans in space. However this goal cannot stand alone, it in turn depends on a prior claim that exploring space is justified. After all, if space exploration is not an adequately justified goal, then the permissibility of measures to achieve this goal may be called into question. To help understand how this goal functions in the context of space research, comparison to the case of medical research is instructive.

In medical research the argument that justifies animal experimentation runs something like this:

- Using nonhuman animals in research is essential to test the safety and efficacy of new medications and treatments;
- New medications and treatments enhance the health and longevity of humans;
- Health and longevity are good things that we ought to aspire to;
- Therefore using nonhuman animals in medical research is justified.

The argument appeals to weighty goals – that a better quality of life for humans results from medical research, underpinned by animal experimentation. Some scholars push this further and make an argument that good health care (presumably underpinned by medical research in an environment dominated by Evidence Based Medicine) is essential to full participation in social, economic and political life, so that health care has a high moral priority, even when societal resources may be scarce (Daniels 2002). Can a similarly compelling argument be made to support space exploration?

Understandably, perhaps, people tend to talk 'big' when considering space exploration. For instance scholar Stephen Pyne claims that '[t]o survey the motives for exploration is to survey all the motives that animate a thriving civilization' (quoted in NASA 1994, p. iii). Even if this is true, it is not an especially helpful statement in the context of articulating justifications for space research; it is just too general and nonspecific.

The reasons given for space research tend to fall into two main categories – those that appeal to a tangible or more measurable benefit and those that rely on appeal to more abstract or esoteric phenomena. In the former category are outcomes such as enhanced scientific knowledge (including regarding cosmology and threatening phenomena like asteroids); development of new technology; political (local) and geopolitical (international) advantage (including regarding security and expansion into new territories); international collaboration and economic benefits (including through employment, developing technology and in the future by resource mining, for instance from asteroids). More intangible reasons for space research and exploration include a sense of national identity and pride. In the case of the United States, this ties into a pioneering/frontier narrative as reflected in this proclamation by President Bill Clinton: '[s]pace exploration has become an integral part of our national character, capturing the spirit of optimism and adventure that has defined this country from its beginnings' (quoted in NASA 1994, p. iii). Space exploration has also been said to inspire people, including into careers in science, engineering and mathematics, and to offer perspective – a sense of our place in the universe. Consider, for instance, the impact on the environmental movement, of images of the Earth viewed from space. Others have suggested a more general cultural and aesthetic value attaches to space exploration (NASA 1994).

When compared to the justifications given for medical research, those given for space exploration appear less convincing for a couple of reasons. First, although both medical and space research claim to use animals to prevent harms to humans, the underpinning rationale of these enterprises is quite different. While travel to space is a discretionary goal (we could easily imagine a world in which space travel did not occur and so there was no need to prevent the harms associated with it), evidence based medicine is not viewed as discretionary. Medicine itself has a long history and evidence based health care is often seen as essential to human well-being. Second, many of the goals of space research (such things as national pride, inspiration and so on) are quite abstract and can be met in other ways. Space research does not have to exist to achieve these outcomes. Although there is some debate over the extent to which research on animals contributes to improvements in human health (public health and sanitation measures also play a role, as do nonanimal models in research) (LaFollette and Shanks 1996), nonetheless animal models have delivered benefits unattainable by other means. It can be argued that animal models are essential to improvements in human health and well-being in a way that does not parallel their role in contributing to phenomena like national pride via space research.

Conclusion

Animal astronauts are vulnerable research subjects on the account of vulnerability developed by *MRD*. Yet unlike human research subjects, identification of animal vulnerability is not a catalyst to significant protection, but rather is downplayed in favour of adopting a utilitarian approach to their experimental participation. However, while the 'greater good' offered up for the use of animals in medical research has some traction and plausibility, the fundamental justifications given for space research are not of a similar kind and cannot license the harms inflicted on animal astronauts.

References

Bergwin, C.R. and Coleman, W.T. 1963, *Animal Astronauts: They Opened the Way to the Stars*. Englewood Cliffs, NJ: Prentice-HalL.

Birke, L., Arnold, A. and Michael, M. 2007, *The Sacrifice: How Scientific Experiments Transform Animals and People*. West Lafayette, IN: Purdue University Press.

Daniels, N. 2002, 'Justice, health, and health care', in R. Rhodes, M.P. Battin and A. Silvers (eds), *Medicine and Social Justice: Essays on the Distribution of Health Care*. Oxford: Oxford University Press.

Figliozzi, G.M 2014, NASA's New Rodent Residence Elevates Research To Greater Heights, viewed 26 June 2014, http://www.nasa.gov/mission_pages/station/research/news/rodent_research/#.U7IMhECceaR.

Ghosh, P. 2010, *Experiments with Genetically Modified Animals Increase*, viewed 1 July 2014 http://www.bbc.com/news/science-environment-10774409.

Harvey, J. 2007, 'Moral solidarity and empathetic understanding: The moral value and scope of the relationship', *Journal of Social Philosophy*, 3: 22–37.

Hoban-Higgins, T.M., Robinson, E.L. and Fuller, C.A. 2005, 'Primates in space flight', in G Sonnenfeld (ed.), *Experimentation with Animal Models in Space*. New York: Elsevier.

LaFollette, H. and Shanks, N. 1996, *Brute Science*. London: Routledge.

Mackenzie, C., Rogers, W. and Dodds, S. 2014, 'Introduction: What is vulnerability and why should it matter for moral theory', in C. Mackenzie, W. Rogers and S. Dodds (eds), *Vulnerability: New Essays in Ethics and Feminist Philosophy*. New York: Oxford University Press.

NASA 1994, *What is the Value of Space Exploration? A Symposium*, viewed 1 May 2014 http://www.hq.nasa.gov/office/hqlibrary/documents/o33273018.pdf.

Nozick, R. 1974, *Anarchy, State and Utopia*. New York: Basic Books.

Pearson, N. 2004, *When Welfare is a Curse*, The Age, viewed 16 April 2013, http://www.cyp.org.au/downloads/noel-pearson-papers/when-welfare-is-a-curse-230403.pdf.

Rogers, W., Mackenzie, C. and Dodds, S. 2012, 'Why Bioethics Needs a Theory of Vulnerability', *International Journal of Feminist Approaches to Bioethics*, 5(2): 11–38.

Russell, W.M.S. and Burch, R.L. 1959, *The Principles of Humane Experimental Technique*. London: Methuen.

Satz, A. 2009, 'Animals as vulnerable subjects: Beyond interest-convergence, hierarchy, and property', *Animal Law* 16(2): 1–50.

Sonnenfeld, G. 2005a, 'Use of animal models for space flight physiology studies, with special focus on the immune system', *Gravitational and Space Biology* 18(2): 31–5.

Sonnenfeld, G. 2005b, 'Overview', in G. Sonnenfeld (ed.), *Experimentation with Animal Models in Space*. New York: Elsevier.

PART VI
Responsibility, Governance and Other Concerns

Chapter 20

The Independent Entrepreneur and the Terraforming of Mars

Chris Pak

From 1964–71, Pan Am enrolled almost 100,000 people onto their First Moon Flights Club, a waiting list for the first of their tourist spaceflights (Cater 2010, p. 838). This publicity drive capitalised on the public expression of desire for spaceflight that had its roots in science fiction (sf) and the first forays into space. As one Pan Am publicist recounts, '[d]uring those months [between the Apollo 8 launch and the Apollo 11 Moon landing], the concept of scheduled passenger service to the Moon quickly shifted from science fiction to the realm of the possible' ('93,000 passengers waiting for first Pan Am Moon flight' 1989). That Pan Am was able to position itself as a pioneer of astrotourism speaks to the optimism surrounding space travel at the time, but it also provides a precedent for contemporary prospects for privately funded ventures into space, thus raising questions over the shape of future public policy with regard to this potential field for human exploitation.

Public policy must now deal with an assemblage of issues and activity related to space colonisation at a scale far exceeding that of the 1970s. Entrepreneurs have once again begun to raise support and funds for private spaceflight. While Jeph Mathurin and Nicolas Peter point to the role of partnerships between private industry and government agencies in funding projects for space exploration, they also mention the entrepreneurs who are transforming traditional models for investment in space exploration (2006, pp. 439, 443). Throughout 2006–07, 14 space agencies opened interagency discussion on the future of spaceflight, culminating in the publication in 2007 of the Global Exploration Strategy (GES), which outlines a vision for future exploration of the solar system that places much emphasis on the important role that private industry could play (Hufenbach 2013, p. 132). Companies such as *Virgin Galactic*, *Bigelow Aerospace* and *Space-X* are developing technologies and securing funding for astrotourism, *Moon Express*, *Planetary Resources* and *Deep Space Industries* are developing space mining technologies infrastructure and *Mars One* is planning for the colonisation of Mars (Cater 2010, p. 839 and Mathurin and Peter 2006, p. 443). As a promotional video from *Deep Space Industries* declares, 'for space, right now is the time' ('Mining the universe for the future' 2013).

Sf has long engaged in speculation about entrepreneurial space exploration. The origin of rocket science shares some of the same roots as sf, with such sf writers as Laurence Manning, David Lasser and Edward Pendray co-founding the American Rocket Society, which merged in 1963 with the American Institute of Aeronautics and Astronautics (AIAA). Their amateur engagement with space exploration was transformed into the professional organisations and agencies that eventually put the first man on the Moon in 1969, but it was the sf imagination that fuelled the myths that were called upon to legitimate the landing project. As Istvan Csicery-Ronay explains, 'rocket heroism has been the domain of the rocket clubs and pulp sf', and when they felt the need to answer to the launch of Sputnik in 1957, 'the U.S. response had to be built from the ground up, as a grandiose just-in-time public relations campaign sold by men who had little interest or understanding of space, rather than a well-established element of state policy' (2008, pp. 240–41). Sf helped provide a language that could be used to communicate with and inspire support from the public. Sf also propelled the technological innovation that led to the success of this iconic American moment, but adequate space policies to complement research into the practicalities of space travel lagged behind.

Given the reflection on space exploration and entrepreneurship that sf engages, it makes sense to see what these narratives can offer by way of thinking about the future of private space exploration, and to consider the potential impact of these explorations on policy. Susan Harmeling bases her analyses of the stories of several entrepreneurs on the idea that their narratives offer alternatives or counterfactuals that can aid in thinking about the notion of contingency (2011, p. 294). Sf stories can function as counterfactuals when compared to our contemporary context, although it is important to remember that considering them as such does not exhaust their meaning as cultural and artistic productions. I consider the portrayal of entrepreneurs who engage in space exploration, colonisation and the adaptation of planets for human settlement, or terraforming, with a view to exploring how these stories can aid in thinking about space policy.

The Space Entrepreneur in Science Fiction

Entrepreneurial endeavour has been central to sf, not only for its formation as a mode of storytelling, but also for its content. Hugo Gernsback established the first sf pulp magazine, *Amazing Stories*, in 1926, and this entrepreneurial venture into sf publishing would have resounding effects on the field. Entrepreneurs as characters were central for early sf, and they have left an indelible mark on the way that space exploration has been conceived. The *Edisonade* is a popular adventure narrative that features an independent inventor who successfully overcomes, through his own ingenuity, the challenges that he is faced with. This type of story is named after Thomas Alva Edison, an epitome of the American dream and a prototype inventor-entrepreneur figure. The online *Encyclopedia of Science Fiction* tells us that such heroes possess 'the conviction that to fix is to own', and that once they begin to see themselves as heroes of an Edisonade, 'the form turns sour, self-serving and entrepreneurial' (Clute 2013).

This identification of the entrepreneurial with the 'sour' and 'self-serving' reflects distrust of private enterprise and its impact on society. Private space exploration has begun to gain popular currency through recent sf films such as Duncan Jones' 2009 *Moon*, in which a private company has established a base on the Moon in order to harvest clean burning helium-3 to support Earth's energy needs. Ridley Scott's 1979 film *Alien* involves a corporate outfit who are sent by their employers to investigate an interplanetary mining facility. Unbeknownst to them, the company is fully aware of the presence of a dangerous entity aboard the facility. Scott's 2012 film *Prometheus* reprises this theme, but here a successful private entrepreneur who is nearing death funds a mission to investigate a planet in the hopes of finding a life-extending treatment: a fountain of youth and the ultimate corporate product. Sebastián Cordero's 2013 *Europa Report*, in which a private company sends a manned expedition to extend the initial exploratory probes' investigation of Jupiter's moon, overturns the image of an impersonal corporation by providing a human face for the company through the entrepreneur and CEO responsible for the project. Her reflection on the significance of the mission and her regret over its outcome attempts to speak back to the common sf image of a self-interested and exploitative entrepreneur. From as early as the 1940s, some examples of sf have made legislation and policy relating to space central to the way their stories developed. If any entrepreneur should spend the money to open space up to investment for mining and settlement, issues of property, monopoly trading and public protection through the regulation of industry or services are central considerations. Entrepreneurial activity can sometimes be driven by a sense of social justice and emotion in addition to desire for profit, and thus recognising the possibilities for developing opportunities to satisfy those needs through investment in space is important. Entrepreneurs create desire that can change economic and social relations, and so attention should be paid to the ways in which such activity in space could work in tandem with – or confuse and negate – other governmental policies.

Jack Vance's 1947 short story 'I'll Build Your Dream Castle' tackles the issue of the entrepreneur's responsibility to the public. It is an ironic tale of corporate exploitation and one-upmanship between designer-entrepreneur Ernest Farrero and his employers Douane Angker and Leon Marlais, owners of a construction and design business. Farrero resigns to pursue an independent and secretive venture involving the design of private planets for wealthy customers. Two factors motivate his decision: Angker and Marlais' single-minded focus on profits and their readiness to appropriate Farrero's research as the company's own property curtails his creativity and sense of social justice. Farrero argues that '"The average man never gets all he wants of the most desirable products, never makes his life fit his dreams"' (Vance 2005, p. 39). The domiciles that Farrero ends up designing are constructed on meteorites suspended 30,000 feet above the Earth's surface. Marlais calls them '[i]ndividual worlds to suit any conceivable whim' (Vance 2005, p. 56). 'Out here' [Farrero] said, 'beauty – grandeur, whatever you choose to call it – comes a lot at a time' (Vance 2005, p. 56). The beauty and the malleability of these worlds, marketed as cheaply as Farrero is practically able to, are still available only to the wealthy, but Farrero is confident that further expansion coupled with a sense of social justice will drive down costs for private worlds. Farrero files for ownership of the 1,132 asteroids whose unique composition makes them essential for the maintenance of gravity on these worlds under the fictional 'Space Claims Act', which 'defines and authorizes mining development of the asteroids' (Vance 2005, p. 59). The entrepreneur's project to improve the quality of life for the majority leads him to engage the law to support his claim of ownership over the physical world.

Imagined Space Policy in Science Fiction

Comparing the ideas raised in this story to the *United Nations Treaties and Principles on Outer Space* (2002) show a contrast between the way early sf imagined space policy and the way policy has been formulated since the 1960s. These principles establish some of the interests and concerns raised by the prospect of space travel first being opened up during the Cold War space race. This document collects treaties, principles and other items related to space policy produced from 1967–2007. Modelled against the UN Antarctic Treaty which came into force in 1961, the first of these policy documents was the 1967 'Treaty on Principles Governing the Activities of States in the Exploration and Use of Outer Space, including the Moon and Other Celestial Bodies'. One of its key themes is that of 'the common interest of all mankind in the progress of the exploration and use of outer space for peaceful purposes' (United Nations 2002, p. 3). Vance anticipates this principle by exploring how entrepreneurs could fit into such a framework and addresses the issue of their responsibility toward 'all mankind'.

In 1999 the UN Conference on the Exploration and Uses of Outer Space (UNISPACE III) recognised the importance of ecological integrity with regard to such activities as monitoring Earth's climate. This 'peaceful' use for space relates back to the 1986 'Principles Relating to Remote Sensing of the Earth from Outer Space', which establishes guidelines that answer to some of the ramifications of access to data that could avert loss of life and damage to property on Earth. The first principle defines remote sensing as the use of electromagnetic waves, 'for the purpose of improving natural resources management, land use and the protection of the environment', while Principle X states that '[r]emote sensing shall promote the protection of the Earth's natural environment' (United Nations 2002, p. 40). An injunction that reflects the sense of an international movement toward cooperation is appended to this statement (United Nations 2002, p. 40):

> To this end, States participating in remote sensing activities that have identified information in their possession that is capable of averting any phenomenon harmful to the Earth's natural environment shall disclose such information to States concerned.

This framework offers an example of how entrepreneurs could respond to the issue of their responsibility to society. Sf dealing with space exploration and terraforming features many instances of the remote sensing of other planets. Kim Stanley Robinson's *Red Mars* (first published in 1992), *Green Mars* (first published in 1993) and *Blue Mars* (first published in 1996, all referred to throughout as the *Mars* trilogy), for example, contain reflection and speculation on the future of Earth's climate that is based on data obtained through such means.

Article 7 of the 'Agreement Governing the Activities of States on the Moon and Other Celestial Bodies' would curtail terraforming based on heavy industrial models as it prohibits significant change to the Moon's environment (United Nations 2002, p. 25):

> In exploring and using the Moon, States Parties shall take measures to prevent the disruption of the existing balance of its environment, whether by introducing adverse changes in that environment, by its harmful contamination through the introduction of extra-environmental matter or otherwise. States Parties shall also take measures to avoid harmfully affecting the environment of the Earth through the introduction of extraterrestrial matter or otherwise.

This agreement does not offer a similar precaution with regard to the other planets of the solar system, although the COSPAR Planetary Protection Policy does outline policies to prevent the biological contamination of Earth and other planets, so long as they are of 'direct interest for understanding the process of chemical evolution or the origin of life' (2011, pp. 1–2). The term 'people and the environment' we learn from the safety framework of the 'Principles Relevant to the Use of Nuclear Power Sources in Outer Space' is synonymous with 'people and the environment in Earth's biosphere' (United Nations 2002, p. 75). Environmental concern for the Moon and Earth is too narrow where potential access to other bodies within the solar system is actively being pursued by entrepreneurs. If these environmental prohibitions were extended to other planets, there would be significant restrictions on mining and perhaps little reason for corporations to invest in the exploration and exploitation of space. A major theme of Robinson's *Mars* trilogy is reflection on how the corporate exploitation of Mars leads to the contravention of the Antarctic Treaty on Earth (Robinson 2001c, p. 249). Once corporations begin to exploit Mars for its resources, the pressure of climate change and resource scarcity on Earth makes it reasonable in the eyes of governments and business to abandon the treaty and begin industrialising Antarctica. This, however, results in an acceleration of climate change that melts polar ice and contributes to rising sea levels and the resulting submersion of coastal cities. Such episodes show how the actions of private business in space may have consequences that redound upon practices and legislation pertaining to Earth.

The Space Settlement Prize Act from the Space Settlement Institute (SSI) is framed as an answer to the lack of policy and legislation regarding space. It aims to put in place a framework for property rights on other planets, and offers to private industry an incentive for embarking in the risky business of space exploitation. At the present moment, however, no major space powers have ratified the treaty. The one direct reference to the environment is phrased in such a way as to distance it from the Antarctic Treaty that the UN Space Treaties were themselves based on (Wasser 2012):

> (4) Recognized ownership of land under this law shall include all rights normally associated with land ownership, including but not limited to the exclusive right to subdivide the property and sell portions to others, to mine any minerals or utilize any resources on or under the land, as long as it is done in a responsible manner which does not cause unreasonable harm to the environment or other people.

It is the slippage of the word 'unreasonable' that the contravention of the Antarctic Treaty in the *Mars* trilogy is based on. Such a principle could provide the motivation for corporations or individuals to direct their actions so as to continually extend the boundaries of the reasonable in ways that do not benefit society as a whole. Given the fact of climate change, what may be reasonable will change in response to the demands placed on society by a changing environment, but this slippage may also serve as a way to legitimate action that is not entirely reasonable in the context of sustainability science. In the light of breaches of current environmental policy, the responsibility of corporations to regulate the environmental effects of their own industry on other planets – constraints which may interfere with profit – may easily be overlooked.

One noteworthy aspect of this draft proposal is that the right to claim extraterrestrial property is limited in an attempt to overcome issues of monopoly ownership. In addition to stipulations regarding the overall amount of land any one company can claim on a given cosmic body, the Space Settlement Prize Act includes the condition that '[n]o entity (nor two entities which are effectively under the same control) shall receive recognition for a controlling interest in two land claims on the same body' (Wasser 2012). Vance's entrepreneur, who is able to claim all of the asteroids within the solar system, would be unable to do so under this proposal.

The notion of Mars colonisation as a break from Earth is one of sf's classic themes. The first terraforming novel, Robert Heinlein's *Farmer in the Sky* (first published in 1950), portrays the colonists' libertarian rejection of Earth's governmental influence, and while corporations are not frequently mentioned in this novel, his 1966 *The Moon is a Harsh Mistress* features an independent Martian colony whose free-market entrepreneurial system stands in opposition to Earth's over-regulation. In each case, inequalities and injustices on Earth prompt this rejection. The employees of Walter M. Miller, Jr's 'Crucifixus Etiam' (first published in 1953) are not so lucky. Their bodies are painfully and irrevocably modified for life on Mars and they are exploited and confined to sub-standard living spaces with no possibility of escape from their contracts. Likewise, in Jerry Pournelle's *Birth of Fire* (first published in 1976), corporations on Mars brutally exploit their workers, but unlike Miller's short story, free Martians and contracted workers engage in an uprising and oust the corporations from their stranglehold so that an independent nation can be formed. Sir Travers Foxe of Michael Allaby and James Lovelock's *The Greening of Mars* (1984) recalls the hero of the *Edisonade*: Foxe develops an ingenious proposal that offers to remove dangerous waste from Earth. Making use of decommissioned greenhouse gases to begin a transformation of Mars and lay the groundwork for an independent Martian government (Allaby and Lovelock 1984, pp. 22–7), Foxe demonstrates how the genesis of the Martian community in the story is rooted in contingencies that Earth's governments overlook.

These two sf histories, of colonies gaining independence from Earth and of corporations creating independent dystopian regimes on other planets, perhaps helps to account in part for why the current space treaties insist on the benefits to 'all mankind' of space travel and exploration, and not for the private profit of a few. As the SSI points out, the lack of ratification by many US states and countries of portions of the UN's bundle of treaties means that there are no real international frameworks for the exploitation of space. What, then, does this mean for space policy now, and in the future? What should entrepreneurs take heed of by way of their responsibilities 'for all mankind' and, implicitly, for their environments?

Frederick Pohl and C.M. Kornbluth's *The Space Merchants* (first published in 1953) is a classic sf story that deals with issues of a globalised corporate world. This satire of corporations and the figure of the entrepreneur addresses anxieties regarding the excesses committed by businesses driven to expand and gain mastery of the world; at one point, Fowler Schocken of Fowler Schocken Associates tells the protagonist Mitchell Courtenay that, '[l]ike Alexander, we weep for new worlds to conquer' (Pohl and Kornbluth 1985, p. 6). Courtenay is a high-ranking advertising executive who works for one of the largest multinational corporations. Fowler Schocken Associates are expanding into a new market – the colonisation and terraforming of Venus – and so Courtenay is placed on the project and charged with raising public support for the endeavour. Carl Iain Cater claims that the contemporary desire for space is still embedded in a traditional view of it as analogous to a new American frontier: 'we should not see astrotourism as completely "out there", and treat it more as the natural progression of a human practice that continually seeks new frontiers' (2010, p. 845). Sf has long reflected on this association between space travel and the westward expansion of early American colonisation, a theme encapsulated in *Star Trek*'s 1966 slogan, 'to boldly go where no man has gone before' (Roddenberry 1966). The colonisation of America, then, offers a history that could inform the formulation of new space policies.

As a satire, *The Space Merchants* addresses the issue of the irresponsible entrepreneur who, whether thoughtlessly or mercilessly, exploits their employees across the globe. While this exploitation is hidden from Courtenay at the beginning of the story, a plot by the conservationists – in this world a radical group who are marginalised by the corporate world and the global population, and who thus do not have a public voice – results in Courtenay's capture, the erasure of his identity and his forced employment as an indentured labourer at the Chlorella plantation in Costa Rica. On his return to Fowler Schocken Associates with his new knowledge about the way corporations are run, he attempts to tell his naïve employer of the realities of corporate espionage and conflict, and goes so far as to admit that '[e]ntrepreneurs don't play a hard, fair game by the rules' (Pohl and Kornbluth 1985, p. 135). Although Mitch understands the crimes that Schocken has committed in order to achieve corporate dominance, he is unable to break away from the deeply ingrained respect for his employer's ability to make money. Given his investment as an important advertising executive, Courtenay's admission points to an assumption about business that needs to be addressed through an appropriate space policy, or otherwise overturned or transcended in some other way before an ethical exploration of space can be attempted.

This negative image of the entrepreneur in sf is balanced by other images of a responsible entrepreneur represented by such stories as Vance's 'I'll Build Your Dream Castle'. Conservation is another important issue in *The Space Merchants*, one that receives increasing attention in sf from the 1960s onward. Addressing this image of the entrepreneur and of environmentalism is Allaby and Lovelock's *The Greening of Mars* (1984), briefly mentioned above. The narrator of this account points out that, unlike early expectations of space colonisation that presented space as a new frontier, his history as a native of Mars does not repeal that of colonisation on Earth: 'I am descended from neither convicts nor political subversives. My ancestors were not even "cowboys". It was all rather dull, I suppose, but highly respectable' (Allaby 1984, p. 126). This dismissal of the myths of space colonisation serves to underline its realities. Habitation and exploitation of other planets may bear some affinities to Earth's history, but it represents a dramatically new historical context.

The narrator discusses the significance of Mars as a field for entrepreneurial endeavour and explains why terraforming is central to incorporating the planet into Earth's economy (Allaby 1984, p. 136):

> The transformation of the martian climate had given the planet a monetary value. It had become real estate, land that could be bought and sold. Those who wished to migrate were asked to buy land on the planet.

An adequate policy on the ownership of property in space, as the SSI outlines in their draft proposal, is essential for corporate expansion into space. It is only the physical possibility of inhabiting, owning and trading land and its resources that makes entrepreneurial endeavour not only possible but worthwhile. What is interesting is that the narrator's emphasis on property also goes hand in hand with Martian independence, and so ownership of land on Mars will not necessarily make other planets annexes of Earth. Furthermore, this emphasis on the necessity of property does not lead to the extensive mining of Mars for its resources. In fact, the ecological management of the planet becomes the colonist's main priority.

Lovelock has championed ecological issues as an environmental scientist since at least the 1970s. As an independent scientist in the 1960s, he worked with NASA to develop methods of detecting life on Mars, where he first thought of his idea for the Gaia hypothesis (Lovelock 1992). The Gaia hypothesis claims that Earth's environment forms a single interconnected system, and that impacts to the environment are regulated via a complex of feedback loops that maintain a stable state. This stable state, however, can be perturbed, causing it to settle into a new state, perhaps uncongenial to humankind. This idea has been influential on sf and on ideas of terraforming in particular; on works such as Frederick Turner's *Genesis* and Robinson's *Mars* trilogy, for example.

This shift toward the ecological management of Mars makes habitation of the planet possible, and this is tied to the utopian aspect of the novel. It is utopian not because it proposes a perfect society on another planet but because it aims to improve living conditions for all of the planet's inhabitants. This flourishing begins with the entrepreneur, Sir Travers Foxe, and his private obsession with Mars: '[t]he planet had become accessible and sooner or later it would be exploited. It needed official protection' (Allaby 1984, p. 23). In order to affect this protection, Foxe engineers a way of utilising technologies that could threaten Earth and turns them to the task of terraforming Mars. Offering to dispose of the unwanted rockets and CFCs owned by Earth's governments, Foxe launches them to Mars, where they begin a runaway greenhouse effect that would warm and eventually transform the planet. Susan Harmeling proposes that 'contingency is an essential element of entrepreneurship because it explains not only the residue of historical accidents that constitute today's playing field but also the makeup of the players who seek to impose their will upon it' (2011, p. 295). This idea accounts for Foxe's entrepreneurship, which is based on fulfilling a private obsession by transforming potential environmental threats on Earth, in this case abandoned weapon systems with dangerous fuel, and harmful CFCs. Harmeling's discussion of contingency as the basic resource and feature of entrepreneurship is suggestive for sf and space policy because of the way she connects these ideas to that of 'truth making' and 'worldmaking' (Harmeling 2011, p. 301):

> The modern pragmatist Nelson Goodman took the idea of 'truth making' a step further, asserting that human beings don't discover worlds; they create them. 'Worldmaking as we know it always starts from worlds already on hand; the making is a re-making'.

She goes on to explain that 'entrepreneuring means taking a piece of the landscape and then collaborating with willing "accomplices" to remake some portion of the world' (Harmeling 2011, p. 302). This suggests that successful entrepreneurs necessarily transform society in ways that are tied to the current 'landscape', whether political, social, environmental or some other characterisation. What this means for space policy is that it should continue to recognise what Harmeling's discussion highlights in a wider context, that the exploitation of space is based not only on the opening up of economic markets, but on the resources associated with a market of ideas, 'in the sense of fostering "human hope" as progress is borne of often painful human contingencies' (Harmeling 2011, p. 299).

In Turner's epic poem of terraforming, *Genesis* (1988), the entrepreneur Chancellor 'Chance' Van Riebeck is brought to trial on Earth for his crimes against the environment of Mars. Earth's governments are subject to a global Ecotheist rule that prohibits any kind of development, especially of the sort proposed by the SSI. Riebeck, against the wishes of the leader of the Ecotheist Gaean Church, has begun the long transformation of Mars by using microbes to adapt its atmosphere to start the process of turning Mars green. Mars' environment in this transitional phase, however, is of a landscape of foul sludge, the product of teeming microbes living and dying. Such an action – a contamination enacted at variance with Earth's policy – shows a disregard for the environments of other planets. Riebeck, however, is attempting to answer a call to his conscience. Under the Gaean theocracy Earth's populations have stagnated, their societies have shrunken and innovation has slowed. His act is intended to revitalise Earth, or at least to provide a space where humankind could develop a less subservient relationship to nature, one in which beauty and respect would strike the keynote of relationships between people and the environment. The colonisation and terraforming of Mars is an attempt to break away from Earth's confining and ultimately destructive strictures. The entrepreneur is, in this context, someone who reaches outside of the frameworks of Earth – an Earth subject to many faults – and works to disconnect it from the Mars colony, perhaps to show the rest of humanity a way out from Earth's deadlock. While this narrative move often leads to interplanetary conflict through war, many other works explore this conflict in terms of political and economic relationships and interaction.

Robinson's *Mars* trilogy provides us with examples of alternatives to war that can help us understand the significance of how sf can help us think about space exploration and space policy. In *Green Mars* and *Blue Mars* the corporation Praxis, led by the entrepreneur William Fort, begins to build relationships with the various Martian communities. Praxis is a late arrival to the exploitation of Mars, as larger multinationals have already begun establishing infrastructure for mining and transporting resources back to Earth. Praxis, however, develops a different business strategy that is based more on markets of ideas than on that of the business-as-usual approach of other corporations. In *Green Mars*, Fort recruits Art Randolph in order to 'acquire Mars' for Praxis (Robinson 2001b, p. 87). His plans for investment are based on a contrasting business model that operates only at the level of the economic market (Robinson 2001b, p. 88):

> Mars isn't just an empty world, Randolph-in economic terms, it's nearly a nonexistent world. Its bioinfrastructure has to be constructed, you see. I mean one could just extract the metals and move on, which is what Subarashii and the others seem to have in mind. But that's treating it like nothing more than a big asteroid. Which is stupid, because its value as a base of operations, as a

planet so to speak, far surpasses the value of its metals. All its metals together total about twenty trillion dollars, but the value of a terraformed Mars is more in the neighborhood of two hundred trillion dollars. That's about one third of the current Gross World Value, and even that doesn't make proper assessment of its scarcity value, if you ask me. No, Mars is bioinfrastructure investment, just like I was talking about. Exactly the kind of thing Praxis is looking for.

Although described in language that reframes bioinfrastructure in economic terms, Fort and Praxis are concerned with the possibilities of addressing climate change and with a host of associated social and environmental issues such as overpopulation and resource scarcity. This discussion takes place during a series of workshops designed to induct new employees into Praxis, and the culture of the corporation emphasises a democratic, experimental and ideas-driven approach to business strategy. Profit, at least immediate profit, as Harmeling argues in her discussion, 'shifts from being the purpose of the project to a byproduct of its success' (2011, p. 304). The entrepreneur able to turn contingency into a resource, as Praxis attempts to do by responding to climate change through an expansion of their market into environmental restoration and sustainability, will find ways to refigure the landscape and, if successful, make a profit from doing so.

Conclusion

These works of sf explore the relationship between the entrepreneur, governments and the public, turning on issues of contingency and raising concerns regarding the responsibilities of the entrepreneur. They consider different ways in which private space exploration relates to 'the common interest of all mankind', as inspiration for improving life in material and social terms (space as a profitable future), as a potential warning about the pitfalls attendant on space colonisation and a suggestion as to the kind of thinking that will be required when formulating policies appropriate to private space exploration. The entrepreneur becomes, in these works, a figure through which the future of Earth is created and shaped. These figures build new worlds through which others follow, but they warn that the direction in which such figures lead is not necessarily tied to a sense of social justice. Both sf and entrepreneurship deal in the business of building new worlds. Innovation, then, should be considered across material and social dimensions with a view to formulating policies that would take seriously the futures that space exploration could open up, and the long-lasting impacts on technology and society that such endeavour leads.

References

Allaby, M. and Lovelock, J. 1984, *The Greening of Mars*. New York: St Martin's Press.

Cater, C.I. 2010, 'Steps to space: Opportunities for astrotourism', *Tourism Management*, 31: 838–45.

Clute, J. 2013, 'Edisonade', in J. Clute and P. Nicholls (eds), *Encyclopedia of Science Fiction*, viewed 1 July 2014, http://www.sf-encyclopedia.com/entry/edisonade.

Committee on Space Research (COSPAR) 2011, *COSPAR Planetary Protection Policy*, viewed 25 February 2015, https://cosparhq.cnes.fr/sites/default/files/pppolicy.pdf.

Europa Report 2013, motion picture, Wayfare Entertainment, Misher Films, Start Motion Pictures, USA. Produced by Ben Browning; directed by Sebastián Cordero.

Csicsery-Ronay, I. 2008, *The Seven Beauties of Science Fiction*. Middletown, CT: Wesleyan University Press.

Deep Space Industries 2013, 'Mining the universe for the future', Youtube, viewed 1 July 2014, http://www.youtube.com/watch?v=pIY_fmvFDhM&feature=youtube_gdata_player.

Gernsback, H. (ed.) 1926, *Amazing Stories*, 1, no. 1.

Harmeling, S. 2011, 'Contingency as an entrepreneurial resource: How private obsession fulfills public need', *Journal of Business Venturing*, 26: 293–305.

Heinlein, R.A. 1967, *Farmer in the Sky*. London: Gollancz.

Heinlein, R.A. 2001, *The Moon is a Harsh Mistress*. London: Gollancz.

Hufenbach, B. 2013, 'Considerations on private human access to space from an institutional point of view', *Acta Astronautica*, 92: 131–7.

Moon 2009, motion picture, Xingu Films (in association with), Limelight Fund (in association with) (as Limelight), Lunar Industries, UK. Produced by Trevor Beattie; directed by Duncan Jones.

Lovelock, J. 1992, *The Evolving Gaia Theory*, United Nations, viewed 1 July 2014, http://archive.unu.edu/unupress/lecture1.html.

Mathurin, J. and Peter, N. 2006, 'Private equity investments beyond Earth orbits: Can space exploration be the new frontier for private investments?', *Acta Astronautica*, 59: 438–44.

Miller, W.M. 1973, 'Cruxifixus etiam', in *The View From the Stars*. Hertfordshire: Panther, pp. 58–78.

Pohl, F. and Kornbluth, C.M. 1985, *The Space Merchants*. New York: St Martin's Griffin.

Pournelle, J. 1987, *Birth of Fire*. New York: Baen.

Robinson, K.S. 2001a, *Blue Mars*. London: Voyager.

Robinson, K.S. 2001b, *Green Mars*. London: Voyager.

Robinson, K.S. 2001c, *Red Mars*. London: Voyager.

Alien 1979, motion picture, Brandywine Productions, Twentieth Century Fox Productions, USA/UK. Produced by Gordon Carroll, David Giler, Walter Hill; directed by Ridley Scott.

Prometheus 2012, motion picture, Twentieth Century Fox, Dune Entertainment, Scott Free Productions, Brandywine Productions, USA/UK. Produced by David Giler, Walter Hill, Ridley Scott; directed by Ridley Scott.

'93,000 passengers waiting for first Pan Am Moon flight' 1989, *Sun Sentinel*, 3 September, viewed 1 July 2014, http://articles.sun-sentinel.com/1989–09–03/features/8903010181_1_moon-flight-requests.

Star Trek 1966, television program, Desilu Productions. Created by Gene Roddenberry.

Turner, F. 1988, 'Genesis: An epic poem', Frederick Turner's Blog, web log post, viewed 1 July 2014, http://frederickturnerpoet.com/?page_id=166.

United Nations Office for Outer Space Affairs 2002, *United Nations Treaties and Principles on Outer Space: Text of Treaties and Principles Governing the Activities of States in the Exploration and Use of Outer Space, Adopted by the United Nations General Assembly*, viewed 1 July 2014, http://www.unoosa.org/pdf/publications/STSPACE11E.pdf.

Vance, J. 2005, 'I'll build your dream castle', in *The World Thinker and Other Stories*. Oakland, CA: The Vance Integral Edition, pp. 37–60.

Wasser, A. 2012, '(Draft of) an act', *The Space Settlement Institute*, viewed 1 July 2014, http://www.spacesettlement.org/law.

Chapter 21

A Place in Space: Marking Emptiness

Meera Baindur

In an ancient Jain geography text, the universe is described as a large 'discworld', 800,000 miles approximately in circumference. The vast area however is an illusion, for the text informs us that humans who act morally are limited to two and a half spheres of this disc world. And we must also share this space in harmony with others of our kind and other living beings. The story of infinite space that is commonly available to all humankind is similar to the story of the disc world. What does it mean for us to share outer space with everybody else? It is increasingly clear that there will soon be contestations and challenges to this seemingly unlimited resource by various nations. When we think about the object of such contestations, one can't help wondering how empty space beyond the Earth's surface can be claimed or marked by territorial boundaries. How can one draw lines in the sky? This chapter will first examine the concept of place in space and then explore how nations can claim rights over what is the emptiness of outer space. Following this, finally some concepts around placement and displacement will serve to understand the responsibilities of nations in the use and sharing of outer space.

As we commonly understand it, 'place' is linked to some surface (like that of the Earth) and is described in terms of orientation, position and direction. The relationality of one's own position to the positions of other objects and people is also used to locate or designate a place. Here I diverge to a different understanding of 'place' as presented in the Indian traditions of thought. In Sanskrit, two very different terms are used to describe the concept of place. Though the terms themselves are not important and may be culture specific, the conceptual meanings they carry are universal and have a direct relevance to the idea of place in space. One term for place (*sthala*) refers to the cultural meanings, the geographical location and the amount of space (in terms of accommodation) used by an object on any give surface. I would use this term in the sense of 'accommodative place' (*sthala*) in conversations such as 'Is there place for one more box in the van?' As such, accommodative places are named and demarcated to distinguish them from the general surfaces. A chess board example would clarify this. There are many empty squares on a chess board that one may occupy as *sthala*, places where pawns are accommodated. One may use cardinal and ordinal points to describe precisely the location of different entities. On the other hand, place referred to by the term stana as place creates a political context to understand the ideas of perspectives and relationships. For instance, the specific piece based on its identity such as a rook or a knight can only move along designated spaces as given by chess notations. The designated place 'stana' is determined by the presence of other pawns on the chessboard, from perspectives that are one's own and the opposing team's. It is a created place, a 'designated place' often connected to ethics and rights of occupancy. When one asks about one's designated place, it has a meaning closer to its use in the metaphor 'to put someone in their place' or 'to know one's place'. This idea of 'designated place' is specifically used to create boundaries and exclusions. According to me, the contestations and claims in outer space lie in the gap between the place available as 'accommodative place' and the 'designated place'. These two conceptual meanings of place can help us understand how infinite space can be limited and suggest to us the ethical implications of 'designated places'.

Understanding of Space as Landscape and Location

The process of implacement or making a space into a place (Casey 1993, p. 37) is easily understood through a description of landscape, boundaries and landmarks. Individual human beings create territorial boundaries through markers such as fences, lines and other symbols that establish rights and strategic claims over landscapes that are represented through maps or descriptions. Nations also follow the same processes to mark their territorial boundaries, though on a larger scale. However when it comes to outer space, we may have to understand strategic boundaries through newer symbolic and associative categories.

There has been an increased permeability of outer space, somewhat closer to the Earth, above the airspace due to increasing satellite networks, particularly those on geostationary orbits (GEO) or medium Earth orbits (MEO). One might suggest that space closer to the Earth is associated with meanings and concerns that are technical, strategic and political rather than artistic or cultural. Moreley and Robins (1995, p. 1) write:

> Patterns of movement and flows of people, culture, goods and information mean that it is now not so much physical boundaries – the geographical distances, the seas or mountain ranges – that define a community or nation's 'natural limits'. Increasingly we must think in terms of communications and transport networks and of the symbolic boundaries of language and culture – the 'spaces of transmission' defined by satellite footprints or radio signals – as providing the crucial, and permeable, boundaries of our age.

Though space is a void with no surface for us to mark our boundaries, nations are creating territorial rights over it. Just like the airspace above a particular country, the space above the nation's boundaries may be claimed by a country as belonging to that particular nation. For instance, eight equatorial nations – Brazil, Colombia, Republic of the Congo, Ecuador, Indonesia, Kenya, Uganda and Zaire – claimed the equatorial arc of the geostationary orbit (GEO) over their respective territories in the Bogota Declaration of 1967 (Peterson 2005, p. 63). These claims did not receive international support or recognition, but the fact that such claims were made is based on presuppositions of space as territorial.

If we imagined space like the airspace, there are pathways or transit areas in space, such as flight paths of space-bound vehicles or rockets and shuttles. On the other hand, like in the case of land or water, there are also stationary nodes in space that are occupied by human-made objects for longer periods of time. Within the first category of pathways and transit zones that is clearly defined by trajectories and flight paths, the contestations are related to launch time and launch areas and also to liability for technology failures causing crashes and collisions. It is likely that the space launch vehicles may crash into another nation's territory or may endanger other traffic if the debris is floating around without control. Under the category of nodes, satellites and other such orbiting objects are present in regulated positions in space along particular orbits. We shall examine later how the ideas of space as similar to airspace or as ocean surface lead to different issues in international laws. Another kind of place that is also particular to outer space is the space station that is basically a form of habitation for humans in outer space. There is only one international space station right now but one may envision a future where many space stations could be set up as experimental and training stations for space exploration.

Locations of space objects, satellites and space stations are closely related to ideas of place-making and are not understood merely through mathematically constructed coordinates and orbital paths. This is because they have also created a sort of landscape in space. Landscape can be defined as 'a cultural image, a pictorial way of representing or symbolising surroundings' (Cosgrove and Daniels 1988, p. 1). A cultural landscape perspective as suggested by Gorman (2005b, p. 87) is useful here and one could extend its scope to include political and ethical meanings. She lists three principal categories off a cultural landscape:

1. The designed or intentionally created landscape, such as a garden or parkland.
2. The organically evolved landscape, resulting from human action within the natural environment, both past and ongoing.
3. The associative cultural landscape, with religious, artistic or cultural associations rather than evidence from material culture alone.

Gorman (2005b, p. 86) suggests that interplanetary space is now a spacescape. She also suggests that historically it was an imagined place of celestial bodies; but with the advent of space technologies, it is now a vast area of human interaction that includes launch sites, satellite orbits, interplanetary space and surfaces of other planets. Such placescapes by presence of human objects become designated places. Metaphorically speaking, the chess board of space is no longer empty but it is like a game in progress. Gorman writes: 'No longer the last wilderness or the last frontier, interplanetary space can be seen as a cultural landscape forged by the organic interaction of the space environment and human material culture' (Gorman 2003, cited in Gorman 2005b, p. 86).

Gorman (2005b, p. 88) refers to this particular space landscape as a vertical three-tiered one, second tier of which is the '... organic landscape in orbit and the surface of celestial bodies (satellites, rocket stages, landers, debris) ...' The geostationary orbit (GEO) is an example of a space landscape which has evolved out of the interaction of satellites and the space.

How have the experts articulated the idea of place in space? Are these descriptions tangible place-markers of space or does space get divided in equal portions in some other ways? Many of these descriptions are not about accommodative places but are about designated places for space activities. According to Peterson (2005, p. 41) International Space Law like other legal systems has to apply two categories of classification for regulations and policies. One category is the 'types of activities' and the other is to establish the 'location of activities'.

Peterson (2005, p. 42) lists the three typical location categories of international law:

1. *res nullius* (areas currently outside the control of any individual state but open to appropriation by the first one that establishes effective occupation of the area),
2. *res communis* (areas outside national jurisdiction not open to state appropriation but to be used in common by nationals of all states), and
3. state domain (areas within the territorial, maritime or aerial jurisdiction of an individual state).

International law about the locations of activities, he suggests, cannot be 'mere extensions of laws' that we use to define territorial, maritime and airspace domains. However he points out that analogous thinking about space by law and policymakers has influenced is of two contradictory types:

> The air analogy was favoured by the location of outer space: in human perception formed by the effects of gravity it lies 'above' the Earth. Vehicles travelling in space could cause damage by crashing or by dropping things on those below and their motion was invariably described as 'flying'. The high seas analogy was favoured by the vastness of space and the evident difference between the near vacuum of space itself and the more solid natural bodies found within it. ... By dealing in some way with two major physical attributes of the realm beyond the Earth's atmosphere – being 'above' Earth and containing both void and solids – rather than one, the high seas analogy gained an edge in mental plausibility over the air analogy (Peterson 2005, p. 49).

In an earlier work, Kayser (2002, pp. 27–8) points out that there is a legal framework for airspace but only a set of 'looser' UN regulations for outer space, despite the principles created for equal sharing:

> By depriving States of the attribute of sovereignty in relation to outer space, these principles have also worked against the motivation of States for establishing a detailed regulatory framework, since such a framework is not needed to ensure their compliance with the international framework which governs their activities in the space sector, and is therefore not a prerequisite to the performance of any business related to space, in particular the launch operations.

The GEO particularly is an economically valuable location in space. Macauley (2004, p. 182) also suggests that though space may seem infinite, there are some locations such as the GEO that are owned by none but are in high demand and therefore need to be managed as a common resource.

In conclusion, we find that understandings of place in space as locations are linked to analogous thinking, and the ambiguities over political control as designated places. We also notice that certain areas of space are subject to more contestation in these designations than others. In the next section we will examine other kinds of places created by the spacescape, particularly the GEO.

Creation of Orbits as Places: Physical Laws and Frequencies, Slots and Parking

The spherical nature of the Earth requires the transmission of data to be received by a middle point and then sent out to the next point. For a good and clear transmission, many towers must be built tall and also at regular intervals. Such a function of receiving and transmission can also efficiently take place by reflecting signals off the ionosphere or by using a telecommunications satellite instead (Jamalipour 1998, p. 5).

Continuous transmission of data through satellites requires that it is receiving and transmitting such data across time. Given the fact that the Earth is rotating, it also important that the satellite be positioned at the same angle over the surface where the transmitters and receivers are located. When it comes to place in space, for these geostationary satellites, we are looking at space to the Earth, within a narrow band of a single orbit around the Earth called the Clarke's orbit or the geostationary orbit. It is here that place is scarce as satellites of different nations jostle each other for space at a distance of about 35,780 kms above the Earth's surface. The first concept of a place in space occupied by our satellites is created by the necessities of physics of rotating celestial bodies, as laid out by Johannes Kepler's (1571–1630) and Isaac Newton's (1665) laws of motion (Jamalipour 1998, p. 711). Depending on the distance from the Earth's surface, inclination and eccentricity, there are different orbits used for different purposes. There are also Low Earth Orbits (LEO) and Medium Earth Orbits (MEO), both of which have some value, but not for telecommunication purposes:

> Because the Earth is continuously rotating, the satellite should also rotate with
> the same angular speed and in the same direction as the Earth, in order to be fixed
> with any objects on the Earth. That is the concept behind launching satellites on
> the geo stationary Earth orbit. (Jamalipour 1998, p. 6)

Each nation wants its satellite to receive and transmit over its own sovereign territory, creating a nationscape in space, a political place in GEO that can be claimed by the nations on the Earth's surface below. The preferred width of this GEO is directly proportional to the width and length of a country (the area to be serviced by satellite).

So in simpler terms one could say that in order for a satellite to transmit and stay above the country it belongs to, it must ideally be placed in geosynchronous orbit, its transmitters creating what is commonly referred to as a 'footprint' over the area it services. The term 'foot print' is an important place-marker of the satellite range on the Earth's surface and is defined by the frequency and the range of coverage of a satellite. From the satellite's perspective, it can 'see' the area it covers. Roberts (2000, para. 8) explains that a geostationary satellite has an 'unobstructed access to as much as forty per cent of the Earth's surface'. Therefore he points out that satellites placed in GEO are 'ideal for the distribution of broadcast signals to large regions'. On the other hand, from the terrestrial perspective, the footprint covers the area that can receive the signals through the receivers. An accommodative place available for satellites the GEO becomes important. However, space satellites have a terrestrial correspondence to the places they occupy in space, creating designated space-conflicts. Later in this chapter I will speculate as to how these two perspectives create a twofold strategic response in the countries below a satellite.

The aim of scientists and engineers working with telecommunication satellites is to try and set up an array of satellites whose footprints do not overlap much and as much of the area possible is covered. Recent technology has allowed satellites to be placed at different angles to each other, allowing for two satellites to occupy the same vertical band, one above the other. Each place that a satellite occupies is called a slot by the international agency that registers the slot, the International Telecommunication Union. A slot is the optimum area around a satellite that it can occupy, linked to a frequency range, without disturbing the frequency of other proximate satellites. The distances between each slot is determined by the physics of frequency, the footprint coverage of the satellite and the other technical consideration of laws of motion in the geostationary orbits.

These narrow slots become available within the narrow band of space above the Earth, and they become unavailable because of these factors:

1. Physical factors such as magnetic space matter, frequency, coverage area and orbital laws of nature.
2. Other satellites 'parked' within these slots (they are not merely in transit through them).
3. Presence of debris or space junk.

One of the ways in which the orbital slots are described is like a parking lot. Each satellite is like a parked vehicle that prevents other vehicles from parking in the same place and other transit objects cannot pass through the same area that it occupies. Satellites can also be wilfully parked in slots to occupy and appropriate the slot. Orbital slots are usually allotted by the International Telecommunications Union in Geneva on a first come, first serve basis. The current situation is that these 'parking lots' have become overcrowded, particularly over the Asia Pacific region with its dense populations.

Within the GEO, the stationary satellite becomes a self-marker of its place. One could say that every satellite casts a territorial ring around itself which other satellites cannot occupy. However, unlike the accommodative metaphor of a parked vehicle, one might imagine the satellite more like a predator with its territory. The satellite size alone does not exclude the other satellites from moving closer, but due to frequency interferences satellites cannot have (like predator territories) electronic proximity.

How does a satellite reach and keep its place in the GEO? We know that satellites are launched using shuttles and are undocked in their slots. Using tiny movements to control them, they are placed in their positions and at angles of the right inclination. Though a satellite in its geostationary orbit continues to rotate around the Earth, it tends to wobble and slowly be drawn towards the Earth's surface little by little (it may take years). This is called orbital decay. If the satellite comes close enough to the Earth, it may re-enter the Earth's atmosphere and burn up or crash into the surface of the Earth. Orbital decay can be measured and calculated, so tiny rockets are fired regularly to keep the satellites at the right distance from the Earth and maintain its place in the slot for coverage and non-interference from adjoining satellites. The wobbling and orbital decay of satellites becomes a significant form of displacement. As long as the satellite is functioning, the countries are bound to restore the satellites back to their orbits. But once the satellites cease functioning, they are to be placed permanently in a safe high Earth orbit (HEO) according to international regulations. Another kind of place in space is created by HEO called junkyard orbital or 'graveyard orbit'. Unlike the strict requirements of distances between the satellites in the slots of GEO, the main requirement is that the satellite be moved about 300 kms beyond GEO (Jehn et al. 2005, p. 37).

Displaced Space Objects: Debris and Dead Satellites

When satellites are no longer functional or they have served their time, they are displaced. Each satellite has a lifetime of active service and it is possible to accurately predict the end of a satellite's active period. A particular amount of fuel is reserved for the last journey of the satellite. Boosters are used to 'displace' the satellite from its spot and move it into the HEO. From slot to a drifting grave plot, the satellite is almost imagined a living being, albeit technological and nonhuman.

The displaced satellite is abandoned and neglected unless it drifts into designated places of the other satellites and useful places in space.

Most nations have to follow procedures and move their satellites away from the lower orbits into the outer orbit. However most countries do not follow these norms and just let their satellites drift away or blow it up into many small bits (as it happened in the case of one particular nation's weather satellite). Jehn et al. (2005, p. 373) assess the risk of such displaced objects in their study and remark:

> In view of these guidelines and recommendations one would expect that the geostationary ring is a well protected and unlettered space. However only about one third of all satellites follow the internationally agreed recommendations. Two out of three satellites are reboosted into an orbit so low above the GEO that they will sooner or later interfere with geostationary satellites or they are completely abandoned without any end of life disposal manoeuvre.

Based on their study of objects recorded in the Database and Information System Characterising in Space (DISCOS), they found that out of 117 satellites that had reached the end of their life, about 37 were abandoned (p. 378).

In the regions of outer space, any displaced object like a non-functioning satellite or small debris from a space mission stage is considered to be out of human control. Such 'displaced' objects form a collision threat to other satellites and space vehicles. While larger debris (such as satellite parts or launch vehicle stages are easier to spot, smaller and free-floating objects in the orbits can cause much worry to space engineers.

Gorman (2005a) points out that:

> Earth orbit has accumulated more than 10,000 trackable objects, including satellites, launch vehicle upper stages, mission–related debris, human remains and 'space junk'. For space industry, these objects fall into two classes: operational spacecraft, and orbital debris, which has now become a serious problem for the continued use of high density orbits. (p. 338)

We now find that displaced objects in the outer space need to be 'placed' or located. The displaced objects are 'placed' by scientists into a volumetric cube representing avoidance measures guidelines for the danger zone or threat of collision. According to the NASA website the placing of these objects is through a 'pizza box' model:

> These guidelines essentially draw an imaginary box, known as the 'pizza box' because of its flat, rectangular shape, around the space vehicle. This box is about a mile deep by 30 miles across by 30 miles long (1.5 x 50 x 50 kilometres), with the vehicle in the centre. When predictions indicate that the debris will pass close enough for concern and the quality of the tracking data is deemed sufficiently accurate, Mission Control centres in Houston and Moscow work together to develop a prudent course of action.

Global Treaties and the Ethics of Sharing Space as a Resource

Space has always been seen as a territory that belongs to no nation in particular. Not unlike the territory of Antarctica, whose treaties have inspired other treaties such as the Moon treaty, the idea is that space and planetary surfaces belong to 'humankind' in common. The ethical and moral concerns of human beings that were mainly focused on terrestrial and territorial integrity have to now increase their scope to include the outer space. Sadeh and Lester (2004, p. 155) detail some of the concerns and issues around space ethics:

> Important questions to consider include: what is the role of human beings in the cosmos; how can links between Earth and space be organized; who is to determine the priorities and choices of science and on the basis of which objectives to society; and what is the level of moral responsibility to which individuals, groups, organizations, and governments must aspire for present and future generations.

So we do find that issues are somewhat balanced between rights and responsibilities of those nations which are competent in space activity with additional accommodation promised to nations of the third world added later.

The space treaties of international cooperation such as article 1 of the Outer Space treaty call for peaceful exploration and use of Outer Space. However the limitations of both human technology and the laws of nature together make the places in space a kind of limited area of commons. As Mineiro (2012, pp. 156–8) points out, there are many challenges to global civil space cooperation in the current priorities of security concerns of different countries and also the lack of a world space organisation as a common platform for managing space.

The normal way to understand the ethics of space sharing is to look at the ways in which countries cooperate and share the places allotted to them in the GEO or cooperate on board the modules of a space station or on a mission to the Moon. The perspective of the treaty is still confined to that of peaceful uses of space for non-military benefits. In fact Kayser (2002, p. 23) points out that the outer space treaty was formulated during the historical period of the Cold War where disarmament of space was the main concern. She suggests that due to this it is possible that the creators of the treaties did not envision the rapid commercialisation of space, particularly in the area of telecommunication satellites:

> They [space treaties] were developed by States to govern activities of States. They did not address the commercial activities and the activities downstream of the activities of States, mostly due to the fact that at that time, space applications were not commercialised and non-governmental entities activities were seen as sort of a science fiction prospect. The texts were elaborated essentially to

maintain a balance between States carrying out space activities and avoiding that
those be used as instruments of conquest, war and domination.

Responsibility to the equitable use of space in the current scenario has focused
on placing objects of different nations in space and assertion of the rights of
nations to develop and expand their own space programs to the best of their
technological abilities.

Place in space based on analogous thinking parallels space with either airspace
or with the high seas, both of which have some lacunae in addressing the claims over
space and the liabilities and responsibilities towards space-related activities. We
have seen how place is imagined as a slot with the GEO for functioning satellites,
as a graveyard orbit for the non-functioning but properly disposed of satellites and
as a dangerous cuboid pizza box for the displaced and dysfunctional satellites.
All these images of placed, displaced and rejected objects could form a new basis
for the ethical concerns around the use of outer space. In all of these descriptions,
relative distances become important. The placement of objects is always relative
to each other so interference and collisions are avoided. While distances from
Earth are important, they signify accommodative space, the available resource
that can be used by humans profitably. They also come to represent an idea of 'far-
away' from the terrestrial home place. We can also note that the further an object
is from the Earth, the lesser it is perceived as a threat or as the personal property of
a nation. The distant object hurled into the infinite space becomes representative
of all of humankind's aspirations. The smaller numbers of human-created objects
in the space path of the long voyage to Mars or out of the solar system occupy
neither a slot, nor a graveyard or a box. Instead they are imagined as pioneers
exploring the nonhuman wilderness of space. How can we use the concept of
designated places to address issues in outer space management? Here I provide
a small example of what may be possible in the area of space when we alter our
understanding of 'accommodative place' to 'designated place'.

Understanding designated place can for instance change our idea of displaced
objects in space that is relevant to our one of our immediate ethical concerns.
The relative places that are like slots, graveyard or the box are the designated
places (*stana*) creating inclusions, exclusions and threats. While one might use an
environmental perspective to study this problem of 'space junk or debris', it is also
possible to see such debris as objects that are not located in their proper places.

The above rationale requires us to recognise and give significance and
eligibility to these displaced objects as deserving of a designated place. While it
is utopian to imagine we will have a zero junk policy for space, pragmatically it is
not possible. To acknowledge these objects of non-use as genuine components of a
spacescape is the first step towards fulfilling the spirit of the outer space treaty. One
of the ways is to recast the displaced objects as cultural artefacts. Gorman (2005a,
p. 349) for instance makes an argument that these objects in space are not just
isolated artefacts but are a part of the cultural heritage of the human exploration

of outer space and they should not be eliminated. Speaking about these artefacts she insists:

> In this case its significance is assessed as part of a cultural landscape. This question hinges on the importance of place. Rather than regarding spacecraft and orbital debris as unrelated objects in an empty substrate, they can also be regarded as related by location, history and function. They are not separate from the space they inhabit, but part of it. They form a new kind of cultural landscape. (Gorman 2005a, p. 349)

While it is interesting to preserve artefacts located in their places historically and perceive them as cultural landscape, not all of these drifting objects have heritage value. An argument that one could make about litter or junk is that they are objects that are out of their own place and obstruct other activities in another object's place. Litter is nothing but a form of clutter. Displaced objects in space are in that sense unclaimed and neglected. Moral responsibility of nations using outer space requires they not place objects in 'non-designated places'. The non-fulfilment of this ethical responsibility has a twofold impact. Firstly, one is causing litter in space; the defaulter is allowing things to be ' out of place'. Secondly, the displaced object is likely to cause other displacements of legitimately placed objects. A rogue drifting satellite could collide with a functional one, causing that to be damaged and drift away. Each displaced object (envisioned as the dangerous pizza box) can create further displacements.

Conclusion

We are designating places for our objects in space and as humankind we need to put things where they belong, even in outer space. It is imperative that nations stringently follow norms of international regulations to park dead satellites in their graveyard orbit in order to make sure we do not have too many of those pizza boxes floating around in our functional orbits. Unfortunately, if the current scenario of negligence towards these displaced objects continues, we may find ourselves with infinite space that we have no place in.

References

Casey, E.S. 1993, *Getting Back into Place: Toward a Renewed Understanding of the Place-world*. Bloomington, IN: Indiana University Press.

Cosgrove, D. and Daniels, S. (eds) 1988, 'Introduction: Iconography and landscape', in *The Iconography of Landscape: Essays on the Symbolic Representation, Design and Use of Past Environments*. Cambridge: Cambridge University Press.

Gorman, A. 2005a, *The Archaeology of Orbital Space*, in Australian Space Science Conference 2005. Melbourne: RMIT University, pp. 338–57.

Gorman, A. 2005b, 'The cultural landscape of interplanetary space', *Journal of Social Archeology*, 5(1): 85–107.

Jamlipour, A. 1998, *Low Earth Orbital Satellites for Personal Communication Networks*. London: Artech House.

Jehn R. and Hernández C. 2001, 'Reorbiting statistics of Geostationary objects in the years 1997–2000', in Sawaya-Lacoste, H. (ed.), *Proceedings of the Third European Conference on Space Debris, 19–21 March 2001, Darmstadt, Germany*, ESA SP–473, Vol. 2, ESA Publications Division, Noordwijk, Netherlands, pp. 765–70, viewed on 30 June 2014, http://adsabs.harvard.edu/full/2001ESASP.473.765J.

Jehn, R. Agapov, V. and Hernández, C. 2005, 'End-of disposal of Geostationary satellites', in Danesy, D. (ed.), *Proceedings of the 4th European Conference on Space Debris (ESA SP–587). 18–20 April 2005*. Darmstadt: ESA/ESOC, p. 373, viewed on 30 June 2014, http://articles.adsabs.harvard.edu/full/2005ESASP.587.373J.

Macauley, M.K. 2004, 'Economics of Space', in Eligar S. (ed.), *Space Politics and Policy: An Evolutionary Perspective*. New York: Kluwer Academic Publications: .

Mineiro, M.C. 2012, *Space Technology Export Controls and International Cooperation in Uuter Space*. New York: Springer.

Morley, D. and Kevin, R. 1995, *Spaces of Identity: Global Media, Electronic Landscapes and Cultural Boundaries*. London: Routledge.

NASA, United State Government, public website information/ resources pages on 'Orbital debris' Viewed on 30 June 2014, http://www.nasa.gov/mission_pages/station/news/orbital_debris.html#.U66gpm34LyE.

Peterson, M.J. 2005, *International Regimes for the Final Frontier*. Albany, NY: State University of New York Press.

Roberts, L.D. 2000, 'Lost connection: Geostationary satellite networks and the International Telecommunication Union', *Berkeley Technology Law Journal*, 15(3), viewed 15 June 2014, http://www.law.berkeley.edu/journals/btlj/articles/vol15/roberts/roberts.html.

Sadeh, E. and Lester J.P. 2004, 'Space and the Environment', in Sadeh, E. (ed.) *Space Politics and Policy: An Evolutionary Perspective*. New York: Kluwer Academic Publishers.

Chapter 22

Outsourcing Space

Christopher Ketcham and Jai Galliott

India may be about to change the economic equation for private space exploitation with its launch of a Mars orbiter. The cost of the launch and spacecraft are such that they could bring asteroid mining into similar cost-revenue alignment as earth-mining of precious minerals. However, India's capabilities produce two important ethical questions. First, while a space player, India is also plagued by poverty, famine, corruption and human trafficking among other maladies and is a recipient of a significant amount of humanitarian aid, especially from Britain. Therefore, the first concerns what India's foray into space means for economical space exploitation and how this complicates the need for humanitarian aid to the country. The second concerns regulation. If India is to develop a cost structure that encourages foreign governments and international firms to outsource the design, manufacture and launching of space mining equipment to it shores within the near future, what sort of treaty will be required to both protect the space environment and ensure that the Indian economy can make fair progress towards self-sufficiency and one day compete on a level playing field with other developed nations engaged in the commercial space race? And finally, this chapter will explore the requirements for a space treaty in the context of the International Law of the Sea.

The Launch Heard Around the World

Cost and daunting technological challenges still plague both public and private space initiatives. However, this may be about to change. On 5 November 2013, The India Space Research Organisation launched an unmanned Mars orbiter. The mission involves the exploration: 'Mars surface features, morphology, mineralogy and Martian atmosphere by indigenous scientific instruments' (Indian Space Research Organisation 2014). According to a *Time.com* article on the day of the launch, there have been 40 Mars missions by the US, Russia and European Union countries, but only 45 per cent, or 18, have been successful (Bhowmick 2013). The orbiter successfully achieved orbit around Mars in September 2014 and since then has been providing data.

   The major news for the November 2013 launch is that the Indian probe cost only 75 million US dollars, approximately 47 million British pounds at the time of writing (Rai 2014). Contrast this with the American Maven Satellite orbiter also for Mars climate research which cost 671 million US dollars.

India is no stranger to space exploration. Its space research organisation was founded in 1962 and to-date has successfully launched 35 Earth orbiting satellites. According to some statistics, India graduates three million students from universities each year, about the same as the United States, with the US and India having about the same proportion graduating from college with science and engineering degrees. India is also the leading country in the world for outsourcing, with information technology its largest outsource service (The Sourcing Line 2013). India is an English-speaking democracy of a billion inhabitants and in 2010 had a middle class, as defined by its National Council of Applied Economic Research, of 228 million persons (The Sourcing Line 2013). While India's middle class may earn less than middle classes in the EU and US, the US had a *total* population of 317 million in 2013.

Poverty Versus Space?

Britain gave India 280 million pounds in humanitarian aid in 2012. India spent 47 million pounds to launch the Mars probe. The question of ethics that arises from this is whether Britain or anyone should be giving aid to India if it has a space agency, presumably something that only wealthy nations should have (Pollard 2013). Indeed, even in the US where there are far fewer people living in abject poverty, the poverty versus space debate simmers and has done for decades. But there are multiple sides to the ethical question as it pertains in India.

The money devoted to the space agency could have been spent to improve education, fund research on a potentially curable disease or otherwise help the poor and disadvantaged. Harsh Mander, Director of New Delhi's Center for Equity Studies, has said that 'we continue to have something like 230 million people who sleep hungry every night, and millions die because they can't afford healthcare. Yet these are not issues that cause outrage' (Magnier 2013). The question, then, is whether India can ethically spend money on a growing space program when it could be spent on education, or research on a potentially curable disease?

In answering this question, we cannot ignore that India's space program may actually be crucial to the country's overall economic enhancement. While we cannot ignore India's persistent poverty problem, we must ask whether a space agency might provide opportunities to increase national wealth so that it can become self-sustaining somewhat more quickly than it otherwise would. Still, could Britain have provided more useful aid to another country? A simple utilitarian answer might be that Britain could have better served another country because aid would have been distributed to more starving people.

Peter Singer illustrated the concept of marginal utility in the ethics of distribution with an example of administering morphine to two patients when the doctor only has two available doses (Singer 1993, p. 24). The first patient is in excruciating pain, the other is in some pain. Giving a shot to each would be considered an equal distribution. But it would be much more than what the patient who has some pain needs (above the marginal utility) and not enough to help the patient who has excruciating pain (below the marginal utility). While not an equitable distribution, giving both doses to the patient with excruciating pain will put both patients at about the same pain level (Singer 1993, p. 24). Since giving aid to India essentially takes aid away from another country, perhaps in more dire straits, is this a giving that is above India's margin of utility?

Which is a more ethical investment in the long run: providing resources towards nudging the Indian economy towards self-sufficiency or giving them to another country for a temporary solution to starvation or disease? Likely there is a balanced answer to this. There is a time and place for humanitarian aid and a time and place for prudent investment in another country. Problems occur when 1) humanitarian aid is given without investment to mitigate or eliminate the underlying maladies, and 2) when investing above the receiving country's point of marginal utility in efforts to produce effective solutions to these problems.

We ask: what is the economic value of the investment India has made in its space agency? What is the prognosis for profitable space exploration? Are we still at the pure-science stage of the journey into space or are we nearing the point where we can produce a positive net present value from the investment in space technology beyond the Earth-orbiting satellite? And, can India perform the same cost-efficient services for private space exploitation ventures as it has for outsourced IT?

Establishing the Value of Space

The difference with the 2013 India Mars mission is that its costs are more in line with what commercial ventures will require for extended missions into space. A hypothetical example illustrates this. Let's assume that science has identified a near-Earth orbit asteroid that is made of nearly pure (86 per cent) platinum (Zolfagharifard 2013). The New York price for platinum was US $1,499 per ounce at the time of writing. On Earth, platinum is expensive to mine. The Stillwater Mining Company of Billings Montana, USA, noted in its 2012 annual report that its cash cost[1] to mine one ounce of platinum and palladium in 2013 was forecasted to be US$560 (Stillwater Mining Company 2012, p. 6).

Let's assume that a start-up group in India and the Indian space industry (government and private) agree to build an asteroid miner and reusable space dump truck that has a capacity of 10,000 lbs or 5 tonnes (4.5 metric tonnes) for the price of 79 million US dollars.[2] For this price, the miner and dump truck are launched by India and sent to the asteroid, with the dump truck later returning to

---

1 Cash costs in mining include cost of production; but do not include depreciation, royalties, refining, transportation or non-site administrative costs.

2 The space shuttle had a cargo capacity of more than 50,000 lbs or 25 tonnes. So even if the cost to build the miner and dump truck were 2.5 billion US dollars and the

Earth with a platinum cargo. Let us assume that the price of platinum stays where it is and, if out of 10,000 lbs of asteroid, 8,626 lbs of pure platinum is expected to be extracted. The cash cost to SpaceMine, Inc. of producing this platinum is US$572.36 per ounce, which is comparable to what Stillwater forecast for 2013.

There will be risks. Platinum is a commodity and pricing changes moment to moment (in late 2008 the price was just short of $800 per ounce). Increasing the supply of platinum if there is no increase in demand will depress prices. The mission may discover that while there is platinum it is only a surface sheen or it is very difficult to mine. There is also the risk of the project blowing up on the launch pad or otherwise failing in route. But the future is already here.

In 2012 a company called Planetary Resources was formed to mine asteroids.[3] A similar operation in India could be a start-up company or, for the sake of argument, may have a track record in satellite construction like Plantary Resources, but does not have the sunk costs of a traditional mining company. By contracting with India's outsourcing capabilities for both design and manufacture of space technology, our India start-up overall costs could be in line with comparable Earth-based mining operations.

Sunk costs may or may not be a problem for India. The US and Russia may never recoup their costs from the innovations they created for space (both peaceful and Cold War-era) that are in today's consumer and industrial products, even taking into account taxation revenue. India may consider the cost of R&D as something it can eventually recoup by becoming preeminent in manufacturing and launching space mining technology.

India's space program is renowned for running on the cheap. The Mars mission used recycled technology. The agency simplifies design to reduce cost, waste and weight. Costs for many parts of future space missions will likely be much lower than today, simply because considerable design and experimentation has already been done. However the cost of failure is high, even with insurance. 'Economical but safe' will need to be the watchwords for space exploration, manned or unmanned.

The India Advantage

The first advantage is that despite a few failures, India has a proven track record in getting payloads into space. Second, they have a lower cost structure than competing

---

dump truck could return 30,000 lbs (15 tonnes) of raw ore, the cash cost per tonne would be $520.83, or less per tonne than the 5-tonne project.

3   Planetary Resources' mission as stated on their website is: 'Planetary Resources' mission is clear: apply commercial, innovative techniques to explore space. We will develop low-cost robotic spacecraft to explore the thousands of resource-rich asteroids within our reach. We will learn everything we can about them, then develop the most efficient capabilities to deliver these resources directly to both space-based and terrestrial customers. Asteroid mining may sound like fiction, but it's just science' (Planetary-Resources, 2013).

programs. They are leaders in outsource solutions for technology companies and have a large and well-educated population in science and engineering. India's track record with Earth orbiting satellites will garner it more satellite business in the future.

Another advantage in India is the difference in rates of pay (2013) for engineers between the US and India. Aeronautical engineers in the US average $105,000 in annual salary, India $20,000. For electronic engineers, the US averages $120,000, India, $12,000 (Neuman 2013).

Business and industry will need to determine how space projects can provide economic benefits that are similar to, if not better than, those projects conducted on Earth. Can India create an economics for space that will encourage profit-seeking firms to enter space for purposes other than to deploy satellites?

Making India an Attractive Space Partner

What India will want to do to attract private space exploration projects

1. Reduce the cost of risk in space:
    a. Develop and deploy reliable launch technology;
    b. Design durable and redundant space vehicles, equipment and technology that can survive the harsh conditions of space;
    c. Develop durable and reusable unmanned craft for mining and other activities associated with resource acquisition.
2. Innovate: create the need for additional communication and other near-Earth orbit equipment that can be deployed, including space junk recycling applications.
3. Recycle technology; simplify technology for space.
4. Identify resource-rich planets, asteroids, moons or comets where high-value and rare Earth minerals, chemicals or other elements can be mined/extracted for return to Earth and work with industry to design economical means to acquire these assets.
5. Align costs of asset acquisition in space with that of Earth, taking into account commodities issues such as market variability and scarcity.
6. Continue to provide the necessary number of educated and trained professionals who perform quality work and ramp up this effort to meet growing industry needs for Outsource, Inc. to supply Space, Inc.

The commercial space industry today is a small part of the world's economy. However satellites and other advances have vastly improved earthly communication and entertainment, and made entrepreneurs wealthy.[4] Should more distant ventures prove to be achievable and profitable, commercial space activities may become a greater engine of economic growth. If a country like India can become a leader in

---

4 Of course there have also been spectacular failures such as the satellite phone venture of Motorola called Iridium which resulted in loss of five billion dollars in 1999 when Iridium declared bankruptcy.

providing services through its vast outsourcing capabilities, then this might move the economic and political centre of gravity closer to Asia.[5]

Protecting India's Advantage

Despite the advantages on offer to potential government and non-government clients and buyers, if India's investment in the space industry is to be justified by appeal to the idea of long-term economic enhancement and the idea that the Indian space program might one day deliver benefits similar to those derived from the American space program, or indeed if there is to be any defence of the decision on the part of a developing nation to accept aid and then spend it on sending robots to Mars, there must be some general protections offered to India and other developing countries in the form of a treaty or generally agreed space ethic.

As things currently stand, access to space is currently politically unhindered and no government or group has yet claimed ownership of any particular space resource. However, without regulation, we are likely to see developing nations come late to the game and the allocation of space resources between countries, between groups of people, within governments and within agencies based on something mimicking Charles Darwin's theory of evolution. That is, while there will be winners and losers, successes and failures, events are likely to be messy and chaotic as the space age moves forward. Billionaires like Richard Branson[6] are building for space tourism while others are still incapable of launching a rocket, and these kinds of technological disparities must be formally addressed if space is to benefit all.[7]

Current treaty mechanisms deal primarily with the militarisation of space and do not focus on matters of access and fairness. To fill this gap, there are a few other ideas under consideration by the international community, but all fall short of establishing an actual treaty. One of these comes from the Group of Governmental Experts (GGE) on Outer Space Activities. This group was established by the Secretary-General of the United Nations in 2012 and has already submitted its final report, which has now also been made public (GGE 2013). Since outer space is inherently a multilateral domain, this group has proposed various transparency and

---

5   Planetary Resources recently acquired a company that estimates profit values for asteroids that can be mined for minerals and other precious elements. See http://www.asterank.com/. Whether fantasy, wishful thinking or reality, the profit estimates for single asteroids range into the trillions in US dollars.

6   See www.virgingalactic.com/ for details about the progress of one space tourism firm. Note that in December 2014, the Virgin Galactic spacecraft exploded in flight.

7   There are other ventures that have been formed to provide launch platforms for space cargo. Space-X is a commercial rocket venture that has a contract from NASA to resupply the International Space Station. It's rocket Dragon in April 2014 successfully launched in such an attempt. The company was founded by Elon Musk of PayPal and Tesla Automobile fame. Information about Space-X can be found at http://www.spacex.com/. Note that in January 2015, their Falcon 9 spacecraft aborted during launch and exploded.

confidence-building measures. These involve exchanging information on national space policy and goals, activities in outer space and details of any risk reduction manoeuvres, such as high-risk re-enteries and intentional orbital breakups. The GGE expects states to review and implement these assorted measures through relevant national mechanisms on a voluntary basis. However, it is important to note that another GGE report was submitted to the UN in 1992, but no progress was made to contextualise this report for developing any effective space policy mechanism (Lele 2013).

The European Union-sponsored Space Code of Conduct (CoC) is perhaps the most comprehensive draft document (Council of the European Union 2013). The sixteenth version is currently circulating and may be enacted in the near future. It does include a provision for all states to access and explore outer space without harmful interference, but still falls short of providing specific guidance when compared with conventions governing exploration of other traditional domains.

The United Nations Convention on the Law of the Sea

For thousands of years, humanity has migrated by land and sea and established colonies on virtually all land masses of the globe (except Antarctica). While humans have left their garbage piles, exterminated local flora and fauna, introduced invasive and destructive species and killed millions of fellow humans with our colonising diseases, we have also sought to bring order to our own chaotic behaviour and it is these previous efforts that we must look to for guidance in bringing order to the commercial space race. One of these ordering endeavours has been The United Nations Convention on the Law of the Sea. The seas are not unlike space, covering vast distances between land masses. The right to travel unmolested in international waters is a centrepiece of this legislation. The sea, sea floor and other oceanic elements are considered the heritage of humanity.

While a 'freedom of the seas doctrine' has been a long-standing concept in international law, after World War II, countries, beginning with the United States, began unilaterally expanding their territorial waters. To mitigate this 'encroachment' and other problems associated with the increasingly important use of the sea for expanding international trade, the United Nations convened a group in 1967 to study and develop an international law of the sea. The resulting law has been amended numerous times since then. The convention summarised the treaty as accomplishing these things:

> In short, the Convention is an unprecedented attempt by the international community to regulate all aspects of the resources of the sea and uses of the ocean, and thus bring a stable order to mankind's very source of life (United Nations 2012).

Key features of the treaty that may also have some merit for a treaty of space include:

- Rights of innocent passage, meaning: passage is innocent so long as it is not prejudicial to the peace, good order or security of the coastal state;
- Right of transit passage: transit passage means the freedom of navigation and overflight for continuous travel between locations;
- Conservation of the living resources with coastal states required to optimise utilisation of living resources in their locale;
- Freedom of the high seas: the high seas are open to all states, whether coastal or land-locked;
- Reservation of the high seas for peaceful purposes;
- Invalidity of claims of sovereignty over the high seas;
- Duty to render assistance within reason:
  - to render assistance to any person found at sea in danger of being lost;
  - to proceed with all possible speed to the rescue of persons in distress, if informed of their need of assistance, in so far as such action may reasonably be expected of him/her;
  - after a collision, to render assistance to the other ship, its crew and its passengers and, where possible, to inform the other ship of the name of his own ship, its port of registry and the nearest port at which it will call.
- Duty to cooperate in the repression of piracy on the high seas or elsewhere;
- Common heritage of mankind: the seabed, ocean floor and other elements of the sea.

Considerations for a Convention on the Law of Space

These are some of the questions that we should be posing and developing answers for in preparation for a law of space:

- Piracy in space seems to have similar issues to the law of the sea. However, space is so vast that it likely will be impossible to police in the near term. While countries are cooperating to suppress piracy in the oceans, much of the policing of oceanic piracy is done by local navies and coast guards. How economical or practical could this be in space? Is there a need for a universal space piracy police agency and grievance body that can pool resources for this purpose?
- Assisting others in space. The issues of distance in assistance to others become a real concern in space. Are we required to divert a spacecraft millions of kilometres and for a duration of many months (or even years) to assist another? Our vessel is small and confined with resources only for the persons we carry. What are the practical limitations of assistance and are there alternative solutions that may be more relevant for space?
- The rights of innocent passage and pollution present other issues. Space flotsam and jetsam (space junk) can produce navigation hazards as they do on the high seas today.

- What is considered salvage in space? What can be taken by collectors and private ventures without recourse to previous owners? Can we seize goods from an inoperable space shuttle as some people illegally do from beached cargo ships?
- There is the question of ownership of space bodies. The sea, its flora and fauna and the seabed are the heritage of humanity. While space itself may be conceived as free, what planetary bodies should be subject to the common heritage of humanity and which elements of them should not?
    - What rules, for example, would we require for planets and moons for the inhabitation and exploitation of their resources?
    - What about asteroids, comets and other planetary bodies and even natural debris? Should they be part of the common heritage or can some be owned and exploited?
    - Can countries acquire any of these by arriving first?
    - What about taxation of these resources and by whom?
- Should there be an international space agency and/or a World Space Council?
- The oceans are to be used for peaceful purposes but countries have orbited military satellites with impunity perhaps even to shoot other countries' satellites from the skies. Can the peaceful purposes of the law of the seas be translated into a law of space?
- What about life forms? What are the requirements for preventing the unwanted introduction of earthly life-forms on other planetary bodies or into space itself? What is the protocol when life-forms are discovered on other planets, both in the collection and use of these life-forms and the removal of these life-forms to space, Earth or other solar-system bodies? In other words what are our ethical responsibilities to extraterrestrial life and to the protection and preservation of life on Earth?
- What are the conservation and resource optimisation requirements for space exploitation?

Currently, many nations are found reluctant to opt for any strong space regime based on hard law. Any soft approach is expected to have inbuilt limitations and may bring in ambiguity to the global space arrangement. Perhaps the ethics of space requires a new moral code or convention that not only denies the thought of piracy or war but also finds both to be so distasteful they are no longer possible to consider. And what will it mean if such an ethics only exists in the space outside of Earth because the Earth refuses to ratify such an idea for itself?

Enhancing Justice

The law of the sea has a rich history and has received much attention from governments, international bodies and the maritime industry. Humanity has spent and continues to spend time and energy to perfect the law of the sea. However, this same proposition is not as easily applied to human justice especially when it comes to India and the commercial space industry. As Nobel Laureate, Amartya Sen, said in the beginning of his book, *The Idea of Justice*, it is more important 'to address questions of enhancing justice and removing injustice, rather than to offer resolutions of questions about the nature of perfect justice' (Sen 2009, p. ix).

What has been lacking is the enhancing of human justice and removing of the human injustice part of the equation in places where much groundwork for the private and commercial exploration of space will be conducted in the future, that is, through countries like India who can perform highly technical tasks for less money. As humanity has an opportunity to create an ethical space for the universe, it also has the opportunity and the *obligation* to provide justice for those who will labour on Earth to supply the needs of space travellers and robot explorers. A robust ethic of space is one that considers the needs, rights and justice for both Outsource, Inc. and Space, Inc. along with the idea that such exploration and exploitation will benefit all humanity and not just the wealthy few.

Humanity can use space as an extension of Earth – something to exploit with impunity – or it can decree that the universe will be understood in context of an ethical space. Humanity's beginning efforts in this ethical space have not been exemplary as we have polluted near-Earth orbits with many tonnes of space junk. There is still time to overcome our adolescent excesses and create a durable social license to operate in space. In this ethical space not only is there the possibility to explore and utilise the riches of other worlds but there is also the opportunity to improve the conditions of humanity. Space opens the long-term possibilities of reducing overcrowding on Earth, and if the economics of space can begin to show profits then there is also the opportunity to lift from poverty those people on Earth who will labour to supply the engine of this transformation.

An ethics of space considers that the universe is something that cannot be owned by humanity but at the same time it is like a world heritage site on Earth, a place where humanity is given over and bound ethically to respect rather than exploit without recourse. If the outsource industry in India can become the engine that enables private space exploration, it is important that both outsourcers and outsourced alike develop an understanding of what this effort can mean to humanity both here on Earth and in space. The world must engage in a dialogue to develop a robust ethic for countries like India and commercial space exploration and development. Their joint efforts will need to produce benefits for persons on Earth and elsewhere. At the same time we must make clear that space is vast and that control of governments across millions if not billions of kilometres will be limited.

References

Bhowmick, N. 2013,. India Races To Space With a Mission to Mars Time.com. Retrieved from http://world.time.com/2013/11/05/india-races-to-space-with-a-mission-to-mars.

Council of the European Union (2013). International Code of Conduct for Outer Space Activities, version 16, viewed 6 January 2015, http://eeas.europa.eu/non-proliferation-and disarmament/pdf/space_code_conduct_draft_vers_16_sept_2013_en.pdf.

Group of Governmental Experts on Transparency and Confidence-Building Measures in Outer Space Activities (2013). U.N. GAOR, 68th Sess. U.N. Doc A/68/189, viewed 6 January 2015, http://www.un.org/ga/search/view_doc.asp?symbol=A/68/189.

Indian-Space-Research-Organization. 2014, Mars Orbiter Mission. Retrieved 4/24/14, from http://www.isro.org/mars/objectives.aspx.

Lele, A. 2013, Space security: Possible options for India, *The Space Review*, viewed 5 January 2014, http://www.thespacereview.com/article/2390/1.

Magnier, M. 2013, India set to launch Mars mission, provoking criticism over cost. Los Angeles Times. Retrieved from http://articles.latimes.com/2013/nov/04/world/la-fg-wn-india-launch-mars-mission-20131104.

Neuman, S. (2013, 11/5/13). Why India's Mars Mission is So Much Cheaper than NASA. Retrieved from http://www.npr.org/blogs/thetwoway/2013/11/04/243082266/why-indias-mars-mission-is-so-much-cheaper-than-nasas.

Online-Library-Of-Liberty. 2014, Hugo Grotius. Retrieved 4/24/14, 2014, from http://oll.libertyfund.org/people/hugo-grotius.

Planetary-Resources. 2013, Mission. Retrieved 11/6/13, from http://www.planetaryresources.com/mission.

Pollard, S. 2013, Why give aid to a country sending rockets to Mars. Express. Retrieved from http://www.express.co.uk/comment/expresscomment/441612/Why-give-aid-to-a-country-sending-rockets-to-Mars.

Rai, S. (2014). From India, Proof That a Trip to Mars Doesn't Have to Break the Bank. New York Times. Retrieved from http://www.nytimes.com/2014/02/18/business/international/from-india-proof-that-a-trip-to-mars-doesnt-have-to-break-the-bank.html?_r=0.

Sen, A. 2009, *The Idea of Justice*. Cambridge, MA: Harvard University Press.

Singer, P. 1993, *Practical Ethics* (Second ed.). Cambridge: Cambridge University Press.

Stillwater-Mining-Company.2012. Stillwater Mining Company Annual Report 2012. Stillwater Mining Company. Billings Montana. Retrieved from http://investorrelations.stillwatermining.com/phoenix.zhtml?c=99837&p=irol-reportsannual.

The-Sourcing-Line. (2013). India. Retrieved 11/6/13, from https://www.sourcingline.com/outsourcing-location/india.

United Nations. (2012). The United Nations Convention on the Law of the Sea (A historical perspective). Retrieved 11/15/13, 2013, from http://www.un.org/depts/los/convention_agreements/convention_historical_perspective.htm.

Zolfagharifard, E. (2013). Nasa launch mission to investigate whether it is possible to mine asteroids for precious metals – and add TRILLIONS to the economy. Mail Online. Retrieved from http://www.dailymail.co.uk/sciencetech/article-2387955/Nasa-launch-mission-investigate-possible-asteroids-precious-metals--add-TRILLIONS-economy.html#ixzz2jyrsyjIW.

Chapter 23

Forty Hectares and an MU:
Towards a Colonisation Ethic

Christopher Ketcham

This is a story about the future, how distant a future remains to be seen. The question this story asks is whether we can learn from our past to not make the same mistakes in the new promised land of Mars.

It may be that it is humanity's manifest destiny to be the stewards of and the colonisers of the planets of this solar system and in some versions of this doctrine into planetary systems beyond. There are two ways of looking at this. We can do to the other planets as we have done to our own, simply use up resources without impunity as an ever-expanding population requires. Or, we can begin a dialogue that considers the nature of humanity not only in its prodigious will to power and will to expand its population and territory, but as a responsible steward of universal resources. We construct alternative scenarios and simulations for use with technology applications, war scenarios and space missions; why not with behaviour and sociology such as will be required for habitation on other worlds or to prevent our own Earth from galloping into unsustainability?

As this story begins, scientists, politicians, religious and business leaders have come together to discuss global population at a conference which many are calling 'From Here to Where?' While most scientists have predicted that the maximum amount of human population that the Earth can sustain is 10 billion persons, within the year of this coming together, the world's population is expected to hit 12 billion. Cities have sprawled over sprawl, poverty has been deemed an intractable problem in many sectors and personal wealth is concentrated in only a few families. Famine, strange weather, drought and plagues in many forms have all strained Earthly resources to a point where something must be done now, not tomorrow.

The Earth is ruled by a representative Consortium government whose authority extends substantially over all the Earth and its peoples. This Consortium was deemed necessary because the combined wealth of the nation had been declining for quite a while and a more streamlined form of government was calculated to be more efficient. It's not a European Union or a republic of states like was the United States of America, but is a single federal system that includes delegates from formerly constituted countries. This is a democratic 'federation' that no longer supports or permits local sovereignties.

While government, science and business have spent the better part of the previous century in projects to produce sustainable sources of non-carbon-based fuel and energy, have introduced more and more genetically engineered super producing plants and mega-waste consuming microbe families and have developed an efficient wind-powered seawater reclamation system to provide (some of) the water needs for the burgeoning population ... another aspect of the Consortium's efforts – population control – has failed miserably. Modelled after the earlier Chinese one-child policy, this population control effort has been successfully resisted because the Consortium has dedicated few resources to enforce this policy; the original mandate passed by only one vote and many representatives and succeeding administrations have turned a blind eye to the regulation; religious leaders have strenuously objected and urged its violation; the poor see large families as their only means to provide just enough income or labour to maintain their subsistence; and businesses have continually used advertising to promote fertility to feed their ever-increasing need for more customers in a highly competitive but low profit-margin economy. The tipping point for action came when the Pope said that maybe it is time to consult God and the heavens for answers.

The conference is expected to meet regularly over its three-year charter in order to map out strategies to deal with unsustainable population growth. No topic is deemed off the table, though euthanasia, mandatory sterilisations and genetically engineered life-span governors are unlikely to gain any traction. In fact where the buzz is in the conference at this moment is colonisation, the colonisation of Mars. Scientists have called on their colleagues at universities and research labs to develop plausible scenarios for making Mars inhabitable. Ideas are streaming in. Economists are looking at feasibilies of more promising schemes and the politicians are engaged, but they remain as a whole, sceptical.

What about Mars?

At this moment in time, exploration of the planets has been limited to government-sponsored and a few private forays, some manned and some not, that have resulted in a still minimal and somewhat controlled footprint on other worlds. Certainly the Earth is ringed in space junk and derelict craft but humans have yet to establish a permanent colony anywhere outside of Earth. The suggestion that humans could inhabit a planet as desolate and unforgiving as Mars, while intriguing, seems so far-fetched as to border on the ridiculous. The hearings are public; the press is sceptical. But things are about to change.

A virtually unknown lab in the Sahara region has just provided the committee with a report on the terraforming project it has perfected in an experimental plot on this boundless desert. The results are profound and a delegation of committee members has been dispatched to review the project. The Dust to Dawn Reclamation Project, as the lab calls it, produces copious amounts of water which feeds drought resistant but highly productive grain that has also been engineered to produce an oxygen byproduct at twice the level of other plants. And it does all this in desert sand that has been fortified by a complex, but minimal, chemical slurry of nutrients. More importantly this soil additive also includes a beneficial bacteria, bugs, mould and other environment-building and self-sustaining microbes. And, as a Nobel-laureate economist, speaking to reporters at the inspection has just said, 'Using a remarkably cost and energy efficient process'. There is a renewed interest in Mars … the buzz is back.

The difficulty is not in replicating the Dust to Dawn process on Mars, but in terraforming Mars so that even this process and others like it can be deployed in the open atmosphere and not just under manufactured shelters.

Other resources to accomplish the initial terraforming of Mars have been theorised, but the cost to prepare the Martian atmosphere so that it can sustain life with adequate carbon dioxide for plants which, in turn, will produce adequate oxygen levels to support animal life … and where the unrelenting cold can be kept at bay is deemed to be without precedent in the annals of human history. 'Unfathomable and impossible to articulate or quantify', said the influential representative from the area once called South Africa.

The Conference Drags On

The conference has met continuously now for almost three years. No solution or combination of solutions other than Mars colonisation has been shown to provide enough of an adequate (as in have enough votes to pass) solution to reducing Earth's population quickly enough to avert a collapse of the ecosystem, the food system and the economic system of Earth.

BREAKING NEWS: on one side the economists have repetitively wrung their hands over how this grand and risky venture will be financed. On the other hand, the politicians have, over the last six months, built support – despite the costs – from hungry and weary constituents tired of living under government subsidy or in subsistence that has become the regimen of Earthly existence. Scientists all over the world (with the encouragement of politicians) have begun clamouring for opportunities (crudely translated into financing) to assist humanity in 'its most daring adventure of all time'. Religious leaders are calling for the end of poverty. The votes have been cast in the two houses of the Consortium.

The president of the Consortium of Nations has just concluded the most anticipated and watched news conference ever conducted on Earth. In it she proclaimed, 'It's humanity's manifest destiny to be the stewards of all the planets of the solar system. As we begin this stewardship, we look towards Mars as our first outpost and our best chance to begin civilizing the planets of our cosmos'. Mars will be colonised.

Manifest Destiny

John O'Sullivan coined the term Manifest Destiny in an article in 1845 titled 'Annexation' his *United States Magazine and Democratic Review*:

> Why, were other reasoning wanting, in favor of now elevating this question of the reception of Texas into the Union, out of the lower region of our past party dissensions, up to its proper level of a high and broad nationality, it surely is to be found, found abundantly, in the manner in which other nations have undertaken to intrude themselves into it, between us and the proper parties to the case, in a spirit of hostile interference against us, for the avowed object of thwarting our policy and hampering our power, limiting our greatness and checking the fulfillment of our manifest destiny to overspread the continent allotted by Providence for the free development of our yearly multiplying millions. (O'Sullivan, 1845, p. 5)

Millions immigrated to the United States in the nineteenth century. The cities would become desperately overcrowded by the turn of the twentieth century and good arable lands in the east had already been snapped up by the early nineteenth century. By 1845, the United States had thrown the British out of the colonies, purchased the Louisiana Territory from France and was about to engage Mexico in a war over the US annexation of Texas. Yet the colonisation in the English-speaking new-world had begun in the 1600s as a replica of British society (Stephanson 1995, p. 3). The Consortium of Nations has this same idea in mind for Mars – Earth, Jr. Early on after the momentous vote, leaders began invoking the Louisiana Purchase as a guide to how to begin the process and chronicle the terraforming of Mars.

Thomas Jefferson wasn't sure what he had when he made the Louisiana Purchase in 1803, so he dispatched Merriweather Lewis and William Clark on an expedition to explore the continent from east to west. Their chronicle was instrumental, not only in damping critics of the purchase regarding its usefulness, but also it painted a detailed picture of what riches (and dangers) potential settlers might find in these lands and this spurred the country into beginning its westward expansion.

The Consortium has begun a similar process, incorporating cinematographers, writers and others into the terraforming project design. These chroniclers will be tasked with assembling grand panoramic pictorial exposés on the wonders of Mars. The sales pitch has begun, but migration is still many years away.

Yet there are those who do question whether humans have a moral right to disrupt the natural forces of another world towards our own ends. Do we have the right to introduce Earth's brand of life and humanity to other worlds? Others counter that there is some scant (but controversial) evidence that Mars first introduced life to Earth and we are simply returning the favour. While this argument and debate has produced protests in universities and lamentations in religious circles, for the most part the general mood of the world reflects the urgent need to act now.

Who Owns Mars?

Just after the vote to initiate the terraforming process on Mars was announced, many retired space scientists received calls from a 'top secret' Hellas Project that offered employment to build a Martian space lander that would be used to perform an important geological survey of a large swath of the red planet. No expense was spared and within six months of the President's manifest destiny speech a lander cobbled together from old lander parts and designs was on its way to Mars, ostensibly to scout for ore deposits that could be mined by potential inhabitants.

The geographic surveyor robot has just landed. The Hellas Project organisers have revealed themselves in a news conference as Metalonic, the largest metals company in the northern hemisphere. The lander will travel around the Martian landscape and survey a large chunk of topography for purposes of claiming it as Metalonic property, principally for the mineral rights. Metalonic argues that by discovering this vacant land that no other interstellar probe has ever visited that they have a right to claim this land for the corporation even if the land is later annexed to Consortium jurisdiction in the terraforming project and subsequent colonisation. Metalonic claims that by virtue of maintaining an active lander they are, and will be, inhabiting this piece of Martian landscape. And they are the first to send a private space probe to Mars.

Metalonic's claim has met with resistance. Editorials decrying subterfuge and trespass abound. Other businesses are scrambling to build their own landers but the government has responded with legislation that annexes the entire planet of Mars as a territory of Earth, putting a hold, at least temporarily, on these projects.

Metalonic's claim prior to annexation is being challenged by the Consortium and this litigation will wind slowly through the courts. The Consortium has asserted a 'common heritage' argument that the Moon, Mars and other planets are part of humanity's common heritage and cannot be possessed by other than humanity itself and since the Consortium is the official arm of humanity, it serves as the protectorate of its common heritage (The Hague, 1954).

Many consumer advocates like the 'common heritage' argument. However, the courts have just ruled that this is without merit because the common heritage argument, as outlined by the government, is so broad that it can be applied to any property anywhere in the universe, including Earth which could ultimately void real property ownership anywhere. The government has decided not to pursue a modified 'common heritage' argument.

The Consortium is now considering the 1967 Outer Space Treaty which prohibits countries from owning interstellar bodies and which was passed by a number of predecessor countries but was never ratified. Most see little merit in pursuing this strategy because the UN treaty is silent on private ownership claims (UNOOSA, 1966).

Undaunted, the Consortium has resurrected the 1984 International Moon Treaty which forbad private ownership of parts of the Moon (UNODA, 1979). Even though some of the nations that were absorbed into the Consortium had ratified the treaty, most others had not. Private mineral rights on the Moon have been sold by the Consortium for three small plots which the courts have just ruled is proof that the Consortium has no desire to carry out the terms of the treaty and they have declared the treaty unenforceable. With the Moon treaty gutted, the Consortium has said that it will not propose a similar treaty for Mars. The truth is that the business lobby is very close to changing the balance of power in the two legislative branches and the current administration is wary of proposing new legislation.

The Consortium has another tactic it is has deployed, one begun further back in the court system, this time claiming that the Consortium had assumed most non-conflicting common law precedents of its predecessor nations when the Consortium constitution was enacted. These rights include prior discoveries on Mars from its predecessors' landers and other probes. The Consortium has effectively argued in lower courts that these landers and explorers have covered the planet sufficiently to confirm the Consortium's intent to possess as territory the entire planet.

One of the most influential cases in the John C. Marshall-led US Supreme Court was Johnson & Graham's Lessee v. McIntosh, 21 U.S. 8 Wheat. 543 543 (Johnson & Graham's Lessee v. McIntosh, 1823). The McIntosh case asked whether private citizens could purchase Native American lands directly. The court found that it could not which, of course, would have profound effect on Native Americans throughout the nineteenth century and beyond. There are no indigenous humans on Mars. However, what is important in this case to Mars is that the government has the power '… to dispose of the national domains, by that organ in which all vacant territory is vested by law (Johnson & Graham's Lessee v. McIntosh, 1823)'.

The higher court has agreed with the Consortium that they have maintained a more-or-less continuous presence on Mars and can legitimately claim the planet as a territory of the Earth under control of the Consortium of Nations. The court's opinion says that by constitutional adoption of predecessor nations' common law, the Consortium can use the McIntosh precedent. Mars is a territory of the Consortium. Metalonic's claim is denied.

Terraforming – The Next 300 Years

The highly technical nature of the Mars Reclamation Project (as terraforming was officially titled) will not be discussed here.[1] Liken it to the Manhattan Project to produce the atomic bomb in World War II but much greater. The cost of the project was projected to consume a fifth of the Earth's wealth. To date it has consumed half. Many believe the actual costs have been even higher.

───────────────

1   Of great concern is the issue of radiation. The thicker atmosphere that results will help reduce solar radiation but the lack of a strong magnetic field on Mars likely will require some form of shielding during times of solar flares and other radiation events.

The effort had been forecast to take 100 years maximum but has stretched into 300. Equipment has broken down frequently in the fluctuating temperatures and critical parts were sandblasted into dereliction from incessant winds and violent storms. Dust storms undid much of the initial 'green' terraforming and crops have not performed as expected because growing seasons have been short and cold.

The Earth has been nearly bankrupted by the effort but population growth has at least stabilised, though conditions for the masses are no less precarious from when the project began.

Finally, however, on Mars there is now just enough oxygen for certifying bodies to declare that humans can exist with the use of personal auxiliary life support systems. A compromise, yes, because the original goal was human self-sufficiency without mechanical supplement. While the planet is still frigid by Earth standards, advances in genetic engineering have accelerated plant growth and oxygen production.

The Ramping-up to Migration

Like Australia, Mars could have been first colonised as a 'one way' penal colony, and even though this approach has been hotly debated, in the end it has been judged that this will be too expensive for the Consortium to finance. 'Forty hectares and an MU' (Mobile Utility[2]) has become the slogan to lure would-be colonists and their families to emigrate to Mars for 'free' land ownership if the colonist can produce at least three annual crops of Martian grain. The cinematographers have outdone themselves documenting the beauty of Mars. Books, movies, posters and even songs tout the wonders of the red planet and all it has to offer humanity. Government sensors have cut dust-storm pictures and panoramas that portray the effects of category eight winds on man-made equipment.

Conestoga

Formed recently by trillionaire speculators after the government's announcement of the basic rules and conditions for Mars colonisation by people, the Conestoga Transportation Group will provide exclusive one-way transportation to Mars and supply (through subcontractors) the government-required Mars survival kit in

---

2   So named because the device uses the soil and mineral resources of Mars to produce energy without a nuclear component and is relatively safe for relative amateurs to operate even in a hostile environment. However, colonisers will be required to take extensive classes in how to operate, maintain and repair their MUs. Forty hectares and an MU is a reference to the call for land reform after the US Civil War when freed slaves believed they had a right to own the land they had worked as slaves, and where the rallying cry became – 40 acres and a mule (History.com-Staff, 2010).

exchange for 'all the Earthly assets' of its passengers. On the return trip Conestoga will ferry back to Earth Martian produce, ore, metals, manufactured goods and returning governmental officials for agreed-upon fees.[3] Cost of a return trip? Quite frankly, the government is not interested in seeing people return to Earth once they have left so it has made little effort to address this issue.

The expectation is that for some Conestoga-bound émigrés, 'all Earthly assets' is enough to pay the fare and the cost of the required survival kit; for most others a lien on the 40 hectares will be established and a mortgage with terms favourable to a financier will be inked. But the regulations have not yet been written and financing has not yet been secured.

As a result, the take-up rate on emigration to this point has been disappointing and has been limited to the wealthy few for whom a mortgage is not necessary. Any financing that could be had is on hold because the courts have intervened.

The Klondike Requirement

When prospective miners of the great Klondike gold rush arrived at the daunting Chilkoot Pass in the Yukon in 1898, the Royal Canadian Mounted Police inspected their kits to make sure that each miner carried a year's worth of provisions and food, about a tonne for each miner (Berton 1958, pp. 244–6). Miners trekked up and down the steep path again and again carrying as much as they could on their backs to a Mounty-guarded storage area called *the scales* before they could begin their journey to the gold fields in the rivers beyond. Many Klondike hopefuls were unprepared for the rigours of sub-arctic living. Most who made it to the gold fields made little money but at least they had provisions to live on. Miners grumbled, but many lives were saved as a result.

Lawsuits and civil liberties challenges have been filed against the Consortium 'Klondike Requirement' for Martian émigrés. Litigation arguments range from discrimination through the doctrine of disparate impact which argues that the cost of such requirements preclude the poor from participating in the migration, government restrictions against individuality and loss of freedom from the outfitting rules and government reaching too far into individual lives. Federal price controls for the trip's passage from the Conestoga monopoly has also been litigated. And it has been argued that the 'Klondike Requirement' is a form of taxation without representation because the people have not voted on the requirement.

The most effective challenge to the requirement has been that there is no agreement between business, government and the financiers on how trip and kit financing will work for the hordes who will need to depart Earth to meet the

---

3   Suffice it to say an incredibly efficient space elevator has been deployed that can lift tonnes and tonnes of heavy grain to awaiting cargo holds with a minimum of cost. This same device also transports people and their belongings to and from the surface of Mars. A similar device is used on Earth.

Consortium's emigration quotas. And there has been no agreement as to what protections the bankers and businesses will have if émigrés default on their mortgages. The emigration for the masses has been just too risky for private enterprise to finance and government has used most of its available resources to conduct the terraforming. Politicians have been recalled in special elections and the tangle in the courts has delayed the general emigration by more than three years.

During the delay, financially secure émigrés simply paid cash and have staked claims to the most desirable Martian properties. Some of the 'firsties', as they are now called, have acquired other parcels for resale in advance of the anticipated waves of migrants or have built Brobdingnagian ranches and stations prevalent in early Texas and Australia.

While there have been court 'victories' on both sides, gold was discovered on Mars six months ago. The clamour from the public has reached fever pitch, drowning civil libertarian arguments in a populous rush to judgement.

Gold

Gold on Mars means that the waiting lists for passage on the Conestoga Wagons, as the space vessels are called, has stretched into decades. Conestoga does not have enough ships to provide berths for all who want to emigrate. Those on the list can move their names up by paying a non-refundable fee which Conestoga is using to finance the building of a larger fleet. Conestoga has also negotiated a tax deal with the Consortium: instead of paying taxes, Conestoga has agreed to transport a required number of prisoners on each flight to new penal colonies near the Martian poles without any fee to the Consortium.[4] This is seen as win-win for both government and industry. Other suppliers, including suppliers of the required survival kits, have been lining up to negotiate similar tax abatements. As the government receives a portion of each émigré's fortune in return for credentials that permit the departing to board the vessel, the Consortium has more cash now and has granted many abatements or tax swaps.

The Rush is On!

It's the 30th year of the great migration. Conestoga continues to build ships which are beginning to depopulate Earth. But emigration is not outflowing at a rate that will satisfy the Consortium.

While there are no indigenous peoples to displace, the conditions of manifest destiny on Mars are similar. Tax-advantaged corporate ventures (transportation companies; goods suppliers on Mars) are becoming wealthy while the colonists

---

4   Also, passage fees have been waived for certain outbound and returning 'essential' bureaucratic officials and their staffs.

struggle to eke out a life on Mars. Financing has become available for more middle-class homesteaders for significant fees and high interest, but a percentage of these homesteaders have failed to produce the required number of 'adequate' harvests and financiers are selling foreclosed territory. Much of this foreclosed land has been sold at discount to the wealthy 'firsties'. Some of those unfortunate families who have been forced to foreclose have negotiated share-cropping contracts with these 'firsties'; other displaced families have joined bands of marauders euphemistically called Robin Hoods, that steal crops and otherwise terrorise the countryside.

Conestoga vessels return to Earth with holds filled with Martian grain and processed gold which is sold at a premium to a starving Earth. The penal colonies on Mars breed anger and resentment both within the walled camps and with the neighbouring communities. The scene on Mars has become a 'wild west' – a patchwork of laws, communities, territories and vague municipalities run by self-appointed administrators, and judges who announce themselves as the law. Socio-economists on Earth are predicting that within a few decades the trappings of a civilised law-abiding society could begin to emerge from the chaos of colonisation, but into what is not certain. As one conservative upper chamber leader exclaimed before a vote to increase bureaucracy and protective forces, 'This is a time for rugged individualism, not wimps!'

As the migration and the various support industries have grown to support the rush to migrate, costs have begun to come down. Yet the costs have not been coming down fast enough for prospective émigrés on long waiting lists who are losing any wealth they do have because the waiting list is a public list. Not only must émigrés pay a substantial down payment to move up the list, once Earthly employers find an employee's name on the list, the employee is laid off, permanently. There are plenty of others who can perform the duties of the laid-off employee and who will 'guarantee' that they will not put their names on any list. Unions have been eliminated because of the passage of the 'willing to work' law that is an employment-at-will statute with a negotiated salary provision without minimum wage. Individuals bid for jobs using salary as their bargaining chip.

Conestoga is worried that its increased capacity will mean vacant berths on outbound flights so it has combined forces with émigré associations which have petitioned and lobbied legislators to ease lending requirements.

Regulators have just lowered restrictions on mortgage lending requirements. Legislation authorising less restrictive lending requirements and a minimum floor of protection for lenders in the form of government-backed loan guarantees has started a flood of trip financing, so much so that today to even get on the waiting list, the down payment has become 60 per cent of the final charge.

Because the guarantees do not cover all of the risk, a private mortgage insurance industry is emerging to insure catastrophic exposures such as a ship exploding on route or from natural disasters on Mars that ruin reclaimed land. Mortgages are packaged together to mitigate default risk and are being sold in unprecedented volumes throughout the financial services industry. This combined government-private industry financing and insurance initiative means that more people can qualify to emigrate, even providing a means for some of the poorest families to leave. Nor is financing limited to banks and other regulated institutions: the Conestoga Transportation Group also has a financing arm.

However, hidden in many lending documents that have been enabled by this legislation are balloon payments and interest bumps. But, more people are now eligible to migrate and some on Mars are making enough money to overcome these hurdles.

Mortgage Meltdown

Years after the Martian exodus financing boom began, the chairman of the Consortium's legislative lower house has just replied to a reporter's question about the emerging mortgage meltdown. He said that this current mortgage challenge that the Earth, and of course Mars, has been experiencing, has not been the fault of lawmakers because no legislator was ever informed of even the possibility of such a condition. This mess, he said, has occurred because the incompetent legislative budgeting office had failed to point out these loopholes or ignored how the laws as written could be controverted by greedy lenders.

Foreclosure panic is looming now in the thirteenth year of the migration (just as balloon payments are coming due). Legislators are excusing themselves from blame because they claim that no-one could have predicted how the productivity of Martian homesteaders would lower inter-global commodities pricing to levels not before seen; and nobody, not even the economists, predicted that the price of gold would have plummeted to levels where production costs have become much higher than the product can be sold for in the open market.

Storm Clouds

While the welfare state on Earth is extensive, there is no such institution on Mars. There is no floor through which a person or a family or a community cannot fall. Many homesteading ventures have failed. Martian weather has claimed some of the terraformed land, and dust-storms have returned territory to its primordial red hue, making the land useless for many years while dwindling terraforming robots painstakingly nurse the land back into condition. Homesteaders cannot survive for long on barren land and many have abandoned their stake. The abandoned land has been repossessed and sold at deep discount to speculators and wealthy landowners who have the means to weather a long-term investment.

Then as suddenly as it had begun, the government-backed mortgage financed emigration has stopped at the end of its 30th year. The high number of foreclosures and the collapse of the mortgage insurance industry on Earth have virtually bankrupted the bi-global economy. Those who have planned, staked their live savings on and wanted to emigrate no longer have the means to do so as loan availability has dried up. The interplanetary commodity market is moribund because the economics of transportation to and from Mars requires that the trip be financed by émigrés on the outbound flight and by the grain, gold and other harvests on the return flight. On Earth the cost of commodities has soared in hyperinflation; on Mars the price of commodities has fallen so low that many farmers have stopped producing crops for other than personal use, often in violation of government homestead terms.

Even though the need for Martian commodities has reached a famine's peak on Earth, the collapse of the financial market means that there are no Earthly means to purchase Martian goods at any price, let alone the price adequate for Conestoga to resume its scheduled flights between the Earth and Mars. Talk of 'nationalising' Conestoga is just that, because even if the government took over the monopoly it could not afford to fly the ships. The bi-global depression has virtually cut each world off from the other, leaving each to find its own solution to the crisis. Pundits are calling this difficult period the beginning of a 'great divergence' between Mars and Earth.

Most of the administrators, bureaucrats and security forces of Mars are not immigrants. Most have signed on for specific tours of duty. As it became clear that the Conestoga ships would soon stop commuting between the two worlds, many of these temporary expatriates have petitioned to return on the final scheduled trips.

Most petitioners have been granted their forbearance. Their departure has created a void on Mars, disrupting markets and transportation, and has eliminated what little security existed on the planet. Without adequate guarding, the polar prisons have rioted and emptied. The Robin Hoods have grown in size, invading properties, stealing food and other goods and in some cases have killed the inhabitants to take over the lands. Private protection schemes have emerged for working homesteaders that are little better than the Robin Hoods and are costly and deadly to both homesteaders and the Robin Hoods.

A few of the larger landowners have assembled to discuss the growing lawlessness on the red planet. They reportedly have secretly agreed to certain reforms and each has purportedly partitioned an autonomous territory in which the large landowner is the chief executive who will not only administer the territory but protect it from marauding bandits, the Robin Hoods and the lawless private protection enterprises. Landowners have given themselves the power to tax territory inhabitants.

Epilogue

We are very good as a species at designing technology that serves us to do extraordinary things. The problem is that even if technology is developed that will make space travel more available to the masses, the masses bring along all that is good and bad of humanity. Societies tend to continue to replicate past failures because while some individuals may learn from mistakes, not all experience the situation that caused the problem in the first place, and the problem continues or reappears later on. Bolstering this argument are the boom-bust cycles, periodic economic bubbles, wars and other socio-economic breakdowns that occur regularly, even after causes are identified, and cures implemented. Warnings and forecasts are ignored or are simply forgotten ... but at our peril.

References

Berton, P. 1958, *The Klondike Fever, The Life and Death of the Last Great Gold Rush*. New York: Basic Books.

History.com-Staff. (2010). Sharecropping. Retrieved 4/24/2014, from http://www.history.com/topics/black-history/sharecropping.

Johnson & Graham's Lessee v. McIntosh, No. 543, 21 (U.S. Supreme Court 1823).

O'Sullivan, J. (1845, July–August). Annexation. *United States Magazine and Democratic Review*, 17, 5–10.

Stephanson, A. 1995, *Manifest Destiny: American Expansionism and the Empire of Right*. New York: Hill & Wang.

The Hague. 1954, Convention for the Protection of Cultural Property in the Event of Armed Conflict with Regulations for the Execution of the Convention 1954. Legal Instruments. Retrieved 4/24/14, 2014, from http://portal.unesco.org/en/ev.php-URL_ID=13637&URL_DO=DO_TOPIC&URL_SECTION=201.html.

UNODA. 1979, Agreement Governing the Activities of States on the Moon and Other Celestial Bodies. Retrieved 4/24/14, 2014, from http://disarmament.un.org/treaties/t/moon/text.

UNOOSA. 1966, Treaty on Principles Governing the Activities of States in the Exploration and Use of Outer Space, including the Moon and Other Celestial Bodies. Retrieved 4/24/14, 2014, from http://www.unoosa.org/oosa/SpaceLaw/outerspt.html.

Index